The Golden Age of Opera

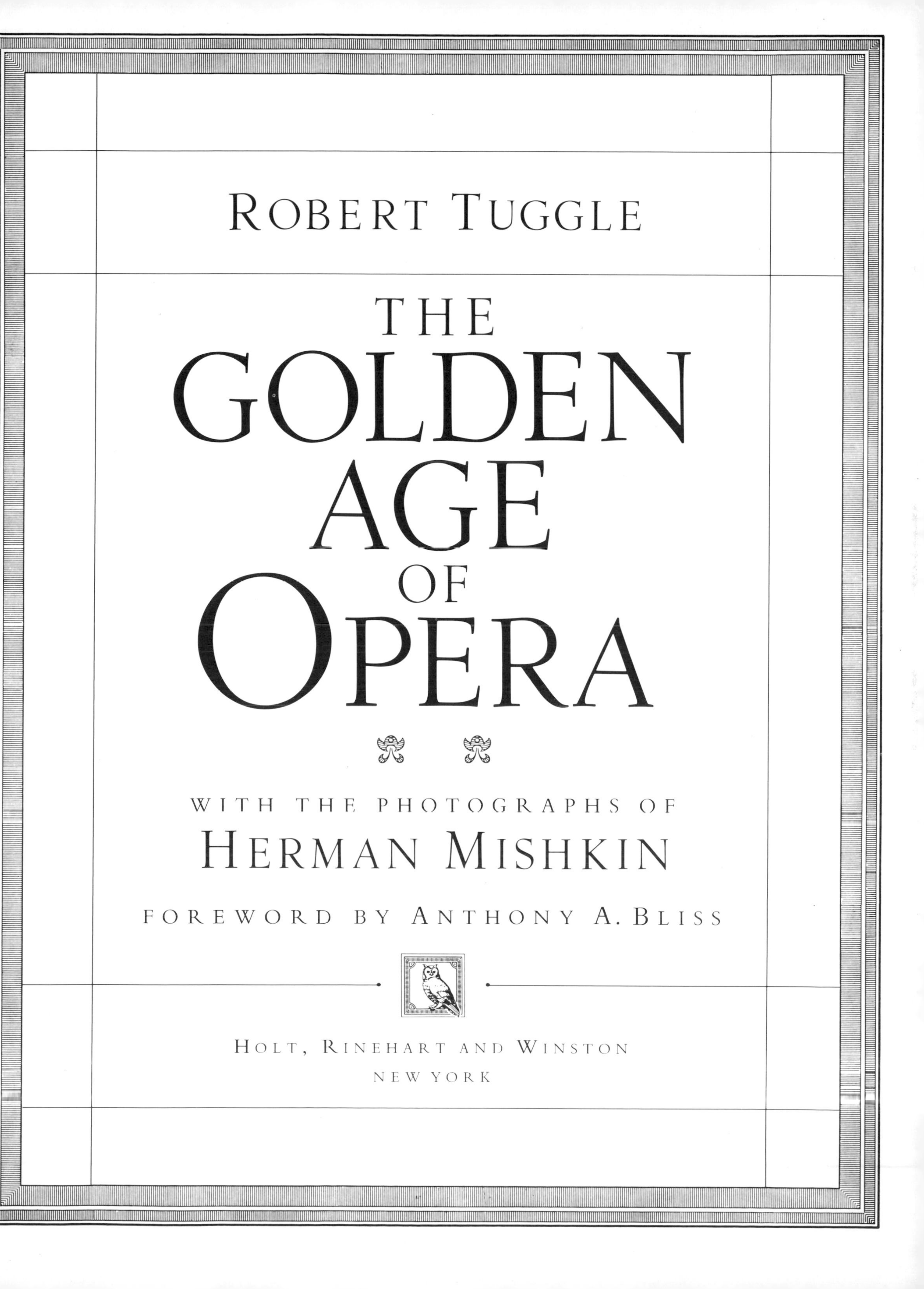

ROBERT TUGGLE

THE GOLDEN AGE OF OPERA

WITH THE PHOTOGRAPHS OF
HERMAN MISHKIN

FOREWORD BY ANTHONY A. BLISS

HOLT, RINEHART AND WINSTON
NEW YORK

IN MEMORY OF UNIQUE FRIENDS,
HARRY TUGGLE AND BOBBY GRAVELY,
WHO SHARED THEIR LOVE OF
GOOD SINGING

Published by Holt, Rinehart and Winston,
383 Madison Avenue, New York, New York 10017.
Published simultaneously in Canada by Holt, Rinehart
and Winston of Canada, Limited.

Library of Congress Cataloging in Publication Data
Tuggle, Robert.
The golden age of opera.
Includes index.
1. Singers—Biography. 2. Opera—New York (N.Y.)
3. Metropolitan Opera (New York, N.Y.) I. Mishkin,
Herman. II. Title.
ML400.T855 1983 782.1′092′2 [B] 83-7895
ISBN 0-03-057778-0

FIRST EDITION

Designer: Amy Hill
Printed in the United States of America
1 3 5 7 9 10 8 6 4 2

Photo Credits:
Except for those photographs in the Introduction
that are identified as the work of other photographers,
all photographs herein are by Herman Mishkin.

Author's collection: 4, 5, 7, 10, 11, 13,
14 (all), 15, 16, 17, 18, 30, 37, 42, 45, 46,
47, 50, 51, 52, 53, 55, 58, 60, 66, 76, 83, 86, 100,
104, 107, 109, 115, 145, 155, 156, 157 (right),
159, 161, 171, 173, 186, 191, 196, 197,
202, (both), 207, 211, 215, 216, 217.
Bettmann Archives: 131, 182 (left).
Michael Bavar: 153, 169. *George Cehanovsky*: 218.
Culver Pictures: frontispiece, 35, 36, 39,
40, 43, 54, 59, 67, 68, 69, 70, 71, 73, 77, 81,
82, 87, 88, 90 (all), 92 (all), 93, 94, 98, 103,
106, 108, 110, 111, 112 (both), 114, 116, 118,
119, 122, 123, 124 (both), 125, 127, 128, 129, 130,
132, 133, 138, 139 (both), 144, 148, 149, 150,
152, 154, 157 (left), 160, 164, 174, 176, 177,
181, 187, 188, 189, 193, 195, 198, 200 (right),
203, 204, 205, 209, 210, 219 (both), 221.
James Heffernan: 21.
*Hoblitzelle Theater Collection of the
University of Texas*: 84.
Metropolitan Opera Archives: 19 (both),
20 (right), 22, 24, 27, 28, 41, 48, 56, 75, 95, 101,
117, 121, 135, 136 (both), 141, 142 (both),
143, 146, 162, 178, 180, 200 (left), 201.
New York Public Library: 72, 96, 182 (right).
Opera News: 20 (left), 79, 170, 172, 184, 212.
Henry Y. Porter: 38.

ISBN 0-03-057778-0

CONTENTS

INTRODUCTION
THE GOLDEN AGE OF OPERA

PART I

THE HAMMERSTEIN YEARS: 1906–1910

PART II
THE GATTI YEARS: 1910–1921

Part III
The Gatti Years: 1921–1932

FOREWORD

WHEN I READ THE FIRST FEW PAGES OF Robert Tuggle's manuscript, I was carried back to the first time I became conscious of the word *opera*. I am afraid it took me an inordinate amount of time to read those pages, because almost every sentence caused my mind to indulge in long periods of reminiscence.

I recall my first opera, at the age of eight, when my father took me to hear Caruso in *Pagliacci* because he felt that the tenor's career was at an end and wanted me to have the experience of hearing him in person. I remember listening to Flagstad's first performance during a Saturday matinee broadcast while I was in a car driving to Long Island. I turned the car around and returned to New York, knowing my father would be in the Director's box and I would be able to get in before the performance was over. Later in the 1930s I had my first part in bringing an important singer to the Metropolitan. One day at home I played for my father a new recording of a young tenor singing "Celeste, Aida." He immediately called Edward Johnson, then the General Manager, who said that the tenor's agent had offered him to the Metropolitan that morning but was told the company had enough tenors. Fortunately, Johnson changed his mind, and there was another impressive Met debut, that of Jussi Bjoërling.

As many other memorable performances and great experiences flooded my mind, I began to think of the problems of running an opera company in the 1920s, the 1930s, and the 1940s, as compared with the 1980s. I remember being taken to performances in the 1930s where my father counted the number of people in the house rather than the empty seats, because there were more empty seats than members of the audience. Today, with the box office averaging over 90 percent, we fortunately are not faced with rows of empty seats. It is the only major problem of the past that is no longer with us.

Running an opera company today poses larger and more complex problems than in the early years of the Metropolitan, but the repertoire and [illegible] are not much different. I envy Giulio Gatti-Casazza's freedom to explore new repertoire—a freedom that the Metropolitan Opera lost to economics at the beginning of the Great Depression and has never fully regained. New problems have arisen with the development of radio, television, the credit card, the computer, and the jet plane. The jet plane in particular has had an enormous and devastating effect on the availability of great voices. Gone are the days when major singers would remain with an opera house for its entire season. Today a singer can, and does, appear almost simultaneously at many opera houses and concert halls all over the world, and the complications that this imposes on artistic planning create major problems beyond anything imagined in Gatti-Casazza's days. Add to the difficulties of artistic planning the necessity of raising over $24 million in contributions to cover the annual operating deficit. Giulio Gatti-Casazza enjoyed many seasons that ended the year with a profit; in those years, when a relatively small deficit was incurred it was made up by a few individuals. In the 1980s the Metropolitan's deficit is made up through contributions from over 200,000 sources.

The title *The Golden Age of Opera* implies that the golden age has come and gone. I do not agree with this perspective. While at times in the history of the Metropolitan Opera there have been greater concentrations of major singers in different voice categories, these singers were known to a relatively small public. Today the very factors that make the management of an opera house so complicated and costly have produced a real golden age. We are at the beginning of an era in which millions of people have the opportunity to hear and see great opera in opera houses all over the world on television. The great singers from the founding of the Metropolitan in 1883 to the middle 1970s were known by a comparatively small audience living in the vicinity of a few major opera houses. Singers were recognized by the rest of the world only through recordings, via radio broadcasts, and by accounts of the more flamboyant stars in the daily newspapers. Now in the 1980s our telecasts bring audiences of millions to a single performance. [illegible] by more people than the combined audiences that have seen that opera since it was composed. We are only at the threshold of the real golden age of opera.

ANTHONY A. BLISS

ACKNOWLEDGMENTS

THE HISTORY OF OPERATIC PERFORMANCE is a quagmire surrounded by bog. Just when the historian believes himself on firm ground, he discovers that information long accepted as fact is actually fantasy. The apocryphal story flourishes in opera as nowhere else. Writers believe what anyone tells them. Stories from information never verified are repeated in book after book. Opera singers themselves perpetuate their myths. When young, they declare themselves younger; with age, their stories become legends and about as reliable. Disasters become triumphs; rivals, nonentities.

Metropolitan Opera history has its readily available crutches. Two distinguished works of scholarship, Irving Kolodin's *The Story of the Metropolitan Opera* and William Seltsam's *Metropolitan Opera Annals,* are basic sources for anything written about the company. If either of them has a fault, it is an accessibility that has allowed lesser historians to proceed while investigating nothing on their own. The information and reviews in both Kolodin and Seltsam have been quoted endlessly. The same reviews have been repeated so often as to give the impression that many major artists were covered by the press only once or twice in an entire career.

In planning this book, I set as a goal to balance unknown and familiar photographs with information that hadn't been recounted time and again. The Metropolitan Opera Archives is the basic source for anything written about the Metropolitan Opera. Mrs. Mary Ellis Peltz established the archives in 1957. In her long tenure she had the help of two remarkable assistants, Marietta Fuller and Heloise Pressey. Fortunately, I have known all three. Mrs. Peltz and Mrs. Pressey found for me a quiet nook where I spent four happy years going through the Metropolitan Opera press books with clippings dating back to 1903, pay books dating to 1896, contract files for artists and other employees, and especially the unpublished official correspondence of Giulio Gatti-Casazza. This book is, I believe, the first to make extensive use of all this material, preserved so lovingly by Mrs. Peltz et al. As will be seen in the notes, some of the Gatti-Casazza correspondence resides in the Otto Kahn Papers of the William Seymour Theater Collection of Princeton University's Firestone Library, which is directed by Mary Anne Jensen. I am grateful to her and to Mrs. John Barry Ryan, daughter of Otto Kahn, who encouraged their use.

Gatti's correspondence with friends and colleagues in Italy was in Italian; with Norbert Salter in Berlin it was in French. Gatti corresponded with Otto Kahn and Edward Ziegler in letters put into English by Luigi Villa, his secretary. Most of the translations in this book are the graceful work of my friend Orlando Rigono, who numbers several languages among his gifts. Several others were the contribution of the inimitable Sissy Lindner. Selma Kurz's letter to Gatti was translated by Michael Rubinovitz.

I was extraordinarily fortunate during the early stages of this book to meet Charles Mintzer, a striking example of that familiar phenomenon, the individual working in one field but consumed by interest in another. His encyclopedic knowledge of historical recordings and literature, performers and their career histories, and opera house chronologies, as well as his overall perspective, was shared with me hourly at every stage. I consider the result a collaboration in which any flaws are mine, all balance and accuracy his.

Few people have immersed themselves in this period with the dedication of William Seward. Bill provided me with rare information; he also enabled me to discuss the latter part of the period with that unique soprano Bidú Sayão. Probably no one knows as much performing history as Charles Jahant; the only problem for an author is to find a way of using the vast amount of information he freely makes available. Gustl Breuer donated the shipboard story of Frieda Hempel and Elisabeth Schumann, obtained directly from Mme. Schumann. From Mrs. William Rogers Herod, I had a musician's insight into Claudia Muzio in 1920s Chicago.

Valuable research and advice were provided by Richard Miller, Paul Gruber, Bruce Kellner, Karen Luten, Dinah Daniels, Dr. Helen Strauss, Nina Keller, Luta [illegible], David Hamilton, Robert [illegible] Stewart, Richard Boehm, Clara Rothier, Nick Dowen, Leslie Carola, Jenny Grazzini, José Doménech, John Scarry, Henry Wisneski, and the entire staff of the Music Division of the New York Public Library.

Important source material included *Oscar Hammer-*

stein's Manhattan Opera, by John F. Cone, a book without flaw; Quaintance Eaton's *The Boston Opera Company;* the two-volume *The Record of Singing,* by Michael Scott, a fascinating critic even at his most infuriating; every issue of *The Record Collector,* an invaluable English publication edited by James F. E. Dennis; *The Concise Oxford Dictionary of Opera,* by Harold Rosenthal and John Warrack.

In 1979 I had a few wonderful days discussing Herman Mishkin with his son and daughter-in-law, Mr. and Mrs. Leo Mishkin, and his daughter, Mrs. Helen Burstein. An adorable man, Leo encouraged me from the start of the project. All generously shared memories of their father and mother; this material appears in the Herman Mishkin section.

Many of Mishkin's surviving prints and most of his negatives reside at Culver Pictures under the watchful eye of Robert Jackson. As someone who would rather look at old opera photographs than do almost anything else, I spent long fascinating hours at Culver, benefiting from Bob Jackson's knowledge, patience, and encouragement. A book of Mishkin photos could be done without his participation, but it probably wouldn't be especially worthwhile.

Many of the Mishkin photographs reproduced here have been newly copied from the original negatives stored at Culver Pictures and the Metropolitan Opera Archives. Most labs lack the skill or interest to deal with glass negatives. The superb quality of the prints recently made from the negatives is the product of Sara and Dave Archer of Gallery West Custom Labs, 189 Columbus Avenue, New York City.

Photographic historian William Welling made valuable improvements. Michael Bavar lent original photos of Feodor Chaliapin in *Boris* and Giulio Crimi in *Il Tabarro,* and Henry Y. Porter provided the portrait of Eleanora de Cisneros in *Gli Ugonotti* and provided a great deal of information on singers and photographers besides. Quaintance Eaton lent the print of Beniamino Gigli in *Mefistofele.* I was able to discuss Metropolitan Opera photographers with Irving Kolodin, who, with his awareness of the visual past, is unique among critics. Others who helped with photo research were George Cehanovsky, Andrew Karzas, Robert Tollett, Edwin McArthur, Lucy Voulgaris, Nancy Toff, Charlotte Daniels Harris, Gerald Fitzgerald, Vivien Liff, Martin Sokol, Rhonda Neu, Mamie Tsong, Marylis Sevilla-Gonzaga, Aida Favia-Artsay, Mary Henderson, and Moselle Broderick. Many Mishkin photographs in my own collection result from the special consideration and thoughtfulness of James and Constance Camner of La Scala Autographs.

The inspired suggestion for creating a book around Mishkin rather than Claudia Muzio came from Paul Thomason. Gregory Downer devoted time and imagination to helping me begin the project. Carol Mann believed in it and found a receptive spirit in Natalie Chapman of Holt, Rinehart and Winston. I am grateful to them all, but especially to Natalie for her patience and her unfailing sense of what more could be said and what was better omitted. The book's appearance is the result of Amy Hill's discreet and elegant sense of design.

To take five years to research and write a book is unusual. Fortunately, I have an extraordinary mother who helped me survive, and a group of friends who provided what can only be called moral support. In no particular order they are Marcia Lazer, Jarmila Packard, Robert Ader, Lonnie Kennett, Richard Dawe, Glenn and Christine and Nicholas Ross, Betty Miller, Tom and Laurence Rimer, David Reuben, Ted and Jean Uppman, C. J. and Carol Luten, Yvetta and Malcolm Graaf, Lisa Neuman, Howard Siegel, Hildegard Stein, Robert Armstrong, Philip Caggiano, Elaine Kones, Larry Peters, Robert and Ellen Leverone, Gertrude A. Fellner, Pearl Guzik, Gail Frohlinger, Mary Ruttenberg, Mary Chinnery, Estelle Ross, Robert Wilheim, Stanley Pearl, Henry Jacobs, Erika Davidson, Jeremiah Murray, Aris Morelli, Kermit Love, Philip Williams, Betsy Garry, Anthony Balcena, Dennis Dilno, and Paul Jeromack.

I am also grateful to Madame Elda Ercole for teaching me to listen to the human voice and to Frank Dunand for giving me lessons in how to look at photographs.

Finally, a word on procedure. Wherever possible, the order of entries has followed the chronological development of Mishkin's photography. To determine when photographs were taken, I have checked the dates an artist performed a role in New York, the year Mishkin could have photographed him or her, the first traceable publication of the photo, and evidence on the paper wrappers of the negatives. The result should be historically accurate and permit us to observe time move forward through the eyes of one photographer.

To ensure quality, all photographs in the book have been reproduced from original images—that is, prints made directly from negatives—with the following unavoidable exceptions: Adelina Patti, Dinh Gilly as Sonora in *Fanciulla,* Geraldine Farrar, and Toti Dal Monte.

Original spelling and usage has been maintained within quotations. In Mishkin's letters to Gatti-Casazza, the photographer's sometimes unusual spelling is printed without the editor's obtrusive "[*sic*]."

Opera titles are generally given in the language in which they were written. To maintain the feeling of the period, however, I have often used the language of performance. Thus, Meyerbeer's *Huguenots,* an opera written in French, is listed as *Gli Ugonotti* when the text refers to the period in which it was most frequently performed in Italian. *Die Meistersinger* becomes *I Maestri Cantori* at La Scala in the 1920s. *Les Pêcheurs de Perles* is *I Pescatori di Perli* at the beginning of Caruso's career but reverts to its original in 1916 at the Metropolitan. *La Fille du Regiment* is the German *Regimentstochter* when Florence Easton sings it in Berlin, becomes *La Figlia del Reggimento* with Frieda Hempel at the Met in 1917, and finally returns to its original with Lily Pons in 1940.

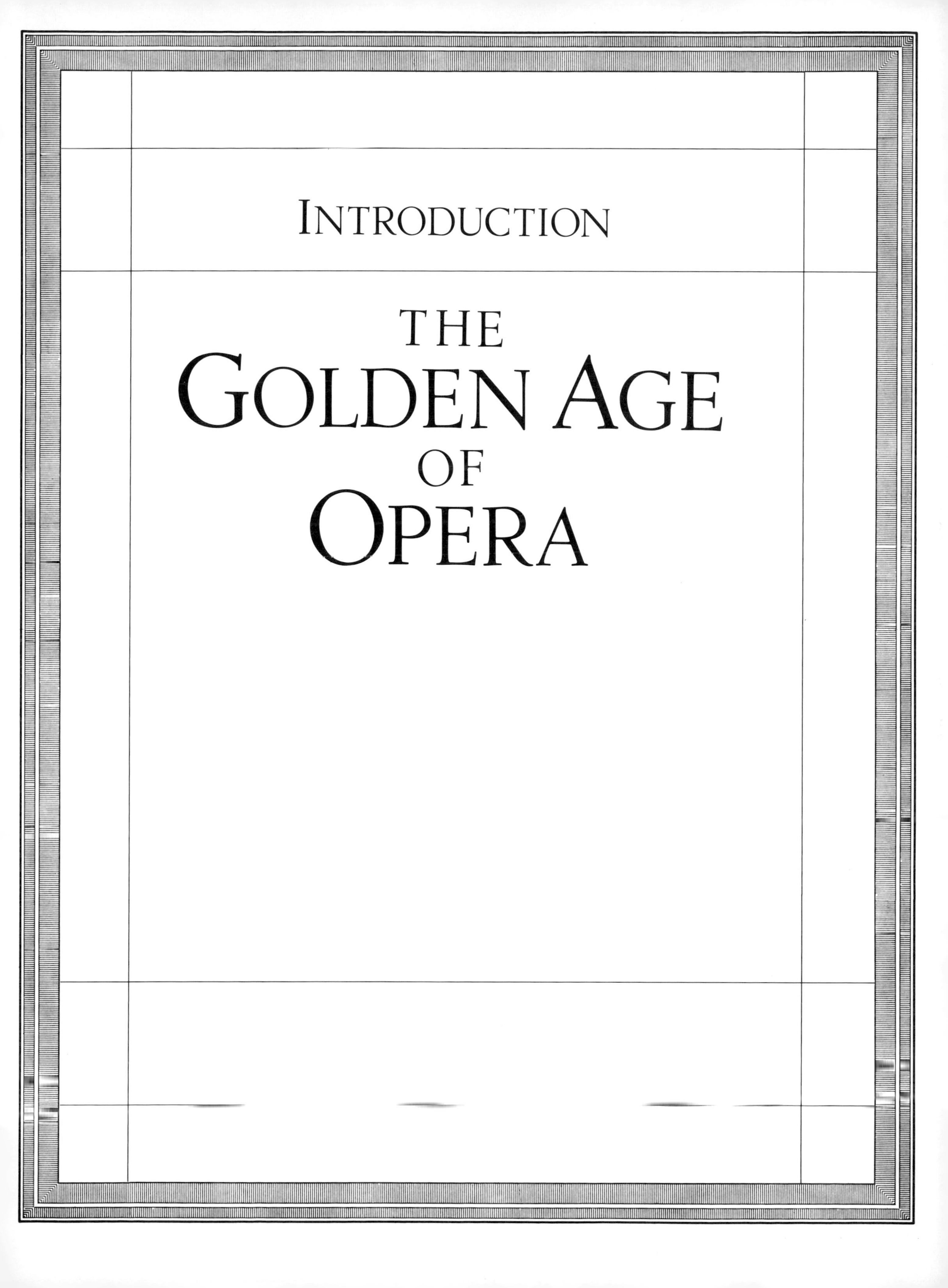

INTRODUCTION

THE GOLDEN AGE OF OPERA

N 1906 NEW YORK WAS ONE of the world's great seaports. The many daily newspapers printed shipping news on their front pages; storms over the North Atlantic sailing routes aroused almost universal interest. Each autumn, docking ocean liners poured forth a volume of passengers that included major opera singers. Once in New York a singer would stay until the spring, giving stability to his opera house and creating a secure atmosphere for his own artistic growth. At the Metropolitan Opera, at 39th and Broadway, orchestra seats sold for $5; a one-sided 78-rpm recording of Enrico Caruso singing "Celeste Aida" cost $3. Between 1906 and 1932 New York heard *Madama Butterfly, Salome, Pelléas et Mélisande, Elektra, Der Rosenkavalier,* and *Turandot* for the first time. In this period before radio, television, and long-playing records, audiences streamed into theaters again and again to hear a score and become familiar with it. The large numbers of churches and theaters throughout the country shared with opera houses a common perception of what the singing voice should be; it was still possible for well-trained voices of choir loft and musical comedy stage to move directly up to the Metropolitan.

On the other hand, in the world of opera some things never change. There were fat sopranos and thin ones, pretty ones and those who were less so. Although close attention was paid to how a performer acted, New York has always been conservative in its tastes, and was only slightly more receptive to the animal drama of Feodor Chaliapin in 1907 than it was to the passionate intensity of Maria Callas in 1956. There has always been the lemminglike compulsion of contraltos and mezzo sopranos to sing soprano roles that were not meant for them, with the same predictable results. Then as now, there were American singers who went to Europe to train and gain reputations, as well as those who stayed; between 1906 and 1932, Paul Althouse, Mabel Garrison, Rosa Ponselle, and Lawrence Tibbett remained at home for training and performances without damage to voice or career. And in 1906 just as today, the onlooker made the faulty assumption that if a longed-for singer was not on the roster, he had not been asked, negotiated with, or wheedled for.

Most of all, opera has always provoked disagreement on what constitutes a beautiful voice, who is a great conductor, what operas should be in the repertoire, and what is an appropriate setting for a specific work. Consider one of the glorious seasons in Metropolitan Opera history. During 1913–14 the Metropolitan revived *Un Ballo in Maschera* with the stellar cast of Enrico Caruso, Pasquale Amato, Emmy Destinn, Frieda Hempel, and Margarete Matzenauer; gave the American premieres of Strauss's *Rosenkavalier* and Montemezzi's *Amore dei Tre Re;* mounted a new staging of the four parts of Wagner's *Ring* cycle; announced Giovanni Martinelli for the first time on a memorable roster that featured Frances Alda, Lucrezia Bori, Geraldine Farrar, Olive Fremstad, Johanna Gadski, Adamo Didur, Antonio Scotti, and Jacques Urlus; and had Arturo Toscanini conducting sixty-one performances of works that ranged from *La Gioconda* and *Ballo* to *Boris Godunov* and *Die Meistersinger.* At the end of the season, the eminent critic Algernon St. John-Brenon pronounced an epitaph for the operatic year: "It must have been a success, because nobody is satisfied."

OPERA SINGERS IN NEW YORK

IN OPERA THE SINGING VOICE WILL always come first. When we tell of opera companies, we must list the fabled voices on their rosters. When we report on audiences, we must know whether they appreciated what they heard. And when we fancifully dream of when we would most happily have lived, we find names rising unbidden from the past, most often names from the first third of the twentieth century, names such as Enrico Caruso, Titta Ruffo, Feodor Chaliapin, Rosa Ponselle, names from an unparalleled era of voices, when all that had gone before in New York burst into a golden age.

New York has known many periods of extraordinary singing that can only tantalize the present-day lover of opera, but perhaps none so romantic as the season of 1825–26, in which the Spanish tenor Manuel Garcia and a small band of eight singers, including himself, his son Manuel, and his daughter Maria-Felicita sailed across the Atlantic in twenty-nine days to present the first season of Italian opera in America. Five works of Rossini, then the rage of Europe, were performed, along with two by Garcia himself, Zingarelli's *Romeo e Giulietta,* and *Don Giovanni,* sung in the presence of its librettist, Lorenzo da Ponte, then an old man teaching Italian at Columbia University. Opening night at the Park Theatre in lower Manhattan was *Il Barbiere di Siviglia.* Garcia, who had created the role of Almaviva at the world premiere in Rome nine years before, was the tenor, his son sang Figaro, and his daughter sang Rosina. An ordinary New York theater orchestra played the music, and the chorus was said to be a stage crew drilled to sing words they didn't understand. But Garcia had in his seventeen-year-old daughter one of the legendary singers of the nineteenth century. In her portrayal of Rosina, "the silver tones of the Signorina poured forth without effort or distortion." "Compass, sweetness, taste, truth, tenderness, flexibility, rapidity, and force do not make up half the sum of her vocal powers; and her voice is only one of the rare qualities with which nature has endowed her." A sparkling actress, beautiful of face and figure, she became the feature of every performance. To New York she was known familiarly as "La Signorina"; to a world that would corroborate New York's judgment she became known by the name of the elderly and bankrupt wine merchant she married halfway through the season, Malibran.

As New York grew, its theaters moved uptown. By mid-century, Italian opera was well established, insofar as any entertainment depending on profit-seeking impresarios, quixotic singers, and a fickle public could have permanence. Jenny Lind, billed as the Swedish Nightingale by her promoter, the showman P. T. Barnum, reached America in 1850 but sang only in concert, having renounced opera for religious reasons. In May 1852 Marietta Alboni, a large, unknown contralto, made her American debut. The timing of her arrival was unfortunate, and she didn't have the promotion that Barnum had provided for Lind. In Alboni's case, however, press and public had no need of instruction. Her first number was an aria from Rossini's *Semiramide;* the composer himself had been one of her teachers. At the end of the second line, the audience, so overwhelmed by her vocal beauty, could no longer restrain itself and burst into shouts of "Bravo, bravo." Long after her brief career had ended, it was maintained that in nineteenth-century America "excepting Malibran, no singer, not even Jenny Lind, did so much as Alboni did to elevate and purify the taste of the higher class of music-lovers. She became the model, the standard by which others were to be tried."

In 1854 New York welcomed the era's most widely known singers, the soprano Giulia Grisi and her husband, the tenor Giovanni Mario, known simply as Mario. She had created the role of Adalgisa in *Norma* twenty-three years earlier at La Scala; together they had sung in the world premiere of *Don Pasquale.* In the title role of Norma, Grisi revealed vocalization that was "incomparably fine—brilliant, powerful, impetuous. Her voice seemed unrestrained by consciousness, and abandoned to the sway of her all-controlling rage. The notes flashed out like lightning, and when they were arrested with the same suddenness with which lightning vanishes into darkness, there was just an appreciable instant of utter silence; and then the thunder shook the house. Few who saw it will forget it."

To Mario and Grisi fell the honor of opening the newly built Academy of Music at 14th Street and Irving Place. Their opening *Norma* was succeeded by more Italian opera, *Lucrezia Borgia, La Favorita,* and *Don Giovanni.* As Edgardo in *Lucia di Lammermoor,* Mario sang "with such exquisite appreciation of light and shade, such a sustained and symmetrical flow of voice . . . that it seemed as if nothing audible could be more exquisitely shaded."

The Academy of Music's most significant event came five years later, Thanksgiving night in 1859, when Adelina Patti, then barely sixteen, made her operatic debut in *Lucia di Lammermoor.* "Her appearance was that of a very young lady," wrote the music critic for the New York *Herald,* "petite and interesting, with just a tinge of the school room in her manner. She was apparently self-possessed, but not self assured. After the first few bars of recitative she launched boldly into the cavatina, one of the most difficult pieces in the opera. This she sang perfectly, displaying a thorough Italian method and a high soprano voice, fresh, full and even throughout. . . . Miss Patti sang with sympathetic tenderness—a rare gift in

Two legendary nineteenth-century sopranos meet in a rare photo: Adelina Patti, approximately twelve years old, and Jenny Lind, on the cover of sheet music. Circa 1855.

one so young—and increased the enthusiasm of the audience to a positive *furore,* which was demonstrated in the usual way—recalls, bouquets, wreaths, &c. &c. The horticultural business was more extensive than usual."

Patti soon converted floral tributes into something more enduring. In Europe she was received by royalty and presented with precious jewels; in America she traveled by private railroad car. Her fee was probably the largest of any singer in history: $5,000 per performance, delivered in gold to her dressing room before she would sing a note.

Born in Madrid the day after her mother had performed the arduous role of Norma, Patti was not strictly an American singer though she grew up and received her musical training in New York. However, her contemporaries Clara Louise Kellogg, Minnie Hauk, and Annie Louise Cary were American singers with international successes. Kellogg, New York's first Marguerite in *Faust,* sang in London but achieved her greatest fame during the 1870s and 1880s with her own company, touring the United States to perform opera in English. At sixteen Minnie Hauk sang Gounod's music for Juliette for the first time in America; she introduced Carmen to London and New York and was known on both sides of the Atlantic as the role's unequaled interpreter. The mezzo-soprano Annie Louise Cary trained in Europe with Garcia's younger daughter, the distinguished Pauline Viardot, and was Amneris in the first American *Aida* in 1873. As Ortrud in *Lohengrin* she was the first American singer of a Wagnerian role.

Easily moving between Wagner and the standard repertoire, all sung in Italian, was New York's tenor idol of the seventies and eighties, Italo Campanini. Cary sang with Campanini in his 1873 American debut as Gennaro in Donizetti's *Lucrezia Borgia.* The New York *Herald* raved over his performance: "He is young; he has a fine presence; nature has given him a magnificent organ, which art has already done much to perfect; and, finally, he evinces something of that magnetic spirit which enters into the conception of sympathetic acting. . . . *Une voix de velours!* . . . For the first time in many years at the Academy of Music was heard a tenor who could produce *diminuendo* or *crescendo* in the highest *di petto* notes with ease and effect." Campanini remained the idol of all who heard him, even during the succeeding tenor reigns of both Jean de Reszke and Enrico Caruso; his qualities were a powerful standard against which less artistic singers could be measured.

Not every great singer was heard in New York in his prime. Mario came alone after Grisi's death with only scraps of his voice remaining. Enrico Tamberlik, Verdi's first Don Alvaro in *La Forza del Destino,* was famed for the high C's he had added to "Di quella pira" in *Il Trovatore.* He sang Donizetti's *Poliuto* at the Academy of Music in 1873 with thrilling declamation but with little music left in the voice. Though already ill from the cancer that would take her life the next year, the German dramatic soprano Therese Tietjens sang New York concerts and opera in 1876 with glints of such conviction and intensity that the *Herald* welcomed "a style that reminded the hearers of those days when there were real schools of singing, not unhealthy vocal hot houses or lyric force pumps."

Enrico Tamberlik in the title role of Donizetti's Poliuto, *a Gurney photo dating from Tamberlik's 1873 American debut.*

And, of course, not all the major singers of the nineteenth century came to New York. Angelo Masini, the Italian tenor for whom Verdi wrote the tenor music in his *Manzoni Requiem,* demanded a contract that would cover the expenses for a valet, a journalist, a doctor, a lawyer, a baker, a secretary, an under secretary, an agent, a cook, and a treasurer, all of whom would wait on him and also serve as his claque. Even in America there were not enough dollars to pay for his engagement.

The Academy of Music was the center of New York opera for almost thirty years. However, the limited number of box seats were unavailable to the socially ambitious among the city's newly wealthy. In 1880, a prominent group, with such now familiar names as Vanderbilt and Roosevelt, met and formed a new organization for the production of opera.

The Metropolitan Opera House opened at 39th Street and Broadway in October 1883; despite fire, personal tragedy, and financial and artistic crises, the Metropolitan brought a sense of permanence to the New York opera scene that had been lacking before. Three general managers have accounted for sixty-two of its one hundred years; their taste has dictated the singers that New York has heard in opera for a century. The first season, however, reflected not so much the taste of the first manager, Henry E. Abbey, as it did that of the rival company downtown at the Academy of Music. Starring in the Met's opening-night *Faust* were Italo Campanini and the Swedish soprano Christine Nilsson, a local favorite who had first been heard in New York in 1870. The real star of the first Met season was the young Polish soprano Marcella Sembrich, who made her debut in *Lucia di Lammermoor* the second night. At the end of the season Sembrich revealed further talents at a performance that Abbey held for his own benefit. "Mme. Sembrich was announced to play a violin concerto by De Bériot. It was expected that this would be a prima donna's caprice, requiring good-humored indulgence on the part of the audience. To the contrary it proved to be a notably beautiful piece of violin playing and not only the audience but also the players in the orchestra went into a rapturous demonstration over it. After a dozen recalls Mme. Sembrich seated herself at the piano on the stage and played admirably a nocturne by Chopin, proving beyond question that she was great also as a pianist. The audience now went quite wild, and to satisfy it Mme. Sembrich finally sang 'Ah, non giunge' from *La Sonnambula.* Such a tripartite musical performance was surely never witnessed before."

In a year of unusual richness, the concurrent season at the Academy of Music was built around Adelina Patti and her bitter rival, the Hungarian soprano Etelka Gerster, and included performances by a young American named Lillian Norton, soon to be known as Nordica. In later years both Nordica and Sembrich became vital contributors to music in New York.

Opera that was sung at the Metropolitan in Italian—even *Faust* and *Lohengrin*—lost money and gave way in 1884 to seven triumphant years of German-language opera, even for *Carmen* and *Aida.* Making her 1885 debut in *Carmen* was a young German soprano, Lilli Lehmann, who had broken away from the Berlin Opera so that she might escape from the lighter lyric and coloratura soprano roles and perform the music that moved her. Her tall stature and almost military bearing were not what audiences were accustomed to; she emphasized the serious, more sinister side of Carmen's character. Yet her singing cast all previous Carmens into the background: "Her voice is true, flexible and ringing, and of most telling quality. She sings with perfect ease and her high notes have a fairly electrifying timbre and power. She has the ability to fill it with the passionate expression and warmth of color which the music of the part often calls for, and utilizes this ability with rare judiciousness and taste." Although surrounded by distinguished artists, Lehmann dominated New York musical life, singing in the American premieres of *Tristan und Isolde, Siegfried,* and *Götterdämmerung,* and displaying her total stylistic mastery in *Don Giovanni* and *Norma.* Ninety years later, Lehmann's reputation maintains her supremacy as the paragon of musical integrity.

Careful attention to musical and theatrical values, which were emphasized during the German seasons, was banished in the 1890s by society's demand for a repertoire selected according to how many stars each opera could display. Leading the stellar array was the Polish tenor Jean de Reszke. The most romantic of roles were his: he opened four Metropolitan seasons as Roméo and two as Faust. Here is an 1895 tribute: "His noble stage appearance, his graceful, manly bearing, his sympathetic comprehension of every role, his nice adjustment of vocal and histrionic means to the end in view, his artistic sincerity, and his constant exercise of a cultivated and naturally keen discrimination, have combined to make him the greatest favorite the operatic stage in this city has ever known." Jean was usually accompanied by his brother, Edouard de Reszke, "the greatest basso of the time.... For breadth of conception and style, coupled with subtlety of details, nothing on the contemporaneous stage, either operatic or dramatic, excels M. Edouard de Reszke's Mephistopheles."

On the same vocal plane as the De Reszke brothers was the Australian soprano Nellie Melba, who was generally regarded as "the foremost living exponent of the art of bel canto. She is a walking epitome of the art of singing.... It is possible that some of the famous singers who died before men now living were born had finer voices, but it is not likely." Melba was said to have limited powers of characterization, displaying her temperament more often offstage than on. Emotional leagues from Melba was the French soprano Emma Calvé, "a singer of true dramatic instincts, unfailing musical and magnetic eloquence in pose, action and vocal utterance." Calvé has become synonymous with vocal fire and dramatic conviction, Melba with a standard of pure song uninvolved with emotion.

Finished vocalism during this era also came from two dissimilar American sopranos, Emma Eames, a cool and graceful beauty with much of Melba's repertoire, and Lillian Nordica, by now a star of dazzling virtuosity, who ranged from the coloratura demands of *La Traviata* and *Mignon* to the heroism vital to Wagner's *Ring* cycle and *Tristan und Isolde.*

At the bottom of the staff was the elegant French bass Pol Plançon, who with his trill and coloratura easily demonstrated that the male voice could have all the technical facility of the female. Also present were Francesco Tamagno, Verdi's first Otello, with a voice that could be harsh, nasal, and bleating but could also peal "with the splendor of the trumpet and the anguish of the human heart," and Victor Maurel, a supreme actor with a worn voice, the first Iago and Falstaff, who could still sing Cassio's dream in *Otello* with exquisite delicacy.

Sarony's portrait of the versatile American soprano Lillian Nordica as Elsa in Lohengrin, *a role she was the first to sing at the Wagner Festival in Bayreuth.*

Many of the finest singers from the period retired from the operatic stage during the first decade of the twentieth century. Many left no valid evidence on recordings of their vocal excellence. Jean de Reszke, for instance, though long rumored to have made commercial recordings, can be heard only on the precious wax cylinders made high above the stage by the Metropolitan's adventurous music librarian, Lionel Mapleson, during De Reszke's last performances in 1901.

Between 1906, the first season of Oscar Hammerstein's Manhattan Opera, and 1932, the middle of the Depression, when profound changes took place at the Metropolitan Opera, New York gloried in a golden age of opera unequaled anywhere else in the twentieth century. Consider the era's unparalleled richness in tenors, that most precious of operatic resources. Towering above everyone else was Enrico Caruso, the vocal god of Italian opera who was at the heart of New York musical life. But Caruso was merely the supreme tenor among many. From Italy alone came his more delicate rival, Alessandro Bonci, and his sweet-voiced successor, Beniamino Gigli. A procession of powerful Italian tenors, including Giovanni Zenatello, Giovanni Martinelli, Aureliano Pertile, and Giacomo Lauri-Volpi, dominated the dramatic repertoire. Ireland sent its finest singer, John McCormack, with his unique combination of finesse and broad popular appeal. From the Austro-Hungarian empire came the commanding Leo Slezak; from Russia, the totally dissimilar voices of Hermann Jadlowker and Dmitri Smirnoff. Spain sent the temperamental Florencio Constantino and Miguel Fleta; and America produced Orville Harrold, Paul Althouse, and Charles Hackett. The Dutch Jacques Urlus and the Danish Lauritz Melchior were heldentenors unequaled since.

The age between 1906 and 1932 boasted equally impressive rosters of sopranos—dramatic, lyric, and coloratura—contraltos, and lower male voices. Chosen randomly, a modest selection of artists from the period would form an enviable company for any of the world's opera houses in the late twentieth century.

The sheer number of significant voices was but one distinction of the years between 1906 and 1932. The age also saw something new and special: a whole breed of singing actors where before there had only been isolated figures such as Victor Maurel and Emma Calvé. Now there were artists with dramatic and vocal techniques ideal for the Italian verismo works of Mascagni and Leoncavallo, the modern French school encompassing both Massenet and Debussy, and those strange nineteenth-century works that began to emanate from Russia. Calvé endured well into the new century; Maurel had his natural successor in Maurice Renaud. Mary Garden claimed the whole of French lyric drama as her own and mesmerized audiences with it; Geraldine Farrar moved with enormous theatrical flair between French and Italian repertoires; Claudia Muzio had a voice and stage personality of smoldering fire, created for melodrama; and Feodor Chaliapin combined a magnificent voice and presence into something unique in operatic history. Even Caruso himself developed during this period from a purely vocal phenomenon into a masterful singing actor.

The world of opera changed in 1932, the low point of the Great Depression. Otto Kahn had just retired as chairman of the Board of Directors. The Metropolitan Opera was forced to cut back from its traditional five-month season. All artists were asked to take a reduction in pay; Beniamino Gigli refused and left the company. Gigli's first season, 1920–21, had been Caruso's last; now a unique Italian vocal line—the first half formed by Enrico Caruso, the second by Gigli—was broken. Never again would the Metropolitan have the season-long services of comparable Italian tenors. In 1932 Maria Jeritza left the Metropolitan, and another tradition, one embodied by a special kind of glamorous soprano whose presence on the roster dated back to Geraldine Farrar's debut in 1906, also vanished from Metropolitan history. And 1931–32 was also the last of baritone Antonio Scotti's thirty-two regular seasons with the company. Although he returned the following season for an isolated farewell performance, it was as though the building itself, not just its inhabitants, had shifted.

Two 1932 headlines reflected changes at the Metropolitan and in the whole social fabric of America: "Is This the Twilight of Opera?" and "What Is Left for Society but Opera?" Franklin Delano Roosevelt and his New Deal were swept into office in 1932. In keeping with popular change, the Metropolitan Opera took a giant step toward becoming an opera company for the entire country in 1931–32 when its regular matinee broadcasts began with *Hänsel und Gretel* on Christmas Day of 1931.

(Coincidentally, the Chicago Opera ceased to exist in 1932. The company had been formed in 1910 from the artistic assets, repertoire, productions, and many of the artists of Hammerstein's Manhattan Opera. With the dissolution of the company, the authentic French repertoire introduced by Hammerstein also disappeared from American stages.)

After 1932 the production of new operas would never again be near the center of the planning for a Metropolitan season. Most of the works that form the Metropolitan's permanent repertoire were already written. Giacomo Puccini was dead and Richard Strauss had completed his masterpieces. Only Alban Berg, Igor Stravinsky, and Benjamin Britten would produce works worthy of standing side by side with those of the past. The fertile flowering of opera in nineteenth-century Italy, Germany, France, and the Slavic countries was over. A creative vitality that had made opera the leading form of musical expression was exhausted. With that vitality inevitably vanished the common assumption that all the best voices would naturally train for opera.

However, just when one assumes that no more good singers exist, opera always surprises. In May 1932, W. J. Henderson, writing of opera's remarkable powers of regeneration, recalled "that Jean de Reszke left the Metropolitan when he was the most famous tenor in the world and that the opera went on. Mme. Melba departed; so did Mme. Sembrich and Mme. Eames. The opera went on. Mr. Caruso died, and the opera went on. Not only did it go on but, until the present period of world wide depression began, it made money. In conversation with this writer Mr. Gatti-Casazza said with his habitual solemnity: 'No one is indispensable. I am not indispensable.' All of which seems to have some relation to the sorrows of Beniamino Gigli, who is now about to show how his dignity can be preserved by singing somewhere other than the Metropolitan. We predict that the opera will go on. The secession of Mme. Jeritza from the company has been an open secret for several weeks. Even without her the opera will go on. The discovery of little unsuspected prima donnas, like Lily Pons, reveals the mysterious way of providence in keeping operas going on. Even when the captains and the kings depart, the tumult and the shouting do not die."

Over the horizon was the Wagnerian renaissance of the 1930s spearheaded by Kirsten Flagstad and Lauritz Melchior. The rich burgeoning of American singers that had begun tentatively in the nineteenth century and had triumphed under Gatti-Casazza with Rosa Ponselle and Lawrence Tibbett in the 1920s became a flood of talent in the late thirties and forties. And during an extraordinary six-year period, between 1955 and 1961, the Metropolitan Opera witnessed the debuts of Renata Tebaldi, Maria Callas, Leonie Rysanek, Christa Ludwig, Birgit Nilsson, Joan Sutherland, and Leontyne Price. Recently, with the preeminence of Placido Domingo and Luciano Pavarotti, the tenor has reemerged as the focal point of operatic attention. And just as one is assured that the dramatic soprano no longer exists, along comes Eva Marton, with a soaring voice worthy of opera's highest compliment: comparison with her glamorous predecessors.

THE CRITICS

SOMEWHERE IN THE EARLY REACHES of history, a singer first raised her voice in song. Listening to her and forming an opinion was the first critic. Ever since, the relationship between these natural antagonists has been that of two unhappy souls locked in eternal marriage. Their complaints are always the same: the other lacks sensitivity.

The enthusiastic and sometimes astute reviews that welcomed the Garcia family to America in 1825 suggest that the writers not only had heard voices previously available in New York but had themselves braved the Atlantic and heard Italian opera in London. By 1850 good voices were frequently heard and operatic activity in New York was flourishing, making the sea voyage unnecessary for critical experience. Standards could be applied and comparisons made on the basis of what was performed nearer home.

Two themes dominated New York reviews of opera and singing in the nineteenth century. Along with an emphasis on vocal technique, to be expected of a period rich in singers with such facility, was a surprisingly constant demand that technical ability be matched by emotional expression. In 1851 the poet Walt Whitman, who frequently wrote about Italian opera and was strongly influenced by it, appraised the singing of Jenny Lind: "The Swedish Swan, with all her blandishments, never touched my heart in the least. I wondered at so much vocal dexterity; and indeed they were all very pretty, those leaps and double somersets. But even in the grandest religious airs, genuine masterpieces as they are, of the German composers, executed by this strangely overpraised woman in perfect scientific style, let critics say what they like, it was a failure; for there was a vacuum in the head of the performance. Beauty pervaded it no doubt, and that of a high order. It was the beauty of Adam before God breathed into his nostrils."

Not everyone expressed himself as well as Whitman, but the twin demands for technique and emotion permeated American nineteenth-century vocal criticism and survived handsomely in the first decades of the twentieth to cope with the vocalism and the newly emerging singing actors.

In a 1913 article for his newspaper, the New York *Sun,* the music critic W. J. Henderson, in a flight of fancy, spoke of his concern for good descriptive criticism as a record for succeeding generations: "When the twenty-first century New Zealander sits on the ruins of the Williamsburg Bridge and gazes at the ragged outlines of the wreck of the Woolworth Building, when he wanders uptown and plucks flowers which the forgotten floral tributes of a bygone age sowed among the tumbled yellow bricks of what was once the Metropolitan Opera House, and when he is seized with a desire to know what manner of music was given and what sort of interpreters give it in this year of grace 1913 he will on his return to New Zealand go to the *Triad* office and borrow the files of the New York papers of today. And as he searches through them with the diligence of a patient historian he will from time to time mutter swiftly: 'Why didn't the fool tell us something?' And when he happily comes upon a column of good descriptive criticism of Geraldine Farrar or Mary Garden, or of Olive Fremstad or Emmy Destinn (with pictures, of course), he will rise up and call the writer of it blessed."

Henderson need not have worried. If we may call the years from 1906 to 1932—a vocal era beginning with Caruso and continuing with Ponselle—the golden age of opera, we may with equal justification hail it as a golden age of music criticism. The writing of the period has not been equaled since; together, the criticism, recordings, and photographs make it the first era in operatic history that may be recalled with some degree of reliability.

Henderson, a graduate of Princeton University who not only had studied the theory of music but had taken extensive singing lessons, was the most distinguished music critic in the United States. He spoke with tremendous authority and set standards that made little allowance for differences of opinion. Of singing: "If it is out of tune, it makes no difference who 'thinks' that he thinks it is not. The only question is, 'Can you hear it or can't you?' Whether an orchestra is out of tune, whether it is out of balance, whether its tone is coarse and vulgar, whether the men are playing with precision and accuracy, whether the strings are poor or the brass blatant are not matters of opinion at all. These are matters of fact and due to be reported upon by persons trained to hear them. Whether a singer has a voice equalized throughout, whether the lower tones are white and sombre, whether her coloratura is broken, spasmodic and labored; whether her cantilena is marred by inartistic phrasing, whether she sings out of tune or not, whether she sings the music according to the score or according to her own caprices—these are not matters of opinion; they are matters of fact. In short, nothing is more clearly known than the results which technic in performance can attain, and the only question that can ever be raised about a critical report is, 'Did the man hear correctly?' If it can be shown that he is in the habit of hearing incorrectly, then he is as unfit for his business

The formidable Nellie Melba as Marguerite in Faust, *her most frequent role at the Metropolitan. Photo by Aimé Dupont, circa 1896.*

as a color blind man would be for the calling of art critic."

Like other critics of the day, Henderson had an unusual gift for vivid and precise writing. In discussing Luisa Tetrazzini as Elvira in a 1909 performance of *I Puritani,* he found a devastatingly accurate yet amusing way of describing the brilliant top of her voice and the undeveloped lower register: "Mme. Tetrazzini has many gifts, but in one she stands entirely alone. She is the only singer now before the public who has her chest tones at the top and her head tones at the bottom. This alone is worth going miles to study, and it is a gift which enables the soprano to produce vocal effects both novel and astonishing."

Writing at the same time as Henderson was Richard Aldrich, whom Henderson had recommended for the position he vacated at *The New York Times* to move to the *Sun.* When Aldrich reviewed a 1913 Carnegie Hall recital by Nellie Melba, he took the trouble to describe the state of her voice with a specificity as sure as the finest recording: "It has not perceptibly lost anything of its most beautiful quality, its lusciousness, its spontaneity of utterance. In its middle range it still has that greater richness that was heard at her last visits here. It would be idle to maintain that the dazzling brilliance of her earlier days is wholly unimpaired. Her upper tones are not quite what they were in power and freedom; some of the lower ones seem to have gained. Nor can it be said that everything in her coloratura has the flawless perfection that was hers. Certain ornamented figures yesterday were produced with some effort. On the other hand, her scales and arpeggios came limpidly and fluently from her lips, and trills upon her most advantageous tones were brilliant and even. Her legato was beautiful, her phrasing of delightful finish."

If Henderson's stringent standards focused more on the vocal abilities of a singer than on theatrical and emotional values, *The New York Times'* critic, Richard Aldrich, showed a breadth of concern that could encompass both dimensions. In writing of the *Götterdämmerung* Brünnhilde of Olive Fremstad, a singer whose vocal and dramatic orientation were light years away from Melba's, Aldrich revealed his dual approach to criticism: "In this impersonation, attention is not centered upon the voice; for all its beauty, its dramatic color, its noble declamation and phrasing seem indissolubly mingled with her action, gesture, pose, and facial play as essentially a part of one and the same expression. A more poignant and profoundly moving interpretation of that scene of tragic bewilderment and despair in the second act, where, conducted home by Gunther, she confronts Siegfried, is not to be witnessed upon the operatic stage. It is a revelation of the subtlest, and most potent resources of a great tragic actress's art."

Music criticism of the age was not only precise and vivid, but it was also more detailed than the writing we find today. On a larger scale than the daily coverage or even the Sunday feature to which the present-day operagoer has become accustomed was the extended essay. This full-scale article on a singer, mixing biography, humor, and criticism in a discussion of the artist by a critic who regularly reviewed him or her, has no current counterpart. If one finds it at all today, it is usually written by an all-purpose journalist who does not know the material as well as his readers. For command of a subject as well as an affectionate regard for it, consider these excerpts from Pitts Sanborn's 1913 essay on Luisa Tetrazzini, which appeared in one of New York's vanished newspapers, the *Globe.*

"Madame Tetrazzini is not 'chic,' she is not a fashionable prima donna. Whether she is an intelligent and reflective artist, or whether she is just an imbecile singing by the grace of God alone, or what she is, those that write most about her are not in a position to know positively, for she is an Italian, and operatic Italians, with rare exceptions, are about as available for purposes of psychological observation as a skylark singing in high heaven. It has been necessary to study her art across the footlights.

"Luisa Tetrazzini has been quoted as saying that she taught herself to sing. Her voice and her trill she had from God. . . . A few months of repertory (and her repertory is not the ten or the dozen parts she has sung in New York and London, but some thirty or forty), completed her preliminary studies. Such training is a contrast to the seven laborious years of the great tradition, and might account for the crudities in her singing, which were most evident the first night she sang here, and which have been harped on ever since, but does it account for her perfect attack, her wonderful control of breath, her clean execution of ornaments, her exquisite portamento, her proficiency in sustained singing, especially her ability to phrase with the roundness and incomparable grace of the pure old Italian style?

" . . . In the autumn of 1907 she suddenly emerged at Covent Garden, and people that walked in darkest London saw a great light. [The Manhattan Opera's] Oscar Hammerstein lost no time. First he engaged her for the next season, then he decided he must have her at once, and he did. Despite the [Heinrich] Conried threats of a previous contract [with the Metropolitan] she faced a New York audience on the Manhattan stage early the following January, and the rest is plain sailing.

"What Tetrazzini was in Russia, what befell her in the South American hill towns, what in the jungles of Mexico, it is impossible for the present writer to say. Whether she had only high notes in Russia, whether the hill dwellers can only hear above the staff he knoweth not. But certain it is when she first sang at the Manhattan she was chiefly admirable for her extraordinary upper octave. In it the tones were perfectly produced, strong, pure, dazzling in their flame-like play of color. When she sang a thing like the 'Carnival of Venice' variations, her staccati, her chromatic runs, her echo effects, her swelling and diminishing of a tone, the ravishing curve of her portamento showed a vocal virtuoso in that exalted region without a peer. The feats of Sembrich and Melba paled in comparison. But those inexplicable crudities and inequalities! A woman who in *La Traviata* had just sung 'Ah! fors' è lui' surpassingly well could declaim 'Dite alla giovine' in a choked, metallic parlando that would not be tolerated in any respectable vocal studio. Some of the sounds she emitted in the lower portion of her voice were like nothing but the clicks of an old-fashioned talking machine before those devices had been perfected. However, Tetrazzini never sang here so badly as that first night.

"When she returned the next season the crudities had largely disappeared, and her medium register, previously deficient, she had recovered or developed. The return to vocal civilization, singing in London and New York under the guidance of Campanini and in competition with such singers as Melba and Sembrich, were doing their work. But the apotheosis of Tetrazzini came last spring when, after a year's absence, she returned here to sing in concert. Then the voice was almost perfectly equalized, a glorious organ from top to bottom. Even in the lowest register she was ready with a firm, rich tone, as in 'Voi che sapete.' She not only sang great florid arias with perfect command of voice, technique and style; she sang Aida's 'Ritorna vincitor' as scarcely a dramatic soprano has sung it here; she sang Solvejg's song from *Peer Gynt* like a true Lieder singer, and the page's song from *Figaro* she sang with an adorable and Mozartean simplicity. It was an astonishing and enchanting display of great soprano singing in every style, and the most wonderful display of sheer vocal virtuosity New York can have heard since the prime of Adelina Patti."

Sanborn goes on to compare Tetrazzini with Sembrich and Melba, to consider her costuming, and to describe her stage presence. The reader knows from reading this that its author adores opera, attends more than isolated performances in the pursuit of duty, and understands the capacities and glories of the human voice.

In addition to Henderson, Aldrich, and Sanborn, the New York reader could follow Henry Krehbiel, the foremost chronicler of New York operatic history, in the *Tribune;* his successor, the learned and witty Lawrence Gilman, who had previously written for *Harper's Weekly;* Henry T. Finck, whose all but mutually exclusive loves were Wagner and Geraldine Farrar, in the

E. J. Foley's 1908 photo of Luisa Tetrazzini as Philine in Mignon, *whose aria "Je suis Titania" was one of the soprano's spectacular concert numbers and recordings.*

Evening Post; and a younger-generation critic, Herbert F. Peyser, who wrote for several dailies and eventually wound up with *Musical America.* Even New York's racing paper, the *Morning Telegraph,* had a music critic, an all but forgotten Irishman named Algernon St. John-Brenon, who was both eccentric and clever. There were at least a dozen others who wrote about opera almost every day.

In applying standards and making demands upon the singers, the critics were outspoken when offended and operated without the good manners that govern later writers. Their flair for expression was comparable to the theatrics of their best subjects.

In 1903 Estelle Liebling, later to become a noted teacher whose pupils included Jessica Dragonette and Beverly Sills, sang at the Met in a *Bohème* with Caruso singing his first New York Rodolfo and Marcella Sembrich singing Mimi. The *Times* commented: "The fly in the ointment was the appearance of Miss Estelle Liebling as Musetta, which in that companionship and to that audience was little less than affront. A voice of gruesome quality and diminutive volume, a characterization that vulgarized the part and crippled the effect of every scene in which it appeared made up the sum of what she contributed." The *Tribune* was briefer: "Miss Liebling's voice and manner do not call for serious comment, nor could they endure it." When Ellen Beach Yaw, a tall, slim soprano who advertised her voice as soaring past the highest notes of Nilsson and Patti up to E above high E, made her solitary Metropolitan Opera appearance as Lucia in 1908 and fell on the stage at the conclusion of the Mad Scene, one critic, obviously not in sympathy with what had gone before, observed, "The lady looked for all the world like a pan of spilt milk."

The honesty of the New York press could be depended upon. Not so with other cities' critics. The Metropolitan Opera must have been shocked during its first visit to Paris the summer of 1910 to encounter critics who ripped apart New York's gods, Toscanini and Caruso. Inspired by the French contralto Marie Delna, who had tangled with Toscanini during her New York engagement the previous winter, one Paris journal, *Gil Blas,* was particularly vituperative. With a sharp reference to Toscanini's procedure of conducting without a score, Delna maintained in an interview that the only person who liked him was the prompter. Midway through the Paris season, however, *Gil Blas* made a complete about-face. All the season's reviews from *Gil Blas* were collected on one page of the Metropolitan's press book; at the bottom appear some astonishing handwritten lines from the then new press officer, William J. Guard: "Note: This 'change of heart' on the parts of the Editors of *Gil Blaș* cost exactly 2000 francs the price arranged for by me. Paris July 1910."

Truth and dependability, knowledge and technical skill, humor and understanding—all the qualities demanded by New York critics of their subjects were their own to dispense bountifully to their readers. If the critics evoked the glamorous names of the past too frequently, it was only for the maintenance of standards. And even that could be treated with humor. Another distinguished critic, James G. Huneker, writing of a 1918 Metropolitan Opera performance of *Aida* in Philadelphia with Giovanni Martinelli and Claudia Muzio, mocked the critics themselves: "But, then, everyone who goes to opera has always heard *Aida* sung better! There were doubters in the glorious days of Italo Campanini, and no doubt some critic shrugged shoulders in Cairo the night of the premiere, 1871, insinuating Rhadames might have been in more competent hands if Larynxini had been confided the role."

We constantly revert to this age for the grandeur of its artists. Its critics, too, were giants.

THE OPERA PHOTOGRAPHERS

OPERA SINGERS HAVE NEVER BEEN timid about publicity. The familiar spectacle of Hollywood stars and their agents battling for top billing in movie advertising was anticipated at least two hundred years earlier by singers who made certain their boldly printed names were on the playbills that announced forthcoming performances. With the increased popularity of the piano in the early 1800s, sheet music excerpts from popular operas were widely sold; their covers featured printed likenesses of the most famous opera stars. The only difference between a printed duet from *L'Elisir d'Amore* with soprano Henriette Sontag and bass Luigi Lablache cavorting in costume on its cover and the 1978 American Express TV commercial starring Luciano Pavarotti is one of time and place. The intent is the same: to make use of a performer's name and image to sell a product. It is more than incidental that the performer benefits from the exposure. Not every singer has had the delicacy of soprano Maria Jeritza, who went to court in the 1920s to have her name removed from a cigar.

British and French discoveries in the 1830s resulted in commercial photography; the opera singer soon recognized the photograph as a wonderful new vehicle for publicity. The daguerreotype, that early, vivid photograph in which the mirrorlike image is created on the silver-coating of a metal plate, was introduced to this country in 1840. It was significant that upon Jenny Lind's arrival in New York in 1850 P. T. Barnum would take her across the street from his museum on lower Broadway to the studio of his friend Mathew Brady and have her sit for him. Lind subsequently posed in every city on her triumphant tours, and the resulting images can still be seen today. Brady's photograph of Marietta Gazzaniga, Verdi's first Luisa Miller, may be the first American portrait of an opera singer in costume.

In the beginning, the transaction between photographer and singer appears to have been one in which the singer posed in exchange for free prints; the photographer would then profit from selling his own copies to the public.

When Marietta Alboni first sang in New York in 1852, she went to the studios of Jeremiah Gurney & Son at Fifth Avenue and 16th Street for her portrait. During the 1860s and 1870s Gurney photographed the tenors Mario, Victor Capoul, and Enrico Tamberlik as Poliuto, as well as Christine Nilsson as Mignon.

By 1860 the paper photograph had largely replaced the daguerreotype. Gurney's flashy competitor, Napoleon Sarony, of 68 Broadway and later of 37 Union Square, turned out an estimated 40,000 different portraits of musical and theatrical personalities and helped popularize photograph collecting. Sarony is credited with having pioneered less restrained poses, and his portraits of Charles Santley as Rigoletto, the Canadian soprano Emma Albani in several roles, and Christine Nilsson in roles from both *Huguenots* and *Gioconda* show a slightly less rigid style.

The Cuban-born José Maria Mora, whose studio was at 707 Broadway, specialized in using interesting backgrounds and accessories in his portraits. In a studio said to resemble the backstage area of a repertory theater, Mora photographed Therese Tietjens in *Lucrezia Borgia,* Minnie Hauk as Carmen, Clara Louise Kellogg in most of her repertoire, and Annie Louise Cary as Amneris. From just the Metropolitan's first season, Mora provided an unparalleled visual record of Christine Nilsson in her opening-night role of Marguerite in *Faust,* Franco Novara as Méphistophélès in the same performance, Marcella Sembrich in both *Lucia* and *Puritani,* Italo Campanini as Don José, Roberto Stagno as Manrico, and Giuseppe Kaschmann.

Also from that first Metropolitan season is a portrait of Giuseppe del Puente as Figaro in *Il Barbiere di Siviglia* by B. J. Falk, first of 949 Broadway and later of 13 and 15 West 24th Street. Falk, who around 1870 had photographed Giorgio Ronconi, Verdi's first Nabucco, as Méphistophélès in *Faust,* is most closely identified with the Met's German seasons, beginning with his portrait of Leopold Damrosch, the second general manager. Most of the German artists posed for Falk, including Lilli Lehmann as Brünnhilde and Marianne Brandt as Fidès in *Le Prophète,* and he worked into the 1890s, with Emma Calvé as Carmen and Santuzza, Nellie Melba in *Roméo et Juliette,* Francesco Tamagno, the Swedish soprano Sigrid Arnoldson, and Emma Eames as Santuzza.

Aimé Dupont's socially significant addresses of 574 Fifth Avenue and Newport, Rhode Island, helped him become the first New York photographer who, without official Metropolitan Opera connection until 1907–10, worked for most of the artists on the roster. It is difficult to think of a Metropolitan singer who did not pose for Dupont in and out of costume between 1895 and 1910. Jean de Reszke as Tristan and Siegfried in the 1890s gives way to the first New York photos of Caruso, including the role of his 1903 debut, the Duke in *Rigoletto.* Melba, Milka Ternina, Sembrich, Aïno Ackté, Eames, and Pol Plançon are joined by Puccini, Mahler, and Toscanini. In quality, Dupont's work shows no photographic advance; the average Mora image is sharper and more interesting than Dupont's work.

Marietta Gazzaniga, probably as Norma, in Mathew Brady's photo dating from her 1857 American debut season.

Curiously enough, the first official Met photographer was the little-known Frank C. Bangs, of 20 West 38th Street, whose name appears in the 1906–1907 programs as "Photographer to the Conried Metropolitan Opera Company." Few examples of his work exist today except for a strikingly dark and dramatic series of Riccardo Stracciari as Amonasro and a portrait of Celestina Boninsegna, an Italian dramatic soprano whose one Metropolitan season was hampered by illness.

Dupont was the last of the Metropolitan Opera photographers to work only on the creation of portraits in a studio. Singers were first photographed onstage early in the century by the New York photographer Joseph Byron. He shot scenes from several 1906–1907 productions, Geraldine Farrar and Louise Homer in the first Metropolitan *Madama Butterfly; Fliegende Holländer* with Johanna Gadski; Olive Fremstad in the notorious performance of *Salome;* and Farrar and Riccardo Martin in a

Gurney's photo of Christine Nilsson as Mignon dating from her first New York appearance in the role in 1871 at the Academy of Music on 14th Street.

The American Minnie Hauk, who dazzled both New York and London with their first sight of Bizet's Carmen. *Sarony photo, circa 1878.*

Mora's 1883 portrait of Marcella Sembrich as Lucia, showing her left profile, which she preferred to have emphasized. Sembrich was the most successful artist in the Met's first season.

One of a series of Falk photos of Lilli Lehmann as Brünnhilde in Die Walküre, *one of several roles in which she dominated the Metropolitan's German opera seasons.*

The incomparable Jean de Reszke as Siegfried in Götterdämmerung, *photographed by Aimé Dupont around 1899 when the tenor first appeared in the role in New York.*

Frank C. Bangs's 1906 portrait of Riccardo Stracciari as Amonasro in Aida, *the Italian baritone's most frequent role with the Metropolitan.*

Opposite: *Herman Mishkin's well-known portrait of Beniamino Gigli as Vasco da Gama in the 1923 revival of* L'Africana.

series from *Mefistofele,* which is significant for its demonstration of a problem that has plagued stage photographers ever since: the failure of an artist—in this case, Feodor Chaliapin—to appear at the dress rehearsal in makeup.

Lande, another New York photographer, was officially engaged by the company in 1908-1909 "to perpetuate the artistic side of the new productions.... When some impresario of the next century feels for instance that the public is ripe to hear *La Wally* and is even clamoring for more of *Tiefland,* it will be possible to find out all the Metropolitan's traditions of costume and scenery in these operas." The following season he worked on *Orfeo* and *Pipe of Desire.* Lande's work is uniformly bad. Nonetheless, the New York *Sun* raved at this innovation: "It would probably never have been possible for the new book of records to have existed in the old days of the Metropolitan. The proud spirit of the star would have resisted. Jean de Reszke would not even appear in the tableau that opens *Roméo et Juliette* on the ground that it was beneath his dignity to pose in the picture while the chorus sang the chant. Imagine him, then, batting his eyes before the flashlight."

Between 1910 and the early 1920s, while Herman Mishkin was photographing most of the major Met stars in portraiture, onstage photographs were the responsibility of the noted stage photographers of White Studio. The quality is a significant improvement on Lande's; White's photographs have frequently been reproduced in articles on the Metropolitan. White's work began with the 1910-11 opening night *Armide* with Caruso and Olive Fremstad, continued through the world premiere of *La Fanciulla del West* (including a famous shot of the final scene that shows Caruso with a noose around his neck), and concluded sometime around 1923-24 with *Fedora,* with Maria Jeritza and Giovanni Martinelli.

Between 1920 and 1935 Carlo Edwards (1889-1948) was an assistant conductor at the Metropolitan, playing both piano and organ and probably prompting some performances. At some point during the 1920s he began to bring his camera to rehearsals. In November of 1928 his *Campana Sommersa* rehearsal shot appeared in the *Evening World* as part of a layout with Herman Mishkin's portrait of Elisabeth Rethberg as Rautendelein; the following November a full page of his work appeared in the *Herald Tribune.*

Edwards had the immense advantage of being on the spot, able to move freely about the opera house. While his early portraits are stilted and unbecoming, he soon developed a sophisticated style of softly flattering portraiture, presumably photographed backstage, that brings

Carlo Edwards's portrait of Kirsten Flagstad as Sieglinde, taken backstage the day of her astonishing Met debut, February 2, 1935.

Jussi Björling in his 1938 Metropolitan debut role, Rodolfo in La Bohème, *taken by the New York Times Studio in the late 1930s.*

Sedge LeBlang's portrait of Zinka Milanov as Leonora in the Met's 1952 production of La Forza del Destino.

us some of the best images we have of Beniamino Gigli, Kirsten Flagstad, and others between 1927 and 1935.

It was inevitable that Edwards's ability to provide on-stage scenes and Mishkin's distance from the opera house should eventually lead to Edwards's appointment as the Met's official photographer. Ironically, the position was his alone for only the 1932–33 season; a foot had to be amputated as the result of an accident in Oklahoma, where he was conducting. During 1933–35 he shared the duties at the Met with New York Times Studio.

Under its director, William Freese, the Times Studio had a large setup, with photographers on staff covering a variety of news events. In his proposal to the Metropolitan in November 1933 Mr. Freese, perhaps remembering how his and Carlo Edwards's work had undermined Mishkin's position there, asked "that other picture syndicates, excepting the Associated Press, not be given the privilege to make photographs there."

The New York Times studio contract with the Metropolitan lasted through 1946–47. Toward the middle of that season Louis Mélançon began to take costume portraits, production scenes, and informal shots backstage. He was official photographer during 1948–50, but the larger body of his work was produced after 1957.

Sedge LeBlang was a superb studio photographer who also took production shots as part of his duties. After World War II, LeBlang set up a studio in New York and worked at the Metropolitan during the first six Bing seasons, 1950–56. Those were the years of Zinka Milanov, Robert Merrill, Leonard Warren, Mario Del Monaco, Ettore Bastianini, and Renata Tebaldi. There are brightly lighted, well-realized photographs of them all by LeBlang, who believed that excessive retouching was akin to embalming. His negatives were given to the Metropolitan Opera Archives after his death.

For a brief period, from November 1956 to January 1957, Frank Lerner was the official photographer. He made a few studio portraits—Warren and Siepi in *Ernani,* Theodor Uppman and Patrice Munsel in *La Périchole*—as well as rehearsal and full stage scenes of Maria Callas in *Norma* and color slides for the Metropolitan Opera Guild's first color filmstrip, Callas in *Tosca.*

So vivid is the memory of Louis Mélancon, with his white hair, red sweater, and ebullient, irascible personality, that one must be reminded of his absence from the opera house since his death in 1974. The photographic studio in the new house was designed to his specifications. With his theatrical background, Mélançon was

Right: *Louis Mélançon's formal portrait of Leontyne Price as Cleopatra in the 1966 world premiere of Samuel Barber's* Antony and Cleopatra, *which opened the new Metropolitan Opera House.*

Frank Lerner's photo of Cesare Siepi as Silva in the 1956 production of Verdi's Ernani.

well suited to opera. Between 1957 and 1974 he photographed all the new productions and all the artists; he was at his best taking action shots from the wings during performances.

As house manager for the Metropolitan beginning in 1966, James Heffernan sharpened his photographic skills and succeeded Mélançon in 1974. The detailed documentation of productions and revivals credited to Lande in 1908–1909 has actually been carried out by Heffernan for the first time. While he performs all the functions of the official photographer, working both onstage and in the studio, his speciality is the glamorous full-color portrait of singers in costume.

In 1983 the black-and-white studio portrait of opera singers is all but dead. The last studio photographs to celebrate fully the extravagance of the operatic personality were taken by Richard Avedon for *Vogue* in 1955 and featured Marian Anderson and Zinka Milanov in *Un Ballo in Maschera.* A less formal journalism demands the action photograph taken either at rehearsal or in performance. Formal substitutes have sprung up in the luridly colored portraits featured prominently on record jackets. With subjects seemingly fresh from Madame Tussaud's, they are not worthy of serious comparison: movie magazines have always done the same thing, but with more flair. Perhaps styles will change, but this would require of singers a better understanding of their own personalities and a more individual approach to character portrayal.

James Heffernan's photograph of Placido Domingo as Otello, taken in September 1979 for Domingo's first Met performance of the role.

Opposite: *Claudia Muzio in Madama Butterfly's death scene, a photo Mishkin took to publicize her 1918 performances at the Ravinia Opera near Chicago.*

ulated that he was to furnish the company with all "photographs necessary to advertising purposes in exchange for the exclusive right to exhibit my photographs in the lobby of the Metropolitan Opera House in frames specially adapted to harmonize with the interior decorations." The number of photographs for distribution to the press would not exceed fifteen hundred copies. Additional copies, either 6 × 7 inches or 7 × 9 inches, would cost ten cents each. The number of subjects was limited to principal artists and new members of the company. He agreed to release the copyright on all photographs for publication. He was to be given two seats for one performance a week. With minor changes in the numbers and charges for photographs, these are essentially the terms under which he worked until 1932. There was no salary; this was a concession under which both he and the opera company were to benefit. Best of all from Mishkin's point of view, he was listed in the Metropolitan programs as "Official Photographer."

For Hammerstein, Mishkin had posed most of his subjects against a neutral background; Maria Labia's portrait as Tosca was taken in front of a stained-glass backdrop that later served Emmy Destinn, Olive Fremstad, and Giovanni Martinelli in the same opera. A classical column appears in some of the Hammerstein work. Before his Met contract, Mishkin purchased a pastoral backdrop, closely resembling Dupont's, and many of his most famous images have this background. At least two Metropolitan artists, Leo Slezak and Emmy Destinn, had been photographed by Mishkin in this setting while he was still with Hammerstein. Caruso posed against it for the first time in December 1910 as Dick Johnson in *Fanciulla.*

The pastoral background is the surest guide in identifying Mishkin's work. Unfortunately, the white "Mishkin" signature is not. As a service to Met singers Mishkin often copied the work of other photographers and invariably marked them with his own signature, the original signature sometimes showing through. Geraldine Farrar's German and French photos and onstage portraits by White of New York were often copied by Mishkin; Maria Jeritza tried out most of her repertoire in Vienna and then brought to New York the atmospheric portraits taken of her by Setzer. Mishkin seems to have had no qualms about putting his name to these photographs; he was probably more dismayed when other photographers did the same to his work.

Mishkin was sometimes careless, as in the ubiquitous oriental rug hastily thrown over some steps for Giuseppe De Luca posing as Rigoletto. At the same time, the images themselves have defined how we remember De Luca and the role itself. One of them was copied in oil by Paolo Ghiglia, a painting that now hangs in Founders Hall at the Metropolitan.

At the beginning of his second season, in November 1911, Mishkin approached the Metropolitan management with an offer to do the onstage photographs then being handled by White Studios. The offer was rejected. His 1918 shot of De Luca and the cast of *Gianni Schicchi* is probably his first use of Met stage settings as background. His most familiar stage photograph shows Maria Jeritza and Giacomo Lauri-Volpi on the staircase in *Turandot;* the best is surely the portrait of Elisabeth Rethberg as Rautendelein in Respighi's *La Campana Sommersa.*

Whatever problems Mishkin had in communicating with his family, his studio personality established an atmosphere that freed his operatic subjects from feeling constrained in that most self-conscious of moments: posing without movement to have a picture taken. With extraordinary frequency Mishkin was able to find the poses that would summon forth the singer's personality and unite it with an operatic character. Although the importance of visual documents has long been underestimated, W. J. Henderson wrote about it prophetically in 1913: "The scores of dead and buried works may be exhumed, but the artist and his effect on his time pass away. . . . The phonograph record alone will not suffice. It cannot reproduce the facial expression, the action, the gesture. It cannot disclose to us the entire impersonation of any one character. We may hear Mme. Fremstad sing the prayer of *Tosca,* but the phonographic record does not yet offer us her whole Isolde. And it never can unless it can be brought to unite with the moving picture in a reproduction of a whole performance of *Tristan und Isolde.*" While it has taken seventy years for television to bring us the complete record foreseen by Henderson, Mishkin at the same time Henderson was writing was ensuring that Olive Fremstad's reputation as a singing actress would endure. His portraits of Fremstad as Isolde with the love potion in Act I of *Tristan* are his masterpiece. Looking at them after the span of many years, who could question her stature as a sublime interpreter of the role? The same immortality clings to Mishkin portraits of Maurice Renaud as Scarpia, Mary Garden as Marguerite in *Faust,* Antonio Scotti as Tonio, Caruso as Samson and as Eléazar in *La Juive,* and Feodor Chaliapin as Mefistofele, Boris Godunov, King Philip, and Don Quichotte.

Mishkin's arrangement with the Metropolitan assured him of sittings with most of that company's fabled singing roster; its general manager, Giulio Gatti-Casazza; its conductors, including Arturo Toscanini and Tullio Serafin; and most of the professional staff. His skill and increasing reputation brought Mary Garden back to him when she was singing in Chicago. Indeed, many singers with the Chicago Opera made a point of engaging Mishkin's services. Maggie Teyte, Riccardo Stracciari, Rosa

Raisa, Giacomo Rimini, and Joseph Schwarz sat for him, and Mishkin photographed Amelita Galli-Curci and Titta Ruffo years before they sang with the Metropolitan. At the Met, Hermann Jadlowker and Feodor Chaliapin, with whom he could speak Russian, were also his friends.

There are, however, some names surprisingly missing from the list of singers Mishkin had contact with and photographed between 1906 and 1932. Geraldine Farrar posed with Caruso in *Carmen,* but there are no other opera portraits, only a few out of costume, and she preferred to use almost anyone else. His family remembers that they fought but recalls no details. In any case, Farrar returned to Mishkin Studios in the mid-twenties for a stunning series of her with graying hair, dog, and pearls. One of them appeared on the cover of *Time* magazine, dated December 5, 1927. While with the Hammerstein company, neither John McCormack nor Luisa Tetrazzini went to Mishkin; McCormack eventually sat for his portrait around 1915, while Tetrazzini is almost alone among the singers who rose to prominence in New York during this period in never having sat for him. Her New York operatic portraits, as are McCormack's, are by E. F. Foley of 164 Fifth Avenue.

Outside opera, Mishkin photographed Anna Pavlova more than one hundred times, often with either Mikhail Mordkin or Alexander Volinine; the Danish-born ballerina Adeline Genée; the great Hungarian violin teacher Leopold Auer and also his three most famous students, Mischa Elman, Jascha Heifetz, and Efrem Zimbalist; the pianists Josef Hoffman and Sergei Rachmaninoff; the conductor Willem Mengelberg; the politicians Franklin D. Roosevelt and Alfred E. Smith; and Albert Einstein. Mishkin did not, however, photograph Nijinsky.

Overriding everything else was the prestige of being able to advertise in the 1920 *Enrico Caruso Souvenir Book* that he was not only official photographer to the Metropolitan Opera House but also "Personal Photographers to Mr. Enrico Caruso."

The cover of the *Souvenir Book* features a rendering in color by Willy Pogany of what has become the most famous opera photograph ever taken. This is the portrait of Caruso as Canio in *Pagliacci,* a forced grin on his face while he leans over a giant bass drum, his right arm raised in the air ready to strike with the beater. The photograph has been reproduced countless times, serving as a readily identifiable image that evokes opera without the need of words. The Metropolitan Opera Guild has had it sculpted in porcelain by Hutschenreuter. Succeeding tenors have felt the need of the Caruso association and assumed the same pose, always with less dramatic effect. Not generally known is that two versions of this photograph exist. At some point between 1912 and 1920 the glass negative plate must have been broken; the first version has a backdrop showing small tents in the background and a more convincing expression on the tenor's face. The second version has the same pose and an approximation of the facial expression. There is a draped background that figures in many examples of Mishkin's late opera work, which may mean that the photographs incorporating it were taken backstage in the opera house. If the negative for the second version still exists, it is probably on the nitrocellulose film that Mishkin switched to around 1919–20. Many more glass negatives have survived than nitrate negatives, which not only are flammable but disintegrate in time.

Mishkin's opera portraits of Caruso began in 1910 with Dick Johnson in *La Fanciulla del West* and continued with most of the great roles of his later career: Canio, the Duke of Mantua in *Rigoletto,* Radames in *Aida,* Rodolfo in *La Bohème,* Riccardo in *Un Ballo in Maschera,* Don José in *Carmen,* Raoul in *Gli Ugonotti,* Samson, Des Grieux in *Manon* and *Manon Lescaut* (the same photos served for both), John of Leyden in *Le Prophète,* and, finally, Eléazar in *La Juive.* There are also portraits of Caruso in the title role of *Julien,* Charpentier's short-lived sequel to *Louise.* Caruso also posed in Mishkin's studio for a variety of portraits that were widely distributed and published. In 1917, when Caruso wanted a special present for the family that had come to his aid in the aftermath of the 1906 San Francisco earthquake, he commissioned a series that included *Bohème, Manon Lescaut, Ugonotti,* and *Samson.* These prints of 11¾ × 19¾ are the finest and most treasured examples of Mishkin's art.

Mishkin sometimes visited Caruso backstage at the Metropolitan and captured him standing on the stage-right staircase leading to the male stars' dressing rooms. The various photos show Caruso in costume and also formally attired for dinner after a performance. The photographer closely observed his most famous subject and treasured throughout his life two notes he received from the tenor. The first one, handwritten in a scrawl on December 31, 1917, said: "Dear Mr. Mishkin Please accept my best thanks for the beautiful fotos present that you sent me which I appreciate very much. With best wishes for the New Year and believe me Your truly Caruso." The second, from December 13, 1920, answered Mishkin's concern about the illness that had struck Caruso earlier that month. Typed and formal, it concluded, "As you know I am very well again and as scheduled will sing FORZA tonight at the Opera House."

Mishkin had not photographed Caruso as Eléazar in *La Juive* when it was first performed the previous season. In connection with the opening-night performance of the 1920–21 season, he made formal studio portraits of the tenor in the Passover scene. Now some premonition led him backstage on Christmas Eve, 1920. Either before the performance or during an intermission, Caruso found a few moments to pause and stare sadly into Mishkin's camera. Concerned and troubled, Mishkin went home and told his family of the experience; his photographs had captured for all time the immortal tenor during his last performance.

At some point between 1921 and 1925, Mishkin Stu-

FIFTEEN CENTS

December 5, 1927

TIME

The Weekly Newsmagazine

GERALDINE FARRAR

Henceforth she works in miniature.

(See Music)

Volume X

Number 23

Editorial Rooms and General Offices, 25 West 45th Street, New York. Circulation Department, Penton Bldg., Cleveland.

Mishkin's photograph of Geraldine Farrar became the cover of Time magazine, dated December 5, 1927.

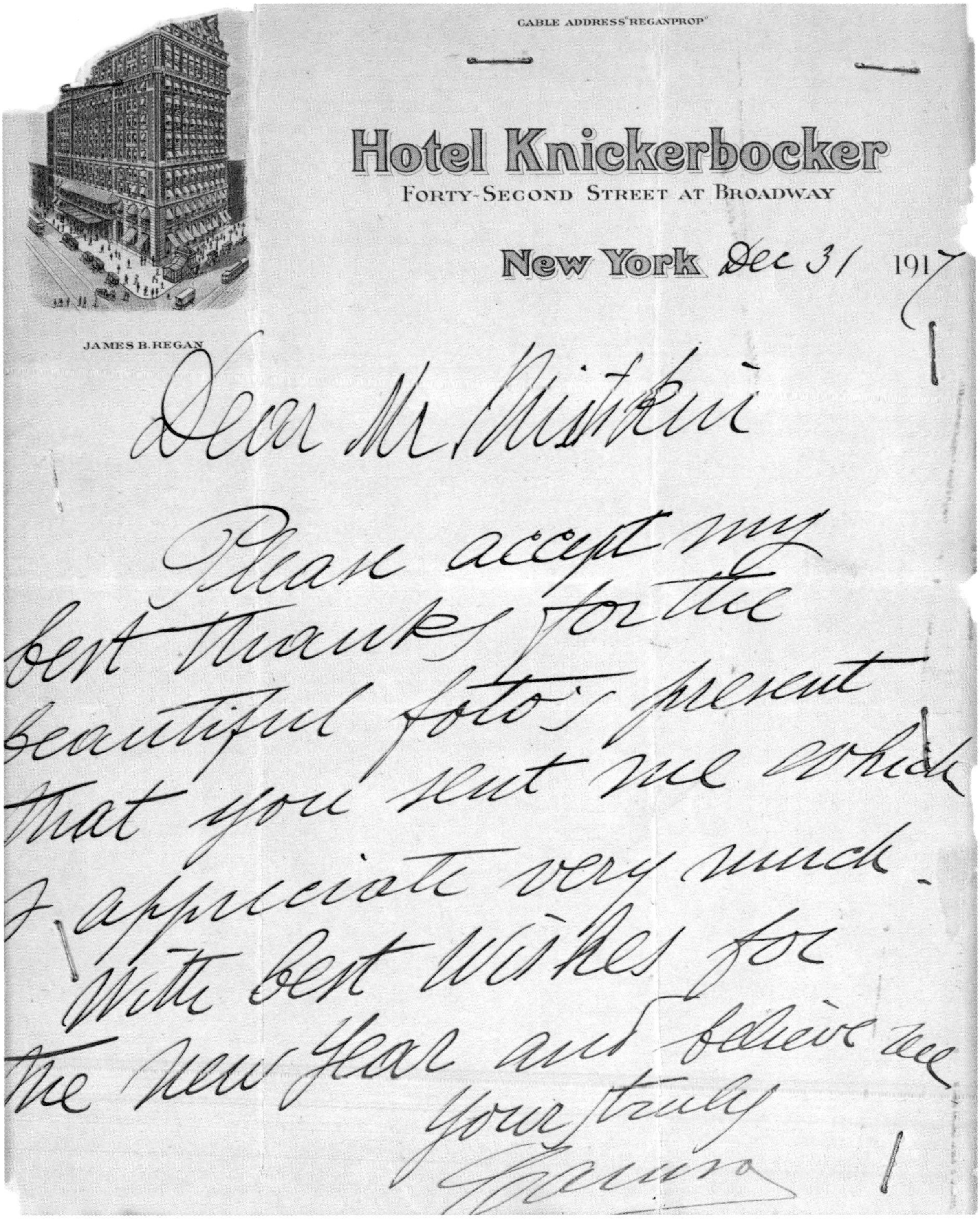

CABLE ADDRESS "REGANPROP"

Hotel Knickerbocker

FORTY-SECOND STREET AT BROADWAY

JAMES B. REGAN

New York Dec 31 1917

Dear Mr Mishkin

Please accept my best thanks for the beautiful foto's present that you sent me which I appreciate very much. With best wishes for the new Year and believe me

yours truly

Caruso

Thank you note from Enrico Caruso to Herman Mishkin.

dios moved from 471 Fifth Avenue, a short distance from the opera house, to 605 Fifth Avenue at 49th Street. There is a marked falling off in the number of costume portraits after this move to a less accessible location. By 1932, when his last contract expired, he was four blocks farther uptown, at 677 Fifth Avenue. The expanded photographic coverage in the newspapers during the late 1920s required a fresher style for portraits and a documentary approach to the activities of the opera house with backstage, rehearsal, and performance shots. None of these were Mishkin specialities. Carlo Edwards, an amateur photographer on the Met's staff of conductors, was on hand to take advantage of Mishkin's physical and technical distance from the theater; the New York Times Studio also began work in the opera during the same period.

Two letters from Mishkin to Gatti-Casazza document the last days of his work for the Metropolitan. May 2, 1932: "Several weeks ago I had the pleasure of a personal interview with you and discussed the photographic department for the future, and you told me, you will think this matter over, and let me know about it. And as I explained to you at that time, the reason for my coming to you direct was, because my original agreement was signed by you personally. I want to impress upon you Mr. Gatti that for the past 22 years I have been associated with you, and your company I put in all my best efforts towards executing and making the best and quickest possible way. I have worked hard and conscieosly to make the finest photographs and best service, and your publicity department will bear me out, that for the whole period, they have never experienced a disapointment no matter how short time I had to turn out the work for them. I do hope you will consider me favorable and reply before you leave for your trip to Europe so I can lay my plans out for next season. Thanking in advance."

May 13, 1932: "Mr. Ziegler informed me this morning that you have promised Mr. Carlo Edwards to do the photographic work next season. And he also told me at the same time, that the reason why I was not asked, whether I wish to continue to do the work, is, because I told him, that I did not care to do it any more, and that is the reason why I was not spoken to. Now Mr. Gatti, I do not want to leave your institution with the vague impression on your mind that I did [not] want to do the work. I never told that to anybody, and if this was my feeling about, I would not have come to you a couple months ago to talk to you and ask you to give me the work, this itself is enough proof that I wanted it, the whole thing was misconstrued, and presented to you in the wrong light. Have never expressed it, and never said it.

However, since Mr. Ziegler told me of your decision, that you promised the work to Mr. Edwards, naturally there is nothing left for me to do. But I do imagine, an institution like the Metropolitan Opera Co., should have a photographer on their staff a proffessial, one who has background color and photographic artistry.

"I am certainly dissapointed the way I was handled about this particular matter, I feel that after putting in 22 years, of hard work, and devotion to the operatic work, I should have at least been asked whether I want to renew the agreement. I feel that I was pushed out, and consider it a shamefull trick on the part of one of two persons who worked against me inside of the opera house, in fact I was once made to understand the fact.

"Now Mr. Gatti, I want you to feel that I leave your organization with the highest respect and best of feeling towards you, and that I have also enjoyed the whole 22 years I served you. Have always considered you a high class Gentleman, and leave your organization with my best salutations and highest respect towards you. . . . P.S. Would appreciate if could mail an aknowledgment of my service and work for your opera co." Gatti's typically perfunctory reply—"You have rendered faithful and conscientious services to the Metropolitan in furnishing photographs of our artists"—took a proud place in the large-sized album that contained the only prints Mishkin kept for himself—autographed photos and letters of Caruso, Pavlova, Otto Kahn, Chaliapin, Mary Garden, Claudia Muzio, Antonio Scotti, and Lily Pons.

This break with the Metropolitan came at the height of the Depression, and Mishkin's wealthy customers had problems of their own. William Guard, the Met's press director, who had come from Hammerstein with Mishkin and was Mishkin's immediate superior at the Met, died during the 1931–32 season. Within a few months, Mishkin had moved his studio to Brooklyn, where he was then living, and set up quarters in Abraham & Straus, on Fulton Street. He offered several times to return to the Metropolitan but was rejected. All the operatic negatives were sold to Culver Pictures, who made it possible for individuals to purchase superb low-priced copies of most of them. Culver gave part of the collection to the New York Public Library after 1950, and most of this collection eventually made its way to the Metropolitan Opera Archives.

Mishkin died in retirement in 1948. His many photographs of opera singers were made for frankly commercial purposes. But as has happened so often with popular forms of expression, the photographs became something more than an immediate vehicle for publicizing the Metropolitan Opera and its singers. All of them are valuable historical documents; many are works of art.

Overleaf: *Mary Garden in the title role of Massenet's* Sapho.

©
Mishkin
Studio
N.Y.

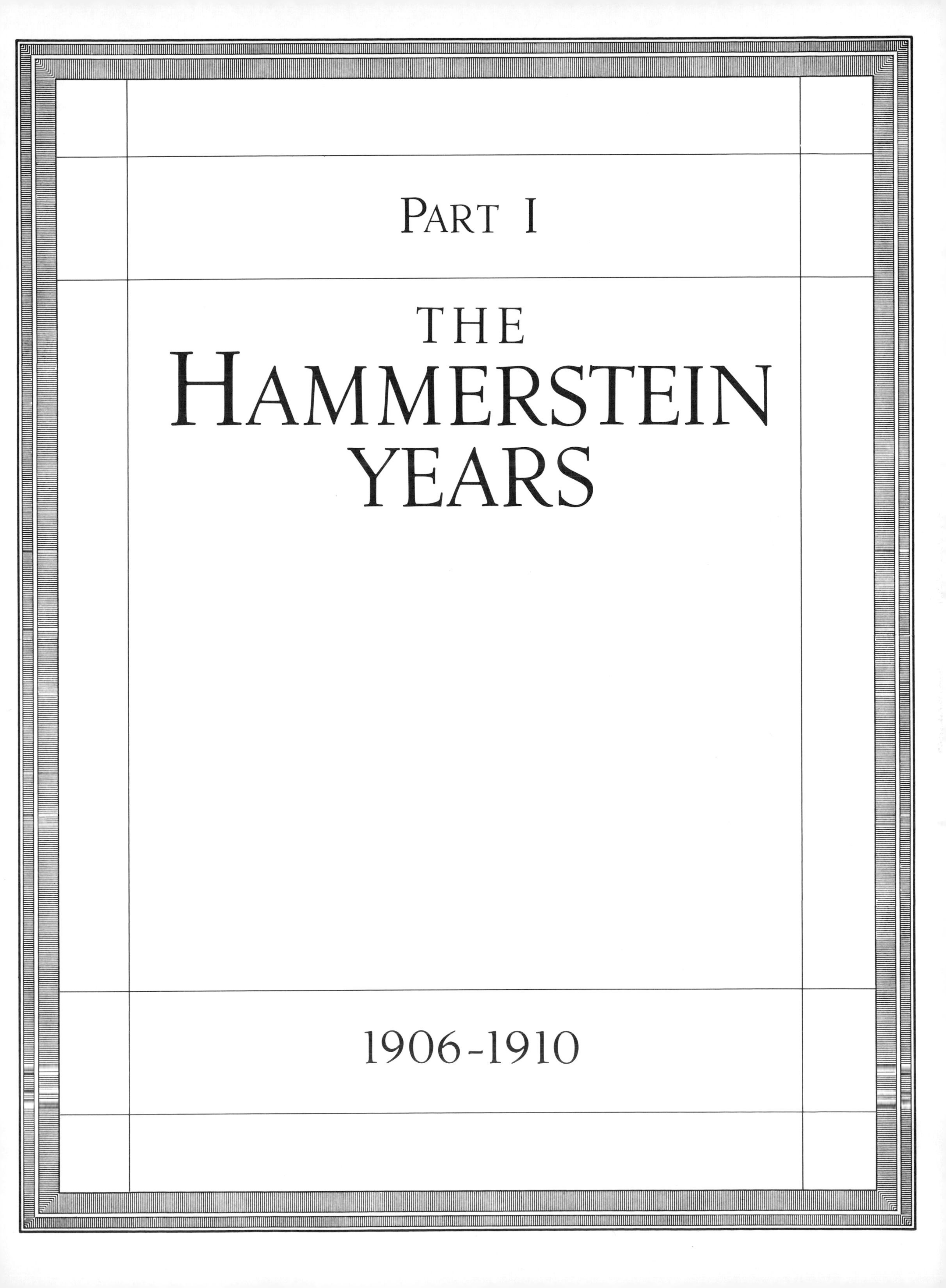

Part I

The Hammerstein Years

1906-1910

N 1906 HEINRICH CONRIED, A German-born actor-manager, was running the Metropolitan Opera. Legend says that Conried had not been inside the Metropolitan before his appointment in 1903. Taking over from an experienced opera manager, Maurice Grau, Conried inherited a number of contracts. He declined to pick up those of Charles Gilibert and Maurice Renaud, and after considerable investigation he approved of Enrico Caruso but reduced the number of performances called for. Eventually he picked up an option on the services of Geraldine Farrar. Conried improved the backstage facilities; in his one memorable success he defied the Wagner family and presented the first staged performances of *Parsifal* outside Bayreuth. In addition to many instances of lack of judgment, he was the victim of very bad luck.

Oscar Hammerstein (1846–1919), also a German immigrant, made a fortune from inventing an assortment of cigar-producing machines, and soon after arriving in New York, he was writing and producing plays and building theaters. Fascinated by opera, in 1889 he opened his first theater, the Harlem Opera House on 125th Street, and during the opening season included the Emma Juch Grand Opera Company on his list of attractions. In the same theater he presented *Les Huguenots* and *Il Trovatore,* as well as Lilli Lehmann in *Norma,* all sung in German. The financial and publicity success opera gave him led him to subsequent ventures in English, with lesser artists and poorer response.

When Hammerstein's plans to build a new theater on the north side of West 34th Street between Eighth and Ninth avenues for melodramas and spectaculars were preempted by the new Hippodrome on Sixth Avenue, Hammerstein halted construction and, perhaps goaded on by Conried, built the Manhattan Opera House in 1906. Hammerstein had presented the young Conried in his first American appearances, had despised him ever since, and thought he could do a better job.

For the opening season of the Manhattan Opera in 1906–1907, Hammerstein attacked the Met on its home ground: the traditional Italian and French repertoires. He engaged as artistic director Cleofonte Campanini, one of the leading conductors of the day. With Alessandro Bonci, Hammerstein quickly proved that there was an Italian tenor other than Caruso. He also hired Charles Gilibert and Maurice Renaud, two of the finest singing actors in the world; produced *Carmen,* first with Clotilde Bressler-Gianoli and then with Emma Calvé; and brought back Nellie Melba, who provided the vocal standard by which New York critics measured all singers. During the same season, Conried opened with Geraldine Farrar's debut; premiered *Salome* and was forced by the ensuing scandal to drop it after one performance; and revealed his new Italian artists, Celestina Boninsegna, Lina Cavalieri, and Riccardo Stracciari, who were generally less successful vocally than Hammerstein's Giannina Russ and Mario Sammarco.

After the 1906–1907 season, during which the Manhattan Opera generated a financial surplus and the Metropolitan had its first deficit in years, the wily Hammerstein saw that the future lay in building afresh rather than merely challenging the past. A whole new repertoire and cadre of artists, unknown to America, were waiting in Paris to burst upon the American scene. He convinced Mary Garden that he was interested in her and her unique repertoire. He already had Renaud, Gilibert, and Charles Dalmorès on his roster; he added Hector Dufranne, Jeanne Gerville-Réache, Jean Périer, and Armand Crabbé. Within the space of two months Hammerstein not only undertook the transplantation of an ephemeral operatic world but also scored a coup in traditional grand opera that stunned New York and the Metropolitan: the debut of Luisa Tetrazzini, the sensational coloratura soprano. Conried had had an option for the services of Tetrazzini that he allowed to lapse; he had also been offered the French works in which Garden was so successful but had rejected them.

Hammerstein's remaining three seasons, from 1907 to 1910, have taken their place in New York operatic history because of the supreme quality with which the French novelties were produced. The American premieres of Massenet's *Thaïs, Jongleur de Notre Dame,* and *Sapho;* Charpentier's *Louise;* and Debussy's *Pelléas et Mélisande* were presented in completely authentic performances that have not been equaled since.

Part of Hammerstein's skill lay in his relationship with singers—his cordiality when he was pleased, his dexterity in shedding them when he wasn't. His ebullient personality matched those of Garden and Tetrazzini, his greatest stars. Once, when planning to sign Garden's contract in the palace at Fontainebleau on the desk where Napoleon signed his abdication, Hammerstein engaged chauffeur and limousine for the trip from Paris. When a wheel flew off the car, they were thrown by the roadside and, on the spur of the moment, signed the contract. On the other hand, he could be sharp. Speaking of a prima donna, he reported one day, "She has been making scenes with me, threatening to do this and do that if I don't consent to what she wants. I told her to take that cat voice *(Katzenstimme)* of hers over to the Metropolitan

Opera House and see what it sounded like over there. That settled her." When Lillian Nordica opened his second season in *Gioconda* and drew neither her society friends nor the public, Hammerstein reacted by standing in the wings, creating a storm of cigar smoke around her during her performances. Apparently this failed to discourage her, so he "sent his secretary to tell her that he had decided to give a series of extra performances at such cheap prices as had never been heard of before in a first-class opera house and that she was to be the prima donna in each and all these representations. That was sufficient to make her resign."

The tenor Zenatello took Hammerstein to court, claiming he was not given as many performances as promised. "He was allowed as many performances," responded Hammerstein, "as his vocal chords [*sic*] could stand." Commented the *Sun,* "Nobody who knows Mr. Hammerstein believes he will ever have to pay him."

At least one Boston soprano's audition, however, must have disconcerted him. "On the morning of the appointment the manager was astounded to see a magnificent grand piano arrive at the Opera House, sent by the young woman for her trial. Presently a perfectly appointed brougham drew up at the entrance with two flunkeys on the box. When one jumped down and, with a flourish, opened the door, out stepped the singer, arrayed as Ophelia in the mad scene, even to the distracted hair and the careless floral adornment." Hammerstein, whose aplomb never left him, told her the voice was one of "splendid promise."

In 1908 the Met replaced Conried with a professional opera manager, Giulio Gatti-Casazza, who came from Italy with Arturo Toscanini. Instead of consolidating to meet the competition, Hammerstein proceeded to build the Philadelphia Opera House. In those days both technology and labor unions were less sophisticated: from razing to opening night took just seven and a half months. The building was an acoustical success, even though critics then did not know how to discuss reverberation time. But by now Hammerstein had seriously overextended himself. He sometimes had the Philadelphia and New York houses and two tour companies going at the same time. His funds were not inexhaustible; in addition, his supply of novel works had begun to run out. One of Gatti's first projects had been to secure the rights to new works of Charpentier and Debussy.

In 1910 the Metropolitan Opera paid Hammerstein $1,200,000 to agree not to be associated with opera production in New York for ten years. He attempted a return in 1913–14, signing up Marthe Chenal, César Vezzani, Maria Barrientos, and Maurice Renaud, but a Metropolitan injunction prevented it. He was planning popular-priced opera for 1920, when he could legally enter the field again; but as Gatti's assistant, Edward Ziegler, reported after a 1919 meeting that "the Oscar Hammerstein of ten years ago does not exist today any more." He died before the year was out.

ALESSANDRO BONCI

FOR THE 1906 OPENING OF HIS NEW Manhattan Opera House, Oscar Hammerstein selected the diminutive Italian tenor Alessandro Bonci (1870–1940) to appear with Polish soprano Regina Pinkert in Bellini's *Puritani.* Bonci was regarded in Europe as the leading Italian tenor after Caruso, and Hammerstein gave him a contract that promised fifty performances, $800 in gold at the conclusion of each performance, and his own choice of repertoire, not to be shared with other tenors except in cases of illness. He was expected to attend only one piano rehearsal of his roles and that could not be held on the day of a performance.

On opening night New York critics and public quickly made up their minds about Pinkert and dismissed her; Bonci, however, though he was not competition for the richer-sounding Caruso as Hammerstein had claimed, made a distinctly favorable impression. "It is a voice that will sound small to most New York operagoers, a slender stream of voice, but of good carrying power, flexible, freely produced, and freely emitted and quite at home in the saccharine cantilena and florid ornaments of Mr. Bellini's music. He has a limpid legato style and his phrasing is good."

By the middle of the season, though, what had begun so idyllically was falling apart. Hammerstein had legal papers served in Bonci's dressing room before a performance of *Fra Diavolo* because the tenor had signed a contract with Heinrich Conried to sing for three seasons at the Metropolitan. But it soon became clear that Hammerstein, who seldom lost a lawsuit, hardly regretted his loss and was actually glad to be out of the contract. Hammerstein said to the *Times* of Bonci: "As a matter of fact his repertoire is limited to the old operas which do not draw. I have asked him to learn new roles, but he says his voice is not suited to the more robust music." It also developed that Hammerstein had signed a contract with another tenor, Giovanni Zenatello, that most robust of singers, well before the incident began.

Initially Bonci was delighted with his Metropolitan contract. At the Met he found a congenial colleague for his debut in *Rigoletto:* "In his first phrases he answered beautifully the question raised as to how his voice would sound in the large auditorium. His tones were quite sufficient. Their light quality was of course in evidence, but the art of the singer who knows how to focus his voice and how to sustain it with a steady column of air made every note float through all the spaces of the house. Added to this was the substantial aid of Mr. Bonci's exquisite diction, which makes every vowel a tone factor and every consonant a perfect link in an unbroken legato. This tenor is an artist of such refinement and skill that it must always be a delight to hear him, but the delight is doubled when he is in company of such a so-

Alessandro Bonci as Arturo in I Puritani, *a performance so successful at La Scala that Hammerstein brought Bonci to New York to recreate it for opening night of the Manhattan Opera.*

prano as Mme. Sembrich. Their duet in the second act was one of the most finished and perfectly balanced pieces of singing that has ever been heard in the Metropolitan Opera House. Every phrase was perfectly made. Every nuance showed a lovely mutual understanding." Shortly after Caruso and Farrar had appeared in *La Bohème,* Bonci and Sembrich performed it: "As an operatic team . . . they are simply unapproachable today. . . . This generation will not see its like again." With his pride in his elegant manners and superior musical background (including several generations of musicians in his family and extravagant European praise from Lilli Lehmann and others), Bonci was offended that he was not permitted to perform more of Caruso's roles during the latter's illness.

Bonci left the Metropolitan at the end of the 1910–11 season after more than one hundred performances. He gave many concerts in the United States but did not return to opera in New York until a 1920 Chicago Opera performance as Riccardo in *Un Ballo in Maschera,* something of a specialty with him. "The most temperate in the audience found themselves moved by the art of the little tenor, which in the interval of his absence has lost none of its exquisite refinement, its aristocratic elegance. . . . He evoked the greatest uproar of the afternoon by his performance of the 'E scherzo od è follia,' delivering the laughing sixteenth notes with a tripping ease past belief and the ornamental effect of exquisite filligree, but barely interrupting the lovely flow of tone thereby." Bonci was then nearing the end of an operatic career that had begun in Parma in 1896 and had included all of Italy, Covent Garden, St. Petersburg, and South America.

MARIO ANCONA

OSCAR HAMMERSTEIN'S CUNNING MIXture of the familiar and the new juxtaposed two older-generation artists, Maurice Renaud, an eminent singing actor unknown to New York, and Mario Ancona (1860–1931), an Italian businessman turned baritone who had started late in 1890 with Massenet's *Roi de Lahore* in Trieste. Ancona quickly progressed to Covent Garden and by 1893 arrived at the Metropolitan to sing Tonio in *Pagliacci* (he had been Silvio at the world premiere in Milan a year earlier). Ancona seems never to have received a bad New York review for his singing. At his debut, Nellie Melba as Nedda was [illegible] as inappropriate and Fernando de Lucia as Canio was said to have great conviction but insufficient voice. Ancona, on the other hand, possessed "a light baritone voice of good compass and carrying power, but of rather reedy quality. He sings with a great deal of feeling and with

Mario Ancona as a debonair Barnaba in La Gioconda, *performed on Hammerstein's 1907–1908 opening night with Lillian Nordica.*

no little breadth of power." Two weeks later, "Signor Ancona as Rigoletto displayed the full measure of his dramatic abilities. He has already shown himself to be a singer of the modern style, who endeavors to make his vocal gifts bend themselves to an interpretation of the meaning of the text."

During the 1890s Ancona became a worthy member for four seasons of a Metropolitan company that included Nellie Melba, Emma Calvé, Lillian Nordica, the De Reszke brothers, Pol Plançon, and Francesco Tamagno.

Hammerstein brought him back from Europe after nine years' absence for his opening-night *Puritani* in 1906. Ancona alternated with Maurice Renaud as Don Giovanni and sang Escamillo, Valentin, and Figaro in *Il Barbiere di Siviglia,* as well as Nevers in *Gli Ugonotti.* In *Aida* he was criticized for costuming the barbaric Amonasro with jewels and a richly brocaded coat. At the end of his first season he fell victim to one of Hammerstein's publicity stunts, when the impresario announced that Ancona had been reengaged for the following season with a stipulation in the contract that he reduce the size of his waistline by five inches. "If Dalmorès can go to a gymnasium every day and keep thin," said Mr. Hammerstein, "why cannot Ancona?" Ancona duly stripped to the waist for reporters who compared his torso to the Farnese Hercules. *Musical America* commented, "The possible effect of this edict against fat is terrible to contemplate. Two sopranos who are eager to appear in New York again next season heard of the edict this week and saw hope recede."

Of course, Ancona sang in Hammerstein's second opening night, appearing in *La Gioconda* with Lillian Nordica, Giovanni Zenatello, and Adamo Didur. As Barnaba, he "sang with beautiful quality and acted with something more of urbanity than of the melodramatic villainy of the Inquisitorial spy."

Indeed urbanity was his style; he epitomized a way of life that was fast disappearing. Each day he would have a late breakfast in bed, then rise in time for an elegant lunch at Martin's that lasted late into the afternoon. After riding home to dress for dinner, which he usually had at the Martinique, where he lived, he'd make his appearance at the opera, after which he could be found entertaining friends at Churchill's or at Rector's. If he did not sing, he went out even earlier.

After two Hammerstein seasons, Ancona did not return again to the United States until the 1913–14 season, when he performed with the Boston Opera. There a reviewer hailed him in the unlikely role of Raffaele in Wolf-Ferrari's *Gioielli della Madonna:* "His clear baritone is imperishable and has all the freshness of tone we heard sixteen years ago." His last operatic appearance anywhere was in the same role, in January 1916 for the Chicago Opera.

MARIO SAMMARCO

MIDWAY THROUGH HAMMERSTEIN'S first season the Italian baritone Mario Sammarco (1867–1930) arrived, having been billed as a replacement for Maurice Renaud but destined to be the Manhattan's standard Italian baritone throughout its existence. His 1907 debut as Tonio in *Pagliacci,* with Amedeo Bassi and Pauline Donalda, "immediately made it clear that he was a singer of uncommon gifts. . . . The newcomer's success was instantaneous. His youthful look and merry eye, his frank confidence and jaunty air as in his suit of motley he came before the curtain to sing the prologue were reassuring. In a few seconds he had won the house completely. At the pause just before the end, it broke into a bedlam of applause. The incident is not uncommon. Scotti at the other house has learned to prevent it by keeping one hand raised in warning. . . . Sammarco's voice is full, round and mellow, of wide range and rich variety."

Hammerstein quickly learned that he could solve casting and repertoire problems by throwing Sammarco's *Pagliacci* into the breach. He was considered superb in *Rigoletto* and "sang the music with great purity of tone and with much power"; H. T. Parker of the Boston *Transcript* commented that "a singing actor who nonchalantly unfastens and pulls off his gloves in the full tide of the singing of 'Di Provenza' has his place and his fitness in music drama."

When he moved on to the Chicago Opera in 1910, Sammarco found further vocal and theatrical success. As

Mario Sammarco as Renato in Un Ballo in Maschera, *one of his many successful Italian roles at the Manhattan.*

the brutal Raffaele in *I Gioielli della Madonna,*"Sammarco was the spirit of Naples incarnate, debonair, corrupt, elegant, with the touch of extravagance in color which puts a green ribbon on its hat, with a flaming red tie. . . . He has the most grateful music to sing, and he gives his voice in song so that the tone always has the color of the word." In a career relatively free from discord, one of his few problems occurred in a 1913 *Tosca* when Mary Garden asked the Chicago Opera manager to replace Sammarco with Vanni Marcoux because she was "animated by the desire to surround herself with the most capable people possible." Sammarco replied publicly: "In London for three seasons I have sung the role with Madame Emmy Destinn and in other cities with others of the greatest Toscas, so I feel I am qualified to sing this role *even* with Miss Mary Garden." A small, dapper man, Sammarco might have added that his credentials for modern Italian opera were comparable to Garden's for the French school. He had created the leading baritone parts in *Andrea Chénier, Germania,* and *Zazà,* and had been a great international favorite in London, Russia, and South America. Sammarco and Garden sang the contested performance together, and it was a notable success for them both.

ELEANORA DE CISNEROS

ELEANOR BROADFOOT, A CONTRALTO from Brooklyn, sang at the Metropolitan during the 1899–1900 season at a salary of $30 a week. Except for an Amneris in *Aida* on tour and again during the Metropolitan English Grand Opera season, her roles were small—Rossweise in *Die Walküre,* Lola in *Cavalleria Rusticana,* and a Genie in *Die Zauberflöte.* When she returned to New York from years of further study and performances in Europe, it was as the Countess Eleanora de Cisneros (1878–1934), Hammerstein's leading contralto. She had discovered in Italy that if she used her husband's name it was not only easier to secure engagements but all criticism of her pronunciation ceased. While in Europe she had studied with Jean de Reszke; sung at La Scala, in Lisbon, and in St. Petersburg; and appeared for several seasons at Covent Garden.

Aida, with Giannina Russ and Amedeo Bassi, served as her 1906 reentry to New York. She was a visual sensation. "To say that Mme. de Cisneros as Amneris is the handsomest woman on the operatic stage in New York seems to insist on too narrow a territory for her supremacy. Like the daughter of the gods, she is, after a florid fashion, 'divinely tall and most divinely fair.' Her drooping posture at the opening of the last act made a picture to be remembered. Her movements are forceful, and her acting, though never showing spontaneity, has

Eleanora de Cisneros as a tall and voluptuous page, Urbain, in the 1907 performances of Gli Ugonotti.

the sureness of good schooling." Her voice, though pleasing, "lacks carrying power, particularly in the lower register, and is not rich in expression."

During her two seasons with Hammerstein, her roles included Ulrica in *Un Ballo in Maschera,* Azucena in *Il Trovatore,* Laura in *La Gioconda,* Urbain in *Gli Ugonotti.* Although both Lillian Nordica and Nellie Melba counseled her to make the vocal move into the higher soprano repertoire, De Cisneros for the most part strayed only into borderline roles such as Santuzza.

After two seasons with Hammerstein, De Cisneros returned to La Scala in 1909 to sing Clytemnestra in the Italian premiere of *Elektra.* She went on to spend four years with the Chicago Opera, singing Amneris on the first opening night, Brangäne in *Tristan,* and Gertrude to Titta Ruffo's Hamlet. She also toured Australia with Melba's company. When war broke out in Europe, her engagements there were canceled, and she returned to America for concerts. A determined campaigner for women's suffrage, she was seen in a pageant as "Miss Columbia," draped in blue, waving a standard. In her vaudeville act she sang opera and concluded with the "Star-Spangled Banner," this time waving the flag. Having raised millions in Liberty Loan drives, she declared bankruptcy in 1919, her operatic career in America at an end. She reappeared briefly at La Scala in 1925 as Herodias in *Salome.*

AMEDEO BASSI

ON HIS FIRST VOYAGE TO NEW YORK from engagements in South America, the Italian tenor Amedeo Bassi (1874–1949) learned the role of Radames and lost a small fortune to card sharks. A wealthy man with palatial homes in and around Florence, Bassi survived the gambling losses but must have soon tired of the odious comparisons that began with his *Aida* debut, in December 1906: "Mr. Bassi, while not a Bonci or a Caruso, made a decidedly favorable impression. His voice is sweet and powerful, well cultivated in its higher register. His impersonation of the part was especially worthy of note in view of the fact that he had never sung it before." And: "It is a strong and flexible organ, well under control and full and sonorous in its upper tones. He sang fluently and effectively.... Mr. Bassi is not a powerful personality upon the stage; he is in fact a conqueror with a somewhat apologetic manner."

He was Hammerstein's Italian dramatic tenor during the first season of the Manhattan and sang in *Ugonotti, Pagliacci, Traviata,* and *Ballo.* During his second season he sang the title role of *Andrea Chénier* with opulence and "a fervor that took the house by storm." However, Giovanni Zenatello had arrived, and Bassi soon departed.

Amedeo Bassi, probably as Raoul in Gli Ugonotti, *a work in which he and Giannina Russ were particularly applauded.*

(Hammerstein was quoted as saying: "I engaged Bassi for my first season and he made a success. The next season he sang for three months in South America and came back to me without any voice. I never reengaged him.")

Bassi was Radames in the opening-night *Aida* of the new Teatro Colón in Buenos Aires, and he repeated the role at the grand opening of the Chicago Grand Opera Company, in 1910, in a cast that included Eleanora de Cisneros, Mario Sammarco, and the Polish soprano Janina Korolewicz. With Carolina White and Maurice Renaud, he was in the Chicago premiere of *La Fanciulla del West* and made his only Metropolitan appearances when he replaced Caruso as Dick Johnson for three performances that same season. In Chicago, he found a role that became his own: Gennaro in Wolf-Ferrari's *Gioielli della Madonna.* It was noted that the voice was worn, had faults of tone production, and was frequently out of tune, "yet where in America is the tenor who could fill the role of the infatuated blacksmith so effectively as he? Others could sing it better, but this was an impersonation, singularly eloquent in its simplicity and earnestness, its native quality." In the 1920s he sang Parsifal, Siegfried, and Loge during Toscanini's reign at La Scala. Back in Florence he taught; one of his pupils was the sweet-voiced tenor Ferruccio Tagliavini.

GIANNINA RUSS

THE WORLD OF OPERA IS FREQUENTLY being assured, usually by a press agent, that a certain type of big and dowdy soprano has disappeared and been replaced by a new, more "stylish" singer with a figure more in keeping with modern taste. Just as frequently the old-fashioned singer lurches back into view, unprepossessing as ever, her only justification being a voice and the knowledge of how to sing. In 1906 Heinrich Conried at the Metropolitan introduced New York to Geraldine Farrar and Lina Cavalieri, two of the most glamorous women ever seen in an opera house. He also had great hopes for Celestina Boninsegna, an Italian dramatic soprano whom he featured prominently in his plans and advertising. Boninsegna, signed for five months and forty performances, was ill throughout her stay and left after five performances. Without her voice to carry her, Boninsegna in *Aida* was merely what one colleague recalled as a large woman in chocolate-colored underwear. The New York public was used to the Aida of Emma Eames—proud and elegant, with her own secret blend of flesh-colored makeup.

Oscar Hammerstein had greater success with his Italian dramatic soprano Giannina Russ (1878–1951), a young woman who had been singing only since a highly acclaimed 1903 Milan concert with Francesco Tamagno,

Giannina Russ as Elvira in Verdi's Ernani. *The soprano's voice was usually praised above her appearance.*

Clotilde Bressler-Gianoli as a wistful Mignon, a role that bore no resemblance to her more extrovert Carmen.

the first Otello. However, she had rapidly gained theater experience at La Scala, Cairo, Buenos Aires, and Covent Garden, singing *Aida* and *Un Ballo in Maschera* opposite Enrico Caruso. Her 1906 New York debut was as Donna Anna in *Don Giovanni,* with Mario Ancona in the title role and Alessandro Bonci as Don Ottavio. In her second performance, Russ "made a far better impression than at her debut. Some of the music—notably 'Or sai chi l'onore'—she conceived in the spirit of Mascagni rather than of Mozart; but she is a dramatic singer of ability and experience, and at times was altogether admirable." Her Aida was proclaimed "so satisfying vocally and dramatically that one forgave her costume and forgot her stoutness." Russ's Act IV *Ugonotti* duet with Amedeo Bassi was declared the best performance of this music since Lillian Nordica and Jean de Reszke had sung it. Always, however, her appearance provoked comment. Her Aida was ungraciously said to resemble "something between an Alaskan squaw and a wooden totem pole." In an Italian-language *Faust* with Bassi, Màrio Sammarco, and Vittorio Arimondi, she was "the most matronly exponent of Marguerite ever seen. Her gowns would well have become the heroine's mother, and her placidly pretty face and self-contained manner disclosed no vestige of coquetry. But her voice was never displayed to such advantage. The Jewel Song was finely done, and in the final trio she showed unlooked-for power."

By the end of his season in 1908, Hammerstein had changed direction. He would concentrate on more dramatically presentable singers, always with the exception of his sensation, the unique Luisa Tetrazzini. Giannina Russ thrived in Italy, where she developed her own special repertoire, concentrating on the title role of *Norma* and operas such as *Nabucco, I Vespri Siciliani, La Vestale,* and *Poliuto,* older works of the sort that would later be revived for Maria Callas. Today the recordings of both Giannina Russ and Celestina Boninsegna, where appearance counts for nothing, are treasured.

CLOTILDE BRESSLER-GIANOLI

ALTHOUGH HAMMERSTEIN DISCOVERED the Swiss mezzo-soprano Clotilde Bressler-Gianoli (1874–1912) when she was singing in Brussels, she was not new to New York. In 1904 she had sung Carmen with the French Grand Opera Company of New Orleans during its ill-fated three performances at the Casino Theatre and appeared in scenes from *Orfeo ed Euridice* in a benefit concert at the Metropolitan. Again as Carmen she was the first real success of Hammerstein's inaugural season. The tight dramatic production conducted by Campanini was extravagantly praised in comparison with the Met's offerings. Without a first-class voice ("I have never known anyone make so much of so little," wrote Algernon St. John-Brenon), she was nonetheless a significant actress: "It was the apparently unstudied naturalness of her movements which kept them alive with beauty and free from offense. And thence she developed the passion and tragic vehemence of the character steadily till the gruesome end. She is not a great singer, but she is a dramatic one, and her voice and diction kept perfect time with her plastic and inspiring delineation." With Charles Dalmorès, the Don José, Bressler-Gianoli provided Hammerstein with his first complete triumph in a performance that was contrasted with the placid performances at the Metropolitan.

Two months later Bressler-Gianoli showed her versatility as she played the heroine of Thomas's *Mignon:* "Bressler-Gianoli's impersonation . . . is startling in its obliteration of every characteristic which seems to make her gypsy cigarette girl a real embodiment. . . . With apparently no effort at make-up, her face is not the same; her figure is different; her voice takes on a different quality; it is a distinct entity that appeals for recognition. And what a beautiful, tender, compelling thing she is as the stolen waif. . . . The opera may be as artificial as you please, but this woman's touch glorifies." Bressler-Gianoli also presented her pungent and vivid Azucena and was the Mother in the first American *Louise,* a part she repeated in Chicago in 1910–11. By then her eyesight and her voice were failing, her parts were smaller, and her brief career was almost over. She died in 1912 of appendicitis.

CHARLES DALMORÈS

THE FRENCH TENOR CHARLES DALMORÈS (1871–1939) was singing at the Monnaie in Brussels when Hammerstein heard him. The next night he went to Dalmorès's apartments, walked into the room, announced, "I want to engage you for America," and without another word put 10,000 francs ($2,000) in gold on the table. Dalmorès sang in all four seasons of the Manhattan Opera, there growing from a badly frightened debutant in *Faust* into an accomplished and versatile artist who figured in many of Hammerstein's important evenings. He was José to the Carmens of Clotilde Bressler-Gianoli and Emma Calvé, Samson to the Dalila of Gerville-Réache, and John the Baptist to the Salomé of Lina Cavalieri in Massenet's *Hérodiade;* opposite Mary Garden, he performed in *Louise, Salome, Grisélidis, Thaïs,* and *Pelléas et Mélisande.* Part of his success was in his superb bearing: "Faust, José, Samson, Pelléas, Julien: He has one particular quality that suits him to all these parts. The quickest appeal of the theatre, be it in drama or in opera, is admittedly to the eye and Mr.

Charles Dalmorès as an eccentric Hoffmann in Les Contes d'Hoffmann, *performed in 1907 with Maurice Renaud portraying all three villains.*

Dalmorès is a believable personage. He keeps the elasticity of youth; his is a vital presence; the air, the glamour of a romantic figure exhale from him."

Saint-Saëns's compliments on his musicianship were echoed by Henderson: "A genuine artist. He has the characteristic traits of the best French singers, who are seldom as excellent in vocal technique as the best Italian and American performers. . . . In spite of a lack of perfect freedom in his emission of tone he produces a quality genuinely good and of musical character. He can sing piano, as almost all French tenors can, and a great deal more artistically than most of them. He phrases elegantly and with insight into the nature of the music. He excels in both declamation and flowing song. He has a certain amount of imagination and not a little poetic warmth. Above all things, he respects the written letter of the score, for he is a thorough musician . . . he sings musically and not mechanically. Taking him all in all, he is the most interesting and accomplished French tenor known in either Europe or America at this time."

Since his early days playing in orchestras in Paris and Lyon (where he had been discovered by a singing teacher while illustrating leitmotifs vocally), Dalmorès had always been interested in Wagner. He sang *Lohengrin* at Bayreuth in 1908 and *Die Walküre, Parsifal,* and *Tristan und Isolde* in Chicago. A musician who played horn, violin, and cello, as well as a physical-culture enthusiast who survived both a train wreck with the touring Chicago Opera and wounds from World War I, Dalmorès performed his most colorful exploit on the docks of New York City in the aftermath of a lawsuit. Unwisely, he had signed a contract with the Metropolitan while a binding one with Oscar Hammerstein was still in effect. The Metropolitan sued for damages and had Andreas Dippel testify against Dalmorès: "I sang tenor roles for twenty years. I consider Mr. Dalmorès one of the greatest of French tenors. He has a great repertoire. We had to hire four tenors to replace him." The judge awarded the Metropolitan $20,000. To escape process servers Dalmorès enlisted in the ship's band of his steamer, the *Potsdam,* and undetected by one and all marched safely aboard, "blowing thousands of dollars worth of wind into a brass cornet."

When he retired from the stage, Dalmorès went to Hollywood to teach.

Jeanne Gerville-Réache as Dalila in Samson et Dalila, *a work she and Charles Dalmorès helped make popular in America.*

JEANNE GERVILLE-RÉACHE

IT IS A COMMON DELUSION THAT GREAT voices are produced only by years of careful study and restraint in the choice of roles, or, in other words, discretion from start to finish. Had she followed the rules, Jeanne Gerville-Réache (1882–1915) would have been dead before her career began. Born in the south of

France to a Spanish mother and French father, she spent part of her childhood in the French West Indies, where her father was stationed in the diplomatic corps. Back in Paris, Emma Calvé heard her rich contralto and insisted that she go on the stage. Her debut, arranged through family influence, was at the Opéra-Comique as Gluck's Orphée. She was seventeen. Two and a half years later her voice and acting won her the honor of singing Geneviève in the world premiere of *Pelléas et Mélisande.*

Gerville-Réache arrived in New York in 1907 for the opening night of Hammerstein's second season. She performed one of her few small parts, La Cieca, in an all-star *La Gioconda* with Lillian Nordica, Eleanora de Cisneros, Giovanni Zenatello, Mario Ancona, and Adamo Didur. Successful in Massenet's *Navarraise,* she was triumphant the following season with Charles Dalmorès in Saint-Saëns's *Samson et Dalila,* a work she had studied with the composer and the legendary Pauline Viardot-Garcia (who had sung Dalila at its first private reading). "Her voice was not to be forgotten for its richness and depth of warm and dark contralto tones, even if, by sheer opulence, they did sometimes seem coarse-fibred. . . . She was a singing actress who accomplished her impersonation by the power of her tones, by the emotional and the characterizing significance with which she colored them and by the kindling force of an ardent temperament. . . . She swept through the part of Dalila . . . in a kind of magnificence of sensual and vocal power, and she knew and could impart the passion of the harried peasant woman in *La Navarraise.* . . . In spite of Parisian training, Mme. Gerville-Réache had Latin ardor rather than French finesse and her best possession was the dark glow of her tones, smoldering and finally flaming into passionate utterance." Her performances as Dalila in New York, Boston, and Philadelphia helped secure the opera's popularity in America. Five months after her first performances, she went to record operatic arias and songs for the Victor Talking Machine Company in Camden, New Jersey. With the closing of Hammerstein's company, Gerville-Réache sang with the Chicago Opera and the National Opera of Canada during the ill-fated 1913–14 season (with Leo Slezak portraying Samson for the first time). Mostly, however, she devoted herself to solo and orchestral concerts and a busy family life with her French husband and two small sons. She died early in 1915 from complications following food poisoning and a miscarriage. She was not yet thirty-three.

HECTOR DUFRANNE

DURING HER NEGOTIATIONS WITH Hammerstein, Mary Garden spelled out what kind of company must surround her in New York: French artists with the style for the works in which she had

Opposite: *Hector Dufranne as the High Priest in* Samson et Dalila, *in which his noble voice was heard with the Manhattan and Chicago operas.*

triumphed in Paris. Fortunately, Hammerstein already had the framework for a strong French ensemble in Clotilde Bressler-Gianoli, Charles Dalmorès, Charles Gilibert, and Maurice Renaud, and he quickly added Armand Crabbé, Jean Périer, and Hector Dufranne. By 1907 the Belgian bass-baritone Dufranne (1870–1951) had been with the Opéra-Comique for seven years and had sung in the world premiere of *Pelléas et Mélisande* in 1902 with Garden, Jeanne Gerville-Réache, Périer, and Félix Vieuille. Following his New York debut as Golaud in *Pelléas* on February 19, 1908, Dufranne was hailed by Henderson as "one of the greatest artists who ever came here from France." Aldrich of the *Times* was equally enthusiastic: "Mr. Dufranne has a baritone voice of resonance, of dark and rich color; his enunciation is of exquisite perfection, his treatment of the phrase most musical, his declamation is of true eloquence. He is an actor of strong individuality and varied resources." A year later he was highly praised in the Manhattan's *Salome:* "As Jochanaan Mr. Dufranne has all the requisites. Here there is singing to do and he intones the sonorous phrases of the prophet with noble tone and deep impressiveness. He is the embodiment of grim asceticism and the one noble and commanding personage in the drama." The word *noble* recurs frequently in assessments of the tone of his voice; his acting was usually praised without qualification except when he repeated roles that were associated with the extraordinary Renaud or Gilibert, such as Athanaël in *Thaïs* or the Father in *Louise.* "That Mr. Dufranne would do vocal and histrionic justice to the role of the Father was a foregone conclusion. He sang with glorious outpouring of tone, and, while he could not efface memories of poor Gilibert, acted with unctuous geniality and a quality of moving sincerity. His raging vociferation 'Va-t'en! Dépêche-toi,' at the close was genuinely thrilling."

Dufranne sang for ten seasons with the Chicago Opera after Hammerstein's company disbanded, recorded excerpts from *Pelléas* electrically, and participated in almost forty seasons at the Opéra-Comique.

Dufranne's remarkable vocal and dramatic skills won him several world premieres in addition to *Pelléas;* among them were Massenet's *Thérèse,* in Monte Carlo in 1907; Prokofiev's *Love for Three Oranges,* in Chicago, 1921; and De Falla's *Retablo de Maese Pedro,* in 1923 at the private Paris theater of the Princesse de Polignac. His farewell to the stage, again as Golaud, was in Vichy in 1939; he had been singing since 1898. With him, a once plentiful breed of deep-voiced French artists renowned for their vocal and theatrical prowess all but vanished.

ARMAND CRABBÉ

THE RICHNESS AND DEPTH OF HAMMERstein's company is best illustrated by the career of the Belgian baritone Armand Crabbé (1883–1947), who made his 1907 New York debut as Brander in a staged *Damnation de Faust* in which "His voice, while not of great power, is a pleasing one and he sings with the delicacy of the French method." The age was so rich in fine singers that for a considerable time his advance was thwarted. In *Le Jongleur de Notre Dame,* Hector Dufranne sang the Friar and Maurice Renaud was Boniface, while Crabbé was relegated to the small role of Monk Musician. His largest part at the Manhattan was probably Escamillo; mostly he was confined to such roles as the First Philosopher and Sculptor in *Louise* and the Physician in *Pelléas et Mélisande.*

When Crabbé moved to the Chicago Opera with many Hammerstein singers in 1910, the more secondary roles were again his. After a 1913 recital, a reviewer complained at the "policy of this organization in shutting up so admirable a voice and so admirable a method of using it in small and ineffective roles. . . . It would be difficult to imagine singing more delicate, more charming than that which was put into those ingratiating trifles [French chansonettes and old Flemish songs]."

Crabbé's patience and determination eventually paid off. His fortunes changed dramatically in 1914 when the Chicago Opera closed for a season and he moved to La Scala for a debut as Rigoletto. Puccini coached him for Marcello in *La Bohème,* Scarpia, and Gianni Schicchi. Known as a skilled actor, Crabbé was awarded roles that required more than a loud voice—Toscanini cast him as Beckmesser in *I Maestri Cantori.* He made a speciality of the title role in Rabaud's exotic comedy about an Egyptian cobbler, *Marouf.* He was a great favorite in Spain, Brazil, and Argentina. His performances in his native Belgium lasted through World War II in Antwerp through the explosions of German V-2 rockets. Crabbé has acquired a posthumous fame for the delicacy of his voice and the rarity of his recordings.

The unfamiliar young face of Belgian baritone Armand Crabbé, taken in New York long before he became well known.

MAURICE RENAUD

"WHERE RENAUD SITS THERE IS THE head of the table." The pronouncement was Krehbiel's, and his sentiment was echoed by the eminent critics of the day, along with anyone else who saw and heard Maurice Renaud (1861–1933), the great French baritone who first sang in New York during Hammerstein's four seasons and then later with the Chicago Opera and on loan at the Metropolitan. (He might have appeared sooner at the Met had Conried, who managed to alienate Johanna Gadski, Charles Gilibert, and Luisa Tetrazzini as well, picked up the contract signed by his predecessor, Maurice Grau.) Renaud's earliest performances were at the Monnaie in Brussels, where he went to avoid French military service (a failing he later atoned for by enlisting and fighting heroically in World War I). Returning to Paris in 1890, he sang the modern French repertoire at the Opéra-Comique, and among other roles alternated performing those poles of magnetism, Don Giovanni and Beckmesser, at the Opéra. In Monte Carlo he was in the world premiere of Massenet's *Jongleur de Notre Dame;* he sang Rigoletto with Melba and Caruso at the latter's Covent Garden debut.

With his delicate vocal resources, Renaud can't have attained his preeminence easily. While the Algerian-born baritone Dinh Gilly was a student at the Conservatoire, Renaud counseled him never to let the public wait to hear what a good singer he might be but to impress the public from the moment of entrance that his "personage" was a real character—advice stemming as

Maurice Renaud as an icy Scarpia performed opposite the Toscas of Maria Labia and Carmen Melis.

Maurice Renaud's Scarpia. Once asked by Oscar Hammerstein for an extra performance, he replied, "Renaud was not contracted to do favors."

much from the actor's insight as the singer's limitations. H. T. Parker, the Boston critic, described Renaud's vocal equipment: "Renaud's voice was not a big voice and even in its prime it had no golden notes, no sensuous splendors. No one ever praised it, even in those best years, for the mere brightness and softness of its texture. He was the singer by dint of intelligence, imagination and knowledge, as well as by grace of voice and labor; and the longer, therefore, did he remain the singer."

Renaud's 1906 New York debut as Rigoletto was "a performance of pathos, of profound tragic power." He played Don Giovanni with "exquisite finesse. . . . He is indeed a fascinating figure in it, and he embodies all the gallantry, the aristocratic grace and insouciance, all the bravado and shamelessness that are the essence of the character." In Raoul Gunsbourg's operatic version of Berlioz's *Damnation de Faust* he made a sad, sardonic Mefisto, "whose high-heeled buskin on the right foot knew not what the left foot's limping and heelless comic sock would do next." As Athanaël in Massenet's *Thaïs,* overshadowing Mary Garden in the American premiere, "he towered above her like an avenging deity; as she cried out to be spared, his eyes burned with an almost insane fire. Then came the fall, and what a fall! From Heaven to hell! His hands, yearning, demanding, terrible, told the story as nothing else could, of those endless centuries of unutterable torture, the soul damned before it had left the body, the face hideous with its unrewarded sufferings, its unquenched desire." And there was his Scarpia, the only one that could be mentioned with Scotti's, not compared with but contrasted as creations of equal power. "Mr. Scotti's is no more than a hard, scrupleless, passionate man who can be cruel, as he can be almost anything else that is evil, when occasion and disposition prompt. To Mr. Renaud's Scarpia cruelty has become second nature and essential pleasure. . . . Mr. Renaud's Scarpia suggests a man of far more acute mind than Mr. Scotti's. In all that he does is a hint of mental finesse and suppleness. Mr. Scotti's Scarpia has become the chief of the secret police because he is brutal and cunning; Mr. Renaud's because he is astute and quietly efficient and can keep up aristocratic appearances withal. . . . Mr. Renaud schemes the part in one long and cumulative design that begins with his musings over the fan, proceeds in his sensuous excitements over the tortures that he employs, and reaches its climax in the suppressed tensities in which he believes he has accomplished his design and in the released frenzy that even Tosca's knife may hardly stay. Mr. Renaud would not be himself were he not minute and subtle."

It may be difficult to reconcile the praise Renaud received for his dramatic abilities with the exacting vocal standards of the time. However, Renaud himself insisted that when sacrifice was necessary, he always sacrificed declamation and gesture to the music. In 1911 W. J. Henderson had occasion to write of a Carnegie Hall recital away from the fantasy world of the opera house: "For those who make no distinction between voice and methods, Mr. Renaud's art does not exist. This is their loss. It is quite true that the material with which this singer has to work is slender, that it shows the signs of much service and that it is often recalcitrant. . . . Over all prevails the unfailing elegance of style of which Mr. Renaud is a master. His art is always aristocratic. It is the singing of a student, a thinker, a man of experience. It is a product of culture and what it lacks in barbaric power it makes up in repose and polish."

Hammerstein liked to observe the habits and superstitions of his artists. He noted that Renaud always went to Mass on the day of a performance but at no other time. A man of great dignity, Renaud was not above a practical joke. With his mastery of the actor's skills, he once astounded his colleagues in Paris by sitting among them backstage unrecognized until he spoke in his natural voice and removed his makeup. Despite Mary Garden's claim that she invented the modern French style of performing, Renaud was, in fact, its greatest exponent.

MARY GARDEN

IN 1907 HAMMERSTEIN SOUGHT OUT one singer with the force of personality, the performing genius, to spearhead a new direction for his opera company. Mary Garden (1874–1967), the soprano born in Aberdeen, Scotland, but brought up in the United States, would become one of the idols of the press (if not the critics), known to the public as "our Mary." Garden's position dated from 1900 and one of those theatrical events dreamed of by every understudy. Asked as a student to study the title role of Charpentier's *Louise,* she worked on it night and day, attending every performance. One evening, seated in the audience at the Opéra-Comique, she was summoned backstage to go on for the ailing Marthe Rioton, the creator of the title role. With an aplomb that was never to leave her, Garden opened the third act with Louise's "Depuis le jour" and conquered Paris in a single evening.

Although adequate in traditional parts such as Violetta, Ophélie, and Juliette, she preferred the new French repertoire, specializing in the operas of Massenet, Leroux, Février, Erlanger. In 1902 Debussy selected her to be the otherworldly heroine in the world premiere of *Pelléas et Mélisande.* In 1907, Garden and Oscar Hammerstein met in Paris and quickly agreed that she would join the new Manhattan Opera.

In rapid succession, between November 1907 and February 1908, Garden highlighted the American premieres of *Thaïs, Louise,* and *Pelléas et Mélisande.* In the Debussy, Hammerstein had the Paris production reproduced for New York, with Jean Périer, Hector Dufranne, and Jeanne Gerville-Réache from the original cast supporting Garden. It showed her at her peak. She "made in it a new disclosure of her art and of the power of her dramatic personality. She is the dreamy, wistful maiden, wandering, uncertain, unhappy; and her denotement of the veiled and mysterious character is of much beauty and plastic grace. In places, as in the difficult scene with the wounded Golaud, and in the scene in which he does her violence, she rises to a height of tragic power that ought to put her among the greatest of lyric actresses." The following season she contrasted the simple piety of Jean in Massenet's *Jongleur de Notre Dame* with Strauss's *Salome,* when Hammerstein took advantage of the latter's proscription at the Metropolitan and performed it in French. Garden announced to *Musical America:* "What a glorious work, and how crazy I am to sing, act and dance it in New York! I will take a dancing lesson each day, and think it will be very amusing to become a ballerina." Henderson reported, "To add to the public interest it had been made known that Miss Garden would not hide her charms under a bushel of garments, and that when she had taken off the seven veils she would take everyone into her confidence." Of the premiere he felt that "without question the important thing was the dance. Salome with Mary Garden as the heroine is a dance with commentary, for the plain truth must be admitted that Miss Garden cannot sing a phrase of Strauss' music. Well and good, but Salome's words must be projected into the auditorium somehow. Miss Garden succeeded best with the lines she deliberately spoke."

Garden's only confrontation with Hammerstein occurred during her preparation of Salome. "I have no objection to Miss Cavalieri in the company," she announced to the press. "I shall be delighted to hear her as long as she confines herself to Italian operas. The day Mr. Hammerstein advertises her as Thaïs he knows what to expect from me." Cavalieri and *Thaïs* were announced, and Garden resigned from the company shortly before the premiere of *Salome.* Privately, she wrote Hammerstein: "In this action you have taken you have violated both the letter and the spirit of our understanding. . . . I shall say nothing at this time of my great disappointment at your extraordinary attitude nor of the injustice you have sought to do me after the loyal manner in which I have seconded your heroic efforts to maintain your position in New York. That you must settle with your own conscience. I am ready and always have been and will be to sing Thaïs whenever and wherever you please regardless of my other work but as I understand your attitude our contract relations have now been severed and I shall not again appear at the Opera House until I receive proper assurances that you withdraw from your present attitude." Hammerstein was forced to back down. Thereafter if anyone sang one of Garden's roles, it was with her permission.

Every now and then Mary Garden would dust off her portrayal of Marguerite in Gounod's *Faust* and proceed to confound her harshest critics. Her first New York performance was in December 1909. "It is an achievement to have made Marguerite something beyond a mere singing doll. It has often been the duty of the writer of musical affairs in these columns to decry Miss Garden's method of singing and to speak in disparaging terms of her voice. Last night, however, she did some of the most carefully considered singing that she has ever given to this public. The 'Roi de Thule' air was almost exquisite in its finish and sad wistfulness. Later in the love duet she again sang in a manner which must call forth praise. In these passages she sang with no effort; there was none of the usual forcing of the tones, and the result seemed to indicate that much of Miss Garden's bad singing has been due to her method of producing her tones, rather than to her voice, itself. Of course, she has not the facility for such music as the 'Jewel Song.' Such singing as she did in it was an expression of the bravado in her nature and little else." Weeks later Garden re-

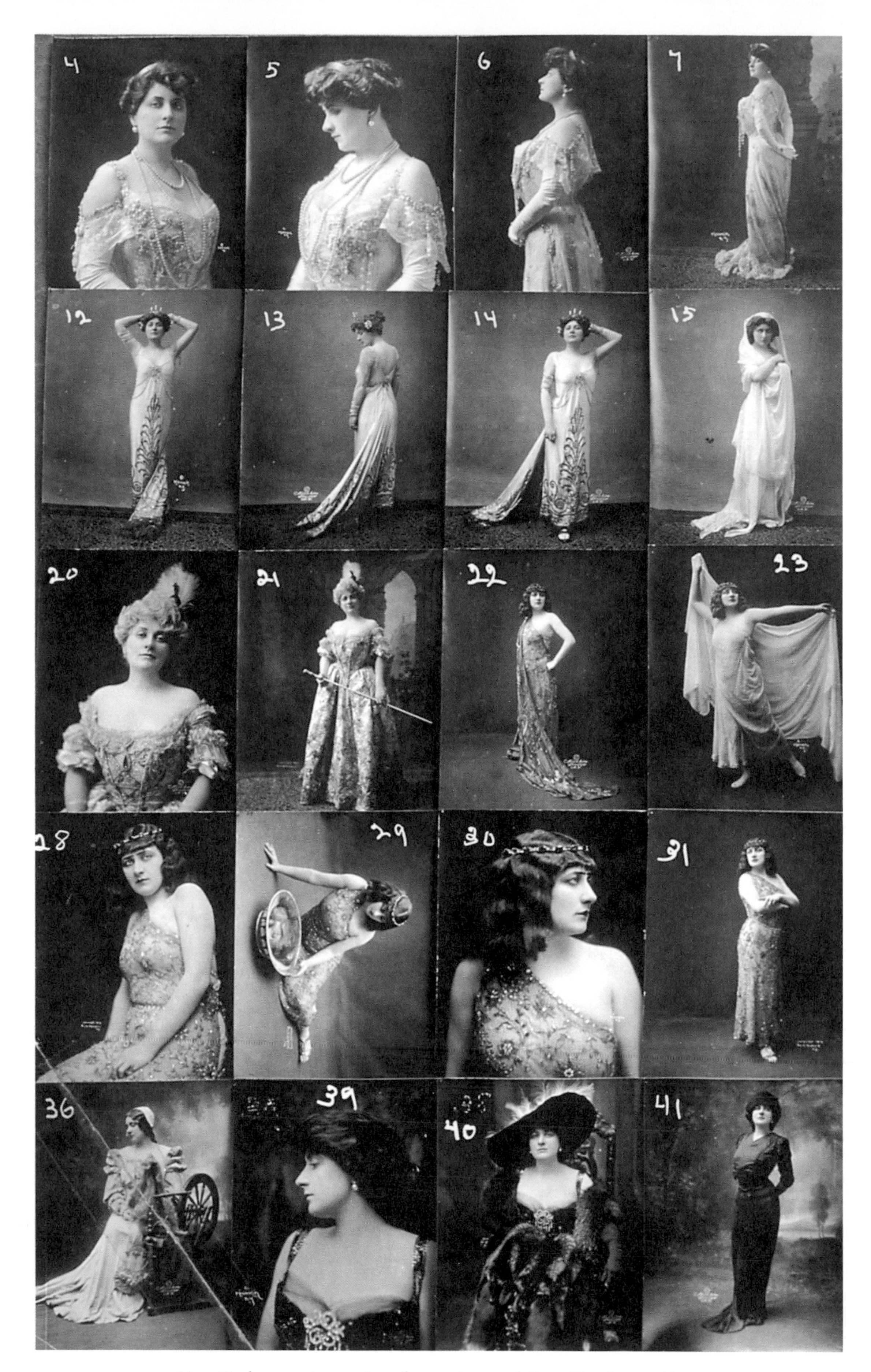

Mary Garden, seen in a variety of poses, in a proof sheet of her first Mishkin photographs. As Mary Garden: 4 through 11; as Thaïs: 12 through 16;

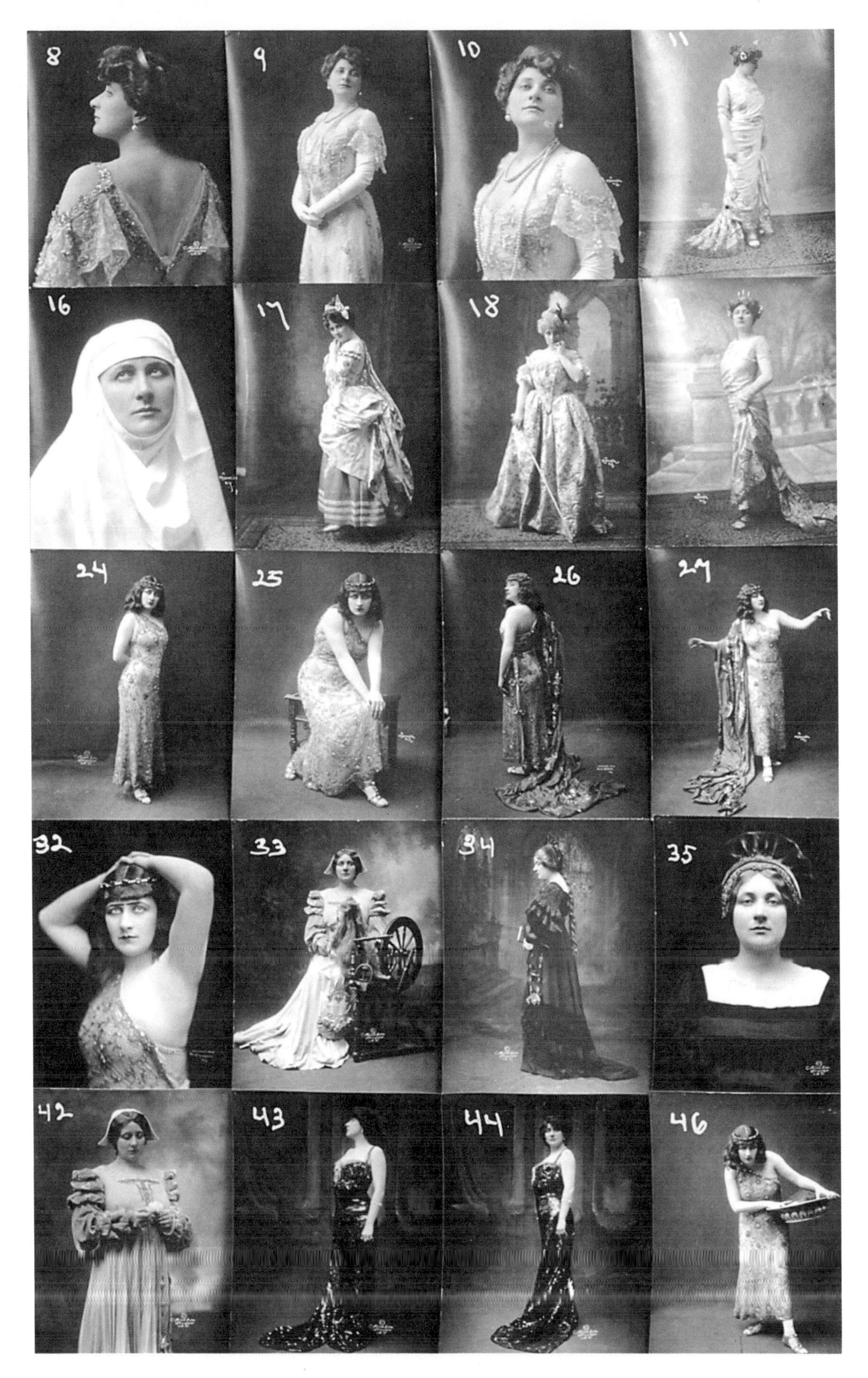

as Manon: 17 through 21; as Salome: 22 through 32, and 46; as Marguerite in Faust*: 33 through 36, and 42; as Sapho: 39, 40, 41, 43, and 44.*

C
MISHKIN
N.Y. 229

Opposite: *Mary Garden as Mary Garden, one of her finest creations.*

plied to the critic of *The New York Times* and others who had hailed her in an interview. "I consider the newspaper reviews of my *Faust* performance most ironic. I was tempted to cry. Here I have been singing the modern French roles with such vocal expressiveness as each of them seemed to demand, but with scant appreciation from the newspaper reviewers. Then I sing the hackneyed *Faust,* which calls for more vocalization than any of the others, and every critic bursts into spontaneous praise. Now I call that downright too bad." Her Marguerite amazed the New York critics again in 1921, and some forty-five years later, on one of her many American lecture tours, she was still having the last word. "Miss Garden then went on to discuss her own voice, and the old charges that she didn't have one. 'Why, I didn't have one voice,' she said with some asperity. 'I had twenty.'" Following the seasons with Hammerstein, Garden spent nineteen seasons with the Chicago Opera, including one in which she managed the company. She called herself "Directa." It was a new and unfamiliar role for her; she hired many more artists than could possibly be used and lost a million dollars in one year.

Her last American performance was in 1935, as Carmen at the Cincinnati Zoo. Thereafter she sang in Europe on rare occasions. At eighty-eight and at the end of her life, while recovering from a fall in which she had broken both arms, Garden sang again for patients, nurses, and doctors packed into a ward of Aberdeen's Royal Infirmary, her music the old Scottish ballad "Annie Laurie." Vincent Sheehan pronounced this epitaph on her death in 1967: "Garden had no school and nothing to teach. She was herself."

FLORENCIO CONSTANTINO

THE CONTROVERSIAL AND ULTIMATELY sad career of Spanish tenor Florencio Constantino (1869–1919) began with training and performances in South America and Italy. He came to the United States in 1906 to tour with Henry Russell's San Carlo Opera Company which developed into the Boston Opera Company. Waiting for the new Boston Opera House to be built, Constantino signed with Hammerstein and made his New York debut in 1908 in *Rigoletto* with Luisa Tetrazzini and Mario Sammarco. Audience and critics alike took warmly to his portrayal of the Duke. "His voice, though not in volume as large as that of Caruso, is pure

The eccentric Florencio Constantino as the Rigoletto *Duke, a role performed with the Manhattan, Boston, Chicago, and Metropolitan Opera companies.*

in tone, brilliant, and of a peculiar caressing quality that eminently fits it for lyric roles. In addition, he uses his voice with great skill." The audience demanded repetitions of two of the Duke's arias, the quartet and "Caro nome."

The rest of the season was an equal success. An unidentified critic from the period describes his stage deportment: "From the glittering diamond upon his little finger to the great flawless stone in his stickpin, Constantino is every inch a tenor. Other tenors might be bankers, brokers or barbers to the unwitting person riding on the same street car . . . but Constantino is always a tenor. . . . I like to see him walk on the stage and occupy his rightful place right where the middle ray of the spotlight will hit him on the probiscus [*sic*]. I like to watch his arms describe graceful circles through ambient atmosphere while his golden voice grapples with high C. Constantino is a real tenor. Long may he wave."

While in New York Constantino also made his debut in court, in a suit brought against him by his agent in Milan for commissions due.

With the Boston Opera he could alternate the florid passages of Count Almaviva in *Il Barbiere di Siviglia* with the dramatic declamation needed for *Aida* and *La Fanciulla del West;* at the same time, he was suing the Boston *Transcript* for saying he used a claque and the Columbia Gramophone Company for avoiding paying him royalties by issuing his records under another name. Apparently drawn to the courtroom by a strong internal magnet, he later sued Henry Russell for various breaches of contract back in his San Carlo days. His big year in the courtroom was 1914, when he was sued in a $100,000 breach of promise case brought by a Weber and Fields chorus girl (for once he won the case); by the bass Joseph Gravina for having put out his right eye in New Orleans during swordplay in *Il Barbiere di Siviglia;* and by Oscar Hammerstein for breaking his Manhattan contract (he not only had to pay $30,000 but spent a few hours in jail). From there his career went steadily downhill, resulting in mostly local performances on the West Coast. In 1918 he was sued, presumably for the last time, for having ruined the Boston premiere of Henry Moore's *Louis XIV* by forgetting his words and drinking cognac between the acts. The following year he broke down in the middle of a Mexico City recital and died a few months later.

CARMEN MELIS

CARMEN MELIS (1885–1967), THE ITALIAN soprano from Sardinia, was in New York singing for Hammerstein within four years of her professional debut in *Iris.* She had studied with Cotogni and Jean de Reszke and was known for performing contemporary

Carmen Melis as Mimi in La Bohème, *performed for Hammerstein in 1910 with John McCormack as Rodolfo.*

roles such as Thaïs, Butterfly, and Tosca (Aida was about as far back into musical history as she ever ventured). Of her Tosca, which she sang frequently during Hammerstein's final season in 1909–10, it was said "she possesses to an unusual degree the qualifications necessary to the successful portrayal of the intense style of singing acting embodied in the operas of realism. Her voice, while neither fine in quality or musical in compass, yet is sufficiently pleasing to answer all demands. It is as an actress that her genius stands out. With a rather awkward physique, she yet contrives to produce the impression of considerable grace. She also possesses the very rare quality of looking remarkably beautiful while singing." Acting seems always to have been her first concern. In *Cavalleria Rusticana* at the Manhattan Opera, she had suggested to John McCormack, that most placid of actors, that he show a little more realism of gesture, only to be thrown crashing into the wings during one of their scenes together.

After Hammerstein's last season in New York, Melis moved on to the Boston Opera for three seasons. Early in 1911 she was Minnie in the Boston Company's premiere of *Fanciulla,* a month after the Met unveiling. Philip Hale watched her admiringly in a succession of performances: "Mme. Melis lays aside the usual devices and conventions of operatic acting for the sake of securing the simplicity, genuineness and directness, essential to a true representative of Mr. Belasco's 'American' heroine. . . . Her voice expresses with unfailing accuracy the color of her experience, whatever it may be . . . the purity of her tones, vitalized by her naturalness in the dialogue passages, commanded admiration. . . . Throughout the evening [she] was by gesture and facial play supremely eloquent.'' In Boston it was also noted that her singing and acting were not always in balance. "Her Tosca can be almost as distinguished for the acting as for the singing; her Butterfly she can ornament with vocal subtleties as refined as the tints of Japanese painting. But her voice, excellent as it is, is one which yields its best tones only to suave wooing. . . . Repeatedly, during an impersonation of Desdemona so adept on its acting side that one often ceased to think of it as acting and watched it as the natural conduct of a woman under torment, Mme. Melis overdrove her voice into hoarseness and stridency.''

Melis sang in San Francisco (*Zazà* under Leoncavallo) and in Chicago. Back in Italy she occasionally took on heavier roles, including Salome and Sieglinde. At the end of her career she was reduced to performing parts for a singing actress, such as Adriana Lecouvreur and Francesca da Rimini most of the time. When she retired from the stage, she taught voice in Pesaro, one of her pupils being Renata Tebaldi.

MARIA GAY

AMONG THE ARTISTS GATTI FOUND ON his roster when he arrived at the Metropolitan for the 1908–1909 season was the Spanish contralto Maria Gay (1879–1943). At sixteen Gay had been jailed briefly for singing revolutionary songs during a republican uprising. Her Paris debut a short time later was at an afternoon concert singing Catalan folk songs while wearing a black riding habit. Impressed by the success of her Carmen in Paris and London and perhaps by her offer to sing one performance as a test, Conried had contracted Gay the previous January as an answer to the Carmen of Bressler-Gianoli at the Manhattan.

It had been said in Paris that Gay sang with liberty and acted with license. This did not appeal to most of the New York critics. "Her Carmen may or may not be Spanish; it is vulgar and common.'' "A big woman, not [illegible] the stage, she has as yet neither style nor finesse to aid any native fitness for the Spanish gypsy.'' For also singing Azucena, Lola, Dame Quickly, and Amneris, she was paid much more than Louise Homer, the other major contralto on the roster in 1908–1909. When Gatti did not take up her contract option for the next season, she moved on to Boston. There Henry Russell's Boston Opera Company provided a five-year operatic banquet not rivaled since. Gay sang in every Russell season, and her Carmen became a fixture. "Last night at the Boston House, Maria Gay put on an old hat and danced on a table, blew her nose violently and significantly when dissatisfied with the amount of ardor displayed by José, played pitch and toss with apples and other fruits, sucked oranges, and on one occasion at least, threw the peeling into the orchestra. . . . It is no wonder that Mme. Gay's finished portrayal of a certain kind of Spanish girl met with such applause, for such as her conception of the character is, she develops it inimitably, in masterly style.'' She was also admired in Chicago ("the voice when correctly used is one of such warmth, such lusciousness and such sensuous suggestiveness'') and in many tour cities in the United States.

Whatever the roles—Dalila, Suzuki in *Madama Butterfly,* Charlotte in *Werther,* or the Mother in *Louise*—Gay maintained her passionate intensity, her animal force. On her retirement she became a teacher and talent scout. She found a more lasting influence on the Met-

Maria Gay in a portrait made about the time of her 1908–1909 Met performances and her first meeting with her future husband, Giovanni Zenatello.

Giovanni Zenatello, famous for his Otello, sang Radames for Hammerstein opposite the Aidas of Lillian Nordica and Giannina Russ.

ropolitan Opera during the late twenties when she and her husband, the tenor Giovanni Zenatello, discovered a young French soprano taking voice lessons in Paris. On their recommendation, Gatti listened to the soprano's recordings, invited her to an audition, and immediately offered her a contract. She was Lily Pons.

GIOVANNI ZENATELLO

WHEN HAMMERSTEIN LOST BONCI TO the Metropolitan, he boasted that there were plenty of tenors and that he had engaged a finer one who wasn't limited to the light parts in the older operas. His prize was Giovanni Zenatello (1876–1949), an Italian dramatic tenor who had begun his operatic life as a baritone singing the second baritone role, Silvio, in *Pagliacci.* Aware that his voice should be placed higher, Zenatello worked alone and was ready when the classic situation presented itself: the leading tenor is ill, who will replace him? Zenatello's successful Naples debut as Canio in 1899 was followed by more study. He was soon appearing at La Scala, singing Pinkerton in the disastrous first performance of *Madama Butterfly* there as well as in its successful rebirth in Brescia shortly after. After singing with Zenatello in *Faust* at Covent Garden, Melba recommended him to Hammerstein. She sang Desdemona at the Manhattan Opera when Zenatello's Otello was first heard in New York: "Her voice, with its original freshness and purity, despite its want of emotionality, and her impeccable vocal art came like a soothing balm after the blows dealt by Signor Zenatello who in his brutal but still thrilling forcefulness of song and action is really an admirable successor of Tamagno [for whom the part was written]." By Zenatello's second season in New York, Otello had come to be considered his most successful interpretation: "This, too, was because he treated the music honestly. He has precisely the right kind of voice for this role, a hard, brilliant pealing tenor, with far reaching high tones. . . . Mr. Zenatello met these requirements freely and with a youthful fire and magnetism which made themselves felt."

By 1909 Zenatello's prestige was such that the Metropolitan had to come begging Hammerstein for his services as a tour replacement for the ailing Caruso. Hammerstein grandly agreed but exacted as his price the use of the Auditorium in Chicago which had been denied his company. Because of Caruso, Zenatello never sang with the Met in New York, but his keen intelligence and forceful expression secured him engagements almost everywhere else. There were four years with the Boston Opera Company. In 1913, inspired by performances in the amphitheater at Orange, he created the summer opera tradition at the Verona Arena and sang Radames in the first *Aida* there. In 1926, after two decades of performing the most strenuous roles of the Italian repertoire, he returned to Covent Garden as Otello in one of the first live performances to be recorded. "What discount ought we to have allowed for the passing of years in the case of Zenatello? In point of technique, none at all, and probably most of us, mentally, allowed for more in the matter of tone than was warranted by fact. Zenatello is a great artist. His method is equal to all emergencies and if he nursed his resources at times, there could still be no denying the purity and freedom of his production in the great moments."

His farewell came seven years later in New York at the Mecca Temple on West 55th Street, his career ending, as it had begun, with *Pagliacci:* his "impersonation of the betrayed barnstormer had all its old time fire and frenzy, his voice retained much of its former power and brilliance and the cleanness of his enunciation made every word tell." Shortly before his death Zenatello recommended Maria Callas to the management of the Verona Arena, and it was there that she made her Italian debut as Gioconda.

MARGUERITE D'ALVAREZ

MARGUERITE D'ALVAREZ (1886–1953), the Peruvian contralto born in Liverpool, England, might have sung more opera had she not encountered Oscar Hammerstein early in her career. Engaged for the Manhattan five seasons after her Rouen debut as Dalila, she made her first New York appearance in 1909 as Fidès in *Le Prophète.* "A really excellent contralto . . . made the hit of the evening at the eleventh hour. From the omitted last act, she had lifted one melodious cavatina over into the church scene. Coupled with her dramatic interview with a thankless child, it made all the close of the opera hers, and she fairly outsang her 'Ah, mon fils' of an earlier episode. A big woman as Fidès can't fail with the public." Backstage there were complications, as Hammerstein, madly infatuated, alternately courted and persecuted her. When she rejected him, he punished her by withholding performances. Divorcing his wife to continue a hopeless pursuit, he obtained her services for his London Opera House in 1911 only by promising in the contract to leave her alone. She did not sing opera again in the United States until 1913–14, when she appeared with the Boston Opera and was hailed in *Aida:* "To Amneris the composer has given music of [illegible] pride, malicious innuendo, amorous entreaty, passion, raging despair. The Music is there, and Mme. d'Alvarez understood it and by it made Amneris a creature of flesh and blood, a haughty princess—but a woman. She has a glorious voice, rich, velvety, sonorous; a voice of gen-

Marguerite d'Alvarez's youthful portrait taken during the 1909–10 Manhattan season suggests one reason for Hammerstein's infatuation with her.

erous compass, with tones that are even throughout and full and round. The voice was used skillfully for dramatic purposes, but the actress never forgot that Verdi's music is to be sung, not declaimed." In *Samson et Dalila,* with Edoardo Ferrari-Fontana and José Mardones, "She did the greater feat. She carried off not merely Samson and his gates, but the whole of Saint-Saëns. Throughout the performance Mme. d'Alvarez sang as if she were in opera and not in glorified oratorio in costume.... It is seldom that the Opera House has contained within its ample walls so much and believable seduction as Mme. d'Alvarez crowded into those moments of reducing the mighty Samson to his original masculine rubbish."

After 1922 and two seasons of opera with the Chicago, d'Alvarez's operatic career in America was virtually finished. In one of those seasons she brought the title role of *Hérodiade* to New York: "To the singing of words she brings a tonality, a diction and an awareness of music rhythm in support of the meaning of her song which lifts her performances far above the level of the ordinary singer or actress, gives to her impersonation the distinction of creative individuality and exalted artistic fidelity."

Some of her strong dramatic instincts carried over into her recitals. At Carnegie Hall in 1920, "Robed in lustreless black amid flowers and palms on a dim-lit platform, she was herself the vivid contrast, often heard but not seen, until from the shadow she suddenly emerged with salient gesture and climax of tone. Her powerful voice was not without vibrato, it was at times strangely modified by emotion, yet effectively in control for the artist's purpose, and eloquent in sustained pianissimo." As extravagant of speech as of gesture, she is reported by her English accompanist, Ivor Newton, to have had a real flair for verbal flights, complimenting a hostess for a soufflé that tasted of "angel's saliva" and comparing a gift of large full chrysanthemums to pregnant swans. In song recitals, which she gave into the 1930s, she was known for her interesting repertoire, even programming Gershwin songs with the composer at the piano. Once she debated a Baptist minister in Town Hall on the subject of "What Shall We Do About Jazz?" She of course defended.

MARIETTE MAZARIN

ALMOST FORTY YEARS AFTER ITS PREmiere, Léon Rothier remembered that the first Louise, Marthe Rioton, was shy, very demure, not at all aggressive, with a gorgeous, full voice; the second, Mary Garden, had been slender, dominating, elegant, sure; the third, Mariette Mazarin (1874–1953), was more statuesque than the others, tragic and powerful, giving the impression of great inner strength. Mazarin was Rothier's wife at the time of these Opéra-Comique performances; the two had met and studied together at the Paris Conservatoire. All her training, her acting lessons at the Comédie Française, the succession of Gluck's classical heroines that she performed at the Monnaie in Brussels—everything coalesced in her appearances during Hammerstein's final season. Although Hammerstein had sensed in her the resources for Richard Strauss's Elektra, he first cast her in two unsympathetic roles, Aida and Carmen.

During the month of January 1910 she studied the score of *Elektra* (because of its difficulty, Hammerstein had Maria Labia and Eva Grippon working on it at the same time) and visited a madhouse as part of her research. She sang the title role in French at its American premiere. It was Hammerstein's last operatic sensation. The music was even more dissonant than that in Strauss's previous work, *Salome,* and the figures on the stage were equally uninhibited. Of Mazarin's contribu-

Mariette Mazarin created a sensation in her performance of Richard Strauss's Elektra, *which she introduced to New York in 1910.*

tion *The New York Times* reported "in nothing has she shown the dramatic power, the intensity of conception, or the manifold resources of interpretation that shine in this achievement of hers. She is a figure of strange and haunting horror; pale, with staring eyes, expressing in features and in every movement the frenzy that rules her being." Her musical performance was equally stunning to W. J. Henderson: "This French dramatic soprano had given little more than a hint in previous appearances here of the vocal skill or of the intellectual and emotional power exhibited in this characterization. For page after page of the score she sang with astonishing accuracy an interminable series of notes and intervals bearing scarcely any relationship to one another in the old fashioned melodic or harmonic sense. She endured these utterances with clear and positive expression, and she emphasized their meaning by movements and gestures and facial expression that made the fearful woman of the new old tragedy live again before the spectators. As a test of endurance, physical and mental, Mme. Mazarin's performance was one of the most remarkable seen on the local stage for a long time. Her dance of mad ecstasy at the conclusion had in it a veritable touch of genius." At the fourth curtain call, exhausted by her concentrated preparation, Mazarin fainted in full view of a screaming audience and had to be dragged to the wings by Gustave Huberdeau, the Orest.

Mazarin never sang again in the United States after that one Hammerstein season. Although she sang all three Brünnhildes in France and was the first French-language Salome, she never again achieved the success or notoriety she had in her union with Strauss's tragic Greek heroine, and today it is for her stunning performance in that role that she is chiefly remembered.

Overleaf: *Enrico Caruso as Samson.*

©
MISHKIN
N.Y.

Part II

The Gatti Years

1910 - 1921

T WAS INEVITABLE THAT Heinrich Conried would not last as general manager of the Metropolitan. Even without the distraction of Hammerstein there were too many deficiencies of personality and skill for him to survive. Giulio Gatti-Casazza (1869–1940), an Italian of distinguished family, came to New York as his replacement in 1908. Though trained as a naval engineer, Gatti had been director of the Teatro Municipale in Ferrara for five years and director of La Scala, in Milan, for ten. Arriving with Arturo Toscanini, he found a theater torn apart by competition and internal dissension despite the presence of many distinguished singers and the conductor Gustav Mahler on the roster.

Gatti was hired by the Metropolitan Opera Board of Directors and was directly responsible to its chairman, Otto H. Kahn, an astute financier uniquely gifted with an appreciation of all the arts. Gatti quickly discovered that although he was general manager, the board had also saddled him with one of the Met's most useful tenors, Andreas Dippel, as administrative manager. The prospectus for 1908–1909 described the season as "under the joint direction of" Gatti and Dippel. Gatti soon secured the support of the board and the loyalty of the company, all the while battling Hammerstein and planning for the future.

In 1909–10, during Gatti's second season, Hammerstein was demolished by the sheer weight of numbers. The Metropolitan operated two complete companies, with chorus and orchestra, putting on an extraordinary display of operatic activity. The six performances a week at Broadway and 39th Street were supplemented by a ten-week season, four performances a week, at the just opened New Theatre, on Central Park West and 61st Street. Brooklyn, Philadelphia, and Baltimore performances were fitted into the weekly schedule. And the Met continued one of its less staid traditions, the Sunday-night concert, which dated back to the company's opening weeks in 1883. A contemporary account of these once-frequent events described them as containing "all sorts of snippets and tags from all sorts of operas, alive, dead, and moribund. They are vocal vaudevilles. Everything is applauded and everything encored, with the exception of the intermission and the ushers." Not just Metropolitan artists performed; among the guests in 1909–10 were two distinguished violinists, Mischa Elman and Fritz Kreisler, and the composer-pianist Sergei Rachmaninoff.

Between November 8, 1909, the season's opening night in New York, and the final night of its triumphant visit to Paris, June 25, 1910, the Metropolitan Opera gave 356 performances, including 23 concerts and galas. This eight-month average of one and a half performances a day, including Sundays, is probably without equal in the history of opera.

In 1908 Gatti had made a subtler move in operatic warfare, one that would deprive the Manhattan Opera of a crucial part of its success, its unique repertoire. Gatti had grown up in a nineteenth-century Italy in which the production of new operas was the rule rather than the exception. During the summer of 1908 he took a series of steps to ensure that the Metropolitan Opera had exclusive access to the major European composers. Contracts were signed for Paul Dukas's *Ariane et Barbe-Bleue,* Maurice Ravel's *Heure Espagnole,* and the entire five-year output of the prestigious German music publisher B. Schott's Söhne, who handled Engelbert Humperdinck, among many others. Most intriguingly, Gatti visited Claude Debussy in Paris and secured an agreement, in return for a payment of 2,000 francs ($384) to the composer, that gave the Metropolitan Opera options for three music dramas that were never to be realized: *La Chute de la Maison Usher, La Diable dans le Beffroi,* and *La Légende de Tristan.*

Otto Kahn provided the $1,200,000 with which Oscar Hammerstein was paid to quit the field of opera in New York for a period of ten years. Of Hammerstein's personnel, Gatti signed only the exceptional character bass-baritone Charles Gilibert (who died before coming to the Met); his enterprising press director, William J. Guard; and his superb photographer, Herman Mishkin. The creation of the Philadelphia-Chicago Grand Opera in 1910, using Hammerstein's assets, productions, repertoire, and many of his artists, solved several problems for the Metropolitan. It took competition and surplus singers away from New York. Thereafter, Hammerstein's operas and singers were heard under Metropolitan auspices in special visits the new company made to the Metropolitan Opera House until 1913. Also, with the appointment of Andreas Dippel as manager of the company, Gatti was relieved of an associate he had never asked for. Singers were lent back and forth between the Metropolitan and Philadelphia-Chicago companies as well as the Boston Opera. In eliminating competition, Kahn and Gatti had established a benevolent operatic dictatorship in the United States.

Free from competition, Gatti opened the 1910–11 season with Gluck's *Armide*, featuring Olive Fremstad, Enrico Caruso, and Pasquale Amato. The world premieres of Puccini's *Fanciulla del West* and Humperdinck's *Königskinder,* and the first American performance of *Ariane et Barbe-Bleue* by Dukas followed. Wagner was represented by *Lohengrin, Tannhäuser, Tristan und Isolde, Die Meistersinger,* the *Ring* cycle, and *Parsifal.* Caruso sang only half the season because of illness. Except for the ban on Wagner during World War I, the pattern remained the same—a mix of strongly cast Italian operas, most of the familiar Wagner, and as many novelties, both new and old, as one could reasonably expect—until the Depression.

In 1910 Gatti presented the first performance at the Metropolitan of an American opera, Frederick Converse's *Pipe of Desire,* with an American cast headed by Louise Homer and Clarence Whitehill; he went on to present more works by native composers than all other Metropolitan regimes put together. In fact, his twenty-seven years were unique for the constant seeking-out of unfamiliar repertoire. If we don't remember Thuille's *Lobetanz,* Wolf-Ferrari's *Donne Curiose,* Blech's *Versiegelt,* and Parker's *Mona,* all performed during the 1911–12 season, it is not because Gatti denied them a hearing or cast them weakly. *Le Donne Curiose* featured Geraldine Farrar, Hermann Jadlowker, Antonio Scotti, and Adamo Didur. During the final rehearsals, the aging basso buffo Antonio Pini-Corsi, who had sung Ford in the world premiere of *Falstaff* long before, was observed backstage in a bit of pantomime, waving one arm in a sweeping gesture and bowing low. When curiosity got the better of a spectator, Pini-Corsi commented on a derivative score: "Merely because I wish to salute the great composers as I hear them pass by in the orchestra." Even the public took for granted the wealth of new music Gatti presented. He was described as "bombarded throughout the year on the one hand by the higher amateurs of new or neglected music requesting him to produce novelties, and on the other by noisy reactionaries pleading for *Pagliacci.* . . . When a novelty is brought forward all these parties [including boxholders and local composers] unite in saying that it is true they asked for novelties and revivals but never for that sort of novelty and revival." Gatti had his own way of dealing with advice. When a board member asked that a performance attended by royalty be changed from an unknown opera to *Pagliacci* with Caruso, Gatti replied that any Metropolitan performance was good enough for any king.

Gatti's ties with Enrico Caruso and Arturo Toscanini had been strong arguments for engaging him in 1908. He had presented Caruso in his 1900 La Scala debut and had worked closely with Toscanini there for seven seasons before coming to the Metropolitan. Toscanini quickly established himself in the eyes of the New York public and newspapers as a conductor uniquely gifted for Wagner and Verdi—indeed, for anything he chose to perform. His discipline and his tantrums have become legendary. Not remembered so well was his regard for the human voice that was singled out by the *Herald* in 1913: "Although he is known as a hard taskmaster, making the most exacting demands upon his musicians at rehearsal, yet when it comes to a performance he knows that his hundred men of brass and strings can produce more sound than a mere set of human vocal chords [*sic*]. So frequently with a characteristic wave of his left hand he 'wipes out,' as it were, the volume of orchestral sound and lets the voice reign. That movement of his left hand is most interesting—as though he held in it an eraser and passed it across a blackboard inscribed with thousands of characters, just so does the orchestral volume diminish and the voices are heard." Toscanini's authority extended to audiences; once he halted the orchestra during a performance of Weber's *Euryanthe* and waited for latecomers to stop talking. In 1915 Toscanini left the Metropolitan after seven seasons. When he blamed artistic differences for his departure, Gatti and Kahn responded by offering him unlimited musical control, but were rejected. Finally, Gatti wrote in exasperation some words that have a special meaning for the music world in the late twentieth century: "One thing is certain, i.e. that the famous Conductors of today, although they may talk incessantly of art and its sacred rights, have become worse than the old-time Prima donna and they do not even have the excuse of belonging to the weaker sex. It is sad but true!"

With its pre–World War I dependence on Europe for leading artists, conductors, orchestra musicians, Italian and German chorus members, even sets and costumes, the Metropolitan faced a serious crisis after the outbreak of hostilities. The company would continue to seek out important singers of whatever origin. However, war encouraged the development of American orchestral musicians and singers for both chorus and solo assignments. Anti-German feeling even raised the question of finding a new repertoire. First, Otto Kahn suggested in September 1914 that the Metropolitan might substitute the Russian Ballet (Sergei Diaghilev's company headed by Nijinsky) for the German repertoire in the forthcoming season. Gatti found, however, that existing artists' contracts did not allow for cancellation because of war and that the artists themselves were eager to reach New York. Writing from Milan in September 1915, Gatti described the old continent as "a mad-house soaked with blood." The war dragged on for two years before the Metropolitan Board of Directors decided to ban all German-language opera. By then, Gatti had new contracts in place with clauses stipulating cancellation in case of war, but he still was not pleased with the timing. He wrote to Kahn in November 1917: "As an Italian (especially in this moment when my country is, unfortunately, invaded), I certainly do not regret that the burden of presenting German opera is taken off my shoulders. I fully understand the sentiments which have inspired the Board to take this decision, but as a responsible manager of this organization, I respectfully call your attention to the fact that the present conditions could have been foreseen by the Board of Directors last April or May, when this country was already at war with Germany. At that time when you submitted to the Board the question whether it would be advisable to give

Opposite: *Mishkin photographed Giacomo Puccini, composer of* La Fanciulla del West, *during his 1910 visit to New York for the world premiere of the opera.*

of re-creating his hit for the Met's big stage. The *Sun* reported at length on the December 5 run-through: "It is 10:30 in the morning and a rehearsal of the second act of Puccini's *Girl of the Golden West* is about to begin. The big auditorium at the opera house is full of ruddy shadows, for only the box lights are turned on, glowing through their sheaths of red silk.

"The orchestra pit, full of men and instruments, is like a cauldron of sound, boiling with preliminary tuning. At the conductor's desk Toscanini, his nose almost touching the score in the intensity of his concentration, is making rapid corrections and interlineations. Puccini himself, in derby hat, brown suit and red necktie, looks over his shoulder and does not interfere. Toscanini takes the corrected sheets to the man with the big bassoon. . . . There are perhaps fifty persons waiting to see and to hear. When the curtain goes up the stage becomes the port for most of their thoughts. But there two sails in their separate offings, the hat of Puccini and the familiar head of Belasco, are the objects of many peering, curious glances. Each is the center of a little group, Puccini quiet, Belasco grumbling ominously, like Vesuvius on the point of eruption. . . . Through the warm shadowy gloom one recognizes faces grown familiar across the footlights. One finds one's self close to Mme. Fremstad and later has a disturbing consciousness of seeing her hands clinched tightly on the top of the seat before her as she follows the music—or you would rather say by way of accuracy that it pursues her with its possibilities. When Emmy Destinn comes on and begins her lines Mme. Fremstad turns and says: 'She sings beautifully. Doesn't she?' And yet they say there is no generosity of appreciation among these men and women. There is not on Manhattan Island a sound so hoarse as Toscanini's voice this week unless it is the raucous bark of an automobile horn. He has talked, he has sung, he has pompommed explanatory phrases till he can scarcely croak. . . . Yet it is gentle as a summer's breeze compared with the Belascan blast over the management of the stage lights during the blizzard. It follows the entrance of Jack Rance and the cowboys who should shout 'Hello. Hello.' outside the Girl's house and then give the usual fateful knock on the door. At the first try they miss their cue. ''Ello. 'Ello' barks Toscanini with hoarse importunity, for the thing is moving with a sweep too good to be interrupted. The tardy singers swagger on with curious European versions of a cowboy's [illegible], shaking stage snow from their hats and shoulders. Even at rehearsal there is a lively dash of realism. Enough snow is dumped to familiarize the stage hands with their work and to remind the singers that snow is to be shaken off.

Mishkin's first photographs of his favorite subject, Enrico Caruso, were as Dick Johnson, alias the bandit Ramerrez, seen here in Act I of La Fanciulla del West.

But the missed cue has brought a halt, and it is at this psychological moment that an unlucky stage person approaching that white spot which is Belasco sets the Vesuvian eruptions going at full blast. He promptly receives the information, adorned with a proper supply of verbal trimmings, that the management of the lights in the episode just finished wasn't fit for a barnstorming performance. . . . 'Why don't you say you'll have them all right next week or next month?' demands Belasco. 'This is the time, right now, for your men to show what they know—if they know anything.'

"Caruso, who has a performance of *Aida* coming on the same evening, uses his voice cautiously. Sometimes the notes are barely audible above the climax of sounds from the orchestra. Again, when these sink to mere whispers, one hears lovely low tones, very soft, very gentle, almost like the drowsy first notes of a wonderful green bird beginning to sing at dawn. And one looks with a sort of painful incredulity at the stout gentleman in a brown business suit, who does not suggest any kind of bird—unless it is a nice plump partridge—yet who is visibly responsible for those tones. . . . He makes few un-

Enrico Caruso as Dick Johnson, dressed for the snowy night of Fanciulla's *Act II, when Minnie saves his life for the first time.*

necessary motions. When he first comes in he takes off an imaginary overcoat and hat and puts them on a chair. When he goes out he possesses himself of these imperceptible articles and departs with them. That episode was repeated several times and he was always most conscientious about handling the make believe raiment. Only in the scene after he is shot does he attempt anything dramatic. This too is gone through repeatedly, and each time he is—apparently—dragged in by Destinn, his knees covered with snow and his motions animated by a sublime disregard of the possible effects on his really admirable trousers of crawling on his knees over the proverbial dust of the stage floor. Both he and Destinn work hard over his painful climb up the ladder to the half loft overhead. That eminence achieved he sits down, Turk or tailor fashion—more sublime indifference to the fate of trousers and knees—mops his forehead with his handkerchief and gazes out into the auditorium. When he has been laboriously assisted to the stage again and has fallen fainting across the table where Destinn and Amato gamble for possession of him, he lies there inert for a while, then sits up, again mops his face and idly watches the game, watches Toscanini, watches the cleaning woman wiping interminable rows of chair backs in the gallery. He seems profoundly indifferent to the whole thing. . . . Destinn on the other hand both sings and acts with more than a mere exhibition of intention. She is in a black velvet frock, almost a hobble skirt, so that she even accentuates the difficult walk called for by the tight slippers of the play. And she sings with dramatic intensity. Of course, she has no performance that night, and that makes a difference. The rehearsal goes on and on. The act is finished and there is half an hour to rest. Belasco goes on the stage, sits down at the table and distributes embroidered advice on assorted subjects; on how to walk like an Indian; on how to 'pull a gun'—a quite different affair, messieurs and signori, from drawing a sword or a stiletto; on how to shut a door in the teeth of the wind; on how to kick one's legs against each other after fighting one's way through a blizzard. . . . Destinn winds her silk scarf, one of the props for that act, around her bare neck and dropping into a chair, puts her head down on her arms outstretched before her; Caruso disappears. John the Baptist (The prompter) emerges from his coop and takes Dinh Gilly's gesticulated assurance that when waiting to ''Ello. 'Ello' outside the house they couldn't get their cue at all. 'Rien. Rien. Rien.' he declares. . . . The act is begun all over again a little before 1 o'clock and goes more smoothly. Caruso sticks to it for a while, but it's a case of 'Don't work, for the night is coming!' and he soon fades away. [Day-of-performance rehearsals are now unheard of.] Toscanini, by means of hoarse fragments of Caruso's part, carries it along, plus the other singers, plus the orchestra. . . . Again the shot is heard outside and at this stage of the game Puccini makes his one and only trip to the conductor's desk and apparently offers some suggestion about the score. He has an unlighted cigarette between his lips. No one smokes either on or off the stage. No one laughs or jokes. What little conversation there is takes place in an undertone. It is evidently a most serious occasion."

"For Act III the stage is converted into a forest of giant California redwoods. Surging among the Italian male chorus are ten men on horseback. 'You mustn't let the Indian tie Johnson,' cries Mr. Belasco suddenly. 'All these men hate Johnson and want to see him hanged, but there is such a thing as caste in the West, and if the Indian bound him they would all let him go!' Time and again they go over the scene, while he makes suggestions. He shows Mr. Amato how to strike Johnson-Ca-

Emmy Destinn as Minnie, the Bible-reading barmaid, a part written by Puccini with her voice in mind.

ruso across the face and then sets them to glare at each other. He shows Caruso-Johnson how to take in with one last despairing glance the whole range of mountains and forest as far as his eye can reach; one thing he cannot show to anybody, and that is how to throw a lasso so that it will knot on a tree limb. It is probable that this will not be done by an Italian on the opening night."

Tickets were at double prices, $3 to $10, but at noon on the day of performance speculators were charging $150. Toward evening their prices came down and their manners improved. Finally the hour of performance arrived: backstage, the last-minute preparations; in the lobby, the eager anticipation of a premiere; in the auditorium, decorated with Italian and American flags, the supercharged excitement of a brilliantly dressed audience. "The dullest imagination can figure the scene in all its eager flurry, its anxiety, its discussions, its movement. Can you not hear the buzz of operatic insects in the lobbies, and the grave booming of directorial guns in the boxes and the offices? Can you not see the delight on the faces of the Italians, on the features of the courtly Roman from the embassy at Washington, in the bright eyes of . . . all of them, prince and proletariat alike, intoxicated with the heady wine of their native music? . . . The honors of the performance fall to Mme. Emmy Destinn. In any part, the issues and passions of which are

Pasquale Amato portrayed Jack Rance, the menacing sheriff of La Fanciulla del West, *in one of his many Metropolitan premieres.*

straightforward, primary, obvious and derived logically from the instinct and natural best of womanhood, Madame Destinn is always more than satisfactory. She is splendid as a peasant. She is insufferable as a duchess. She was delightful as Minnie. With her wonderful musical powers she caught the very essence of Puccini's music. She sang with a liquid beauty of tone, a fine spun delicacy of phrasing, a poetry of vocal interpretation that must go far toward the making of the opera. It was a complete, an irresistible and a personal triumph. M. Caruso's presentation of Johnson, apart from its vocal distinction and qualifications, upon which it is hardly necessary to harp, was clean cut, proper as to costumes properly worn, manly, vigorous and not un-Western. The splendid voice and large, generous, boyish utterance of M. Amato may have seemed out of place in so deliberate, so icy, so harsh a character as that of Jack Rance, but we cannot find it in us to blame him for having so fine and so warm-hearted a voice. The smaller parts will be dealt with in a future notice, though it should be now stated in justice to M. Gilly that he might have lived among the Sierras all his life.

"Applause. The whole night was a hurricane of applause. Who can describe that wondrous tumult as celebrity after celebrity, familiar or new, made his bow before the majestic curtain of old gold.

"Success. This opera was a popular success before it was written. It was never intended that it should be anything else."

Although not mentioned by all the papers, in addition to Gilly the cast was sprinkled with notable singing actors from the roster, including Adamo Didur, Angelo Bada, Albert Reiss, and Antonio Pini-Corsi. In the tiny role of José Castro was Eduardo Missiano, who years before had befriended the impoverished Caruso in Naples, introduced him to the singing teacher Guglielmo Vergine, and taught him arias from *I Pescatori di Perli* and *Cavalleria Rusticana* for his second audition. Caruso had now secured a job at the Met for Missiano.

Fanciulla was an immediate hit, but it never achieved the universal appeal of *Bohème, Tosca,* or *Butterfly*. Caruso kept it in his repertoire for only four seasons; it has reappeared on the Met stage only after long rests.

Ever since the first *Fanciulla,* operagoers have speculated about why Caruso did not record its most familiar excerpt, the third-act "Ch'ella mi creda." At least a partial explanation can be found in the December 17, 1910, issue of *Musical America:* "Tito Ricordi, of the Milan publishing house of Ricordi and Co., and agent and publisher of all of Puccini's operas, has refused to permit American talking-machine companies or music roll houses to reproduce mechanically any of the music of *The Girl of the Golden West.* Selections from *Tosca, Boheme* and *Madame Butterfly* have a large sale in player-piano music rolls and talking-machine records. Some of the interest being taken in *The Girl* by the public is shown by the fact that out of 1,000 scores sent to this country, not one was unsold at the end of the first week." For the sale of a handful of scores, Ricordi not only denied us the sound of Destinn, Amato, and Caruso in their most remarkable creations, but deprived *Fanciulla* itself of these far-reaching builders of popularity.

Dick Johnson, portrayed by Caruso, bound and waiting to be hanged in Act III of Fanciulla.

DINH GILLY

THE SON OF A FRENCH OFFICER AND AN Arab woman described as the most beautiful in Algiers, Dinh Gilly (1877–1940) was graduated from St. Cyr, the French military academy, before his baritone voice took over and led him to study in Italy with Cotogni and at the Paris Conservatoire. The Opéra fol-

Algerian-born baritone Dinh Gilly as a Western cowboy, Sonora, in Act III of Fanciulla, *one of several works in which he appeared with his innamorata, Emmy Destinn.*

Singing Rigoletto on six hours' notice and for the first time in Italian, Gilly showed why Gatti found him so useful: "Mr. Dinh Gilly as Rigoletto was a splendid piece of work, his voice is at once rich and penetrative, youthful and mellow and excellently managed; his acting is pungent and sincere."

As Dapertutto, he was equally successful in one of the first Metropolitan performances of *Les Contes d'Hoffmann*: "The French baritone never has shown the range, quality and flexibility of his voice to greater advantage in New York than he did yesterday in the exacting 'Mirror' aria, and after a concluding high G sharp, spun out in exquisite mezza-voce, the progress of the performance was halted for more than a minute by applausive demonstrations extending from floor to gallery."

Gilly sang with Emmy Destinn for the first time in *Cavalleria* just after his *Werther* debut. It was probably the beginning of their long-lasting liaison. Back in France his wife was heard to complain that he came home only to father another child.

In 1914 Gilly was trapped by the war on Destinn's estate outside Prague. Gatti kept his place open for all of the 1914–15 season, hoping Gilly would be able to rejoin the company. Finally, the Metropolitan secured Gilly's release through diplomatic channels on the condition that he promise not to fight in the French army. He refused and was interned for the duration of the war. Although he and Gatti maintained a cordial correspondence, Gilly was never invited back to the Metropolitan. Instead, he returned to London, where he and Destinn had introduced *Fanciulla* at Covent Garden in 1911, and spent the remainder of his life there, performing and teaching.

lowed for four seasons. His all-round usefulness came to the attention of Gatti-Casazza, who, before even coming to New York, gave him a contract for 1909–10. He sang on opening night of the Metropolitan's season at the New Theatre, November 1909, as Albert in *Werther* with Geraldine Farrar, Edmond Clément, and Alma Gluck. His formal debut at the Met quickly followed in the double bill of *Cavalleria Rusticana* and *Pagliacci,* with Gilly singing both Alfio and Silvio effectively. "He gave them a distinctive and peculiar artistic significance by the admirable skill that he brought to bear upon them. He is an accomplished actor, and while his voice is not of a power and quality that will make a sensation at the Met, it has real beauty and is used with such skill and discretion as to make all its effects tell to the best advantage." In his five seasons with the Metropolitan, Gilly performed almost as often as Amato and frequently substituted for him as well as for Scotti and Renaud in a repertoire that ranged from Sonora in *Fanciulla* to Amonasro in *Aida,* from Germont to Marcello.

EMMY DESTINN

THE OPERAGOER WHO DEMANDS INstant gratification upon hearing a report or recording of a new singer might well recall that the general manager's work has seldom had quick results. In August 1902 Maurice Grau, then manager of the Metropolitan, wrote from Carlsbad to his conductor Nahan Franko in Bayreuth, "I wish you would write to me your opinion of the performances of today and tomorrow, especially what you think of Mme. Destin [*sic*] and Mr. Borgmann, both of whom are in the market and with both of whom I am negotiating." Emmy Destinn (1878–1930) was then in her second Bayreuth season, where she was the

Opposite: *Emmy Destinn as Marie in Smetana's* The Bartered Bride, *performed for the first time at the Metropolitan in 1909.*

MISHKIN
N.Y.

first Senta and also the Forest Bird in *Siegfried.* Only five years earlier she had made her professional debut as Santuzza in Dresden after training in Prague. Her international career flourished with appearances in London and Berlin, but she was not to reach the Metropolitan until six years after Grau had begun his negotiations. Heinrich Conried, Grau's successor, eventually signed Destinn, but by the time she made her Metropolitan debut, Conried had been fired and replaced by Giulio Gatti-Casazza. Gatti chose *Aida* for the gala opening night of his new regime. Appearing with Caruso and Louise Homer in a performance conducted by Arturo Toscanini, Destinn in the title role was immediately hailed as a major artist. "Miss Destinn might have been appearing here for the hundredth time instead of the first such was her seeming self-possession as she made her entrance in the opening tableau. From the first glimpse the audience had of her she was in character, and from the first note she uttered in command of her voice. Since she is an operatic actress of rare skill, endowed with a voice of extraordinary beauty, it is not surprising that her debut here amounted to a triumph. With a figure of ample height and noble lines, a finely poised head, and expressive features she really looked the barbarian princess. . . . In make-up and costume her Aida might safely be a model for all who attempt the part. So might it in action and song. From the proud humility of her entrance till she lay dead in the vault beneath the temple this Aida compelled the attention of the spectators. Never did Miss Destinn step out of the part for a moment. Even when the victorious Rhadames returned, she was not a famous soprano concerned with the disposition of her draperies and anxious about top-notes to come. She was the agonized daughter, searching the group of captives for a glimpse of her father. And she is one of the few operatic actresses who dare now and then to leave their arms at rest, having learned the value of significant repose. The same absorbing dramatic quality pervades her singing. The voice is as expressive as it is deliciously fresh. Remarkably even throughout its range, smooth and sweet in mezza voce, it has also the brilliancy of timbre to ring out like a clarion above the crashing ensembles of the second finale. 'The three requisites of a singer,' a famous vocal teacher is reported to have said, 'are voice, voice and then voice.' These three requisites Miss Destinn has in rare perfection, controlled by art as rare. Her legato is unsurpassable, her intonation (last night, at least) of exquisite purity, she phrases with the poise and certainty of a masterly performance on the violin. And this most appealing voice and finished art are at the service of a woman of temperament and brains."

Although New York soon decided that she was not the actress at first perceived, there was seldom any departure from the 1909 appraisal of her singing in the American premiere of Catalani's *Wally*: "Her face is of that peculiar type and cast that one does not easily forget. Her voice has the same haunting, pervasive individuality. She sang the purely lyric and the absolutely dramatic parts of an opera, the aspects of which are constantly changing—as if Catalani were uncertain he was a Verdian or a Wagnerian—now with skill and taste, and now with such fire that she extracted from Mme. Nellie Melba, who was present at the rehearsal, a generous expression of spontaneous praise."

She and Geraldine Farrar, her rival from Berlin, never acknowledged each other's existence in the corridors of the Metropolitan; however, when Destinn was given Farrar's part in *Butterfly,* Henderson made a point of noting "She at any rate has solved the difficult problem of singing the entrance in tune. . . . It must be admitted that she does not create any visual illusion. One sees Madame Butterfly and is reminded of Little Buttercup, whom Capt. Corcoran pronounced a plump and pleasing person. But when Puccini's sensuous music is sung with so much artistic understanding and so much skill in the management of tone, all may be forgiven."

She was Alice Ford in *Falstaff,* Tosca, and Wagner's Eva and Elisabeth; one evening she even sang the off-stage Priestess to her own Aida. Puccini wrote *Fanciulla* with her voice in mind. She frequently appeared opposite Caruso in *Cavalleria Rusticana* or *Pagliacci, La Gioconda, Gli Ugonotti,* and *Un Ballo in Maschera;* with Leo Slezak she sang in *Queen of Spades* and *Die Zauberflöte. The Bartered Bride,* in German, was one of many works staged for her; dancers were imported from the National Theatre in Prague, and Gustav Mahler conducted the overture as an introduction to the second act. "The climax was the Bohemian village sextet. As a quintet it began, all low voices in effect almost hymnlike. . . . To hear Destinn's clear, ringing treble lift that quintet to a sextet in its closing measures was as thrilling as all her screeches at the two youngsters who wanted to marry her."

Destinn's long-lasting romantic liaison with Dinh Gilly ended during World War I, while they were interned on her estate outside Prague. When a young air captain crashed on the grounds, Destinn nursed him back to health—and married him. Gilly chose to wait out the war in a concentration camp.

After the war years, Destinn sang again at the Met and with the Chicago Opera on tour, gradually tapering off the number of her appearances. After 1921 she confined her singing to Europe, especially in her newly created homeland, Czechoslovakia. She last gave a concert in 1928, two years before her death.

LÉON ROTHIER

WITH HIS PURE DICTION AND REFINED style of acting, the French bass Léon Rothier (1875–1951) was the conscience of the Met's French repertoire for twenty-five seasons. His first opera portraits

Léon Rothier's characterization of Bluebeard in Paul Dukas's Ariane et Barbe-Bleue, which had its American premiere with Geraldine Farrar in 1911 at the Met.

Albert Reiss in an unusual role, the Witch in Humperdinck's Hänsel und Gretel, *performed in 1911 in the presence of the composer.*

had been taken by his father, a photographer in Reims. The striking Mishkin photo documents Rothier's appearance in the American premiere of Paul Dukas's *Ariane et Barbe-Bleue* with Geraldine Farrar, conducted by Arturo Toscanini, during Rothier's first Met season. A student of Paul Lhérie, the first Don José in Carmen, Rothier performed both leading and featured roles in forty works in French, German, and Italian during his long career. Although never a box office attraction, Rothier was so effective as Arkel to Clarence Whitehill's Golaud in *Pelléas et Mélisande* that Pitts Sanborn maintained "it should be called *Arkel and Golaud* when he and Whitehill were in it." After retiring from the stage, Rothier opened a studio in New York and taught. In 1949 he celebrated the fiftieth anniversary of his debut at the Opéra-Comique, where he sang in the first *Louise,* with an acclaimed Town Hall recital attended by many of his former colleagues.

ALBERT REISS

GERMAN TENOR ALBERT REISS (1870–1940), an actor turned singer, specialized in that kind of Wagnerian role not taken by front-line artists but usually spoiled by anyone less than first-class. By the end of the first of his nineteen Metropolitan seasons, in a 1902 *Siegfried* with Milka Ternina, Andreas Dippel, and Anton Van Rooy, Reiss was proclaimed as "the best Mime New York has yet enjoyed. Reiss, who filled the role of the malicious, malignant dwarf, was the very embodiment of the wicked wretch. Physically, with his shaking shanks, his shambling steps, his crooked body, he satisfied all ideals. He sang the music with the suggestive eloquence of cunning, of insinuation and of grotesquery. His speech was distinct and his acting a marvel in the expression of abject cowardice." Mime in both *Rheingold* and *Siegfried,* David in *Meistersinger,* and dozens of other German and Italian parts became his property. When Engelbert Humperdinck came to New York in 1910 for the world premiere of his *Königskinder* with Geraldine Farrar and Hermann Jadlowker, Reiss sang the Witch in *Hänsel und Gretel* performances celebrating the composer's presence. "There is always a certain risk in such a transfer of roles between men and women, even when made with the assent and approval of the composer, as this presumably was since he is here and concerned with the doings of the Opera House. But the result, this time, seemed to be fortunate. There are passages of the music which do not quite lie in Mr. Reiss's voice; but beautiful singing does not happen to be one of the essentials for this witch's role, which has often been sung in a caricatured manner. . . . He made the very properly grotesque and unpleasant person, at once humorous and terrible; and it fits admirably into one side of his versatile talent."

A naturalized American citizen who founded the Society of American Singers for performances in English, Reiss survived World War I, when most German artists had their contracts canceled, only to return to Germany in 1920 after a petty disagreement with Gatti backstage. Although he eventually returned to acting, he sang long enough to record portions of his *Siegfried* Mime with Lauritz Melchior.

ALMA GLUCK

NEVER TOTALLY COMFORTABLE WITH her operatic career, the American soprano Alma Gluck (1884–1938) abandoned it as easily as she had fallen into it. Born Reba Fiersohn in Bucharest, Rumania, she was brought to the United States at the age of six. As a young married woman Alma Gluck studied singing with Arturo Buzzi-Peccia, composer of "Colombetta." One evening in 1909 she came to his home for a lesson to find him entertaining dinner guests—Gatti-Casazza, Alda, Toscanini, and the Amatos. Their curiosity aroused by the handsome young woman, the guests insisted that the lesson proceed; a few days later she signed a five-year contract with the Metropolitan. Her debut performance was the opening-night *Werther* of the Met's 1909 season at the New Theatre. Also debuting were Edmond Clément and Dinh Gilly; Geraldine Farrar sang Charlotte and Gluck was her younger sister, Sophie. She "displayed a very pretty light soprano voice and sang with taste and intelligence." That same season she debuted at the Metropolitan Opera House in a brief appearance as the Blessed Spirit in Gluck's *Orfeo ed Euridice* with Toscanini conducting. Louise Homer sang the title role, and this began a musical partnership that included joint recitals and popular duets for Victor Records. On tour with the Met that first season, Gluck quickly and easily graduated to leading roles—Marguerite in *Faust* and Mimi in *La Bohème*. "With a pleasing personality, an extremely clear and fluent voice of sufficient power for last night's demands, with an intelligent grasp of the character [of Mimi] and with marked ability in presenting her conception of it, she was natural, simple-minded, loyal and unfortunate. Her death scene was remarkable for its naturalness and good taste."

In spite of her favorable reception by the public and increasingly prominent roles, the exacting Gluck became dissatisfied with her musical progress after only one season. When the Met went to Paris for a summer season in 1910, Gluck, uninvited, followed Gatti there and begged to be allowed two years for study and performance in small Italian opera houses so that she might grow more slowly into an operatic career. Gatti laughingly refused. While still appearing at the Met she made a 1910 New York recital debut in Mendelssohn Hall. She was obviously at home in a program that included works by Beethoven, Mendelssohn, and Schumann, as well as a long section in English. "We have few concert singers who would have surpassed Miss Gluck in distinctness of enunciation, purity of intonation and breath control." Two seasons of opera and recitals followed, and finally in 1912 Gatti became convinced that she would profit from further experience. An unusual contract was drawn up and signed. She would proceed to Europe in January 1913 and stay there for two years except for a short vacation; she would "apply herself to the study of her profession as prima donna; shall extend and perfect herself in her repertoire and shall obtain regular employment in opera houses in Europe, singing regular performances. . . . During such two years, the artist shall not make any extended concert tournees nor sing regularly in concert." She was to be paid $5,000 and her original five-year contract extended two years. Unfortu-

Alma Gluck in one of her first important solo roles, the Happy Shade in Gluck's Orfeo ed Euridice, *during her short operatic career before turning exclusively to concerts.*

nately, Gatti had waited too long; her preference for concerts won out decisively over opera. The previous contract was canceled and an extraordinary new agreement drawn up. Gluck promised not to sing with any other opera company in New York without the permission of the Metropolitan; on breach of contract she was to pay $10,000 as partial compensation. All this because, according to the contract, "It is specially stipulated that the artist is a singer of unique distinction, and that this negative contract is necessary to protect the rights of the company." She left opera in November of 1912 after a Philadelphia performance of *Rigoletto* that featured Titta Ruffo in his American debut.

Gluck rounded out her training with extended periods of summer study under Marcella Sembrich. By the end of 1914 the improvements in her voice and repertoire convinced critics that "as Miss Gluck's voice now stands it is the most beautiful lyric soprano before the public. Nature gave her a notably fine organ, and its resources have at last been brought fairly, if not completely, under her command. Her medium and upper tones are now not only ravishing in quality, but they have a splendid fullness and vigor. Her upper scale is now generally well attached and cleanly delivered, and she has been initiated into the school of perfect equalization, to wit, the emission of head tones and the art of carrying them down. Miss Gluck sang sonorous, flute-like high tones yesterday which last January would have been half strangled in her throat and would have been without quality. . . . The truth is that she must be accorded a position among the best young sopranos of this time. If she has not eloquence of utterance, she has much finish, much taste, much delicacy. . . . She possesses in no ordinary measure the power to communicate sentiment, gentle feeling and the varying moods of reflection and meditation."

Her Victor recordings, all made between 1911 and 1919, included a large proportion of light songs that few sing so naturally or spontaneously. In sales she was exceeded only by Caruso and John McCormack. With the royalties from more than a million copies of "Carry Me Back to Old Virginny," she bought a house on Park Avenue. She had married the violinist Efrem Zimbalist in 1914, and her home and family occupied increasingly more of her time. There were few recitals after 1921; her last was in 1925.

LEO SLEZAK

THE DATE WAS NOVEMBER 17, 1909, THE occasion the first performance of *Otello* at the Metropolitan in seven years. Much had been written about the six-foot four-inch proportions of the Czech tenor making his debut, and when he appeared onstage, he quickly captured the audience. "Out of the aggregation of singers, his gigantic figure looming high like a giant out of mythology, emerged victoriously Leo Slezak, the most impressive dramatic tenor New Yorkers have heard since the days of Tamagno." Only Caruso could arouse such acclamation as Slezak did that night, not by his stature but for his equally resounding voice. Although compared to Francesco Tamagno, the original Otello, "his voice is less robust and more lyric in volume and quality, and he possesses just what the great Italian tenor lacked—finish of style and wide range of vocal color and expression. Slezak can thrill you with the real tenor high note, and also charm with a delightfully modulated phrase or bit of mezza voce." It was no coincidence that the memory of Jean de Reszke was also evoked: Slezak had taken off several months the previous year for study with De Reszke in Paris.

New York's standard for acting the role of Othello in Shakespeare's play had been set by Tommaso Salvini, the Italian tragedian, in the nineteenth century, and Slezak's performance was compared favorably with the actor's: "The scenes of his jealousy were conceived and executed with Salvini's tiger-like fury and oriental abandon. Older theatregoers will recall the tremendous moment when Salvini shoved Iago down on his knees. Mr. Slezak last night strode toward Mr. Scotti with the speed of light, crouched, gathering for a spring, literally leaped into the air, landed on that eminent baritone like an avalanche, and bore him to the stage. . . . There were audible gasps from the audience as the smaller man was crushed to the ground."

Slezak had taken the first steps of his career in his hometown. Filling in with the local chorus and singing what he could remember, he was heard by a guest baritone who was performing Tonio in *Pagliacci.* As Slezak recounted, "I was bawling alongside him like a madman" when the other singer turned and asked to see Slezak later. The baritone, Adolf Robinson, had sung at the Met in the American premieres of *Rienzi, Tristan,* and *Götterdämmerung* and was then in the last days of his career. He became Slezak's teacher. Starting with a 1896 debut in Brno and advancing to performances in Berlin and Breslau, Slezak made his way to Vienna in 1901. By May 1909 his reputation was such that the Metropolitan signed him to a contract that called for a salary second only to Caruso's.

A man of great wit, Slezak was an immediate hit with the New York public, who adored him as much for his humor and modesty as for his voice. To the consterna-

Opposite: *The giant tenor Leo Slezak in his American debut role, Otello, performed at the Metropolitan between 1909 and 1913, usually opposite Frances Alda and Antonio Scotti.*

tion of other tenors, he once announced casually that he had problems with "low" notes. He hated posing for photographs; what other tenor would have published a photograph of himself diving into a secluded woodland pond—with only his legs showing? And while legends come to be fabricated about various singers, Slezak indeed was responsible for opera's most famous witticism. Waiting backstage for his entrance in *Lohengrin,* he turned to find the swan boat had moved onto the stage without him. Without a moment's hesitation he asked, "What time is the next swan?"

Slezak had the talent—unique among members of an opera company—of being able to move from all but the heaviest Wagnerian roles into the Italian dramatic repertoire, and to perform both with equal success. Of his first New York Manrico in *Trovatore* with Johanna Gadski, it was written, "Verdi's hero of high C's has several things to express before he comes to the second scene of the third act. Most of these things Slezak sang admirably and in genuine Italian fashion, holding the top notes with true southern fervor and producing, whenever there was sufficient provocation, the most delicious mezza-voce. He even indulged in tones 'morendo,' tones dying away into the faintest sort of whisper. But then came that scene that contains 'Ah, si ben mio' and that irresistible tenoristic battle horse 'Di quella pira.' Admiration then changed to amazement and amazement to tumultuous enthusiasm. . . . On his mettle, putting every ounce of energy into his voice, the great Slezak, chest thrown out and head held high, sang the dramatic rhythms of the familiar aria with irresistible temperament. The first high C, delivered with remarkable freedom and ease, delighted the crowd so much that proceedings were almost interrupted at this point. Quick hisses, however, stilled the incipient storm of noise, and Slezak was permitted to bring the scene to a close. As soon as the last high C had been hurled at the crowd, which Slezak did assuming a heroic posture, with sword held high in the air, the thunder of applause that already had begun to rumble burst forth unshackled. So vociferous a demonstration greeted the tenor it seemed as if every man and woman were shouting, that the prompter, usually hidden from view, peeped out of his box near the footlights to see what it was all about. Every musician in the orchestra pit, too, got up in wonder and astonishment. Ten times Slezak had to return and bow his thanks before the noise could be quelled."

Tannhäuser revealed the opposite end of his expressive abilities: "Best of all he shows imagination. He can conceive not only the personality of the character he interprets but also its relation to the drama. He enters fully into the emotional content of a work and he finds ways to convey to an audience the struggles of the man he pretends to be. It was this that made his Tannhäuser important. It was this that enabled it to stir so deeply an audience usually dilettante in its tastes. His Otello was powerful but his Tannhäuser was melting. Lovers of the opera have to thank him for disclosing in generous measure the deep humanity of the work."

With Mahler conducting, Slezak sang in the first American performances of Tchaikovsky's *Queen of Spades.* These performances are of particular interest to collectors of operatic minutiae: in addition to Slezak, father of the future Met artist Walter Slezak (Szupán in Johann Strauss's *Gypsy Baron,* 1959), the cast contained the parent of another Met star—Anton Ludwig, father of the great mezzo-soprano Christa Ludwig—in the small part of Narumoff. Slezak's repertoire also included Radames, the title role of Von Flotow's *Alessandro Stradella,* Walther in *Meistersinger,* and Tamino in *Zauberflöte.* After four seasons Slezak returned to Vienna, ostensibly to be with his young son Walter but perhaps also to appear with companies for which he would be the only leading tenor. The next season he was touring America with the Canadian National Opera Company. One of the most important singers in the history of the Vienna State Opera, Slezak sang there until 1927. In 1926 he offered to return to the Metropolitan and sing three performances for nothing but no engagement followed. After opera, he found a new career playing character roles in Austrian films.

HERMANN JADLOWKER

HERMANN JADLOWKER (1877–1953), THE Russian tenor from Riga, Latvia, pursued the art of singing throughout his lifetime. At the age of sixteen he ran away from home and was smuggled across the border into Vienna without a passport. After four years of studying and supporting himself by singing in synagogues and cathedrals, he made his debut in Cologne. His international career began when Kaiser Wilhelm heard him in Karlsruhe and invited him to Berlin.

When the Kaiser entertained the state visitor Czar Nicholas of Russia at a command performance of *Lohengrin,* Jadlowker sang the title role. During an intermission, Jadlowker went to the Kaiser's box at his invitation. Proudly, the Kaiser presented him to the Czar, with the words, "This is my Lohengrin." "He might be your Lohengrin," responded the Czar, "but he is still my subject."

Jadlowker was singing in Berlin when the Met engaged him. Many of his vocal qualities were immediately evident during his 1910 debut, as Faust: "A voice of more than usual richness of color, and clearly and equally produced. His stage demeanor was governed by good taste and his vocal style proved well disciplined and sometimes brilliant. He is decidedly an acquisition to the Met, which is already rich in tenors." One Boston critic announced that he was "the first Faust in the memory

Hermann Jadlowker as Faust, his 1910 debut role at the Met opposite Geraldine Farrar and Andrés de Segurola.

of living children who could wear the doublet, hose and blond beard without impersonating a dowdy tailor's dummy."

He was as enthusiastically received by his colleagues as by his audiences. "Had I that voice," announced Antonio Scotti after singing with him in Caruso's opera, *Pagliacci,* "I should be a millionaire in five years." At a *Bohème* performance a member of the audience pointed to two boisterous demonstrators as evidence that claques still existed. He had to be told that the offendors were Caruso himself and Riccardo Martin cheering on a fellow artist. Jadlowker quickly became a friend of Herman Mishkin, with whom he shared a Russian Jewish background.

In three seasons Jadlowker sang in four premieres, two of them opposite Geraldine Farrar: Humperdinck's *Königskinder* in its world premiere and Wolf-Ferrari's *Donne Curiose.* In the first American performance of Ludwig Thuille's unsuccessful *Lobetanz* with Johanna Gadski, Jadlowker "had the title role and disclosed an artistic stature larger than that hitherto supposed to be his limit. His singing is worthy of the warmest praise. His treatment of tone was beautiful and founded on fine skill, while his enunciation of text, his phrasing and his employment of nuance showed dramatic intelligence of no ordinary type." According to the New York *Sun,* he was the most popular youngster since Caruso: "since Jean de Reszke's times this town has not heard a star tenor whose repertoire included the languages German, French and Italian, which he rendered with equal facility."

In January 1912 the manager of the Berlin Royal Opera came to New York and signed Jadlowker for five years at a large annual salary. Shortly after his return to Germany, Richard Strauss selected him to sing Bacchus in the world premiere, performed in Stuttgart, of his new one-act opera, *Ariadne auf Naxos,* with Maria Jeritza as Ariadne and the composer conducting. Jadlowker subsequently attempted even heavier roles such as Otello and Parsifal, and ultimately his voice suffered. In few opera houses was he ever allowed to display fully his extraordinary technique. Fortunately, he made more than 200 records, including demanding passages from Mozart's *Idomeneo,* which reveal a breathtaking florid skill that included a faultless trill.

When his career in Germany ended, Jadlowker returned to Riga to direct music in the synagogue where he had begun. His last years were spent in Israel. To a reporter he declared, "I want to teach young people to sing. I do not need any more money, or praise, renown, or publicity. I had all of these, more than plenty." He taught in Tel Aviv until the day he died.

RICCARDO MARTIN

RICCARDO MARTIN (1881–1952), THE tenor from Kentucky, studied composition for four years with Edward MacDowell at Columbia University before discovering he had a voice worth training. After study in Paris and Milan he debuted as Faust in Nantes, which in turn led to appearances in Italy as Andrea Chénier. Returning to America for a 1906–1907 engagement with Henry Russell's San Carlo Opera, Martin made his first American operatic appearance in New Orleans as Canio and toured most of the major cities of the United States. The following year Conried signed him for the Metropolitan as a replacement for the ailing French tenor Charles Rousselière. Although he tended to be lost in the 1907 *Mefistofele* cast that featured Chaliapin and Farrar, one review did note that "if we are not very much mistaken, he will develop into that unheard-of-thing, a first class American tenor. Indeed, in the last acts . . . his clear pure voice rang out with splendid force and sonority."

When Gatti succeeded Conried, he found that Martin was most useful [illegible] particularly needed for *Il Trovatore* since, as the *Evening Globe* observed, "The prospect of singing Manrico seems to have a particularly irritating effect on Mr. Caruso's health." Martin sang almost fifty performances a season, appeared successfully at Covent Garden, and in 1911 re-

American tenor Riccardo Martin as Enzo Grimaldo in Ponchielli's Gioconda, *one of his seventeen leading roles at the Metropolitan.*

ceived this tribute from Henderson: "Riccardo Martin sang the music of Pinkerton with beauty of tone and elegance of phrasing. . . . His voice, though a tenor, had a character not unlike that of Melba. It is silvery and sparkling, but it cannot take on the fire of red gold."

For a few more years Martin remained a first-rank tenor, earning the tenor roles in the first American operas heard at the Metropolitan—Converse's *Pipe of Desire,* Parker's *Mona,* and Damrosch's *Cyrano de Bergerac.* But by 1913 his voice was being described as constricted and strident. Gatti-Casazza, who throughout his regime always preferred to move on to younger, less expensive singers if there were problems, elevated the newly arrived Giovanni Martinelli to Martin's place during the Met's 1913–14 season. Martin sang less and less at the Metropolitan; in a 1917 *Bohème* featuring Claudia Muzio's first Met Mimi, his voice broke and the claque demonstrated loudly. He annoyed Gatti by pretending to negotiate a new contract while using the offer to achieve a better one with the Chicago Opera. Gatti did not engage him again.

DMITRI SMIRNOFF

EARLY IN 1910 GABRIEL ASTRUC, THE Paris impresario, arranged on behalf of the Metropolitan a three-year contract with Dmitri Smirnoff (1881–1944), the Russian lyric tenor whom Otto Kahn had heard in the 1908 Paris performances with Chaliapin that introduced *Boris Godunov* to the West. The contract provided the usual star amenities, including a deluxe outside cabin on an ocean liner to and from Europe for Smirnoff and his wife, as well as second-class passage for his valet. He was to prepare a number of roles, relearn *Boris,* this time in Italian, and sing twenty-nine guaranteed performances the first season at a fee of 5,000 francs ($965), which made him, after Caruso and Slezak, the highest-paid tenor on the roster.

Gatti arranged for him to debut in 1910 as the Duke in *Rigoletto,* with Pasquale Amato in the title role, in an evening with a strong Russian flavor. Lydia Lipkowska, his soprano compatriot, sang Gilda; in what was then a common practice, the complete opera was followed by ballet divertissements danced by New York's current favorites, Anna Pavlova and Mikhail Mordkin. Among an audience of cheering Russians was Smirnoff's tenor rival, Hermann Jadlowker. Not present to hear the audience calling for an encore of "La donna è mobile" were many of the first-line critics; they were attending a farewell dinner for Engelbert Humperdinck, whose *Königskinder* had just had its world premiere. Those who were there welcomed the new tenor: "Mr. Smirnoff is in many respects a first-rate artist. His voice is of lyrical sweetness and is smooth and even in quality. His phrasing is admirable and his breath control astonishing. Few tenors of late years have been gifted with such a capacious pair of lungs, and it is with the most consummate ease that the singer is able to sustain phrases of almost unbelievable length. His desire to put this faculty to the utmost use results at times in the practice of prolonging high notes far beyond their written value."

The vocal idiosyncrasies that have long endeared Smirnoff to collectors of historical recordings, however, only grated on the ears of the critics. At Smirnoff's second performance, *Roméo et Juliette* with Geraldine Farrar, Henderson was so outraged by the extravagant costuming that he considered the singing second: "If this Juliette had vowed she never saw the streets of Cairo no one would have believed her. . . . As for Mr. Smirnoff it could be said of him that he was a tall and shapely Roméo and his clothes were made by one of the best tailors in Verona. . . . As for his singing it proceeded in a dead, flat, colorless and unmoving stream of pallid tone from the first unto the last. There was not one note of passion, not one phrase of lyric poesy in the whole impersonation."

More important, his performances were badly attended, and in this first year without Hammerstein's competition the Metropolitan was obsessed with its profit. Before Smirnoff sailed home at the end of his first year, Gatti had reduced his performances the next season from thirty-five to eighteen.

The following year, Smirnoff sang better. When the Metropolitan visited the Brooklyn Academy of Music, his vocal control was highly praised. "In the finale of ['La donna è mobile'], for example, he did not, as Caruso sometimes does, cut off sharply the final note, but prolonged it, diminuendo, so that it beautifully gave the effect of distance."

His enormous promise largely unfulfilled, Smirnoff sang only for two seasons. He never had the chance to demonstrate his command of the Russian repertoire, in which the unusual sound of his voice and the music were as one. He left complaining bitterly, "It is a land of Italians." Gatti, however, made it clear that the contract had been canceled by mutual consent because Smirnoff did not know a great part of the repertoire that had been voluntarily included. Gatti did not mention that he was accustomed to paying most of his tenors considerably less per performance—for example, $267 for John McCormack and $550 for Hermann Jadlowker.

After the Russian Revolution, Smirnoff sang a few guest performances in Soviet Russia but offended the government by not returning permanently; he performed frequently in Western Europe instead. Engaged for the Washington Civic Opera, Smirnoff returned to New York in 1926 for an Aeolian Hall recital. He attempted a reconciliation with Gatti, but the general manager, who had a rare capacity for wiping from memory artists he no longer needed, refused to greet him.

Mishkin took this rare portrait of the Russian tenor Dmitri Smirnoff sometime during his two Metropolitan seasons, 1910–12.

GERALDINE FARRAR

THE GLAMOROUS AMERICAN SOPRANO Geraldine Farrar (1882–1967) presents special problems to anyone considering the important singers of the twentieth century's first quarter. So beautiful was she, so dazzling was her personality, that writers have tended to undervalue her other qualities.

From the beginning there was a strong mind at work. At ten she appeared in a Melrose, Massachusetts, pageant as Jenny Lind singing "Home, Sweet Home," but insisted that the audience first listen to her garbled account of Siébel's aria from *Faust.* She quickly left Melrose and came to New York to study and, as a Met standee, to listen to Nellie Melba, Emma Calvé, Lilli Lehmann, and Jean de Reszke. At fourteen she sang for De Reszke. In the spring of 1898, Maurice Grau, then manager of the Met, offered to let her sing in a Sunday-night concert. Only sixteen, she refused; this was no way for a prima donna to begin. Instead, her father, a professional baseball player during the summer, sold his store and borrowed money, and the Farrars sailed for Europe on a cattle boat. In Paris, Farrar went to Reutlinger, the famous fashion photographer. "I want professional rates," she said. Reutlinger objected that she was unknown. "But I am going to be famous," she calmly replied.

Farrar proceeded to Berlin to study and made her debut at the Hofoper as Marguerite in *Faust* when she was nineteen. She became a pupil of Lilli Lehmann's and, more intriguingly, the favorite of both the Kaiser and the Crown Prince. Lehmann had her sing Zerlina in one of her early Salzburg Festival performances of *Don Giovanni.* There were short prestigious seasons in Monte Carlo that included a rare *Don Carlo* with Maurice Renaud and Feodor Chaliapin.

An early photo of Geraldine Farrar, who preferred to sit for photographers not used by other Metropolitan Opera singers. (This may be the work of a European photographer, copied in New York by Mishkin for Farrar.)

Conried brought her home in 1906 for *Roméo et Juliette,* the one Metropolitan opening night without Caruso during his American career. She quickly became a reigning figure in New York opera. The press described her clothes, her food, her travels, her every word, and her performances. On the Met roster she was paid a salary second only to Caruso's. (Melba and Tetrazzini received more for their rare guest appearances.) Soon after Toscanini's arrival in 1908, they argued during a rehearsal. She reminded him that she was a star; he acknowledged only the stars in the heavens. But she quickly recognized that her Toscanini-led performances brought greater rewards than those without him and sang with him whenever possible. A personal relationship grew until in 1915 he left the Metropolitan and returned to Italy to resolve his conflict between love and family.

The first Madama Butterfly in Berlin, Farrar also sang the first at the Metropolitan in 1907 and went on to sing the role more times there than anyone else. In 1916 W. J. Henderson, who greatly enjoyed writing about Farrar, surveyed her variable performances: "She has had her ascents and her descents in the part, for there have been periods in which she seemed to abandon all attempt at sincerity and played with the impersonation as if it were her personal toy. But Mrs. Farrar has changed her attitude toward *Madama Butterfly* in recent seasons. She has realized Cio-Cio-San is one of her best roles and that in order to keep her popularity in it she must bring to it the best resources of her art. The impersonation which she gave last evening was one of great charm and of high musical merit. She was in excellent voice and sang the flaming measures of Puccini with beauty of tone and with elegance and style." On the other hand, three months earlier *Musical America* had criticized her for a Kansas City concert in which she omitted the high B flat at the end of "Un bel dì."

The fluctuations of her voice seem always to have brought out the most vivid language from her critics. In a 1910 *Faust* review, St. John-Brenon observed: "The higher notes of Miss Farrar's voice are still resonant, musical, and eloquent. Her medium voice is frayed, threadbare, open in a painful effort to be eloquent and vigorous, while her lower voice, at least in this part, bears a strong resemblance to the snakes of Ireland. Her acting, as always, was the acting of an instinct of supreme and eager intelligence." There were many similarities to her older colleague, Mary Garden, who was also known for her vivid acting and often unyielding voice but who could find no place at the Metropolitan while Farrar reigned there. Just as Garden created her own special repertoire, Farrar put her unique stamp on "personality" roles such as the Goose Girl in the world premiere of Humperdinck's *Königskinder* (she trained live geese to appear onstage with her) and later as Caterina in the premiere of Giordano's *Madame Sans-Gêne*: "Whatever faults Miss Farrar may have disclosed in her impersonation of Caterina, it is certain that there is no one else on the operatic stage today who could have brought to the role such a combination of theatrical ingenuity, personal charm and vocal excellence." As Thaïs she was more controversial in a role that Garden had just filmed. "She has a new costume which consists entirely of skirt. From the waist up it is exclusively Miss Farrar and two small groups of jewels, inconspicuous but essentially located.... The performance on the whole made Mary Garden in the picture at the Strand Theatre look like a modest missionary."

As Caruso's voice became sturdier and Farrar's increasingly fragile, the Metropolitan's leading box office attractions appeared together less frequently than in their early years. Caruso's progress through a heavier repertoire required associates such as Margarete Matzenauer, Claudia Muzio, and Rosa Ponselle, while Farrar's increasing preoccupation with specialty roles such as Madame Sans-Gêne, Zazà, and La Navarraise needed nothing from Caruso's vocal strengths. But the two were together for a 1914 *Carmen,* and the performance was the sensation of the season, perhaps the triumph of Farrar's career. Henderson was dazzled by it: "She was indeed a vision of loveliness, never aristocratic, yet never vulgar, a seductive, languorous, passionate Carmen of the romantic gypsy blood.... It was full of imagination and delicate touches of art. And above all it was beautifully sung. Miss Farrar has never sung anything else better, and hardly anything else as well. And in Carmen the coloring of the tone, the nuancing, the reading of the line are more than half the battle. If Miss Farrar's Carmen is not accepted by the public as one of her best roles it will be a matter for astonishment."

Indeed the public accepted Farrar's Carmen, screaming approval and thereafter identifying her inextricably with the role. And it was of course Farrar who was awarded the movie version of the Mérimée novel. It was the first production of her movie career—a more successful one than Garden's—and it provoked some malicious tongues to suggest that she portrayed the gypsy better in silence than in song. The film's popularity, however, inspired a Charlie Chaplin parody with the little tramp as Don José.

After Farrar had finished her work in the movie, she returned to the Met for further performances with Caruso and with her newly learned lessons in realism. Act I chorus ladies were not in a position to complain of her slaps and scratches, but Caruso was, and he suggested that she find a new José. There was a reconciliation between the acts but their performances together, even in *Carmen,* became fewer.

Two years before her Met [illegible], Henderson contemplated Farrar's vocal gifts: "Her voice, which last season was dull, unsteady and often recalcitrant, has this season been more free, vibrant and sonorous. The soprano has been able to sing with far less restraint and her lyric art has given something like the same pleasure it

c
MISHKIN
N.Y.

afforded in the early days of her American career. It is not probable that future operatic history will contain a record that Miss Farrar ranked with the celebrated mistresses of the art of singing. But her voice has its own interesting personality. There is not another voice in the Metropolitan company that possesses quite the same combination of individuality with range of color. One has only to note how excellently it has fitted to the requirements of such roles as Ariane, Cio-Cio-San, and Zazà. These are three very dissimilar roles, and yet this particular musical instrument has most admirably performed the music of them all."

Farrar suffered from the sensational arrival of Maria Jeritza in 1921–22. There were rumors of departure. Cheered at the end of her final *Butterfly* that season, she stepped before the curtain. "Are you coming back?" screamed the audience. "Yes, I am," she declared, "and for many years to come." However, for the first time in years the management was able to suggest its own terms for a new contract, and Farrar rejected the offer of only half a season. Her farewell was as Leoncavallo's Zazà, a portrayal that had been described as "Geraldine Farrar with vocal and scenic accessories." Never had the Metropolitan witnessed such an outpouring of love and affection, flowers, confetti, streamers. In another curtain speech, she asked, "Has George Cohan stopped crying? I don't want a tear in this house." Proudly, she proclaimed, "I am leaving this institution because I want to go." She was driven through crowds surrounding the opera house, headlong into a new career of concert tours, speaking over the Metropolitan's early radio broadcasts, patriotic service during World War II, and a vivid correspondence with many friends.

ENRICO CARUSO

AMONG THE CONTRACTS THAT HEINrich Conried found on his desk when he succeeded Maurice Grau in 1903 as manager of the Metropolitan Opera was one for a thirty-year-old Italian tenor from Naples, Enrico Caruso (1873–1921). An actor-manager with slight knowledge of opera, Conried attempted to have the number of performances in the contract of the little-known tenor reduced to ten a season. Fortunately, before changes could be made, Conried chanced to hear one of the remarkable little ten-inch 78-rpm discs that Caruso had recorded on wax in a Milan hotel in March 1902. These single-sided recordings with piano accompaniment were sold in London to promote his debut there that spring and preceded him to New York the following year, arousing tremendous public interest.

The Caruso legend has been told many times. Born to poor parents in Naples, he was the eighteenth of twenty-one children, the first to survive. His mother insisted

Opposite: *Geraldine Farrar as Carmen and Caruso as Don José pose peacefully together in the Metropolitan's 1914* Carmen, *a photo taken before her acting became excessively realistic.*

Caruso as a jealousy-maddened Don José in Act IV of Carmen.

c
Mishkin
N.Y.

Opposite: *Enrico Caruso arrayed as Radames in* Aida, *ready to engage the Ethiopians in battle.*

---

that he attend school, where he won a gold medal as a boy contralto. He sang at church and in cafés. A friend recommended a teacher who was not overly impressed with the vocal material and commented, "It is like gold at the bottom of the Tiber—hardly worth digging for." During compulsory military service, a major heard Caruso singing the "Brindisi" from *Cavalleria Rusticana.* Somehow it was arranged for his younger brother to replace him in the army so that he could sing. At twenty-one, Caruso made his debut in a now-forgotten opera. He had his first photograph taken when his limited wardrobe was at the laundry: the handsome young man is seen draped in a bedspread.

Legends may omit mention of the hard work and disappointments. As professional engagements followed, there was one difficulty: Caruso would crack on a high B flat. His second teacher, Vincenzo Lombardi, cured the problem (it should be remembered, however, that the high C, much sought after by tenors, was never a standard part of his equipment). He was denied the honor of singing in the world premiere of *Tosca* because the soprano wanted her lover to sing Cavaradossi. Whatever the problems, the sound of his voice had him singing in Caserta, Palermo, Salerno (his first *Pagliacci,* in 1896), Genoa, and Rome. In St. Petersburg, the Czar presented him with cuff links of gold and diamonds. Ill with laryngitis but refusing to cancel, he failed in his *Bohème* debut at La Scala but triumphed soon after in *L'Elisir d'Amore.* Toscanini asked him to sing in the *Rigoletto* quartet in the observance of Giuseppe Verdi's death at eighty-eight in 1901.

In October 1902 he complained to his agent in Milan about negotiations with New York: "It also seems to me that Mr. Grau does not have high-salaried artists which is absurd since one must understand that I also take a risk in coming to America and one does not move himself for nothing. In any event if this does not suit Mr. Grau it is of little importance because I prefer to make contracts without strangulation clauses rather than those with articles of death and a lot of money."

Although history recalls the opening-night *Rigoletto* of November 23, 1903, as the occasion of Caruso's American debut, it was also the first performance of Conried's management. Conried had prepared a special surprise for the festive, brilliantly dressed audience entering the theater. This was the night the [illegible] rium first donned its finery of deep red and gold that [illegible] for the elegant, such a cherished frame for the performances onstage.

One of the myths that has grown up around Caruso and the Metropolitan maintains that his acceptance in New York was achieved slowly. Actually, there had been enormous advance publicity about the new tenor, and the public made its feelings known somewhere between the last act of his *Rigoletto* debut—with Marcella Sembrich, Louise Homer, Antonio Scotti, and Marcel Journet—and the tomb scene of *Aida,* his second performance one week later. Troubled by the New York weather, Caruso sang his first few performances with a bad cold and even canceled his second appearance, a *Bohème.* The debut performance began slowly: "In the first act he kept his voice in his pouch. 'Questa o quella' was brisk and melodious—and that was about all. People said, 'Why yes, but'—Caruso changed all that when he reappeared as the eager lover in Gilda's back yard. He sang 'Love is the Sun' with such fire and passion that his sentiment counted almost as much as his execution. People got up and shouted at him. There was danger of an encore right then and there, but the pious devotees to the score hissed for silence severely and the peril passed. But at the end of the act he was recalled four times, together with the equally beloved Gilda, and a lady, whose corsage glistened like the sun in heaven, heaved a big bouquet of pink roses from a box, which Mme. Sembrich bore away scoring the first touchdown. Later, in the famous drinking song, 'La donna è mobile,' he made his greatest hit and did it 'like a gentleman,' as a lady remarked afterward in the foyer. Her escort asked her what she meant, and she said, with wide eyes of innocent surprise, 'Why, he took such liberties with the score.' To be sure he did, but he got in his high C capitally, and when the audience, whose command of the English language was quite lost by that time, shrieked 'Bis! bis! bis!' so insistently, Caruso sang his blackguard chansonette again, and stayed in his chair throughout, tossing off his high C again at the end most nonchalantly, as though he had the whole alphabet at his command." His New York reign had begun.

In the cast for *Aida* were Johanna Gadski; Edyth Walker, making her debut as Amneris; Scotti; and Pol Plançon ("there never could be a finer Ramphis"). Caruso was still suffering from his cold. He "was naturally very careful of his voice, and saved himself whenever it was possible, but when the time came for a climax or a big dramatic effect he was prodigal in his use of it. Any lingering doubt about its loveliness and the artistic way in which he used it were dispelled. Phrasing, management of breath, delicate gradations of light and shade—in short, all those higher elements of the art of singing—he possesses, one is almost tempted to say, in only a less degree than that masterly singer, Jean de Reszke. He can make his voice as lusciously sentimental as a cello, and [illegible] bright color of a trumpet. He seems to be completely the master of his instrument. With exquisite sentimentality he sang 'Celeste Aida.' In the Nile scene he changed this sentimentality to irresistible and overwhelming passion. And then, in the final scene, in the tomb, he compelled his

In Aida's *Act III, Enrico Caruso as Radames, betrayed by Aida, registers surprise, disbelief, and resignation.*

voice to speak in the very accents of despair. It was an astonishing performance. We are not used to such tenors, to such voices, and to such singing by men. Jean de Reszke has a greater art than Caruso has now, but he never had such a beautifully pure and melting voice."

Caruso sang Radames in each of his Met seasons except the last two. It was considered his finest role. Some critics lamented the fact that, like most tenors before or since, he declined to sing the high B flat in 'Celeste Aida' pianissimo, as written. For the public, however, *Aida*—selected for four Caruso opening nights at the Metropolitan—was the work that often relieved its apprehensions over whether the voice had returned without impairment that year. After the first *Aida,* the papers called him a "godsend" and "the year's popular idol." By the time he had sung his third performance, Rodolfo in *La Bohème,* it was declared, "The worship of Caruso has begun. The end of the season only can determine the extent to which it may be carried." The phenomenon diminished not a bit; in fact it grew unabated during his lifetime and continued after his death. For an explanation one returns to that first *Aida* and the prophetic words of a reviewer: "His fire is unbounded. He hurls his heart at his listeners."

OLIVE FREMSTAD

"SHE WAS ALWAYS AN EPIC SORT OF creature, moving most comfortably somewhere between heaven and earth. . . . If she were to come on the scene, wearing an old dressing gown and reading the *Ladies' Home Journal,* you would still rise up in your seat and claim 'Ha, now something important is going to happen.'"

The initiation of Olive Fremstad (1868–1951) into the mysteries of the theater began at an early age in the Norwegian settlement town of St. Peter, Minnesota. Brought to America by her Scandinavian parents, she went with her preacher father and a portable organ to prairie revival meetings. As her companion and biographer, Mary Watkins Cushing, put it, "She was the organist and led the singing too—and at times she was also expected, when sinners seemed reluctant about being saved, to start the procession to the altar." The fanaticism of the father, which had led him to sell all his worldly goods and become a missionary, was found in the daughter throughout Fremstad's career.

[illegible] States, Fremstad went to Berlin to study with Lilli Lehmann and soon ran off with Lehmann's husband, the tenor Paul Kalisch. Following her 1895 debut as Azucena in a Cologne *Trovatore,* she was confined for years to mezzo roles and the lower Wagnerian parts such as Kundry, Venus, and Sieglinde, her Met debut role in 1903. She was enthusiastically welcomed: "Mme. Fremstad's performance was a delight with small alloy. Her accomplishment as both a singer and an actress, the power and depth of her art, were such as to fill the lovers of the German works in which she is to appear with present satisfaction and jubilant expectation. Her voice is of extraordinarily beautiful quality and large range, in the lower notes, particularly of the richest contralto coloring, and its freedom and flexibility, the volume with which she poured it out, the nobility and broad sweep of her phrasing, showed in her the true artist—the artist who comprehends the essence and the significance of Wagner's musical style."

With a consuming ambition that needed little critical encouragement, Fremstad already had her sights on the great Wagnerian soprano parts. Neither the first nor the last woman to decide that her voice could soar higher than nature intended, Fremstad made early forays into soprano territory with poor results. Of a 1906 Sunday-night concert in which she sang the awakening scene from *Siegfried* with Heinrich Knote, St. John-Brenon reported: "Miss Fremstad (last night in green and ecstasy) we have long since given up in despair. She is lacerating her fine dramatic contralto voice, throwing the shreds at us and calling them Brünnhilde."

However, in 1907 both voice and acting won Fremstad the coveted role of Salome in the first American performance of a Richard Strauss opera. In preparation she visited a mortuary to discover the weight of a human head. Onstage, she staggered when the severed head of Jokanaan was handed to her; her brightly lighted byplay with it in the final scene helped result in the twenty-seven-year ban on the work at the Metropolitan. Conried's expectations had been so grand that he had contracted Fremstad for a special short season of *Salome* performances before the start of the 1907–1908 season. With *Salome* prohibited, she sang her first Isolde in 1908, with Gustav Mahler in his conducting debut at the Metropolitan. She had no problems with the music. "Mme. Fremstad's voice is of indescribable beauty in this music, in its richness and power, in infinite modulation in all the shades and extremes of dramatic significance. It never sounded finer in quality and never seemed more perfectly under her control. And her singing was a revelation in the fact that the music was in very few places higher than she could easily compass with her voice. The voice seems, in truth, to have reached a higher altitude and to move in it without strain and without effort." For a few short years she won her battle, adding all three Brünnhildes, Elsa, and Elisabeth to her repertoire, as well as Tosca and Gluck's Armide. She was compared with Lilli Lehmann and Milka Ternina, her Wagnerian predecessors; her Wagnerian contemporary, Johanna Gadski, might sing the music with more ease but could not begin to suggest Fremstad's depth. Contrasted with Mary Garden, Geraldine Farrar, and Lydia Lipkowska, "Mme. Fremstad is the one, all things considered, who has the best sense of proportion in combin-

With subtle gesture and facial expression, Olive Fremstad reveals the shifting emotions of Isolde as she drinks the love potion in Act I of Tristan und Isolde.

©.
H. MISHKIN
N.Y.

©
Mishkin
N.Y.

Opposite: *Olive Fremstad shows her dramatic versatility as the wild Kundry, one of her most memorable characterizations, in Act I of* Parsifal.

ing the arts of the singer and the actor. . . . Mme. Fremstad recognizes that the singing and acting parts must make concessions to each other if they are to work together as one art."

Even so, she continued to have occasional difficulties with her chosen vocal range; of her first Elsa, the *Sun* observed: "Her management of the high tones . . . was clever in the extreme." Fremstad, however, could admit to no mere physical failing and loftily announced, "I do not claim this or that for my voice. I do not sing contralto or soprano. I sing Isolde. What voice is necessary for the part I undertake, I will produce."

Fremstad was adept at putting her forceful personality across to the public. The press adored her. She confided to reporters, "I spring into life when the curtain rises, and when it falls I might well die. The world I exist in between performances is the strange one, alien, dark, confused." She also had enough awareness of the mundane uses of publicity to occasion this 1911 memo from the Met's secretary, John Brown, to Gatti: "Mishkin, the photographer, comes to me stating that Mme. Fremstad wishes him to make for her a life size portrait in colors showing her in the role of Isolde, which she wishes to place in the lobby on Friday Evening, when she appears in this opera. This will mean that Mme. Fremstad would have in the lobby a picture about five or six feet high and before taking any action, Mr. Mishkin wishes to know whether it will be permitted."

This must have been just one more irritation for Gatti, who had not welcomed her grand manner, her requests for precedence, and, most damaging of all, her frequent cancellations. Finally, by the time she departed in 1914, she no longer had her voice to protect her. "The tint and glory of her tones have faded, and she gives us the threads instead of the web of its former valid beauties. Such is the inexorable penalty extorted by the Furies for six years of singing beyond the limitations imposed by nature."

Fremstad requested Isolde for her farewell; Gatti gave her Elsa. There were countless curtain calls, a tearful audience, petitions for her reinstatement, letters in the press. Instead came concerts, a scheduled return to the Metropolitan in 1917 that was ruined by the war, an unanswered request in 1920 that she be permitted to sing either *Tristan* and *Tannhäuser* in English or *Forza,* which she had just learned; and eventually there was nothing. She had been one of the theater's supreme interpreters, trained for nothing else. When Kirsten Flagstad made her Metropolitan debut twenty-one years later, critic Lawrence Gilman could only exclaim, "It recalled to wistful Wagnerites the irrecoverable magic of Olive the Immortal."

American bass Herbert Witherspoon (1873–1935) makes a mournful King Marke in Tristan und Isolde. *Primarily a concert artist and teacher, Witherspoon went on to become the Metropolitan's General Manager upon Gatti-Casazza's retirement in 1935 but died before the beginning of his first season.*

JACQUES URLUS

THE DUTCH TENOR JACQUES URLUS (1867–1935) made his debut as Tristan at the matinee of February 8, 1913; it was one of the great disasters in Metropolitan Opera history. Urlus was not without experience or endurance. A veteran of Wagner and Italian roles, having sung with the Leipzig Opera since 1900 as well as for two seasons at Bayreuth, he had performed four Tristans and a concert within the span of twelve days in his American debut the previous season in Boston. "Much had been hoped of Mr. Urlus, who was to replace Mr. [Carl] Burrian [the Met's resident Wagnerian tenor since 1906]. . . . Mr. Toscanini was said to have expressed himself as delighted with the new Tristan. And when in the first act he strode on the stage, he promised well. At last the audience saw the part sustained by a man who really did convey the illusion of the brave but ill-starred knight. He had the stature and dignity of Tristan. He seemed a hero. Moreover, in his opening scene he had his voice." But midway through the Act I scene with Isolde, Urlus was overcome with hoarseness and was forced to continue almost in a whisper. At the end of the act he turned his back to the audience and wept. Of the two potential replacements, Burrian was on the high seas and (Edoardo) Ferrari-Fontana was replacing Burrian as Tristan in Boston. Urlus gallantly continued and Mme. Gadski, the Isolde, in a "splendid display of nerve in the face of danger," supplied many of his phrases, in effect singing a love duet with herself. Act III was largely pantomime.

Urlus's recovery was equally dramatic. Three days later his first *Siegfried* was a triumph, a nearly ideal characterization that was thought more virile than Jean de Reszke's, with more voice and art than Max Alvary's. While the healthy voice rang out splendidly in the Act I forging songs, "perhaps most gratifying of all was his singing in piano and mezzo forte passages when the quality of his tone and taste he showed in phrasing were such as one scarcely hears from a tenor of German training and experience." His diction was especially clear and "in the final act he finally loosed the full power of his voice and sang gloriously."

By the time Urlus returned to *Tristan* he had consolidated his position with performances of Siegmund and the *Götterdämmerung* Siegfried. This time the bare silhouette of a Tristan became "one of the most profoundly moving embodiments of Wagner's immortal hero ever revealed in New York." Olive Fremstad was the Isolde and "rarely has the love duet been sung more beautifully . . . sung with exquisite tenderness, passion and beauty of tone."

Urlus remained with the Metropolitan for five seasons, the major heldentenor between the days of Jean de Reszke and those of Lauritz Melchior. He performed all the important Wagnerian tenor parts as well as Florestan in *Fidelio* and Tamino in *Zauberflöte.* Only in *Tannhäuser* was he less than successful, for the recent memory of Leo Slezak worked against him. It says much for Urlus's vocal manners that Gatti specified the lighter, more florid role of Don Ottavio in *Don Giovanni* as a part for which he was responsible in his contract. In Europe he was known for his Evangelist in Bach's *St. Matthew Passion* and the tenor solos in Mahler's *Das Lied von der Erde,* which he performed at its 1921 premiere. The hysteria of World War I caused the cancellation of his contract

Jacques Urlus as Tristan, the role of his disastrous 1913 Metropolitan Opera debut opposite the Isolde of Johanna Gadski.

for two seasons, and although there were negotiations with Gatti, he never returned to the Metropolitan. His last performance there was the *Tristan* of April 13, 1917, with the resourceful companion of his debut, Johanna Gadski, as Isolde. It was also her farewell and the last performance of Wagner at the Metropolitan for three years.

JOHANNA GADSKI

ALGERNON ST. JOHN-BRENON, THE EXtravagant Irish-born critic of the New York *Telegram,* once remarked of the German soprano Johanna Gadski (1872–1932) that her head was a kind of operatic department store. "One portion of it," he wrote, "is full of spergiuras and traditores, for use in her Italian repertory; another is full of schmerzens, tods, ungedulds and leise-leises, for the German. Another has birds, love, streams, May nights, for the Middle West. And another is full of Tauscher." Thus did St. John-Brenon neatly sum up Gadski's musical career and her family life with the German officer who was the American representative of the Krupp munitions concern. She had been discovered by Walter Damrosch in Berlin at the Kroll Opera, where she had made her debut at the age of seventeen. Hired under the conviction that as a German she was certainly a Wagnerian, she made her American debut on March 1, 1895, as Elsa in *Lohengrin* in a Damrosch German Grand Opera Company performance at the Metropolitan Opera House. It was her first Wagner performance anywhere, and it made little lasting impression. "Fräulein Gadski, who made her debut as Elsa, has a very light soprano voice too small for such an auditorium as that of the Metropolitan, but of pretty color. She sang the part respectably, so far as conception went, but with frequent departures from pitch. She is not the kind of singer to make a serious impression in a city accustomed to the best, though her work is earnest." Seldom can a review have been less prophetic. That season with Damrosch she sang Gutrune, Elisabeth, and Eva and created the role of Hester Prynne in Damrosch's *Scarlet Letter.* In 1899 she sang at Covent Garden and Bayreuth and at the end of the year with the Metropolitan. From that point on, her career was almost exclusively centered in the United States, where this "small-voiced" soprano went on to sing more performances of Wagner with the Metropolitan than did Lilli Lehmann, Olive Fremstad, Margarete Matzenauer, Kirsten Flagstad, or Birgit Nilsson.

Her first Brünnhilde came in 1903, a performance of *Walküre* that featured the debut of Olive Fremstad as Sieglinde. By this time both Gadski's voice and reputation had grown. "It was full of superb vigor, of life and impulsive energy, of statuesque dignity and thrilling solemnity, as in her scene with Siegmund when she announces to him his impending death, and of tenderness and passion, as in her leave-taking of Wotan. Never for moment did it fall into conventional ruts, and her voice seemed fuller, richer, more resonant, and more perfectly at her command than ever before." The performance was also noteworthy for a frightening accident. During Wotan's Act III denunciation, Gadski fell and knocked herself out, only to be awakened by the cries of the prompter just in time to sing "War es so schmählich." When she sang Aida the following week opposite Caruso's first Radames, she had a badly concealed black eye, which nonetheless did not affect her singing: "Miss Gadski showed herself equal artist with the tenor. Her voice was managed with equal skill and grew in puissance with the progress of the work. . . . She kept her tone true, despite her unsparing dramatic action, and through the swelling choruses no note was denied her delighted hearers. It may be that passages in Brünnhilde's music tax her full artistic powers more than any in that of *Aida,* but she was a glorious Slave, and was called and recalled, with Caruso and all the rest, till even she, with all her ambition and zealous self-judgment, must have felt that she had fairly won her applause."

Drive and determination brought her all she wanted. She balanced a glamorous theatrical career with a well-ordered home life. The Met's stage doorman reported that approximately thirty minutes before the conclusion of a Gadski performance, she would ask him to call her home and have the potatoes put on.

Gadski's Italian repertoire included Valentine in *Gli Ugonotti,* Santuzza, Amelia in *Un Ballo in Maschera,* the Countess in *Le Nozze di Figaro,* Leonora in *Il Trovatore,* and Euridice. As one of Victor Records' most prolific artists she recorded Italian duets with Amato, Caruso, and Homer, in addition to extensive excerpts from her German and song repertoires. Her versatility may have been surpassed only by Florence Easton, who arrived the season after her departure. Gadski left the Metropolitan in 1917 upon the declaration of war with Germany. She had not endeared herself during the early years of the war by the pro-German stance of her husband (who was tried and acquitted of conspiring to blow up Canada's Welland Canal) or by throwing a notorious party at which Otto Goritz celebrated the sinking of the *Lusitania* in a satirical song. When she returned to New York after the war, Gatti denied her the use of the Metropolitan auditorium for a gala resumption of her concert career. She was not heard again in opera in New York until 1929, when she brought her own German company for three consecutive national tours. Never a great admirer of her Isolde at the Metropolitan, W. J. Henderson was forced to admit that "Mme. Gadski reappeared last evening after her long absence with her voice, always one of more than ordinary beauty, in astonishingly good condition. Her upper tones especially had brilliance, res-

c
MISHKIN
N.Y.

Opposite: *Johanna Gadski as Isolde, one of nine Wagnerian soprano roles she sang during her eighteen seasons at the Metropolitan Opera.*

onance and power. Her management of mezza voce was that of an artist and her treatment of color was commendable. Her Isolde had ripened with the years. If there was less unbridled ardor in it, there was more depth and reality of feeling. She was acclaimed by an audience manifestly friendly."

Two years later, thirty-six years after her New York debut, she repeated her Isolde. "Her vocal technique was well-founded, and doubtless to this is attributable the remarkable preservation of her voice. It was strong and brilliant in the higher range last night and serviceable in the medium." The following year she died in Berlin as a result of injuries suffered when her car crashed into a streetcar.

ADAMO DIDUR

WHILE STILL AT LA SCALA, GATTI AND Toscanini had begun planning for the Rimsky-Korsakov version of Mussorgsky's *Boris Godunov* at that theater. Otto Kahn's enthusiastic reports of the 1908 Diaghilev production in Paris encouraged them to begin planning again when they arrived for their first season at the Met later that same year. Dmitri Smirnoff was contracted to relearn his role as the pretender Dmitri in Italian, and the production itself was purchased from the Paris Opéra, which feared to produce it without Feodor Chaliapin. The lavish St. Petersburg production had been copied in Paris. The costumes were unique. Diaghilev sent the painter Ivan Bilibine to search the northern provinces of Russia for handwoven sarafans, headdresses, and embroidery that peasants had stored in chests for centuries. These materials were supplemented by special brocades woven in Moscow, and everything was fashioned into costumes under the set designer's direction.

The sensational Diaghilev production—to which the Inn Scene, painted in New York, was added—finally reached New York in March 1913. Gatti explained to the press that Mussorgsky was a barbarian and that only Rimsky-Korsakov's revision had made the work performable outside Russia. For the Polish bass Adamo Didur (1874–1946), the role of Boris was the summit of his career, a lofty region he inhabited alone during the first eight years of the opera's life in the United States. For a time it had seemed that he would not find the recognition his flowing voice should attract. Hammerstein had brought him to New York in 1907 following engagements with the Warsaw Opera, La Scala, and Covent Garden, as well as performances in Brazil and Argentina. Only his Méphistophélès in *Faust* attracted real attention at the Manhattan: "Maurice Renaud recently gave a striking picture of his Satanic majesty; Chaliapin is physical and horrible when he plays the part; Plançon is a boulevardier; Edouard de Reszke was gay. Mr. Didur is none of these things, and yet all of them. With his costume in the third act, a long black robe which he waved over his head, he achieved weird effects. At times he looked like a gigantic bird." "In action forcible and suggestive, in voice sonorous and emphatic and suggestive, I have seldom heard 'The Calf of Gold' better sung—M. Didur pleased me mightily and can certainly make up a trio of notable impersonations of the role seen this season." However, he and Hammerstein canceled his contract by mutual agreement well before this first season was over.

With his friends Gatti and Toscanini now at the helm of the Met, Didur performed Ramfis in the 1908–1909 season's opening-night *Aida.* The title role in *Nozze di Figaro,* Don Basilio in *Barbiere,* Coppelius in *Contes d'Hoffmann,* and the standard bass repertoire built up to the *Boris* premiere. Didur's *Boris,* with Toscanini conducting and the chorus and soloists singing in Italian, became one of the Met's finest offerings: "Hitherto he has seemed a capable, but by no means remarkable, singing-actor, filling his bass parts with excellent singing and intelligent acting. . . . His Boris was another thing. Even when the Czar merely crossed the scene and spoke a few grave words to the people in the coronation procession, as one stirring out of gloomy brooding, Mr. Didur made the passing figure and the brief declamation seize eye, ear and imagination. Already Boris seemed fated. The larger opportunity came first in the scene in which Boris's grandiose imaginings about Russia and sovereignty yield to the remorseful guilt that tortures him, to the haunting dread that is a recurring agony and finally to the pursuing image of the murdered and bloody boy. Even on the stage of the spoken word, recent impersonations of Gloster and Macbeth have wrought no such illusion of a racked and agonizing spirit writhing in the pit of darkness it had digged for itself. In Mr. Didur's face, body, gesture and accents was such a Boris. To the piercing phrases of the declamation and of the instruments, he added the vividness of his own histrionic imagination and power. It was so, again, in the scene of Boris's death. The wasted figure staggered into the councilroom, with eyes that looked upon its own visions and not upon the assembled nobles; the stammering tongue babbled thickly, strangely, of murders done; the haggard face became yet more ghastly at the monk's narrative of the miracle done at Dmitri's tomb; and the Czar's cry at the end was the voice of the despair that was searing him. Death and fate had come upon this Boris and there

c
MISHKIN
N.Y.

Opposite: *Adamo Didur in the title role of* Boris Godunov, *which he performed in the 1913 American premiere to score his first great New York success.*

was no veil between. He died horribly, straining out his words of warning and pity and love to his son, while all that his eyes had seen and his hands had done was strangling them in his throat. By this time it is agreed that Mr. Slezak's operatic Otello excels all the present Moors on the stage of the spoken word. So Mr. Didur's operatic Boris surpasses its Glosters and Macbeths in the imagination and the delineation of remorseful agony. None had expected these things of Mr. Didur; there had been regret even that such a part as Boris fell to him; yet these things he did. Since the evening in which *Pelléas* first came to the American stage, there has been no such occasion in any of our opera houses and on so many sides as this production of *Boris Godunov* at the Metropolitan."

Some who attended the premiere accused Didur of copying Chaliapin in the role. "This is not true," he replied, "as I have never seen him in the part. If I have reached results similar to Mr. Chaliapin, I can only say that this I consider the highest praise." Most, however, rejoiced in Didur's success. A New York newspaper observed, "Such a triumph as came to Didur last night, comes once in the life of an artist and it is enough." Otto Kahn was equally pleased with the performance: at his suggestion, every chorus member was given $5 extra in his pay envelope at the end of the week.

Eventually public interest lagged, and the performance itself began to fall apart. *Boris Godunov* was dropped for a year during the 1920–21 season; when it was revived the following season Chaliapin took command of the title role and Didur sang it only once again, a Saturday-night performance at "popular prices." After he performed Don Alfonso in the Met's first *Così fan tutte,* his roles became ever smaller. Chaliapin left in 1928–29, but in the meantime Ezio Pinza had arrived on the scene, to be followed by the young Tancredi Pasero, an important Italian bass with much of Pinza's repertoire. By 1931 Didur had been singing publicly for thirty-five years. His final Met performance took place the following year, at Gatti's twenty-fifth-anniversary gala, when he sang Pistol in the fugal finale to *Falstaff.*

Paul Althouse as the Pretender, Dmitri, photographed for his operatic debut in Boris, *the beginning of a long, distinguished career as a singer and teacher.*

PAUL ALTHOUSE

THE ORDERLY CAREER OF AMERICAN tenor Paul Althouse (1889–1954) followed a natural progression from boy soprano in his Reading, Pennsylvania, church, through college and the chorus of

Hammerstein's Philadelphia Opera Company, to study and oratorio in New York City, all leading to a 1912 audition at which he sang "Celeste Aida" for a handful of listeners in the darkened Metropolitan auditorium. He was back onstage the following season in unbilled walk-ons in *Die Zauberflöte,* and his official debut came as Dmitri in the American premiere of Mussorgsky's *Boris Godunov* in March 1913 in which he was able to make a strong impression on audiences and critics in a leading role sometimes obscured by overwhelming pageantry. "He is comely to see and of an easy and elastic stage presence that seems rather of the practised singer than the beginner. His voice is uncommonly full and rich, without a trace of whiteness, shrillness or unsteadiness. He uses it freely and vigorously, but with intelligent control and a keen sense of the musical and the dramatic significance of his declamation and song. So far as the part of the pretended Dmitri went, he showed a clear faculty for operatic impersonation and no lack of modest histrionic resource. He has imagination, too, since he kept the part of the young and dreaming pretender in vivid contrast to that of the old and racked Boris, and made the bright tenor tones of the one the foil to the sombre bass accents of the other." For seven seasons Althouse was Dmitri in every performance of *Boris,* adding many outside engagements and more important roles to his operatic repertoire: the Italian singer in *Rosenkavalier,* Pinkerton in *Butterfly,* and Turiddu in *Cavalleria Rusticana.*

At a performance of *Cavalleria* and *Pagliacci,* Caruso noticed the nervous young tenor standing in the wings in an unbecoming costume. Hastily urging on him one of his own, he said encouragingly, "Go out and sing like Caruso."

Eventually concerts and oratorio occupied more and more of Althouse's time, and he left the Met in 1920. When he returned in 1934, he had studied Wagner, performed Schoenberg's *Gurrelieder* under Stokowski with Rose Bampton in Philadelphia, and sung Act I of *Die Walküre* under both Toscanini and Koussevitzky. Henderson noted how effective the change to heldentenor had been: "Mr. Althouse was not a Wagnerian hero when he left the Metropolitan. His career as an interpreter of the Bavarian drama began with certain concert appearances which revealed the fact that his voice, carefully nurtured, had developed into an organ of more heroic proportions and that his singing had acquired a much larger range of expression and a more confident style. . . . Mr. Althouse looked the part, acted it with youthful animation and emotion, and delivered the music, and also the text, with intelligence and feeling."

In 1935 he was Siegmund on the historic afternoon when Kirsten Flagstad made her Met debut; when his second Met career ended in 1940, he had become the first American to sing Tristan there (the list is still not very long) and he was then able to devote his full time to teaching. His students included Eleanor Steber, Richard Tucker, and Irene Dalis.

ANTONIO SCOTTI

ONE-THIRD OF THE METROPOLITAN Opera's first one hundred years might well be remembered as the age of Italian baritone Antonio Scotti (1866–1936). Puccini had wanted him to create the role of Scarpia in his new opera, *Tosca,* at its 1900 world premiere in Rome; instead, a contract with Maurice Grau brought Scotti to New York and the Metropolitan, where his Scarpia would eventually become the most frequently seen characterization in the history of the opera house. Over the years at the Metropolitan he intimidated a royal line of sopranos in the title role, beginning with Milka Ternina and continuing with Emma Eames, Lina Cavalieri, Olive Fremstad, Geraldine Farrar, Emmy Destinn, Louise Edvina, Claudia Muzio, and Maria Jeritza.

Scotti was singing Rigoletto that night in 1903 when his fellow Neapolitan Enrico Caruso made his New York debut. Through Caruso's reign and Beniamino Gigli's succession, Scotti endured. He witnessed the arrivals of Geraldine Farrar and Maria Jeritza and saw them both depart. Two bigger-voiced Italian baritones, Pasquale Amato and Titta Ruffo, sang at the Metropolitan, receiving cheers for their booming voices, and Scotti survived them both. His total number of performances—more than a thousand—is unlikely to be surpassed by any leading artist.

On January 1, 1924, Scotti celebrated his twenty-fifth anniversary at the Metropolitan by singing a performance of *Tosca* with Maria Jeritza and Miguel Fleta. W. J. Henderson, who had heard Scotti sing each of his thirty-six different roles—everything from the Count in *Le Nozze di Figaro* to Kyoto in *Iris*—summed up the qualities that had made such longevity possible: "When Jean de Reszke left this city he prophesied that Scotti would be still busy at the Metropolitan fifteen years later. Mr. de Reszke knew his man. . . . He did not take this town by storm. He was never a sensation. He made his debut in 1899 as Don Giovanni and fastened public interest upon himself by his fresh, sonorous, but not robust voice, his finish of style, his elegance of action, his grace of manner and his handsome physique. Later when he sang De Never[s] in *Gli Ugonotti* he deepened the impression. He was the beau idéal of the French courtier and made himself a prominent figure in one of the most brilliant casts ever assembled in Meyerbeer's masterpiece. [His associates on March 11, 1901, were Lillian Nordica, Louise Homer, Nellie Melba, Jean de Reszke,

Opposite: *Antonio Scotti as the Count De Nevers in* Gli Ugonotti, *a role performed during his long Metropolitan career with both Jean de Reszke and Enrico Caruso.*

Mishkin
N.Y.

Antonio Scotti shifted easily from the elegance of the Count De Nevers to a scruffy Tonio in Pagliacci*, an opera in which he often appeared with his friend Caruso.*

Pol Plançon, and Marcel Journet.] Still later he astonished those who had come to regard him as the Beau Brummell of opera by his subtly conceived and deftly executed impersonation of Tonio in *Pagliacci.* His Sergeant Sulpice in *La Figlia del Reggimento* revealed yet another side of his art, his delineation of the bluffness, the tenderness and the yearning of the gallant old soldier. His Iago in *Otello* showed that he could be sinister, evasive and crafty. But present day operagoers recognize the existence of these traits in his incomparable Scarpia, an impersonation in which he has been without rival and still is. To the subtlety and craft of his Iago he here unites dread power and elemental sensuality. In the singing actor who has composed two such impersonations one could hardly have looked for the equipment needed for a Falstaff, and yet as the fat knight Mr. Scotti presented a portrait second only to that of the matchless original, Maurel. . . . And the indisputable proof of this success of his art is that while he is on the stage you never take your eyes off him.

"That he is still in the foreground in his twenty-fifth season argues well for his conservation of his vocal gifts. He never had a big voice. He never tried to make it big. He accomplished his ends with it just as it was and treated it with a real singer's discretion, so that, while it is certainly no longer the organ of a youthful singer, it is still a practicable instrument and fully equal to the demands of the graphic and convincing character portraits which he draws with a master hand. In all the years that he has been with us Mr. Scotti has enriched our experience with his consummate mastery of style. . . .

"It is no small part of Mr. Scotti's merit that he has in these twenty-five years withstood the crushing atmosphere of opera. An opera house is not an artistic conservatory. . . . Opera singers seldom make notable artistic progress. They do not need to. Once successful, their safest play is to repeat incessantly that which gained the first approval and to make no ventures. It is only when the singer begins to lose the powers which originally fostered public attention on him that he begins the search after new means of retaining his hold on the public. Mr. Scotti began to widen his artistic horizon when he was yet in the zenith of his ability. One gratifying result of this is that now when his voice has passed its meridian his skill in impersonation, which years ago became the chief part of his stock, still chains the interest of operagoers."

For his 1933 farewell to opera, Scotti chose Chim-Fen in Leoni's *Oracolo.* It had always been the role most distant from his own natural elegance: "Not only in make-up and costume, but in pace, gesture and movement, the great Italian baritone gave a gruesomely realistic characterization of the villainous Chinaman, every detail of his portrayal, even to the forward inclination of his head, the indrawing of his shoulders and elbows and the ghastly limpness of his pendulous fingers, showing careful study and elaboration. Few persons are likely to forget the uncanny sight Scotti presented as he sank, loose and spineless, under the onslaught of his murderer, and later as he flopped forward in a heap and rolled over on the stage." Without Scotti, *L'Oracolo* vanished. Scotti sailed to retirement in Naples and was dead within three years.

ENRICO CARUSO AND *PAGLIACCI*

HE WAS THE GREATEST SINGER IN THE world, the highest-paid and the most famous, and more than a century after his birth, his recordings are still best-sellers. During his lifetime he received almost $2,000,000 in record royalties from the Victor Company. For Victor he sang everything from Rossini's "Cujus Animam" to George M. Cohan's "Over There." Everything touched by his tenor voice turned to gold. At the Metropolitan he performed roles in thirty-seven different operas. But just as "Vesti la giubba," the clown's big aria from *Pagliacci,* is the recording that has endured in the minds of even the most casual listeners, so *Pagliacci* itself was the opera he sang more times than any other. He sang it in Italy for war relief, in London, Mexico City, and Havana. On tour with the Metropolitan, he appeared in it in Paris and Chicago, Atlanta and Milwaukee, Kansas City and San Francisco. In all, Caruso sang more than a hundred performances of *Pagliacci* with the Metropolitan Opera Company, as well as frequent galas featuring Act I, which ends with Canio's great lament.

During the first two decades of this century Caruso as the heartbroken Canio was *the* theatrical event, the experience that everyone wanted to share. The ritual of a Caruso *Pagliacci* called for the prologue to be sung by Antonio Scotti or Pasquale Amato. When Caruso drove the mule cart onstage there was a roar of recognition, "and the more the house cheered, the more Caruso beat the drum. He was again the white clown, all sleeves and tragedy." Riding in the cart was a succession of Neddas that included Marcella Sembrich, Bella Alten, Emmy Destinn, Lucrezia Bori, and Claudia Muzio. While there were those who lamented the way Caruso expended such volume on the strenuous moments, thereby changing an essentially lyric voice into a more robust one, the applause after "Vesti la giubba" usually lasted until the start of Act Two unless an encore was granted.

H. T. Parker saw Caruso's Canio many times in Boston and New York and summed it up in 1922: "From year to year, he amplified it with much illuminating and defining detail. Recall, for instance, the exaggerated whimsies of a strolling player with which his matured Canio cozened the crowd at the beginning of the play; the wiping of the powder from his face as of a player

Opposite: *This Mishkin study of Enrico Caruso as Canio in* Pagliacci *is probably the most familiar opera photograph ever taken.*

An unusual photo of Caruso as Canio showing one of his gestures in the role.

resuming relievedly his own person; the intensity, brooding or ominous, that he threw into his declamation in the play while in action he was but doing the part; the fashion in which he went emotionally dead when he had struck down Nedda; how he returned to himself, dragged out of his throat 'la commedia è finita' and huddled away, distraught, blind, blank again.

"Always, too, Caruso's song was the speech of Canio, as elemental in all his moods, as direct and full-voiced in his emotions, as simple or savage as the character really is. He made tellingly but untheatrically the swift change from playful banter over the lightness of women to the amorous and vindictive words about a wife that he already suspects; he did not overdo the celebrated soliloquy as a Canio might utter it; he sang in the final scenes with the accents of the pain and the passion that rend the clown amid the ironies of the make-believe and the reality." Other critics gave up trying to describe Caruso's Canio; it was an annual phenomenon with which mere words could not cope.

LUCREZIA BORI

IT WAS THE FINEST ENGAGEMENT THAT opera in 1910 had to offer: the title role in Puccini's *Manon Lescaut* in performances with Caruso and Antonio Scotti on the occasion of the Metropolitan Opera's first visit to Paris. Originally scheduled for the part was the beautiful but unreliable Lina Cavalieri, who was off securing a wealthy husband. Carmen Melis was considered, but then, just weeks before the performances, an unknown Spanish soprano had a private audition on the stage of Milan's Teatro alla Scala. Listening to Lucrezia Bori (1887–1960) on the recommendation of the publisher Ricordi were Arturo Toscanini, Giulio Gatti-Casazza, and Giacomo Puccini. That day the Met found its young and graceful Manon Lescaut.

Twenty-three years old, with little more than a year's professional experience, Bori became part of the Met's triumphal Paris season. She declined, however, to come to New York immediately. Wanting more experience, she sang at La Scala for two seasons, where she was Octavian in the first Italian *Rosenkavalier.* Her official Metropolitan debut came two years after Paris, again as Manon Lescaut on opening night of the 1912–13 season.

The immediate spell cast over her first American audience would always be shared by Bori's enthusiastic public and the critics, all of whom reveled in the fresh voice, musical feeling, and warm emotional life of whatever she portrayed. Of her first Nedda in *Pagliacci,* performed a few nights after her debut, Pitts Sanborn wrote, "She gives it the Italian peasant quality that imparts a

Lucrezia Bori as Nedda in Pagliacci, *one of the roles in which she became invaluable to the Metropolitan.*

tang of the soil to the yearning, the cruelty, the passion, the supreme terror that Nedda must convey in the short course of the opera." In the "Balatella," Nedda's song to the birds, "her voice, firm and clear despite a trace of nervousness, soared to capture its highest notes like a falcon unhooded to seek its prey." And later, when she "took her deathblow at the eleventh hour at Caruso's hands she did not, like some melodramatic prima donnas, roll screaming down the toy theatre steps, but sank down slowly, clinging to her strangler."

For Lucrezia Bori at the age of twenty-six, Montemezzi's *Amore dei Tre Re,* with Toscanini conducting and Edoardo Ferrari-Fontana making his debut, consolidated her position among the era's outstanding artists: "It was the most important opportunity this young singer has had since she became a member of the Metropolitan company last season; and she rose to it in a manner that immediately put her on a higher plane as an artist than she has occupied here before, and that raised her greatly in the esteem of discriminating music lovers. Nor was

Lucrezia Bori's haunting portrayal of Fiora in Montemezzi's Amore dei Tre Re *was first revealed in the opera's 1914 American premiere.*

there anything accidental or lucky in the impression she made as the sorely beset Fiora of Sem Benelli's tragedy. It was an admirably wrought piece of tragic acting, thoroughly thought out, finely and skillfully composed in its development of the playwright's conception. Miss Bori showed the possession of hitherto unexpected resources as a tragic actress in pose, gesture, facial expression, the subtle and often minute details whose sum is so important in establishing the character of an impersonation as a whole. She showed also that she possessed a presence that could truly command and dominate the stage when the time came for her to do it. And some of these are part of Miss Bori's equipment. As for her voice, it has always challenged admiration since it was first disclosed here on the opening night of last season, for its purity, clear freshness, and brilliancy; a voice of great and unspoiled beauty. It has seemed a typical lyric soprano, not of great power and ill enduring forcing. And yet in this performance [illegible] ample power for the singer's needs without the ill results of pushing it beyond its natural limits. She was also able, when the time came and when she was no longer the 'little flower' of Manfredo's almost compassionate love, to give her voice more dramatic quality. It had the intense coloring and expression that the superb scene in the second act calls for, as her passion for Avito, at first calmed and dissipated by the knightly gentleness of her departing husband, is rekindled by the ardor of her lover. Miss Bori has hitherto made her successes in parts of a less serious and exacting character. In *L'Amore dei Tre Re* she has given a token that she can be counted on for greater responsibilities."

But it was not her voice alone that so enthralled her audience: "What a flower-like, lily-handed, as from a poem and picture of Rossetti, was Mlle. Lucrezia Bori. . . . In personal appearance she was rich with the possibilities of picturesque illusion. She was in tune with the poetic spirit of the piece. She harmonized with the epoch. She was a woman about whom three kings, as well as a full palace of three kings and two knaves might have contended. . . . She moved in grace, and passed through the sullen and frowning events of the piece in fragrance, light and pathos." A triumph for all the participants, the acclaim was as short-lived for Bori as for Ferrari-Fontana. Penciled in for performances at the beginning of the 1915–16 season, Bori was afflicted with increasing vocal problems that one operation had not cured. She was forced to withdraw from the Metropolitan and did not sing there again until January 28, 1921.

EDOARDO FERRARI-FONTANA

IT WAS IN MONTEVIDEO, URUGUAY, that the Italian tenor Edoardo Ferrari-Fontana (1878–1936), medical student turned diplomat, first discovered his talent for singing. And it was on shipboard while returning to Buenos Aires that he met Margarete Matzenauer, who later married him. Self-taught, Ferrari-Fontana appeared as a baritone in lighter works such as *Fra Diavolo, Figlia del Reggimento,* and *The Merry Widow* in Argentina and Italy. The baritone Riccardo Stracciari urged him to study, and within a short while, he made his formal operatic debut in *Tristano ed Isotta* at Turin. His roles now became those of a strong dramatic tenor's repertoire—Tannhäuser, Pollione in *Norma,* Siegfried in *Götterdämmerung,* Licinio in *La Vestale,* and Dick Johnson in *La Fanciulla del West* in the Buenos Aires premiere with Ruffo. In his second season at the Teatro Colón he sang opposite Matzenauer's Brangäne; at the end of the season they were married, and he canceled most of his season in Italy to be with her in the United States.

His 1913 American debut came about by accident during a year in which he had not planned to perform, when he substituted for a suddenly departed Carl Burrian as Tristano in a Boston Opera performance that was otherwise *Tristan und Isolde* (he sang in Italian, while the rest of the cast performed in German) with Minnie Saltzmann-Stevens. It was a perfect example of the last-minute substitute's erasing the memory of his predecessor. "His voice is unmistakably an Italian voice—warmly colored, full-bodied, largely flowing, of a natural sensitiveness to passionate song. It falls resonantly upon the listening ear; it has power without coarseness, and sensuous beauty without a marring trick of manner, without one of the vices that many an Italian tenor like to cultivate as a virtue." "Mr. Fontana is the most romantic Tristan that we have seen in Boston since Jean de Reszke. He is physically suited in the part, and our Tristans for some years have been matter-of-fact persons if not distressingly globular. He sings, and not only the notes."

His reputation established, Ferrari-Fontana opened the 1913–14 Boston season as Gennaro in Wolf-Ferrari's *Gioielli della Madonna* and sang Samson with D'Alvarez. His Canio in *Pagliacci* was declared the most dramatic seen in Boston since Fernando de Lucia's in 1894. He attempted his first Tristan in German opposite his wife's Isolde, but the result approached disaster. At the end of the second act, he reverted to Italian and never attempted German again, later even singing Beethoven's "Adelaide" in Italian at a Philharmonic concert in New York.

The pinnacle of his career was his portrayal of Avito in Montemezzi's *Amore dei Tre Re,* a role he had created at La Scala (as the eleventh-hour substitute for Bernardo de Muro) and which brought him to the Metropolitan in January 1914 with Pasquale Amato and Lucrezia Bori. "It may be said of him without hesitation that he sent an electric shock through the Metropolitan. He has a magnificent robust voice with pealing upper tones, he sings with admirable technique, with high dignity of style, with much taste and above all with intelligence and inspiring temperamental warmth. His delivery of the mad appeals of Avito to Fiora in the second act were irresistible in their dramatic power and yet there was no offense against the chastity of art. No other tenor in recent years has offered an impersonation making such a quick appeal to the feelings of the audience as this. If Mr. Ferrari-Fontana can repeat in other roles such singing and acting as this we can only wonder where he has been all this time." Ferrari-Fontana had no contract with the Metropolitan his first season there; instead, his five performances were obtained from Boston in return for three performances by Riccardo Martin and a single appearance each by Carl Jörn and Jacques Urlus. He did have contracts for the following two years, but Lucrezia Bori's illness and his own war service intervened to prevent a third season of *L'Amore dei Tre Re.* When he returned it was too late. His marriage with Matzenauer had broken down, and their public squabbles made it difficult for Gatti to engage both. (Among Ferrari-Fontana's complaints was that Matzenauer hired only German-speaking servants so that he couldn't give them orders.) During the 1920 season he sang Tristan and Siegmund at the Colón, a Carnegie Hall *Pagliacci* in 1924 in honor of the Democratic Convention Women Guests, and after that nothing.

Ferrari-Fontana had written to Gatti in 1921 that he was leaving the theater to devote himself to his family, and that is what he did. With his second wife, the daughter of a Cuban sugar planter, and their children, he moved to Toronto, where he taught for many years.

Edoardo Ferrari-Fontana as Avito in L'Amore dei Tre Re, *a role he performed in the world premiere at La Scala in 1913.*

MARGARETE MATZENAUER

"THE MAJESTIC MATZENAUER STRIDES still splendidly amid the shifting scenes of the Metropolitan pageant. Hers is a voice of grand proportions, but they have not been gigantic enough for her ambitions. Heaven created her a mezzo-soprano, but for her only the mountain heights of Brünnhilde and the death devoted Isolde would suffice." Hungarian by birth, German by training and first marriage, Margarete Matzenauer (1881–1963) came to the Metropolitan after a

Opposite: *Margarete Matzenauer as the exuberant warrior maiden Brünnhilde in* Die Walküre.

C
MISHKIN
N.Y. 40

Brünnhilde was one of thirteen Wagnerian roles, both contralto and soprano, in Matzenauer's large Metropolitan Opera repertoire.

long Munich contract. From November 1911 opening-night debut as Amneris in *Aida,* she was a central part of the Metropolitan's planning. With Caruso she sang Ulrica in *Un Ballo in Maschera,* Dalila in *Samson,* and Fidès in *Prophète;* with Urlus she sang Fidelio; with Martinelli and Ponselle in the first Met *Don Carlo,* she was Eboli. She had steady control of all the Wagnerian mezzo and contralto roles, and outlasted both Olive Fremstad and Johanna Gadski on the roster to continue with Isolde and Brünnhilde into the 1920s.

After Amneris, her most frequent role at the Met was the *Walküre* Brünnhilde. The first one she sang there in 1912 "in many respects was strikingly successful. She has done nothing here, in fact, in which she has not shown herself an artist of exceptional and commanding powers. There might have been properly a question whether a singer whose voice is so nearly a well-defined contralto as Mme. Matzenauer's were able to sing the music of this part, which in certain portions mounts to the range of a true soprano. She made it clear, however, that she could compass the music, albeit not without something of effort. The crux in this matter, of course, was the electrifying cry of 'Ho-jo-to-ho,' with which the divine maiden makes her appearance at the beginning of the second act. This Mme. Matzenauer delivered with plenty of power, but with something of heaviness. Nothing could have been finer, however, than her singing of the solemn notification to Siegmund of his approaching death—a passage in which was heard all the nobility and beauty of her voice, all the sustained phrasing, all the eloquence of diction that she commands. She was fine also in the last scene of the third act with Wotan. Such passages showed Mme. Matzenauer's finest powers and most consummate art."

Her second husband was Edoardo Ferrari-Fontana, the Italian heroic tenor, whom she brought to the United States from Buenos Aires. When they separated during World War I, he denounced her as a German sympathizer, and alone among major artists with large German repertoires she survived the crisis quite well. She put herself at the disposal of the government for concerts at army bases, removed all German music from her recitals (even Gluck and Handel), and performed Grieg in English. When Wagner's music returned to the Met after the war, first in English and later in German, Matzenauer was in each premiere. Again the critics were enraptured. In her English-language Isolde she "revelled in the gorgeous opulence of her royal purple voice. Such a magnificence and splendor of vocal tone as she poured out we cannot ever recall to have heard before. . . . It was almost bewildering from a musical, dramatic, and purely vocal point of view." Another described her physical presence architecturally: "She is a cathedral, not a bungalow, and the bungalow type is, thanks to the general decadence of taste nowadays, more admired. But a cathedral is dramatic and Matzenauer belongs to the grand old dramatic school of Lilli Lehmann, Milka Ternina and Olive Fremstad."

During Matzenauer's first decade at the Met, her only rival for mezzo roles had been Louise Homer, who preferred to spend as much time as possible with her family. But in the 1920s Julia Claussen and Karin Branzell began to take a larger share of her repertoire. In 1930 she declined a new contract for operas in which contralto roles were of lesser importance and withheld announcement of her Met farewell until after the performance itself. Never for an instant willing to admit that her career might be finished, she did this, she explained, "to avoid the flowers, speeches, testimonial scrolls and other funereal touches that might have made her feel she was tossing in the sod on her own head."

Outside the Met she sang Jocasta in the American premiere of Stravinsky's *Oedipus Rex* with the Boston Symphony under Koussevitzky, the Verdi *Requiem* with Toscanini and the New York Philharmonic, and Klytemnestra in an *Elektra* conducted by Fritz Reiner in Philadelphia, with Anne Roselle in the title role and a new generation of singers in the cast: Nelson Eddy as Orest and Rose Bampton, Helen Jepson, and Irra Petina as Serving Women. In 1936 she had a small part in the motion picture *Mr. Deeds Goes to Town* with Jimmy Stewart and Jean Arthur, and as late as 1942 Matzenauer sang "Ah, Perfido" with the American Symphony Orchestra and appeared as a comedienne on Broadway.

FRIEDA HEMPEL

A FAIRLY STRAIGHT LINE DIVIDES THE operatic performances of the German soprano Frieda Hempel (1885–1955) from her later career in concerts. By the time she was twenty, she had been brought by the Kaiser to the Royal Opera in Berlin, where she remained until 1912. Gatti-Casazza had contracted her in 1910 and waited two years for a royal release to come. After an illness she made her 1912 New York debut in a revival of *Gli Ugonotti* with Enrico Caruso, Emmy Destinn, Antonio Scotti, and Léon Rothier. It was not a success. As the *Times* noted "It was not the voice of a great singer in the plenitude of her powers." Two weeks later, following a *Traviata* with Pasquale Amato and Umberto Macnez, the same paper was happier: "Hempel has made *Traviata* at the Metropolitan a somewhat less speculative and hazardous undertaking than it has been for some years. . . . She is the first singer of her kind . . . to cope with the music adequately since the departure of Mme. Sembrich. . . . Mrs. Hempel's singing of the coloratura airs that fall to her share in the opera was admirable in its brilliancy and incisiveness and the accuracy with which the vocal ornaments were executed." The same account sheds some light on production standards of the period: "The personages were clothed in this performance in the mixture of ancient and modern costume that has become traditional with the opera; the heroine appearing in the latest models, the others in eighteenth century garb. Better things have twice been attempted in New York, once when the costumes really belonging to the period of the opera—that of the 30's of the last century—and again when those of the present time were used."

Hempel's performance as Violetta was the beginning of a rapport with the New York public that was to continue for decades. Equally at home in German, French, and Italian opera, Hempel mixed Eva in *Meistersinger* with Rossini's Rosina and Offenbach's Olympia, the title role in Weber's *Euryanthe* with Maria in *Figlia del Reggimento.* She was the Queen of the Night in *Zauberflöte* and Susanna in *Nozze di Figaro.* And the presence of her full lyric voice on the roster made the production of three Caruso vehicles possible: *Marta, Les Pêcheurs de Perles,* and *L'Elisir d'Amore.* She is best remembered, however, as the Metropolitan's first Marschallin in the 1913 American premiere of *Rosenkavalier* with Anna Case, Margarete Ober, and Otto Goritz:

"Her impersonation was truly beautiful in every sense. She looked the noblewoman and dressed the part with fastidious taste. Her bearing, her poses, her gestures were all replete with grace, ease, repose and meaning. Her face showed unwonted nobility. Her acting was on the whole most interesting. She sang her music well nigh flawlessly. The style which she employed in the delivery of the dialogue was perfection itself, and in the melodic passages she revealed a poise of the voice, a purity of tone, a breath control and a delicacy of nuance such as she had never exhibited in any other opera. Above all her delivery had the tenderness and gentle pathos required by the scene, and it is but simple justice to say that she put far more of it into the music than Dr. Strauss did. It is a delight to find Mme. Hempel equipped with a role so nicely fitted to her powers, and to behold her in the enjoyment of a pronounced success with the public."

Hempel left the Metropolitan in 1919; soon her life as a concert artist effectively began when she appeared in the Jenny Lind Centennial Concert. Costumed as the Swedish Nightingale and repeating the format developed by P. T. Barnum for Lind, Hempel found a new and popular occupation. After hundreds of Jenny Lind concerts in the United States and Britain, Hempel retreated further in time and became in effect an eighteenth-century court singer: in return for $43,000 a year for life she agreed to forswear public appearances and sing only for the New York millionaire August

© Mishkin
N.Y.

Heckscher's private concerts and charitable events. The arrangement didn't last, Heckscher stopped payments, and Hempel was forced to take him to court twice, winning both times. As a result her public career and image suffered, and in 1934 she wrote Gatti, asking to return to the Metropolitan for a single performance as the Marschallin during his final season: "I have had so many disillusionments," she pleaded, "so much injustice and so much humiliation." Instead, Lotte Lehmann sang her first Marschallins at the Metropolitan that season. Hempel was still singing well some years later. At a 1948 Town Hall recital, when the audience was, no doubt, paying tribute to her past triumphs as one of the leading singers of the century, *The New York Times* still reported "the musicality, the knowing phrasing, the clear diction" of the performance.

German baritone Otto Goritz (1873–1929) as Baron Ochs in the first New York performances of Der Rosenkavalier. *Goritz made his Metropolitan debut as Klingsor in the 1903 performance of* Parsifal; *among his twenty-five Metropolitan roles, only one, Papageno in an Italian-language* Zauberflöte, *was not in German.*

ANNA CASE

THE AMERICAN DREAM FOUND ONE OF its loveliest embodiments in the soprano Anna Case (1889–), who rose from shoeing horses in her father's blacksmith shop in South Branch, New Jersey, to become a leading soloist and, ultimately, a society matron. Discovered singing at a tea in Philadelphia's Bellevue-Stratford Hotel by Met executive Andreas Dippel, Case had had her early lessons financed by a New Jersey grocer who was repaid with the $114 in proceeds from her first concert. At the Metropolitan in 1909–10 she started with a student contract of $300 for the six-month season and appeared onstage thirty-nine times in the smallest of parts. Larger roles were gradually entrusted to her—Esmeralda in *The Bartered Bride,* the Priestess in *Aida,* and Fyodor in *Boris.* In Gluck's *Orfeo* "the happiest of all happy shades was surely Miss Anna Case, who united personal beauty with beauty of voice and beauty of art." Then in 1913 a giant opportunity came with the American premiere of *Der Rosenkavalier.* Case was the Sophie, and opening night was a disaster for her; she was ill, knew no German, and had had only a short while to absorb the then difficult Straussian idiom. Although she went on to sing all eleven *Rosenkavaliers* in 1913–14 to improving reviews, the season marked the effective end of her operatic career. She returned the following year for a few minor roles and in 1917–18 sang three Micaëlas; increasingly, though, the concert stage became her home. From her second season at the Metropolitan on, she had been a frequent soloist at the Sunday-night concerts, singing lyric and florid numbers such as "Depuis le jour" and "Casta Diva." Aside from a brief, unsuccessful foray into motion pictures, she devoted the remainder of her career to concert appearances. Thomas A. Edison declared her his favorite singer and recorded

Opposite: Frieda Hempel's wistful Marschallin contemplates the approach of age at the end of Act I of Der Rosenkavalier, *photographed by Mishkin before the 1913 American premiere.*

One of several Mishkin portraits of Anna Case taken around 1915 when the soprano was leaving opera for a successful concert career.

her many times ("the most perfect scale of any singer," he maintained).

At her first Carnegie Hall recital in 1916, critic Richard Aldrich reported, "It is a light soprano of the most lyric quality, of delightful freshness and transparent purity when it is heard at its best; a voice that is not adapted for dramatic expression nor for the utterance of deep emotions but yet capable within its limits for a variety of color and of manifold charming effects."

Anna Case's life changed dramatically following an engagement to sing at a private musicale given in the home of Clarence H. Mackay. Taken with her beauty, he sent a carload of flowers to her next Carnegie Hall recital, enclosing a small diamond band with an enamel bluebird in the center. In 1931 she reached the summit of New York society with her marriage to Mackay, the millionaire head of the Postal Telegraph and Cable Corporation who served as president of both the New York Philharmonic and the Metropolitan Museum of Art. Mrs. Mackay occupied his parterre box on Monday nights at the Metropolitan Opera. She had said all along she didn't like country boys.

FRANCES ALDA

A NEW ZEALAND SOPRANO FRANCES Alda (1883–1952) was not prepared for the kind of attention she received when she arrived for her Metropolitan debut in 1908. Aware of her affair with Gatti-Casazza, the new general manager, a reporter interviewed her on a New York pier with her sixteen pieces of luggage. "Does the care of home and children call you?" she was asked as he probed into how serious the relationship really was. "Oh, it isn't as bad as that," she replied casually. Unfortunately for her, it became much worse as the New York press subjected her to the attention that only an artist more than contractually involved with the management received. Her December 1908 debut as Gilda in *Rigoletto* with Pasquale Amato and Enrico Caruso was no more successful than her Anna in the Met's first performance of Puccini's *Le Villi,* with Alessandro Bonci, shortly thereafter. For her first *Manon,* W. J. Henderson wrote one of his most scathing reviews. "Mme. Alda was the Manon. She has one advantage over Mr. Caruso and that is in the possession of many more registers than he. [The noted voice teacher] Garcia recognized three registers and some of the early masters found only two. Clara Kathleen Rogers found five, some of which she called 'lower thick' and 'upper thin.' Mme. Alda has at least five, clearly divided, but she has an 'upper thick' and a 'lower thin.' In this at least she is original. The audience heard her last night with much placidity."

There was no reason in Alda's professional background to anticipate such a reaction; indeed, some of her finest recordings date from this period. A pupil of Mathilde Marchesi's in Paris, Alda made her debut in *Manon* at the Opéra-Comique in 1904. Before coming to New York she had sung frequently at La Monnaie in Brussels, appeared briefly at Covent Garden with Caruso, and created the title role of *Louise* at La Scala under Toscanini. In 1909–10 she took the season off, married Gatti, and sang with the Metropolitan every subsequent season until 1929–30. The Board of Directors debated her position on the roster in 1912, when Toscanini interceded with a letter on her behalf. Although she sat in on auditions, she appears to have been discreet in using her influence. The more vivid roles in the repertoire, such as Tosca and Carmen, went to Geraldine Farrar and later Maria Jeritza, while Lucrezia Bori handled the subtleties of Manon, Violetta, and Juliette. Alda found her own specialties to be both Marguerites, Manon Lescaut, and Desdemona and several world premieres of now forgotten American works. While sharing Mimi with Bori, Alda sang Puccini's heroine more times than any other soprano in the Met's history.

Surely Alda's most extraordinary *Bohème* was with the Metropolitan on one of its Tuesday evening visits to Philadelphia. The signs of disarray came in the first act

Frances Alda looking deceptively demure in Puccini's Manon Lescaut, *the opera chosen for her Metropolitan farewell in 1929.*

A playful Enrico Caruso as Rodolfo in Act IV of La Bohème.

limpid, flowing, delicately moulded to the contours and content of melody and phrase. The lightness and brightness of her song made it seem a very speech of Mimi. . . . Mme. Alda has not been content; she has borne many hard sayings and, perhaps, profited by them; now—and in her middle years—she is a new born singer."

Not an emotional actress, Alda usually displayed more temperament offstage than on. As litigious as the Spanish tenor Florencio Constantino, she sued her stockbrokers for mismanaging her account; in turn, she was sued by two of her landlords, two furriers, and two interior decorators, one of whom she had threatened to shoot because of the way he had hung the curtains in her bedroom. She divorced Gatti, saying, "Three is a crowd. . . . Gatti was interested in a ballet dancer." The ballet dancer was in fact the distinguished Italian ballerina Rosina Galli, who was then the director of the Metropolitan Opera Ballet. When Alda got around to using Galli's name, she said, "The chief difference between us is that Galli's weight is all below her waist and mine is all above. I prefer it this way."

Soon after her divorce from Gatti, Alda gave her farewell Metropolitan performance, a 1929 *Manon Lescaut* with Beniamino Gigli. She had never missed a scheduled performance with the company and was "in the best of voice, and her use of the voice was marked by exceptional breath control, admirably placed high notes, an unimpeachable legato and low tones which lately have acquired a 'cello-like richness.'" There were several years of broadcasts and concerts, then retirement. Speaking of Gatti in 1937, she said, "The two most grievous errors I made were when I married him—and when I divorced him." In her operatic autobiography *Men, Women and Tenors,* published the same year, Alda recalled some of the nonmusicians she had known: "Half a dozen kings, and several queens; princes, great ladies, ballet girls; bank presidents and tenors; movie stars, ambassadors, and crooners; debutantes, admirals, advertising men, politicians, lawyers and other thieves."

when Schaunard lifted his hat before exiting and found it full of water. Caruso was a notorious practical joker; he and Antonio Scotti wore monocles throughout the performance, an obvious allusion to Andrés de Segurola, the Colline, who affected a monocle onstage and off. Soon they had Alda joining their antics, singing duets cross-eyed. In Mimi's Act IV death scene, Alda discovered that the cot on which she lay was missing one of its castors. The slightest movement caused squeaks and teetering that were obvious beyond the footlights. After the final curtain an indignant Gatti-Casazza rushed backstage to fine Alda, Caruso, and Scotti $100 each. They agreed it was deserved—and money well spent.

Alda's reviews improved over the years. Of a 1916 Metropolitan *Bohème* in Boston, for instance, H. T. Parker wrote, "It was a night in which Mme. Alda proved herself a singer of voice, style, intelligence and sensibility. . . . Her voice, once thin and sharp, was now all clear softness and gently lustrous timbre. Her tone, which once betrayed many a fault of teaching and practice, was

LINA CAVALIERI

IN *TOSCA* SHE WAS A VISION, COMPOSED of "white Caucasian ermine, glowing white satin, and luscious flesh, topped by the deep green of emeralds of tiara, necklaces and brooch." The voice was usually mentioned last. Lina Cavalieri (1874–1944) billed herself as "the most beautiful woman in the world," and there

Opposite: *The Italian soprano Lina Cavalieri, who billed herself as "the most beautiful woman in the world."*

were many who agreed. For much of her brief operatic career she was front-page news. The titles of her motion pictures summarized her life better than headlines: *The Shadow of Her Past, Love's Conquest, The Eternal Temptress,* and especially *Manon Lescaut.* Like the heroine in the Abbé Prévost novel and the Massenet and Puccini operas, the beautiful girl from a simple Roman background quickly acquired a taste for fine jewels and beautiful clothes. Whether she had begun by selling flowers, folding newspapers, or singing songs on the wrong side of the Tiber was unclear, but by all accounts Cavalieri rapidly made her way to Paris and the Folies Bergère. Her beauty and her various talents developed simultaneously; she had soon acquired her first husband, a Russian prince, Alexander Bariatinsky, and was headed for the operatic stage. Her debut was in Lisbon as Nedda in *Pagliacci.* The first night the public endured the performance; the second night its protests chased the whole company from the stage. She persevered, singing successfully in Italy and Poland; in Russia there were grand dukes and emeralds.

After shedding her husband, she arrived in America in 1906 to sing at the Metropolitan. There she commanded a salary larger than Farrar's. With Caruso she appeared in the first Met performances of Giordano's *Fedora, Manon Lescaut* (Puccini, another admirer, was in the audience), and Cilèa's *Adriana Lecouvreur.* The public, having heard through a dazzled press of her exploits and successes, was prepared to adore her. Critics too were admiring but tempered their judgments with a measure of objectivity. Most often it was her acting they praised, as in a 1907 review of *Fedora:* "She has fire, rapidity of varied movement, impulse, emotion—a dash of originality and an eagerness to do something. What Oliver Wendell Holmes called the 'expression peculiar to the face of gingerbread rabbits' she avoided. She lets her features play and change. About her singing one cannot speak so surely and so eulogistically. Sometimes her high notes are wrong, sometimes her low notes, sometimes her medium notes. She is at least impartial. It almost seems as if half a dozen teachers had worked at her voice and all of them contributed something good and something bad. The voice is good, sometimes ringing, but it has been sorely mutilated. She makes a rare and somewhat enticing figure upon the stage. There is nothing quite like her, with her Madonna face and serpentine, sinuous figure."

In 1910, after singing a few performances for Hammerstein, Cavalieri married Robert Chanler, grandson of John Jacob Astor and a painter of large murals. When Mr. Chanler's brother John, who had been adjudged insane in several states (but not in Virginia, where he made his residence), learned that Robert, whose sanity was never in doubt, had signed away his fortune to Miss Cavalieri before they were married, he sent a telegram: "Who's loony now?" The marriage lasted several weeks and she received only a settlement.

Following a concert tour together in 1913, Cavalieri married Lucien Muratore, the leading French tenor of the day. By this point her operatic career was almost over, and motion pictures, in which she was perhaps more successful, took over. After a stint operating a beauty salon in Paris, she finally settled in Italy with her fourth husband. During an Allied bombing raid on Florence, like Manon Lescaut she became anxious for her jewels and returned to her villa to secure them. She never reached the bomb shelter.

LUCIEN MURATORE

LUCIEN MURATORE (1878–1954), THE French tenor from Marseilles, found equal success as actor and singer. He had already appeared opposite Réjane when Emma Calvé attended a performance of Sarah Bernhardt's in which he had something to sing. Calvé urged him to study and coached him for the role of the King in a new opera by Reynaldo Hahn, *La Carmélite.* With Calvé in the title role Muratore made his operatic debut in the world premiere at the Opéra-Comique in December 1902. He quickly established himself with public and composers as an artist able to exploit fully the possibilities of any part. During his subsequent career he was chosen to create more than a dozen roles in now rarely heard works by Massenet, Fauré, and Février, among others. Prinzivalle in Février's *Monna Vanna* remained his special property; with Mary Garden he introduced the opera to Boston, Chicago, Philadelphia, and New York. By 1918, much of the public and some music critics preferred him to any tenor except Caruso. "There were moments last night when he had to camouflage his method of obtaining a high note, but that was a mere detail; for the most part his voice poured forth full-throated, robust, manly, sonorous, passionate and tender in alternation, and filled with that intensity which opera lovers love. As an actor he is supreme among operatic tenors; on him has fallen the mantle of Jean de Reszke, especially in the matter of graceful, eloquent poses and suiting the action to the words."

Muratore was the ideal partner for Mary Garden at the Chicago Opera, where he sang with her for seven seasons. Like Cavalieri and Garden he had a good sense of publicity and was not above the pretentious gesture: he refused to wear tights as Hercules in Saint-Saëns's *Déjanire,* since it wouldn't be "true to his art"—or to his leg muscles. But he was extremely serious about the artistic details of his portrayals. Told that no one would be able to notice that his fencing in *Les Huguenots* was historically accurate and distinct from *Faust,* he replied, "There's always one person in the theatre who notices and who cares; that is myself."

Lucien Muratore, the distinguished French tenor with the Chicago Opera, photographed during a visit to New York.

LOUISE HOMER

FEW CAREERS CAN HAVE BEEN AS BALanced between the demands of home and theater as that of Louise Homer (1871–1947), the contralto from Pittsburgh. She and Gatti-Casazza must often have been at cross-purposes, as their correspondence during 1918–19 suggests. Gatti to Homer at the beginning of the season: "Of course, if you do not want to arrive in New York until November 11 you are at liberty to do so, but arriving on November 1, you will find a much better distribution of your rehearsals and besides you will have a good chance to go over your role in *Prophète* with Mr. Bodanzky. I do not see what a few days' difference your arrival in New York could mean to you and your family, but it does mean a great deal to your work at the Opera House." Homer to Gatti at the end of the season in which she had sung Dalila, Amneris, Nancy in *Marta,* Marina in *Boris,* and Fidès has a different tone and describes the "blissful quiet" of Boulton-on-Lake George: "The only singing we hear is from the thrushes and robins, with occasionally hoot owls reminding us, in the night, of the duties of the winter!" Homer had married the composer Sidney Homer while studying in Boston, and he had taken her to Europe, where she made her 1898 debut in Vichy as Léonore in *La Favorite.* She sang Lola in *Cavalleria* at Covent Garden and by 1900 was at the Metropolitan in *Aida.*

Singing Amneris more often than anyone else in Metropolitan history, Homer gave probably her most exciting performance at the opening of the company's first Paris visit in 1910. It was not an easy victory. Earlier that season in New York, Homer had collaborated with Toscanini in a notable revival of Gluck's *Orfeo ed Euridice.*

Following Homer as Orfeo had been Marie Delna, the distinguished French contralto. At rehearsals Delna and Toscanini clashed several times, mainly over the tempo of Orfeo's most familiar aria, "Che farò"; at the performance each maintained his convictions and the result was a shambles. Delna's New York career concluded abruptly after one season with a large body of the French public blaming Toscanini and Homer for the failure of an important French artist. Now, at the opening-night *Aida* an organized demonstration protested against both Toscanini and Homer: "During the entr'acte there were savage yells and catcalls, and when Toscanini took his seat and tapped his baton there arose a storm of shouting and hissing. Toscanini ignored the demonstration and started conducting. When the curtain rose not a note from the singers could be heard. The occupants of the stalls and boxes showed their disapproval of the disturbance by applauding, but this merely added to the bedlam. It was in this emergency, which it seemed would end in stopping the performance altogether, that the American contralto, Louise Homer, the Amneris of the evening, arose to the occasion and stilled the tumult. She began her solo with the utmost pluck and coolly continued it until in a pause in the uproar her tones rang out clearly. Never has she sung better, with more wonderful art than tonight, and the effect, when she became audible, was instantaneous. The noise subsided and the audience fell completely under the singer's spell, and when she finished gave her such an ovation as seldom comes to a singer." Interviewed the next day, Madame Delna denied any part in the demonstration but expressed no regret at it.

Homer's forty-two-role repertoire at the Metropolitan included a number of Wagnerian roles, everything from Schwertleite to Ortrud and Brangäne, and the Met premieres of *Manru, Zigeunerbaron, Pipe of Desire, Armide, Königskinder,* and *Mona.* Family and career collided at a rehearsal for the first American *Boris Godunov,* when her five-year-old twins attacked the overbearing Toscanini, screaming, "Don't you make our mother cry!"

The last of Homer's more than seven hundred Met-

Louise Homer as Azucena in Il Trovatore, *among the most popular of her forty-two roles in Italian, French, and German at the Metropolitan.*

ropolitan performances was as Azucena in November 1929. A prolific Victor artist, she recorded everything from "Whispering Hope" and other duets with Alma Gluck to the *Lucia* sextet with Amelita Galli-Curci and Beniamino Gigli. One of her most familiar records is the duet "Ai nostri monti" from *Il Trovatore,* with Caruso.

GIOVANNI MARTINELLI

THE ASSOCIATION OF ITALIAN DRAMATIC tenor Giovanni Martinelli (1885–1969) with the Metropolitan went on for so long—first as singer with more performances of leading roles than any other tenor in Metropolitan history, and then as a jovial, white-maned presence in the audience for many rewarding years—that it is worth remembering that he arrived back in 1913 with a short distinguished career behind him already. Martinelli had benefited from a 1908 agreement in which three Milanese had undertaken to pay all his expenses as a student, including board and lodging, clothing, and piano and voice lessons, until he was able to support himself. They reserved the right "to terminate this contract, if in their opinion, they do not find in Mr. Martinelli all the qualities necessary to make him a first class artist, or in case he shows some vocal, or intellectual or musical defects, or also on account of irregular conduct in his private life." For supporting and directing his career, his sponsors were to share in his earnings for twenty years. Gatti-Casazza heard the young tenor in Italy during one of his annual summer visits and in June 1912 signed him to a contract for the 1913–14 season. Negotiating on behalf of Martinelli was one of his sponsors. On loan from the Met, he made his American debut in a Philadelphia *Tosca* in which the sensational second act of Mary Garden and Vanni Marcoux was inhibited by a sofa that collapsed early in the proceedings. His Metropolitan debut, in *Bohème* with Bori and Scotti, confirmed Gatti's faith in the young tenor. "He sang [the 'racconto'] in a way to win the plaudits of the house and to show New York why London liked him. It is rather Amedeo Bassi, as he first sang here, than Mr. Caruso that Mr. Martinelli suggests vocally, but the comparison cannot be pushed too far. Mr. Martinelli's is a genuine Italian tenor, young, fresh, delightfully free from the baritone shadow, clear and ringing, especially at the top, a voice with plenty of good metal in it."

With his handsome, ebullient presence and his strong unwavering voice, Martinelli quickly became a great audience favorite. Gatti found that he could be cast without worry in both lyrical and dramatic parts thirty or forty times a season. He appeared in the world premieres of *Madame Sans-Gêne* and *Goyescas,* the American premiere of *Simon Boccanegra,* and the first Metropolitan performances of *Oberon* and *Don Carlo.*

Over the years, perhaps because of the unrelenting strength of his voice, the critics were constantly discovering a newly developed artistry. In 1916, it was H. T. Parker at a Boston performance of *Il Trovatore:* "Since the days of Mr. Jadlowker no tenor of its stage in the young prime of his voice and abilities has given such pleasure and promised such ripening. From the beginning, Mr. Martinelli has commanded large, warm, vibrant tones. . . . For a while he sought only power in his singing, for a while he knew not or left unpractised artistry and finesse. . . . Now—by work, study, self-scrutiny and natural ripening, by no other means than intelligence, industry and ambition—Mr. Martinelli in all but voice has become another singer. His tones keep their resonance and penetration the more for the skill with which he uses them. . . . His singing of Manrico's music spun the longdrawn melody in unbroken and astutely shaded line, struck fire, did little feats of sustained tone; enriched the music with its own beauty and with the tenor's just feeling for it as an emotional speech."

Giovanni Martinelli as Manrico in Il Trovatore, *a role his long career enabled him to sing opposite the Leonoras of Claudia Muzio, Rosa Ponselle, and Zinka Milanov.*

In 1923 it was Pitts Sanborn at a performance of *William Tell:* "Arnold is the high part par excellence for heroic tenors, as Arturo in *I Puritani* is the soaring goal of their lyric brethren. I had heard Orville Harrold at the Century and John O'Sullivan at the Paris Opéra do dazzling things in this role. And for Mr. Gatti-Casazza, Giovanni Martinelli sings it with a maximum of splendor and a minimum of forcing, really reaching in it the apex not only of his scale but of his New York career." And in 1928, Martinelli continued his traversal of the heavier Caruso repertoire. During Caruso's lifetime they had shared a number of operas, including *Aida, Pagliacci,* and *Carmen,* and after his death Martinelli added *Forza, Samson,* and *Prophète.*

In *Prophète* he completed his critical conquest of the exacting W. J. Henderson: "Mr. Martinelli ascended to heights loftier than he had ever reached before. In the scene with the Anabaptists in the inn he sang and acted with simplicity, directness and conviction. He gave the scene its true value. In the coronation he rose to a new level, imparting to the episode its full measure of self-concentration, religious delusion and egotistic domination. His dignity of pose and action was paired with the beautiful continence of his singing. It was chiefly to the sustained level of moderate and delicately shaded utterance that the success of the scene was due. His impersonation at this point attained a beauty and dramatic force of high order, and fitted itself perfectly into the well-prepared picture and general action, all uniting in one of the most impressive moments known to the Metropolitan stage in recent years."

Martinelli's career exemplified the value to artist and his opera company of remaining with one theater for several months each season. For the Metropolitan there was the obvious advantage of having a first-class artist available for varied assignments. (Martinelli sang almost nine hundred performances of leading roles at the Met, a tenor record.) For Martinelli there was the artistic growth made possible by a secure environment, enabling a brash young tenor to mature into a remarkable singing actor.

Martinelli's final new role at the Metropolitan was Otello, in the revival of 1937. He last sang there in a 1945 *Norma* with Zinka Milanov, and his final public performance was with the Seattle Opera in a 1967 *Turandot,* an opera Gatti-Casazza would not release him to sing at the La Scala world premiere. Now, however, instead of Calaf, his role was the father of Turandot, the Emperor Altoum.

ENRICO CARUSO AND *SAMSON ET DALILA*

SINCE ITS FIRST OPENING NIGHT, OCTOber 22, 1883, the Metropolitan Opera has enticed writers into testing their descriptive power to evoke the atmosphere, the singers, the audience. The eccentric critic for the New York *Telegram,* Algernon St. John-Brenon, sharpened his account for several seasons until in November 1915, for the opening night with Caruso and Matzenauer in *Samson et Dalila,* he found its perfect expression.

"Never could a season have had a more felicitous and well favored a beginning. . . . The audience that assembled last night was a characteristic one. It is the custom of those ignorant or careless of actual conditions to talk of the opera as a 'social function,' as the luxurious resort of the idle rich, as the paradise of the moneyed Brahmin and as the preserve of our beloved American peerage. This is the ludicrous misrepresentation of irritated sansculottes. One row of boxes and one row alone is reserved for the owners of the building. The rest of the vast theatre is open to anyone and to everybody. There is no plant that is not encouraged to flower there to the richest unfolding of its blossoming. On the one floor the

Enrico Caruso as Samson, first performed by the tenor on opening night of the 1915–16 season. One of the heavier roles he began to sing during the latter part of his career, Samson required Caruso to develop his skill as an actor.

air is heavy with the exotic fragrance of gardenias. The circumambient ether just beneath it is heavy with pungent and tropic essence of garlic. And anybody and everybody was to be seen last night! The dowagers in the parterre were sparkling and beaming in all their precious gems, resplendent 'in what you wears in your "air and calls a tarrara," as the cockney waif says in a touching play. The motley and medley crew of two-dollar promenaders and strutters were enjoying their night of glory. Nearly the whole of musical New York was on view; the conductors of dreary and effete oratorios and sickly cantatas, seedy church tenors and comic opera baritones; the canaille and charlatan teacher flaunting a Sahara of white waistcoat and finding fault with the 'diaphragmatic breathing' of Amato and the spacious phrasing of Mme. Matzenauer; the decayed tenor and the dazed and raw reviewer, the envious and querulous emissaries of singers rival to those in the cast, stating on the one hand that it was M. Gatti-Casazza's well-known prejudice in favor of the Germans that had induced him

to give the prima donna part to a Teuton; or, snarling on the other hand, that it was his gross favoritism for the Italians that had led him to entrust the role of Samson to an Italian. I noticed symphonists, publishers, amateurs, pirates, plagiarists and virtuosos, recitalists and quartetteers, kammersingers from small German courts discontented with everything, men who sang the part twenty years ago satisfied with nothing, contrapuntists, table d'hotists, Greenwich Villagers, second trombones, piano salesmen, brigands, champagne agents, essayists, dress-makers and epigrammatists, philosophers and correspondents. The gaunt and Murgeresque figure of William Guard repulsed with stern resolution the united and impetuous charge of wild-eyed and magazine men, clamoring for admission, and trying to pronounce Saint-Saëns's name with dexterous ease of a glib Parisian familiarity. I heard the broken fragments of violated and distorted syllable fall crashing to the floor. . . . The grave and senatorial figure of Signor Giulio Gatti-Casazza, wrapt in a Catonic toga of austere taciturnity, broke his silence but twice. Once in response to a long hypothetical question, the answer to which would have revealed the secrets of the prison house, he replied in majestic advice with the words, 'Lo spettacolo.' This means 'the presentation.' It is the thing nearest his heart. A second time he was heard to murmur the enchanter's spell: 'Il Boxofficio.' There were $11,000 in it. Then came the sullen and sinister procession of those who had lost in the throbbing and reckless struggle for the laurels and the rewards of prosperous lyric lyfe. With black looks on their faces and sneering contempt upon their lips they trod the fantastical battlefield where they had fought and lost. They rejoiced in the weaknesses and sulked at the validities of their more fortunate successors. Not far from them were those who were nursing the ambition, for the best reasons in the world never to be satisfied, of standing in triumph before the maddening blaze of the footlights, before that sea of faces, as the human supplement of that tide and tempest of glorifying music, surging from that well of exquisitely governed sound. Poor wretches, we know them well. We see them pacing the opera night after night, their finery fading year by year, the slow and poisonous fires of treacherous and deluded hope stupefying their brains and corroding their hearts. And there is something in the world they yet might do passably well. But away with reflections on the legions of the operatic lost. It is the opening of the season, and they were the living issues of the opera who appeared last night. The house was filled shortly after 8.

"You can imagine the hum of society chatter. You can hear the buzz of operatic insects. Then the dark, dapper and familiar figure of Giorgio Polacco . . . appears, a black shadow among the rich and solemn browns of the instruments. There is a ripple of applause. . . . The lights throughout the house, all but the little fairy lamps in the boxes, are suddenly dimmed. The lower line of the stage gleams like distant fire, subdued and mysterious, forming part, in the words of Verdi, of the 'realm of illusion.' The mighty wings of the curtain fold themselves with a majestic sweep. Amid the solemn and ecclesiastic concord of lovely sounds, you find yourself amid the palms and arches of Gaza in Palestine. You have travelled far down the twilight avenue of the ages to the storied days when Samson, iron in muscle and weak in senses and given to luxurious dalliance with treacherous women, was judge in Israel."

St. John-Brenon's opening-night article also provides a convincing explanation for an overweight singer's everlasting survival: "In physical appearance Madame Matzenauer is no obvious Dalila, and the exuberant efflorescence of her figure made illusion on this score at first sight almost impossible. But the moment she opened her mouth there was another story to tell. . . . After all, the contralto is the most beautiful and affecting of human voices, so rich it is, so rare, so capable of the expression of the graver and more wistful emotions. The loveliness, the allurement, the seductiveness, the reverie, and the dream were in the glorious utterance of the singer. We cannot ask for more."

Caruso was not in his best voice for opening night, and the critics, with their well-known candor, mentioned the fact. However, all was well ten days later, as the *Tribune* reported: "Mr. Caruso was in better voice last night than at his two previous performances, which fact must relieve those faint-hearted ones who tremble at each cough the great tenor emits, fearing that the golden voice is about to depart on its last sad journey. Mr. Caruso, on the other hand, is evidently determined to show that each vocal relapse is really a rebirth. The Philistines may try to bind him with their fears, but unlike Samson he does not feel it necessary to pull down the operatic temple about their ears in order to prove his superiority." In the Metropolitan press book in which this clipping is pasted, there is a pencil scrawl over the face of the review: "It is true. Enrico Caruso."

During the last years of his career Caruso revealed depths that had not been suspected when he first came to New York in 1903. One observer reported in awe of a 1919 *Samson et Dalila* that " . . . as the opera progressed he rose to heights of vocal splendor and dramatic intensity in song and action such as even he seldom scales. It was predicted some years ago of his enactment of Samson that it would be recorded as one of the greatest impersonations of the operatic stage. It can be so recorded now. Were his voice but half of what it now is, his Samson would enthrall the hearer and the spectator as few operatic achievements have ever enthralled. He is often at his best in French operas . . . but his Samson tops them all. It ranks as high as Jean de Reszke's Roméo, Siegfried and Tristan. Caruso is now ripe for the Wagner operas. Ten years ago few believed he ever would be. If any one doubts it now, let him witness his fervid exhortations to the discouraged Hebrews; his manly efforts to resist the allurements of the temptress; his utter abandonment to despair when he realizes how he has been entrapped; his woebegone prayer for release through death when blinded, shorn of his locks, barefoot, he turns and turns the mill wheel and finally, his supplication to the God of Israel before he takes hold of the two middle pillars and in making the house collapse slays more at his death than he slew in his life. A touching detail was his kissing the boy who had taken care of him and sending him away to escape the slaughter."

ERNESTINE SCHUMANN-HEINK

LONG BEFORE WE HAD "MEDIA" IN ALL their current manifestations, there was Madame Ernestine Schumann-Heink (1861–1936), the German contralto who became a household name to most of American society. Underpinning the career was the voice itself, described thus by Henderson in 1906 after a Carnegie Hall recital: "The splendor of tone, the magnificent sweep of utterance, the broadlined declamation and the stimulating appearance of reserve power which made her singing a constant joy in days now well remembered. Added to these traits of her singing are her power to express emotion and the lofty sincerity of her art." Of significance to the American people was the way this mother of eight used that voice throughout World War I. "During the war her family was divided, some with Germany, some with America. Yet she was the darling of the cantonments here, where music-hungry doughboys thrilled as her 'Stille Nacht' and other simple pieces rushed with harp-toned wings into the air over hushed regiments. She sang to those boys as if they were all the critics in the world gathered together to render judgment."

And there was that unique personality compounded of warmth and common sense. In response to a questionnaire from *Singing* magazine on the harm or benefit of cigarettes: "I never in my life smoked so cannot proper answer your question." On the general use of tobacco: "Let everyone do as he pleases, why bother over other people's doings! By the way, tobacco leaves are the best protection against moth—of that I am sure."

In all, Schumann-Heink sang fifteen seasons with the Metropolitan Opera but after 1907 her appearances were isolated breaks in concert tours back and forth across the country. At the end there were annual radio appearances singing "Stille Nacht" and even one movie. Her many recordings for Victor illustrate the broad range of her interest and expression, everything from Mozart's "Parto, Parto" from *La Clemenza di Tito* to Root's "Just Before the Battle, Mother."

In 1926, a decade after posing with a Victrola for her Mishkin portrait, she made one of her by then rare appearances at the Metropolitan. An account by Pitts Sanborn documents a career based not on publicity or press but on solidity of achievement.

"Now she is [at the Metropolitan] on the eve of her fiftieth year as a singer. When the great Ernestine utters a tone, let the youngsters listen and ponder well the re-

Opposite: *Ernestine Schumann-Heink posed with the Victor Company's Victrola in a 1915 photograph taken for advertising.*

MISHKIN
N.Y.

lation that 'breath support' may bear to half a century of career. Yesterday her voice was thrilling in its sovereign sonority and color, her every word a sword-thrust, her authority colossal. With the first 'Weiche, Wotan, Weiche!' she tore the trammels from the years, discovering a world where high gods ruled till men grew up in stature greater than the gods. The sentences of Mother Earth she gave in plenitude of Aeschylean grandeur. It is not to be wondered at that Wotan himself heeded and obeyed."

JOHN McCORMACK

PRESUMABLY THERE WERE IRISH TENors before John McCormack (1884–1945), just as there have been pale imitations ever since. The Irish knack for lyric and narrative expression first blossomed in McCormack when at nineteen he won the gold medal in the Feis Ceoil, or National Music Festival, in 1903. (A friend of McCormack's, the writer James Joyce, won a bronze medal for his singing in the next Feis.) McCormack sang in America as part of the entertainment at the Irish Village of the 1904 St. Louis Exposition. Next he went to Italy and made his operatic debut after three months' study in Mascagni's *Amico Fritz*. The Royal Opera at Covent Garden followed and was the scene of the majority of his operatic appearances. Luisa Tetrazzini, his frequent partner there, recommended him to Oscar Hammerstein and, though ill, McCormack made his New York debut in a 1909 *Traviata* at the Manhattan Opera: "He is a pure lyric tenor, with a carefully trained voice; pure, clear, even and flexible, and naturally placed. His tones are always true and sympathetic, and his mezza voce was most effective. At the outset, in addition to his apparent physical suffering, he was palpably nervous, but Madame Tetrazzini came to his rescue by crossing the stage and giving him a gentle pat of encouragement."

Never at home onstage, McCormack had an operatic repertoire ranging from the totally inappropriate Turiddu in *Cavalleria Rusticana* to Faust in Boito's *Mefistofele,* which he sang at Covent Garden in 1914 with both Rosa Raisa and Claudia Muzio in the cast. His one indelible operatic impersonation, solely for its vocalism, was Don Ottavio in Mozart's *Don Giovanni:* "His command of breath, his fine legato, and pure quality of voice" were noted in a series of 1913 Boston Opera performances and documented in the Victor recording of "Il mio tesoro" from the same period. It has remained an unattainable ideal for succeeding tenors. The other extreme of his operatic experience must have been Lieutenant Paul Merrill in Victor Herbert's *Natoma,* a new opera performed in 1911 by the Chicago Opera with Mary Garden as an

John McCormack in a portrait taken in New York around 1916; most of his opera portraits are from the earlier years of his career.

Indian maid: "Mr. McCormack was almost equal to the demands of his role, but not quite, for bad as the role was he was even worse."

McCormack had cracked on a high note when he auditioned for Gatti-Casazza at La Scala and sang only six performances under Gatti at the Metropolitan. Although he lacked the swelling stentorian effects customary to the Puccini roles he sang there in 1917–18, there were redeeming qualities in *La Bohème:* ". . . what Mr. McCormack contributed here, and later in the opera, was much beautiful singing, of its kind unsurpassable in quality of tone, in purity of diction, in finish of phrase, and in most of the subtler graces of the art that are not always the first to be recognized."

Soon he abandoned the opera house for good. McCormack in the concert hall was another story, a master unsurpassed in the history of song. The years 1910 to 1930 were the heyday of concert activity in America; McCormack was the greatest attraction. He could sell out the small-town auditorium. In New York and Boston he could fill the largest halls ten times a season with audiences that acted as though they would never have another chance to hear him. Each audience received a carefully balanced program in which "something for everyone" found its finest expression. As a teller of tales, imparter of confidences, McCormack found material in the popular Irish ballads to enrapture not only his countrymen but the most sophisticated of audiences anywhere. Those who came for the Irish songs were treated to Bach, Handel, and Mozart, which no one had thought to sing for them. His recordings, spanning the period between 1904 and 1942, rivaled those of Caruso in popularity and captured the full range of his repertoire.

Mishkin's 1913 portrait of Margarete Ober in her debut role, Ortrud in Lohengrin, *made before she tore up all his photographs.*

MARGARETE OBER

WORLD WAR I MIGHT HAVE DEstroyed a weaker person than the German mezzosoprano Margarete Ober (1885–1971). An all-round singer with something of Margarete Matzenauer's usefulness in Verdi and Wagner, Ober cast a narrow enough shadow to sing Octavian in *Der Rosenkavalier,* as well as Eglantine in Toscanini's revival of *Euryanthe* and, in English, the Wife of Bath in Reginald de Koven's *Canterbury Pilgrims.* Her 1913 Met debut was as Ortrud in *Lohengrin* with Olive Fremstad and Jacques Urlus. *The New York Times* reported on her quick success as "a singer of uncommon excellence and unusual dramatic gifts. She is young; her voice has the freshness and strength of youth, and she poured it forth lavishly last evening. She has the power of coloring it with vividness and intensity. It is, in fact, a voice of remarkable dramatic quality, a true and immediate reflex of her own quality as an actress, in which her gifts and accomplishments are exceptional. Her Ortrud was an impersonation of hateful malevolence in conception, skillfully expressed with manifold and significant detail of gesture, pose and facial expression. . . . Her invocation to the heathen gods in the first scene of the second act was a passage of surpassing power and eloquence and called forth a burst of applause from an audience that does not habitually so interrupt the progress of a Wagnerian opera."

Ober had been engaged specifically for Octavian in *Rosenkavalier* and was a vital participant in its American premiere two weeks after her debut. Although a procession of Sophies passed, and even Frieda Hempel as the Marschallin was replaced a few times by Melanie Kurt, Ober sang every Metropolitan *Rosenkavalier* until war halted all German performances.

In 1916 the events in Europe began to catch up with her. A New York *Tribune* headline read GERMAN SHE SEVERS PHOTOGRAPH RELATION, with the following article: "Mme. Ober, Opera Singer, Tears Up Pictures Made by

Russian. Mme. Margarete Ober, Metropolitan Opera contralto, is a German, born and bred. Herman Mishkin, photographer, of 467 Fifth Avenue, is a Russian. 'Sole and exclusive photographer for Mme. Ober' has long been one of the prize ads on Mishkin's shingle. Then the war came, and with it wrath. Wrath, last week, became rage, and with her own hands the opera star tore to bits every picture of her that Mishkin had ever taken. Now a new picture hangs in the display window of Adolph Bauman, photographer, of Fifth Avenue. Bauman is of the Fatherland. 'Will the madame sing any more in the Russian opera *Boris Godunov?*' is the question that is now perplexing managers of the Metropolitan. Yes, they think she will, for in *Boris Godunov* she sings the part of a Polish princess, and is not Poland Germany's now?"

In the Spring of 1917 Ober was singing the evening that President Wilson sent his war message to Congress. The entire cast assembled onstage to sing "The Star-Spangled Banner" and Ober fainted in full view of the audience. She had recovered three nights later when, during Act IV of *Aida,* as Amneris casts a curse upon Ramfis and the other priests, Ober turned and clearly directed it to the audience. That fall the Metropolitan canceled the fifth year of her original contract. She sued, lost, and was not able to return to Germany until after the war. Ober survived and returned to the Berlin Opera, where between 1906 and 1944 she sang every season aside from the war years. Character roles were mixed with leading mezzo parts, including Kostelnička in the first Berlin *Jenůfa.* When a second world war caught up with her, she was still effectively singing the Witch in *Hänsel und Gretel* with Erna Berger.

MELANIE KURT

THE STORY GOES THAT AT A 1914 DINner party, Gatti-Casazza, asked how he was going to replace Olive Fremstad, poured out salt on the tablecloth and with his finger spelled out the letters K U R T. This was Melanie Kurt (1880–1941), the German soprano with whom he had signed a contract, perhaps anticipating problems with Fremstad, back in June of 1912. Kurt's musical life began as a concert pianist who studied with Theodor Leschetizky, the teacher of Ignace Jan Paderewski and Artur Schnabel. During the transition to singer she worked with Marie and Lilli Lehmann in Berlin and apparently accompanied Geraldine Farrar at some of her lessons. Her 1915 New York debut in *Tristan und Isolde* came at a time when a company could lose an important Isolde and replace her with another. Describing her voice, Richard Aldrich reported: "It is a veritable soprano, of a truly beautiful quality, of great power,

Melanie Kurt gowned as Brünnhilde in Götterdämmerung, *one of several roles in which she replaced Olive Fremstad.*

ranging upward to a point where she took the highest tones of the part with certainty, without effort, without trepidation. Her intonation is of unusual accuracy. One of the delightful features of her art as she disclosed it in *Tristan* last night was the clearness of her diction and the excellence of her declamation, which she has the subtle skill to fuse with a true cantabile style of singing and with a fine feeling for the molding of the phrase and a command of dramatic accent and poignant expression." Kurt sang Fremstad's roles as well as Fidelio, the Marschallin, and the only performances of Gluck's *Iphigenia auf Tauris* at the Metropolitan. After war caused the cancellation of her contract, she never sang in America again. Fleeing another war, she returned to New York in 1939 and taught until her death two years later.

ELISABETH SCHUMANN

THE WHITE STAR LINER *CANOPIC* reached New York Harbor in early November 1914, from Naples via Boston, and unloaded its riches: Gatti-Casazza, Lucrezia Bori, Enrico Caruso, Geraldine Farrar, Pasquale Amato, Emmy Destinn, Adamo Didur, Jacques Urlus, Toscanini, and seventy-five members of the Metropolitan's Italian chorus.

One day while still at sea a young soprano bound for the Met, Elisabeth Schumann (1885–1952), suddenly found herself face to face with the great Frieda Hempel. "Well, *meine Kleine,* what will you be singing with us?" asked the Diva. "I'm making my debut as Sophie to your Marschallin, *Frau Kammersängerin,*" said Schumann, ingratiatingly, "and then I'll sing Musetta, Gretel, the *Fidelio* Marzelline, a Rhinemaiden, Papagena, and Mr. Gatti told me also to study Oscar in *Ballo.*" "I wouldn't bother," shot back Hempel. "*I* am Oscar at the Metropolitan." As she forecast, Hempel continued to appropriate the role for herself; Schumann sang all the roles in her contract except Oscar.

Debuting as Sophie in the 1914–15 *Rosenkavalier,* Schumann was the only new cast member in the popular opera that had been unveiled the season before. "As anyone who heard Miss Case in *Der Rosenkavalier* must know, the role of Sophie is vocally exceedingly exacting. For Mme. Schumann, however, the difficulties had apparently no terrors. With remarkable ease she coped with Strauss's long-sustained phrases, spinning out her sweetly appealing and expressive tones, even in the loftiest altitudes, in a way that could well have served as an object lesson for students of singing. Mme. Schumann's lyric soprano is not large. But it is admirably placed, finely concentrated and supported by an excellent control of breath. At no time last night did the singer force her voice and not once did she wander from

A very young Elisabeth Schumann as Gretel, among ten roles she sang successfully during her one Metropolitan season.

the correct pitch. In the duets of the second act with Octavian, one almost resented the interference of Margarete Ober. . . . Schumann's presence in the cast accounted in large part for a marked improvement in the performance of Strauss's opera. Certainly her singing in the final terzet added a great deal to the effectiveness of that beautiful episode."

Schumann's first Musetta anywhere followed the next afternoon: "Her artistic sincerity, her simplicity, her freedom from all affectation and exaggeration, were decidedly refreshing and her singing at all times gave unalloyed delight." Schumann left after one season that included a privately organized *Fledermaus* at the Metropolitan in May 1915 featuring most of the company's German stars. Most significant for her future was a Sunday-night concert she appeared at in February. Her three Brahms songs "disclosed the surprising fact, that unlike most opera singers, the German soprano understands the art of interpreting lieder."

It was as a recitalist that she returned to America in

Spanish bass Andrés de Segurola attired in Colline's greatcoat in La Bohème, *the opera in which Caruso sang the Act IV bass aria when De Segurola lost his voice.*

the 1920s with Richard Strauss as her accompanist. The most intriguing concert on their tour was one in which he forgot the piano part of one of his own songs and improvised a completely new song while Schumann bravely continued with the vocal line. She is now recalled as a distinguished singer of German lieder who in middle age retained the charm and girlishness that had enabled Hempel to overwhelm her. If her one obscure Metropolitan season is remembered, it is because her radiant Sophie in the *Rosenkavalier* excerpts with Lotte Lehmann and Maria Olszewska became a classic of recording history.

ANDRÉS DE SEGUROLA

SPANISH BASS ANDRÉS DE SEGUROLA (1875–1953) was not a particularly outstanding singer but a skillful actor who is best known for having discovered and taught Deanna Durbin. At the Met for twelve seasons and with Hammerstein for two, he usually sang character roles, with Varlaam in the American premiere of *Boris Godunov* the most noteworthy: "The best acting of the evening was that of Segurola as the bibulous Varlaam, who went to sleep with his arms around a demijohn and woke to find himself arrested and about to be hanged. It was an excellent genre picture that he gave, and his disguise was so complete that he was unrecognizable save for his voice and his art." His most frequent characterization, Colline in *La Bohème,* is now remembered chiefly for the 1916 performance in Philadelphia during which De Segurola lost his voice completely in the last act and persuaded Caruso, with his back to the audience, to sing the bass aria "Vecchia zimarra" for him.

PASQUALE AMATO

FOR A FEW INTENSE YEARS PASQUALE Amato (1878–1942) was the leading Italian baritone in America. He missed Gatti's opening-night *Aida* in 1908 because of a late sailing, but thereafter he figured in a significant number of first nights at the Metropolitan. He made his debut that November as Germont in *Traviata,* with Marcella Sembrich as Violetta, and "won for himself immediate welcome as a singer of good ability. He has a firm, fresh, sonorous voice of good quality and he sang last night with excellent tone production and taste in style. Mr. Bonci, who was to have been Alfredo, was indisposed, and his place was amiably taken by Mr. Caruso, who, needless to say, was a most acceptable substitute."

Amato sang Jack Rance in the world premiere of Puccini's *Fanciulla del West* in 1910, had the title roles in Damrosch's *Cyrano de Bergerac* and Borodin's *Prince Igor,* and was Napoleon in Giordano's *Madame Sans-Gêne.* Aided by a German-speaking wife and experience in Germany before singing at La Scala, Amato appeared in German-language performances of *Tristan* and *Parsifal* and was soloist in Wagner concerts under Mahler.

Amato's vocal gifts were lavish and he distributed them prodigally. In his first four seasons at the Met he averaged more than sixty performances a season, often appearing four or five times a week. As popular with press and public as with the management, Amato was described in 1910 by that most stringent of vocal critics, W. J. Henderson, as the most gifted of operatic baritones "as far as voice and physique are concerned. He has a natural organ of uncommon beauty, rich, sonorous, well

Opposite: *Mishkin's portrait of Pasquale Amato as Scarpia in* Tosca *has frequently been misidentified as Antonio Scotti.*

C
MISHKIN
N.Y.

equalized and of a peculiarly winning character. His range carries up to the high A flat, a tone practically not required in the occupations of a baritone. His voice production is thoroughly good, though he not infrequently yields to the temptation to 'split the ears of groundlings'. He phrases well, treats melodies with regard for their musical character, and shades with skill. He can sing softly with well-governed mechanism and with charm."

In a 1911 guest appearance with the Boston Opera in *Il Trovatore* he drew from H. T. Parker an evocative description: "Mr. Amato apparelled the baleful count romantically, struck romantic attitudes, made big gestures at big moments and rolled out his music in the biggest, smoothest, the surest of baritone voices that our stage knows. His singing was magnificent in its freedom of flooding tone, the mere vocal power and richness of it made an emotion in themselves. With such a voice and in such music the singer may be as big-toned as he can and will, and as everyone knows the more baleful does the count become in his wicked heart, the more mellifluous is his malevolence."

From New York comes a 1912 description of the "profound and elaborate unction with which he acknowledged the numerous summonses before the curtain, singly and with his fellow artists. He comes into the presence of his audience with an obeisance that would become a courtier entering the presence of royalty; yet all the while there is a subtle smile playing about his lips, as one who knows he is master though he chooses to appear the servant."

Then something happened that probably marked the beginning of Amato's decline. In November 1912, the Philadelphia-Chicago Opera visited New York and performed *Hamlet* with Titta Ruffo at the Metropolitan Opera House. It was not in Amato to ignore the vast acclaim Ruffo's huge voice received. The following evening the Met performed *Pagliacci* to great enthusiasm as Amato attempted to rival Ruffo. The critics took note: "In the prologue he demonstrated that long phrasing and high tones do not have to be imported from Philadelphia," wrote the *Sun*. "With Ruffo's singing of the night before to rouse him Mr. Amato declaimed the prologue with unusual vigor, prolonging some of his tones as if to show that he is the equal of the phenomenal baritone." The oversinging that had been a small mannerism in a strong technique now became a way of life. By 1918–19 the vocal crisis which he later blamed on a kidney ailment had reached its peak. Both audiences and critics had noticed it; that most perceptive of critics, the Victor Company, had stopped recording his voice. Amato, his voice irreparably strained, took a season's leave of absence to recover. (During his absence another baritone, Luigi Montesanto, later the teacher of Giuseppe di Stefano, was brought in to sing Michele in *Tabarro* at the world premiere of Puccini's *Trittico*.) Amato rested, sang in Havana, and then returned to the Met for a season that included Leoncavallo's *Zazà* with Geraldine Farrar. But when his contract with the Met expired in 1921, Gatti did not renew it.

Thereafter Amato was relegated mostly to small companies in the United States and occasional performances in Europe.

In 1926 Gatti and Otto Kahn helped Amato and his wife to emigrate from Italy but did not reengage him. He celebrated the twenty-fifth anniversary of his Metropolitan debut in a popularly priced *Traviata* at New York's huge Hippodrome theater. The cast at his debut had included Caruso and Marcella Sembrich; now, in 1933, he sang with unknowns before an audience that bought tickets for twenty-five and fifty cents. The same season he returned briefly to the Met for Gatti's own twenty-fifth-anniversary performance and led the ensemble in the final fugue from *Falstaff*. With a last *Tosca* at the Hippodrome in 1934, his operatic career ended. He headed the opera department of Louisiana State University in Baton Rouge until his death.

ANNA FITZIU

ANNA FITZIU (1888–1967) CAME TO OPERA from a well-to-do Virginia family that had encouraged her in the theater. After singing in vaudeville with the Powell Sisters Quartet (two of the sisters got married and Anna was left on her own), she appeared in musical comedies called *The Wizard of Oz, Baroness Fiddlesticks,* and *Lower Berth 13* in Chicago and New York. She seems never to have wanted for money: when she reached the age of eighteen an uncle gave her $100,000, of which she spent $17,000 on a birthday party for the cast of *Oz* in Chicago. She married a wealthy Canadian doctor who did not accompany her abroad for her conversion to opera. In Italy, Tito Ricordi, the famous publisher of Puccini, became her patron, arranging a 1912 operatic debut as Elsa in *Lohengrin* in Rimini.

Returning to America with operatic experience and a new name (the Italians couldn't pronounce Fitzhugh), she fell into the world premiere of Enrique Granados's *Goyescas*. This dramatization of a series of piano pieces inspired by Goya had been planned for the Paris Opéra in 1914 but was postponed by the war. Snapped up by Gatti, it was an obvious vehicle for the Met's charming Spanish soprano Lucrezia Bori. In the fall of 1915, however, Bori was in the first stages of vocal problems that would prevent her from singing at all until 1919. Probably at Ricordi's suggestion, Gatti gave the score of *Goyescas* to Fitziu and signed her to a contract only a month before the premiere. It was a success for both Fitziu and Granados, but not a lasting one. Of Fitziu, it was noted that no more beautiful figure ever stepped on the Metropolitan stage. "Miss Fitziu also has a voice, a powerful

The former Broadway showgirl Anna Fitziu as Rosario in the world premiere of Granados's Goyescas, *her only role at the Metropolitan Opera.*

organ, of good timbre, at times a little hard perhaps, but in the main of pleasing quality." Granados, who had been praised for "this full blooded, passionate utterance," gave recitals in New York (one with Pablo Casals and another with Fitziu) and made piano rolls for the Aeolian Company. Fatefully he canceled his return passage on a French steamer in order to play for President Wilson at the White House (a recital with Julia Culp), and returned instead with his wife on the *Sussex.* The boat was torpedoed by the Germans in the English Channel; Granados and his wife were last seen clinging together on a small raft. His American fees, which Granados had insisted be paid in gold, were sewn into his clothing and disappeared with them. Ironically, the opera *Goyescas* rarely appears in the repertoire of any opera house; the piano works remain classics.

Fitziu sang in Cuba and Mexico and for several seasons with the Chicago Opera. There her repertoire included *Tosca, La Bohème,* Henry Hadley's *Azora,* the American premiere of Catalani's *Loreley,* and Mascagni's *Isabeau,* in which she rode adroitly through the city streets as Lady Godiva. In 1919 her husband, whom she was suing for divorce, died and left her a fortune. During the early twenties she sang mostly with the touring San Carlo Opera in productions she is said to have subsidized. In the San Carlo *Tosca,* it was noted that nobody else in the part had spent so much for clothes in the second act. In 1922, while on tour in New York shortly after Maria Jeritza had made a sensation performing part of the second act of *Tosca* on the floor, Fitziu was observed singing "Vissi d'arte" flat on her back. Vaudeville followed again in 1926, and Fitziu spent the remainder of her career teaching, sometimes not charging poor students.

MARIA BARRIENTOS

AROUND THE TURN OF THE CENTURY a flock of teenage Spanish coloratura sopranos was propelled onto the world's stages. There were Maria Galvany, famous for her staccati and brilliant recordings with Titta Ruffo; Giuseppina Huguet, who recorded *Pagliacci* under Leoncavallo; and Graziella Pareto, a graceful singer admired by Sir Thomas Beecham. Elvira de Hidalgo, who toured with Chaliapin and later taught Maria Callas in Athens, was so caught up in the phenomenon of youth that although she was eighteen when she debuted at the Met in 1909, she was only twenty-two when she sang in Paris some fourteen years later.

Maria Barrientos (1883–1946) outdid them all. A year after her Barcelona debut, her mother positioned herself in the lobby of a Milan opera house and exhibited a birth certificate proving that Maria, who was singing Lakmé inside, was only fifteen. Barrientos might have reached the Metropolitan sooner but Gatti, always romantically interested in one of his performers, turned his attention from her to Frances Alda. Hammerstein hired her for his 1914 season that didn't take place, and Gatti got around to her the next year. Lucia was her debut role (although she had requested Amina in *La Sonnambula*), and when she sang it on tour in Boston, H. T. Parker described both sound and manner. "Her voice is exceedingly light in body, exceedingly soft in timbre and exceedingly sensitive to the slightest compulsion the singer or the music may lay upon it. Does she stress it ever so little in her uppermost tones, and they become thin and piercing; does she for ever so little in the middle range and it turns appreciably reedy and 'white.' Touched, however, with the fingertips of the singer's skill and taste (which are delicate, deft and true) and skimming, as it were, the surface of lyric song, it is an exquisite voice to hear—all pellucid flow, gentle lustres and shimmering undulations. . . . To the eye, Mme. Barrientos is as quietly graceful. She is tall, slight, comely in the dark, finely chiselled Latin fashion, past her first youth but

Maria Barrientos as Lucia di Lammermoor, photographed for her 1916 Met debut in the role.

Edith Mason, here as Sophie in the 1915–16 performances of Der Rosenkavalier, *reached the Met three years after her debut.*

still untouched by dulling and thickening middle age. She carries herself with equal grace and gravity. . . . Her costumes, for the most part 'arrangements' in black and white, actually suggested the character. Her gesture was sparing but not always conventional."

In 1916 Barrientos rehearsed *Les Pêcheurs de Perles* with Caruso, but when it was performed the next season Frieda Hempel was the Leila. She was featured in *Il Barbiere di Siviglia, Rigoletto, L'Elisir d'Amore, Le Coq d'Or, Mireille,* and *I Puritani,* but the reviewers did not always take her repertoire seriously. (One reviewer complimented her in *La Sonnambula* for resisting the temptation to copy the recent Havana performance of another prima donna who, under the influence of some latter-day Svengali, had sung the opera in an actual state of somnambulism duly certified by four doctors of medicine.)

Barrientos left the Metropolitan in 1920, having endured the enormous attention given to Galli-Curci and turned increasingly to recitals. Although performing on a smaller scale, she had prestigious associates, Manuel de

Falla accompanying her in the first recording of his *Siete Canciones Populares Españolas,* and the distinguished harpsichordist Wanda Landowska collaborating on concerts in Paris and Barcelona.

EDITH MASON

WHEN ELISABETH SCHUMANN LEFT THE Metropolitan after one season, Gatti found as a replacement a young American soprano whom the war had sent back across the Atlantic. Edith Mason (1893–1973) had made her operatic debut at nineteen while still a student at the New England Conservatory of Music when she substituted at the last moment for an ailing soprano as Nedda with the Boston Opera. Leaving after two seasons and a handful of performances, Mason continued her studies in Paris with the French lyric tenor Edmond Clément, whose artistry had impressed her in the Boston company. Her 1915 Met debut role was Sophie in *Der Rosenkavalier,* and for two seasons she was its only exponent. Mason was a hit with her first audience, although one critic felt she lingered unbecomingly before the curtain. Others had no complaints: "She is pretty and her manner is gracious, and in addition to these she has the charm of youth. Her voice is fresh and high, scaling the dizzy peaks of the difficult role without any sign of stress." The next year Aldrich in the *Times* hailed her: "This part of Sophie is a killing one in the demands it makes upon a soprano voice of the lightness and timbre suitable for its expression, and the disastrous results upon the delicate art of Miss Anna Case, who was the first representative of Sophie in this performance, will be remembered. Miss Mason is the most successful of the representatives of the part, and she realizes what can be made of it, in a charmingly demure impersonation." She appeared eighty-seven times in two seasons, at a salary progressing from $100 to $150 a week, her repertoire ranging from a Flower Maiden in *Parsifal* to Gretel, Micaëla, Musetta, and the Forest Bird in *Siegfried.* Mason then begged Gatti to be released from her contract; she was in the middle of an autumn 1917 season in Mexico City and wired for a cancellation so that she might continue a tour that reached Central America, Cuba, and Puerto Rico and gave her an opportunity to sing more important roles in *Gli Ugonotti, L'Africana,* and *Faust.* Gatti was then in the process of canceling all contracts relating to German opera and probably was glad to be free of the obligation.

In the [illegible] she found her gifts better appreciated in a Chicago debut at the Ravinia Op[illegible] Nedda. "Miss Mason's arrival among us is a cause for rejoicing. Beauty of physique and countenance, a voice of smooth, velvety, luscious, fresh quality, used with consummate artistry. Silver-pure in the upper register and warm in the medium, stage assurance, intelligence and perfect diction are a few of the reasons why Chicago is happy to welcome this charming artist." Chicago, in fact, extended a permanent welcome to Mason. Although she appeared with great success at the Opéra and Opéra-Comique in Paris, sang with Toscanini at La Scala and the Salzburg Festival, and appeared with less impact at Covent Garden and at the Metropolitan in the thirties, Chicago was her artistic home. Her Ravinia performances (including a *Thaïs* at which a reviewer taking a swipe at Mary Garden said, "At last we heard *Thaïs* actually sung. The music was sung—not shouted, or panted, or spoken, not bluffed through—but sung") were followed by the Chicago Opera in 1921–22 where her second (and later, fourth) husband, Giorgio Polacco, was chief conductor. Mason sang with the Chicago company for sixteen seasons, and in everything from *Snegourotchka* to *Mefistofele* and *Iris* there are frequent references to the silvery tone. She returned for a solitary Mimi in 1941 so that her fifth husband might hear her in the role.

GIUSEPPE DE LUCA

ALTHOUGH HE LACKED THE BURLY vocal strength of Pasquale Amato and Titta Ruffo or the histrionic command of Antonio Scotti, Giuseppe De Luca (1876–1950) devoted a lifetime to the cultivation of an elegant baritone voice which rewarded him with more than fifty years of service. One of the earliest Caruso photographs shows him with De Luca in 1898 in *I Pescatori di Perli;* at the time both men had been singing opera for a mere three years. They would renew their partnership at the Metropolitan in 1915. In the meantime De Luca sang at La Scala and Covent Garden, in South America and Russia, and began his important operatic creations with the world premieres of Cilèa's *Adriana Lecouvreur* and Giordano's *Siberia.* De Luca was Sharpless in the memorable premiere of *Madama Butterfly* at La Scala in 1904, when organized opposition to Puccini turned the first night into a historic fiasco. Generally De Luca's career was long, rewarding, and without incident. At his 1915 Met debut as Figaro in a *Barbiere* with Hempel and Didur, he "won the audience with a single aria, his 'Largo al factotum.' . . . He has the most agile baritone voice heard at the opera house in many years. It is beautiful in quality. The [illegible] full and round, the upper tones of almost tenor-like clarity. His breath control is marvelous, for he sang the swirling aria at a tempo that took his hearers' breath, but left his own intact."

Of fifty-two roles in twenty-two seasons, De Luca

C
MISHKIN
N.Y.

Giuseppe De Luca as Rigoletto, from an extensive series of photographs taken by Mishkin before the Italian baritone's first Metropolitan Opera performances of the role in 1916. De Luca was able to take command of the part through subtlety of voice and movement.

dominated three of the most important, Figaro in *Barbiere,* Rigoletto, and Germont in *Traviata.* His first New York *Rigoletto,* with Caruso making one of his increasingly rare appearances as the Duke, was hailed as a masterpiece. "His acting is charged with just the right shade of the melodramatic to make the plot of the familiar opera ring true and hold the audience's interest. His facial expression mirrored at first the cynical mockery, then the tragedy of the part. His singing was superb in its quality of tone, in phrasing, wonderful breath control and dramatic import." In an interesting glimpse of contemporary performance practices, the *Evening Sun* spoke of "a restored duet between the new Barrientos and De Luca. Following the tenor's last 'Donna è mobile,' the curtain didn't fall. Prima donna and baritone instead sang a proper adieu to a world of folly, set to waltz time, it's true, but strangely prophetic of the great Verdi of the Nile scene in *Aida.* The episode was worth waiting for and it ended with two-thirds of the boxholders still there."

In his extraordinary record of "firsts" De Luca sang the world premieres of *Goyescas* and *Gianni Schicchi,* and his Metropolitan premieres included *La Forza del Destino, Eugene Onegin, Così fan tutte, Luisa Miller,* and *Don Carlo.* As Posa in *Don Carlo,* he was said to provide "the most distinguished singing of the day. And in the duo which this grandee has with his king Mr. De Luca measured with Chaliapin, line for line, eyelash for eyelash, and helped turn it into a most remarkably subtle yet dramatic affair."

De Luca left the Metropolitan in 1935 after twenty seasons but returned again in the spring of 1940 for a memorable series of performances at the age of sixty-three. The war years were spent in Italy without performances. "For five years," he said, "I was playing cards with a friend. I refused to sing because I was not in a good humor."

In 1946 at the age of sixty-nine he sang again at the Met and in concert. Irving Kolodin described in the *Sun* what remained: "A life well and continently spent in the nurturing of the gift within him has left De Luca with more than enough mellow, pliant tone to discourse the humors and the sorrows of his many years. There were some who considered the amount of voice he had to work with a small part of its original splendor, but they remember incorrectly. It was never a voice distinguished by size, rather by quality and the deftness with which it was used. As he worked over it, and the richness began to glow, like an iron heated over a slow flame, the colors returned; and the deftness of its use was, if anything, greater than in the past." Near the end he "completely charmed his listeners with a little flourish in the middle of a legato phrase in Montana's 'Dolce Madonna' which reminded us that the good school in which he was reared seems to have closed its doors forever."

CLAUDIA MUZIO

THE RETURN OF CLAUDIA MUZIO (1889–1936) to New York and the Metropolitan Opera in December 1916 was a triumphant homecoming for the Carlo Muzio family. "The baggage master of the company, who is wont to meet the most famous operatic stars of the world at the steamship piers and be interested only in the trunks and boxes they bring with them, took the trouble to greet her, and show his pleasure over her arrival before he paid any attention to her luggage at all. . . . The baggage master, known as 'Frank' to several generations of opera singers, was like all the other old employees at the Metropolitan. To them the new prima donna . . . was the little girl they had seen lingering about the house while her father, one of the assistant stage directors, was rehearsing the company, or when she had come there with her mother, who was a singer in the chorus."

Carlo Muzio was returning to the Met after years with Hammerstein's Manhattan Opera, Covent Garden, and small theaters in Europe; the Met had paid the Geneva Opera House to obtain his release so that both parents might accompany their daughter. In a career only six years old, Claudia Muzio had stridden to the forefront of Italian sopranos with appearances in Milan, London, and Havana. Her starting salary was to be $3,000 a month; in the same theater her father's peak had been $20 a week. Originally scheduled for the Metropolitan in November 1917, Claudia Muzio's arrival had been hastily advanced a season because of Bori's continuing vocal crisis, the failure of her substitute, and Destinn's stay in Europe with Dinh Gilly.

As a child she had watched Scotti's Scarpia from the wings. Now, the first Italian to sing Tosca regularly at the Metropolitan, Muzio was a tremendous success with the public, only partly so with the press. From the beginning it was clear that she resembled no one else: "She has beautiful speaking eyes, mobile, expressive features, and generally knows how to suit her gestures to her words. Better than any Tosca ever seen here, she succeeded with face and hands in expressing her loathing of the villainous Scarpia." Her voice was considered "warm and sympathetic in quality, responsive in emotional impulse, ample in volume and much more pow-

Opposite: *Claudia Muzio in Act I of* Tosca, *in which she made her 1916 Metropolitan debut with Caruso and Scotti, two idols of her childhood.*

erful in appeal because of its timbre." Her acting was generally preferred to her singing, and while the extraordinary carrying power of her pianissimi was noted, in a prophetic way a negative review brings us closer to what became the essence of Muzio: "She was always willing to sacrifice vocal display to the need of coloring a phrase to suit the dramatic intention of the moment." As a child in London, Muzio had reacted angrily to a visitor who had praised her beauty—she didn't want to be beautiful, she wanted to be like Melba. But the eloquence of her diction, her way of coloring tones for emotional effect, took her on a path diametrically opposed to that of Melba's pure vocalism.

An interview with Muzio soon after her debut indirectly gives us our only account of a photo session in Mishkin's Fifth Avenue studio.

"Miss Muzio was entirely too busy to be interviewed on last Thursday—that is, in the regular way. Between periods of study and rehearsals, according to appointment, she was to use her luncheon hour in a photograph studio having her striking characterization of Floria Tosca photographed for William Guard's cabinet in the press room of the Metropolitan to satisfy the demands of the newspapers for her likeness. When found, she had acted the first act of *Tosca* for the photographer and had donned a startling violet gown used in the second act. She had been seated comfortably on a sofa and asked to pose according to his directions. . . . 'But this doesn't mean anything,' she said, 'I'll just smile and you can get me this way. Then we'll begin in earnest.' After that she took things in her own hands.

"Back to the camera, stealthily, impressively, she walked slowly across the room with all the grace and dignity of the proverbial queen toward a table on which [lay] a dagger, the very dagger with which she had stabbed Antonio Scotti, as Scarpia, in the opera. She reached the table, seized the dagger, and turned toward the camera a face filled with anguish but revealing in some strange way the determination to kill.

"'Snap me quick,' she whispered between her teeth. 'I can't hold the pose long. I must feel it or it is lost.' The picture was taken, and Miss Muzio, who for the moment had forgotten herself in the acting before the camera, came back to life, so to speak."

For five of her six seasons Muzio's popularity steadily grew. Enviable assignments became hers: Giorgetta in the world premiere of *Il Tabarro,* Tatiana in the first American *Eugene Onegin,* and Maddalena in the first Metropolitan *Andrea Chénier.* She became Caruso's most frequent partner; in *Pagliacci* they were said to be "like

c
MISHKIN
N.Y. 9

flint and steel together." Still, she maintained second place to Geraldine Farrar in salary and choice of role. One reviewer used *Trovatore* (not a Farrar opera) to compare the two: "as a dramatic soprano she differs from Farrar in her lack of artifice, her very real fervor. She has grown much the past year in histrionic value, putting her strength into her impersonation rather than her clothes. . . . While her voice is not the sweetest in the world, it followed exactly the color of her moods. A certain wild splendor marked her feverish grief in the Tower climax [the Miserere]."

Then, following months in South America, she returned to New York for her sixth season in January 1922 to find a new world around her. Caruso was gone; Farrar was about to leave but Maria Jeritza had taken over the previous November. Gatti explained the situation to Angelo Scandiani of La Scala: "As for Muzio, I don't believe I'll rehire her. In any case, I'll be able to cable my decision within two or three weeks. This artist, who in the past was good-natured and obliging, as well as in command of a varied repertoire, has partly lost her head for two reasons: first, her success in Buenos Aires and Mexico went to her head. . . . Second, because the skyrocketing, absolute, indisputable triumph of Jeritza (which triumph several of our artists staunchly and falsely attribute to German propaganda) has put her in an inferior position she cannot bear.

"Consequently, tantrums, whims, long faces, rebellious attitudes worthy of a prima donna of forty years ago. All trivia I absolutely can't tolerate, I, who have always demanded on principle that the artist be, first of all disciplined and obliging, then, if possible, capable."

Thereafter Muzio alternated between the Chicago company, where she became an enormous favorite although usually in second place to Rosa Raisa, and South America, then, eventually, Rome. For 1933–34 there was a reconciliation with Gatti-Casazza and three now legendary performances that included her Violetta. Suffering from heartbreak and failing health, she died in Rome at the age of forty-six, almost certainly by her own hand. Oblivion might have followed, but because of her recordings, especially a series made late in life and underwritten by her, Muzio's posthumous fame has triumphed over all her antagonists and rivals.

AMELITA GALLI-CURCI

DURING NOVEMBER 1916 OPERATIC New York was shaken by news from Chicago of a sensational young soprano who had just conquered the city with one matinee performance of Gilda in *Rigoletto*. Inquiry revealed that Amelita Galli-Curci (1882–1963)

In Act II of Tosca, *Muzio contemplates the choice forced on her by Scarpia, discovers the knife on the table, and, after the murder, withdraws from the room in anguish.*

was an Italian singer whose ten years of performances in Italy and South America had brought her only an indifferent reputation, and that Chicago had signed her too late for her name to appear in the season's prospectus and given her only trial performances. The Chicago sensation created for Gatti-Casazza the greatest embarrassment of his professional career. Here is his May 1917 explanation to Otto Kahn: "Last year during the winter I received a letter from Cuba from the husband of Mme. Galli-Curci, in which he asked me if there would be a possibility of an engagement for Mme. Galli-Curci for the season just finished. As I was perfectly informed that Galli-Curci was not successful in Cuba and that a few months before in Buenos Aires she was a failure, I replied that owing to the fact that Mme. Hempel and Mme. Barrientos were engaged for the following season there was no position for her. This is all! Since then I never heard anymore from Mme. Galli-Curci and no one else approached me, neither directly nor indirectly, regarding this artist. . . . As to Caruso, the latter has declared to me that he considers her a mere mediocrity." (Caruso's resentment toward Galli-Curci may have dated to their 1915 *Lucias* in Buenos Aires, when she had become the center of attention with her rescue of a rehearsal by dazzlingly taking over and reading from an orchestral score for a missing coach-pianist.) The one group not taken by surprise by the Galli-Curci success was the Victor Talking Machine Company, whose test sessions in October had resulted in several recordings before she headed west to Chicago. When she returned to New York even Caruso was brought back to the studio to redo his famous recordings of the *Rigoletto* quartet and *Lucia* sextet, both of which he had made earlier with both Sembrich and Tetrazzini; it was the only time he sang with Galli-Curci in the United States.

Her long-awaited New York debut with the Chicago Opera in January 1918 was carefully preceded by a series of tantalizing concerts in nearby cities, all of which were canceled at the last minute. The anticipation was such that W. J. Henderson said of her performance of the title role in Meyerbeer's *Dinorah* that she might "have made sounds like those usually offered by her goat, and she would have been crowned . . . wonderful." *The New York Times* ran an editorial reporting on her very real success. "She stole out on the stage, a tiny figure in the brown linsey-woolsey of Breton peasant dress, her oval, olive face shaded in the glossy black of her own long curls, in which flowed scarlet poppies. Nerves tugging at her throat, she sang flat, as she had before she became famous. On the second entrance, drawn by a flute played on the stage, the voice tones brightened to their true lyric quality—still a low voice, that excellent thing in women—till it was doubtful which note was singer and which was flute. New York waited to be assured of the one more thing needed, the miracle of song. It came in the second act, and even then it was just a girl playing

Amelita Galli-Curci in a 1916 Mishkin portrait made in New York before the soprano's sensational Chicago debut. A Mishkin portrait had by then become a requirement for most famous and would-be famous singers.

with her shadow in the moonlight, who sang 'Shadow Song,' smiling, dancing, only momentarily at rest as the voice each time took up a newer, higher flight of dazzling ease and beauty. They heard her through, the silence becoming breathless in a house that had been a bit noisily astir until then, and at the close of a trill like a bird's full-throated outpouring, all the famous stars in town save those singing elsewhere joined with an assembly representing the musical taste and the society of New York in giving the awaited verdict. They gave it standing, waving arms in the air, shouting and applauding. The singer, bowing before the storm, came before the curtain and repeated part of the air, to others difficult or impossible; to her it was simply something to sing, as she had sung all evening, quite naturally, all in character, never a prima donna pose."

Galli-Curci continued to sing until her final Los Angeles concert in 1936, but the years of her greatest success were those early ones with the Chicago Opera. In 1921 she went to the Metropolitan and sang the first opening night after Caruso's death, a performance of *Traviata* with Beniamino Gigli and Giuseppe De Luca. Increasingly, her singing was afflicted by a throat condition that made her sing flat. She remains, however, one of the most beloved singers of the century. Although lovers of the human voice rarely agree on anything, nevertheless a large portion of the public has always preferred a singer who concentrated on purity of tone rather than intensity of expression. For these admirers of the traditionally "beautiful" voice, one of the finest examples will always be the sound of Amelita Galli-Curci, singing on her many Victor records such ballads as "My Old Kentucky Home" and "Home, Sweet Home."

LYDIA LIPKOWSKA

FOR A SHORT PERIOD BETWEEN 1909 and 1911 the Russian soprano Lydia Lipkowska (1882–1955) managed to attract the kind of publicity normally reserved for Geraldine Farrar and Mary Garden. Pretty and outspoken, Lipkowska was the leading soprano of Henry Russell's Boston Opera Company, and between performances there of Lakmé, Lucia, Gilda, and Rosina made pronouncements on life, love, men, etc., and sued to prevent a Boston chef from demeaning her name through using it on the menu (a "Lipkowska cup" and "Lipkowska soufflé"). On a street corner in New York she spoke in German, French, and Russian for women's suffrage. Russell lent her to the Metropolitan, where she made her debut in a 1909 *Traviata* with Caruso and Amato. It was only a partial success: "A more than comely, even a beautiful personality; an actress of gracious parts, an artist of undoubted sincerity, the possessor of a voice of small calibre, youthful timbre, commendable purity, wherefore it carries well, and great flexibility, but without the accents of passion; a singer who has learned to vocalize, a vocalist whose singing is little else than superficial glitter, which can charm but not move. In externals an agreeable representation of Violetta Valery; in the essentials of dramatic song inconsequential. Her hearers refused to be warmed, but they frequently gave evidence that they were pleased." Although Lipkowska did not become the successor to Sembrich that might have been hoped for, she was certainly more effective at the Met and its New Theatre than two other candidates, Elvira de Hidalgo and Bernice de Pasquali. Back in Boston after guest appearances with the Met, Lipkowska merited no reservations from H. T. Parker about her Lucia with Florencio Constantino: "Not within recollection has this 'Mad Scene' been so sung in

The captivating Russian soprano Lydia Lipkowska in an unidentified portrait, possibly for a Broadway performance.

any of our opera houses. There is nothing to compare with it—at least for the younger generation—except Mme Calvé's similar singing of the similar music of Ophelia at the end of *Hamlet.* What usually seems artificial, vocal embellishment had become, touched by the imagination of the singer, the natural, the searching and the haunting expression of a scene, a character and their emotions."

Lipkowska escaped the Russian Revolution via Odessa in 1919, returning almost immediately to rescue her daughter from a convent; the French officer who engineered both escapes became her second husband. She returned to the Paris Opéra, where Russell had discovered her singing for Diaghilev years earlier, before sailing in 1920 for New York performances with the Chicago Opera and the San Carlo Opera. Despite wigs woven with strands of gold and silver, and jewels that had led a reviewer to observe "she wore so many diamonds that the plethora of them inclined one to skepticism as to her powers of song," she did not duplicate her earlier successes. In September 1921 she began a fifty-six-performance run of *The Merry Widow* at New York's Knickerbocker Theater; after that she not only disappeared from the American scene but remained in comparative obscurity the remainder of her life. As with so many of the important singers of Imperial Russia, she wandered for much the rest of her life, singing Violetta in Odessa in 1941, teaching Virginia Zeani in Bucharest, and dying penniless in Beirut, Lebanon, in 1955.

ROSA RAISA

OTHERS MAY HAVE HAD MORE DELIcacy of feeling and finish of phrasing, but among operatic sopranos in the decades between 1910 and 1930 no one could match the sheer vocal splendor of Rosa Raisa (1893–1963).

Fleeing a 1907 pogrom in her native Poland, Rosa Raisa went to live on Capri with relatives. Six years later, at the age of twenty, after study with Barbara Marchisio at the Naples Conservatory, she made her operatic debut in Verdi's first opera, *Oberto,* at the Teatro Regio in Parma. It was the 1913 opening of the Verdi centenary celebrations under the direction of Cleofonte Campanini, who then brought Raisa to the Chicago Opera. Her American debut came that November in a Baltimore *Bohème* with Giovanni Martinelli. In those days the Chicago company toured extensively, including in its itinerary Baltimore and Philadelphia, Des Moines and Wichita, Dallas and Denver, Los Angeles and San Francisco. Back in Chicago she was heard by Covent Garden's manager, Harry Higgins, who took her to London for the 1914 season and *Aida* with Caruso, *Mefistofele* with John McCormack, Claudia Muzio, and Adamo Didur.

Rehearsing for the 1916 La Scala premiere of *Francesca da Rimini,* Raisa gave one of her few offstage displays of temperament. A director instructed her to sing a difficult phrase while descending a staircase, taking great care to finish on the first step. Offended, she replied that she was a spontaneous artist, singing with sincerity, not rules. "I never know what step I will finish what phrase on," she declaimed as she headed for her dressing room. "I am always prompted by instinct." She had her way and began a triumphant association with Italy's first theater.

Following a 1917 Chicago *Aida* performance during which audience enthusiasm forced Raisa to encore "O patria mia," Nellie Melba came backstage with an invitation to tea and some advice: "Luckily your repetition of the aria came out even better, if that could be possible,

MISHKIN
12 N.Y.

Opposite: *Mishkin's classic 1918 portrait of Rosa Raisa as Norma, taken in New York before her first performances of the role at the Teatro Colón in Buenos Aires.*

than the first rendition. It is best to avoid such repetitions—it's too difficult an aria to take any chances with." Returning from Mexico City in 1919, Raisa discovered a less conventional audience when her train jolted to a stop, rifle shots rang out, and statesman-turned-bandit Pancho Villa and his men burst into her coach. Asked to prove her identity as a singer, she rewarded Villa with an unaccompanied rendition of the Spanish song "El Guitarrico" and was rewarded a drink from his bottle of a fiery liquor called pulque, and safe passage.

Raisa had made her New York debut the year before with the visiting Chicago company in *I Gioielli della Madonna. The New York Times* reported: "Miss Raisa has a voice of uncommon richness, power, warmth, and natural beauty, and she displayed the heedless prodigality of youth in her use of it. She seized in extraordinary fashion an opportunity to make the theatre ring with that voice as she climbed the stairs to the Naples hovel in Act 2, while pouring down top notes, plaintive, passionate, hateful, hysterical, less to Gennaro's edification, than to the delight of the house, and to its frankly invited ovation. . . . Maliella is not a sympathetic character, the second act ending, as the girl sinks into one lover's arms while murmuring another name, is a damper to most audiences. Nevertheless, Miss Raisa received a dozen curtain calls." When she first brought her Norma to town in 1920, Henry T. Finck proclaimed her the greatest opera singer of the day after Caruso. Pitts Sanborn didn't like her "Casta Diva" but reported that "in the florid 'Ah, bello a me ritorno,' sung with ecstasy, she began a triumph which went on crescendo through all the inexorable length of the part, a triumph of voice, of singing, of noble mien, of dramatic eloquence. In that final scene of self-denunciation and supreme sacrifice Miss Raisa passed from a passion that was fairly leonine to a tenderness and elevation of the spirit which deserve no less a word than sublime. To pick out just one detail—in the priestess's avowal of her own guilt, 'Son io!' Miss Raisa achieved one of those indescribable feats of vocal expression that seize the listener in his very marrow like the ineffable dignity of Monna Vanna's answer to the implied insult of her husband's doubt as voiced by Miss Garden at the end of the first act of *Monna Vanna,* or Brünnhilde's 'Ruhe, ruhe du Gott!' as pronounced by Mrs. Fremstad in the final speech of *Götterdämmerung.*" On the other hand, W. J. Henderson, who had pointed out that even Lilli Lehmann took "many of the elaborate passages at a very moderate tempo and sang them with very evident labor" said that Raisa in her second New York season of Norma "revealed the fact that she had made no progress whatever. She displayed the same splendid voice and the same ignorance of the style of the work. Her phrasing of 'Casta Diva' covered the stage with the disjecta membra of vocal art."

No one seems to have quarreled with Raisa's natural vocal equipment. When someone commented on the volume she was able to produce, she is said to have replied, "You should hear me in South America, where they really like loud singing." The dimensions of her voice qualified her for her second creation at La Scala, the world premiere of Boito's long-awaited and unsuccessful *Nerone* in 1924. That fall Scandiani of La Scala wired the Chicago manager that Puccini and Toscanini had selected Raisa and Edith Mason for the first *Turandot.* Pregnancy kept Mason from singing Liù, but Raisa did create the title role of Turandot in 1926, for which she is now best remembered. Also in the cast, as Ping, was her husband, Giacomo Rimini, a baritone who usually sang everywhere she did.

Raisa appeared frequently in New York but never at the Met. In 1921 she sent word to Gatti from Rio that she didn't want to return to Chicago because of Mary Garden's directorship and the changes in the repertoire. However, the Chicago Opera remained her home for twenty-one seasons until 1937. When in the summer of 1938 she sang for the last time, at an open air concert, a Chicago critic who had heard singers come and go exulted: "There remained in her singing, besides its unique richness and hugeness of tone . . . that bold unmatched and masterly breadth and decisiveness of line by which she has characteristically staked out vocal proportions quite beyond the capacity of any singer known to our generation."

TITTA RUFFO

WHILE IN PHILADELPHIA FOR HIS 1912 American debut with the Philadelphia-Chicago Grand Opera, the Italian baritone Titta Ruffo (1877–1953) toured a local foundry. Ruffo had worked with wrought iron before becoming a singer; to demonstrate his skill he seized a hammer and quickly transformed an iron bar into an overflowing cornucopia. The horn of plenty might well have been created as a symbol of his own prodigious vocal gifts. At his first Philadelphia performance Ruffo was a sensation as Rigoletto. The applause after Act III with Ruffo and Alma Gluck had forced an encore of the duet "Sì, vendetta" before the curtain. The principals were still acknowledging a screaming audience when a fan seated in the top gallery began to slide down the pillars of each succeeding balcony, finally landing in front of Ruffo on the stage. "What are you doing here?" demanded the startled bar-

Titta Ruffo had the first of his Mishkin portraits made several years before his debut with the Metropolitan Opera in 1922.

itone. "I wanted to see whether you were human," replied the man. "Anyone who can sing like that must be a god." The next morning, Philadelphia newspapers, which for weeks had been trumpeting Ruffo's greatness, were in the happy position of being able to confirm it. "His voice is extraordinary alike for its quality and for its volume. In its middle and upper ranges it has something of tenor timbre, while in its lower register it has all the richness of the true baritone at its best. Its resonance is remarkable. Even in the most piano passages it easily filled the auditorium and it constantly communicated a sense of musical beauty and emotional power. In its clearness and sweetness and fullness and purity, in the evenness of its registers, the extent of its range and the sympathetic eloquence of its appeal, it is as fine a voice in the class to which it belongs as anyone need hope or wish to hear."

Ruffo did not initially appear with the Metropolitan Opera for reasons that reveal the contrasting business principles of Gatti-Casazza and the manager of the Philadelphia-Chicago company, Andreas Dippel, a former tenor who had once been Gatti's assistant. After the operatic war with Hammerstein, the Metropolitan had an understanding with the opera companies of Boston, Philadelphia, and Chicago that no artist except Caruso would be paid more than $1,000 per performance. Early in 1912 Gatti was approached by a New York restaurant owner acting as agent for Ruffo. The terms demanded for a Met contract were so extravagant that Gatti, adhering to the agreement, declined to make a counterproposal. Subsequently, Dippel signed Ruffo for $2,000, the same fee Caruso was paid during the 1912–13 season. Dippel's rationalization was that since one of his supporters, E. T. Stotesbury of Philadelphia, had paid the difference out of his own pocket, the agreement had not been broken.

Dippel brought Ruffo and his company to New York in November 1912 as guests of the Metropolitan Opera. Ruffo sang the title role in Ambroise Thomas's *Hamlet,* an opera that almost every company would trot out at his command. The news from Philadelphia had been circulating for several weeks, and the opera house was sold out with an audience that probably included everyone of musical importance except Gatti. W. J. Henderson went beyond the popular acclaim to analyze the foundation of Ruffo's sound: "He has a splendid pair of lungs and astonishing breath support. But he has learned how to develop the natural gift. His control, which means the government of the expenditure of the air drawn into the lungs, is perfect. He knows how to obey the old Italian command *'filar il tuono,'* spin the tone. When he sings forte he uses just enough breath to create the tone, and no more. Any living singer can profit by observing this man's management of the breath."

In the first third of the twentieth century, three men dominated not only their vocal categories but the consciousness of opera audiences. Enrico Caruso was one; another was the Russian bass Feodor Chaliapin; indisputably the third was Ruffo. Ruffo's 1898 debut was in Rome as the Herald in *Lohengrin,* but he was soon singing the leading baritone roles there and around Italy, in Egypt, and in South America. By 1903 he was at Covent Garden, and in rapid succession sang at La Scala, in Russia, and in Paris. His stature was such that he cannot be described as having been a member of any opera company. Instead, he granted guest appearances.

Ruffo suffered few disappointments in his rise to eminence but one episode in London in 1903 smarted for years. Scheduled for *Lucia di Lammermoor* and *Il Barbiere di Siviglia* during Covent Garden's summer season, Ruffo was asked to replace his ailing colleague Antonio Scotti in *Rigoletto* with Nellie Melba as Gilda. Melba's social and musical influence in London were so all-prevailing then that she did not rehearse with Ruffo but sat instead in the directors' proscenium box observing the proceedings and witnessing the enthusiastic applause of both chorus and orchestra for the baritone. The next morning Ruffo discovered that his name had been removed from the *Rigoletto* posters outside Covent Garden; he was informed that Madame Melba had refused to sing with him because he was too young for such a role.

A few years later, in 1911, Ruffo had his revenge. On a trip to her native Australia, Melba passed through Naples, where Ruffo was appearing at the Teatro San Carlo. After hearing his Nelusko in Meyerbeer's *Africana,* Melba sent word through the local impresario that she would be happy to sing Ophelia opposite Ruffo's Hamlet. Ruffo requested that his reply be delivered verbatim: "Tell Melba that she is too old to sing with me." (The Ruffo-Melba story has been told so often that everyone forgets that in 1914 the two did sing together in Philadelphia—in *Rigoletto.*)

Ruffo finally had a contract with the Metropolitan in 1921–22, when Gatti sought out the biggest names he could for the first season after Caruso's death. In his 1922 debut as Figaro in *Barbiere,* Ruffo showed his lighter side: "The recitative secco, as it is technically called—the rapid Italian dialogue patter—he sang with great facility, with elasticity, with unction and with color. The recitative ... was a significant element in Mr. Ruffo's gay and infectious impersonation.... The florid passages in the first scene ... were hardly in his line, but he showed cunning in turning them to humorous uses."

With the Metropolitan, Ruffo remained more of a guest artist than a company member who appeared many times in a season. However, Giordano's new work, *La Cena delle Beffe,* was mounted for him in 1926, and proved ideal for his dramatic talents: "Mr. Ruffo's Neri dominated the stage; seized the eye; held fast the imagination. To life at last in the theatre had come a recognizable Renaissance bravo—swaggering shoulders, striding legs, hands that were fists, rude-cut features, lowering countenance, great voice—menace, might, savagery, sensuality, all rough-kneaded into a single flesh."

Ruffo left the Metropolitan in 1929 for a $350,000 contract with MGM to film excerpts from *Barbiere, Otello,* and *L'Africana,* of which no trace survives except still photos.

Ruffo did not sing in his native Italy during the last years of his career. Following the assassination of his socialist brother-in-law by Mussolini's henchmen, he made and kept a pledge never to perform there as long as the fascists were in power. His last operatic appearance was the 1932 opening of Radio City Music Hall performing scenes from *Carmen* with Coe Glade. (On the same program was a young tenor listed as "John Pierce.")

Maggie Teyte as a youthful 1918 Mignon, photographed long before she became famous again in the late 1940s.

MAGGIE TEYTE

SO ROMANTIC WAS THE POST WORLD War II career of English soprano Maggie Teyte (1888–1976), when a whole generation of the American musical public fell in love with a singer of French songs who was old enough to be thinking only of retirement, that it has obscured the earlier seasons, between 1911 and 1920, when she appeared frequently in major American cities primarily as an operatic soprano. As a teenager in Paris, Teyte had studied with Jean de Reszke; she sang small roles at the Opéra-Comique and in 1908 was selected to follow Mary Garden as Mélisande, a part she coached for nine months with Debussy, who also accompanied her in song recitals. Performances in London with Thomas Beecham followed, and in 1911 she reached Philadelphia for Cherubino in a *Nozze di Figaro* with Carolina White, Alice Zeppilli, and Mario Sammarco. With her strong, independent mind, Teyte quickly made headlines. Approached by the head of the claque before her debut, she was informed that a payment of $500 would insure the success of her debut, while nonpayment might bring hisses. Pretending great interest, she contrived to have him repeat the terms in her hotel room while reporters listened next door. The resulting press coverage assured that she was already a familiar name at her debut.

She was with both the Philadelphia-Chicago and the Boston companies, singing a variety of roles that one no longer associates with her: Mimi, the title role in Massenet's *Cendrillon* with Mary Garden as Prince Charming; Desdemona to Zenatello's Otello; Fiora in *L'Amore dei Tre Re.* She made headlines again when some of her colleagues started a campaign against overwork; Teyte countered with a drive against underwork. For a smaller company she sang Gilda in Mexico City. Most of her operatic work, in New York, however, was with the Society of American Singers. As Mignon in 1918, with Geraldine Farrar watching intently from a box, she "accomplished a portrait which was a veritable masterpiece. Rarely has the operatic stage witnessed such an exquisite adjustment of acting and singing. It was an impersonation of infinite charm and pathos, and she sang the music with beautiful fidelity. Miss Teyte's voice was rich in color." Later the same season in *Madama Butterfly,* "by virtue not only of pure and artistic singing, but of a deep realization of the power of movement on the stage to enhance the effect of the music, she gave the performance real distinction. As a sort of prelude to her astonishing performance in the second act, she sang the finale of the first act with Orville Harrold, an admirable Pinkerton, so that both singers were recalled again and again. Then, in the first scene of the second, Mrs. Teyte held her audience spellbound. Her grace and ease of movement are rare for the operatic stage. Her body as much as her voice was surrendered to the music with such sensitiveness to the interpretive power of gesture that it seemed as important to the beauty of the scene as was her singing."

With the war over and transportation once more available to civilians, Teyte returned to England and sang only intermittently. She did not visit the United States again until 1937, when she found no managers interested in an almost forgotten British soprano. Her second American career, inspired by a memorable series of French song recordings, began in 1945, when she was fifty-seven. Although her appearances now were primarily in recital or on radio's *Bell Telephone Hour,* she returned to opera in the series of *Pelléas* performances at the New York City Opera that introduced Theodor Uppman. Later, at London's Mermaid Theatre, she sang Belinda opposite Kirsten Flagstad in Purcell's *Dido and Aeneas.* It was a farewell to the stage for both of them.

FLORENCE EASTON

COMBINING THE SKILLS AND RELIABILITY of a singer of secondary roles with the vocal gifts of the prima donna, the English soprano Florence Easton (1884–1955) may have been the most useful artist ever on the Metropolitan roster. During her twelve consecutive seasons, some forty-one parts of her eighty-eight-role repertoire were heard, often as last-minute replacements for ailing sopranos such as Geraldine Farrar, Claudia Muzio, Rosa Ponselle, and Maria Jeritza. She always praised the musical independence that her early piano studies in Canada and England had given her. The voice itself, trained against the wishes of her family, was then a light soprano appropriate for a debut at eighteen as the Shepherd in *Tannhäuser* while touring England with the Moody-Manners Company. She came to the United States when her husband, the American tenor Francis Maclennan, was engaged to tour in *Parsifal* in English for the Savage Opera Company. The next season both husband and wife sang for Savage.

Florence Easton's devout portrayal of St. Elizabeth in the Met's 1918 English-language staging of the Liszt oratorio.

Easton's American debut in October of 1905 in Baltimore as Gilda in *Rigoletto* was noteworthy for her high E natural. The following year she was one of three Butterflys in the Savage company. While they were in Boston, Easton distinguished herself from the rest of the company: "Miss Easton in her turn, seemed to seek first of all as perfect a musical expression, as lay within her powers, of the part. . . . None of Mr. Savage's singers has a voice of such intrinsic musical quality and none has advanced so far and so intelligently in the fine artistry of song.'' All three sopranos were called upon to appear in a special professional matinee given in New York in December 1906 so other performers could hear the new opera. In Act I Easton may well have sung for her most distinguished audience: Farrar (who was to introduce *Butterfly* seven weeks later at the Metropolitan), Caruso (who caricatured Easton for the first time), Lina Cavalieri, Pol Plançon, and Otto Kahn were there from the Met; from Hammerstein's company came Alessandro Bonci, Clotilde Bressler-Gianoli, and Maurice Renaud; the theater was represented by Eleanor Robson, who as Mrs. August Belmont would play such a vital role in the life of the Metropolitan Opera.

With no offers from the Metropolitan or the Manhattan, Easton and Maclennan moved on from Savage to the Royal Opera in Berlin. It was there she acquired her reputation for coping with crises. Karl Muck, the music director, said he would be willing to give her the score of any opera at 8 A.M. and have her sing it at 8 that evening.

By the time Easton reached the Met in 1917, she was trailing successes in Berlin (everything from *Elektra* to *Der Regimentstochter*), England (Covent Garden and a tour of *Elektra* in English), and Chicago. After a debut in *Cavalleria Rusticana* her first great success was in the title role in Liszt's oratorio *St. Elizabeth.* One critic felt the music flowed with the placidity of molasses while another said the "considerable audience bore up bravely under the visitation.'' For Easton, however, there was nothing but praise: "She sang with an emotional expressiveness and intensity that carried her musical message straight to the heart. . . . But the limpid purity and warmth of her lyric voice, the ease of her diction and the skill with which she invariably managed her resources were always in evidence. Singing that conformed so nearly to the best traditions of the past has not often been heard in the Metropolitan Opera House in recent years.'' She soon became invaluable. Her versatility was tested when Farrar canceled *Lodoletta* with Caruso, and Easton sang all but the opening performance. "To accomplish at short notice what she did on this occasion, when she sang Mascagni's heroine for the first time in her life, and without a stage or orchestral rehearsal, requires something more than the typical prima donna has at her command; something more than vocal beauty, personality, histrionic skill and various other patent persuasions that make an immediate appeal. If, therefore, any doubt existed as to whether Mme. Easton combined with her palpable artistic qualities, the musical intelligence, the quickness of memory, the adaptability, the steadiness and assurance which were accredited to her, this doubt was dispelled effectually by her latest and most remarkable achievement.''

The following season she created Lauretta in *Gianni Schicchi;* she dazzled as Fiordiligi in the Met's first *Così fan tutte* in 1921–22; and in 1926–27 she created Aelfrida in Deems Taylor's *King's Henchman.* Pleading ill health, she left the Met in 1929. Gatti spoke with unusual warmth of his regret, "first of all because I hear that your health is not in good condition and secondly because this compels me to lose an artist of your rank and versatility.''

She made up for an earlier failure in *Walküre* when she sang Brünnhilde for a guest appearance in 1936 in which her "Ho-jo-to-ho'' "was voiced in ringing tones alive with exultation. The high B's and C's flowed forth without effort and were admirably true to pitch.'' She gave concerts as late as 1943, often programming an entire evening of lieder in her own English translations. It was a long and distinguished career in which only one thing seems to have been lacking, the public adoration that belonged to singers such as Lotte Lehmann and Kirsten Flagstad.

THE WORLD PREMIERE OF *IL TRITTICO*

DURING THE SUMMER OF 1918 THE Met conductor Roberto Moranzoni sailed to Europe expecting to hear the world premiere of Puccini's three one-act operas, *Il Trittico,* in Rome. But the war forced the cancellation of the Rome premiere, and the two men met instead in Viareggio, where Puccini played over the scores with him and Moranzoni in return taught Puccini the current American rage, George M. Cohan's "Over There.'' Moranzoni came back to a wartime Metropolitan where all German opera and most German artists had been proscribed and where Caruso was about to register for the draft. When hostilities ended with the November 11, 1918, Armistice, Puccini wrote to Gatti of what was to be his second world premiere in New York: "Could I have foreseen the sudden collapse of our enemies, I certainly should have been helping to celebrate the glorious victory in New York.''

This premiere-by-default was considerably less festive than *Fanciulla* had been in 1910. For the first performance on December 14, 1918, Gatti assembled strong casts. In the first one-act opera, *Il Tabarro,* there were three Italians: Claudia Muzio, baritone Luigi Montesanto, and tenor Giulio Crimi. "The opening work provides Claudia Muzio with a role suited to her peculiar abilities. Its opportunities for sustained song are few, and Miss Muzio is ever at home in the delivery of such dramatic speech as Puccini devises.''

And: "Mr. Crimi as the lover . . . sang and acted with genuine fire. Of Mr. Montesanto it may be said that his Michele was too much of a Latin-Quarter poet, yet he sang and acted with vigor and his solo scene was praiseworthy. . . . The other parts were capital; Didur's in particular. Alice Gentle's sketch of the eccentric old woman

I.C.
MISHKIN
N.Y.

Opposite: *Members of the first cast of* Gianni Schicchi, *including Giuseppe De Luca in the title role, captured in what was perhaps Mishkin's first onstage photograph.*

could hardly be improved upon. They were not Parisians, these people, but only Italians on the Seine." As to the opera, "as a one-act thriller, *Il Tabarro* has plenty of dash and go and, well presented, cannot fail of effect."

After the "peppery draught" of the first opera, "the composer administered *Suor Angelica* as a sedative." Geraldine Farrar took the title role in these unusual scenes from convent life. Farrar had sometimes upset the critics with what they considered her dramatic excesses. Now, they praised her sensitive restraint: "Seldom has Miss Farrar seemed so fine-grained an actress as in this suggestion; seldom has she so willingly subdued herself to a whole illusion in which she was but incidental figure. The artist of the opera house as well as the 'movie queen' does still abide in her." "One song . . . is the only notable lyric in the score, and is utilized a little later in the inevitable intermezzo for orchestra which is 'de rigueur' in modern Italian operas."

The third opera, the comic *Gianni Schicchi,* was the unqualified success of the evening. "Even the mechanics of the music-making glint. Even the froth and the spray of it sparkle with comic spirit. Action and speech, voices and orchestra are inseparable in ebullient flood. About an Italian folk-figure, around an Italian folk-fable, in high Italian gusto, Puccini, wont to range the world around for his scene, personages, action, has written his most Italian opera. With not a whit less zest for comic impersonation his Italian singing-players frisked and chattered through it." Leading the cast was Giuseppe De Luca who "made the crafty Gianni Schicchi a likeable trickster, with a gentle sigh at the end for his own craftiness. With that white nightcap and nightgown and the absurd green velvet cap which he wore upon his pretended deathbed he was probably the most mirth-provoking figure the Metropolitan stage has encouraged." As his future son-in-law, "Mr. Crimi as Rinuccio had easily his best part here so far. His comedy was good and the white, metallic, piercing quality of voice he used cut right through any instrumental or vocal racket." One short aria, "O mio babbino caro," became an immediate hit. "The pearl of the evening is, perhaps, a half-serious prayer which the young daughter of Schicchi sings to him on bended knee, to plead the cause of her lover and his miserly crew of elders. Here, for once, comes pure melody: melody, indeed, so plaintive and tender as to verge upon the street ballad—yet it is arch and exquisite, and Miss Easton reaped a triumph and replanted an encore with it." And how appropriate that "O mio babbino caro" should have started life as it has continued on countless soprano programs, as an encore!

Giulio Crimi as the tough stevedore Luigi in the world premiere of Il Tabarro. *Crimi later became the teacher of the important baritone Tito Gobbi.*

Huneker had a final social note: "Mr. and Mrs. Oscar Hammerstein were guests in the box of Manager Gatti-Casazza, who must have slept the sleep of a happy impresario last night."

MABEL GARRISON

LONG BEFORE IT BECAME STYLISH TO make the claim, Mabel Garrison (1886–1963) was one of the first American sopranos to have a successful Metropolitan Opera career without benefit of foreign training or experience. Her progress was sure and steady. In Baltimore she graduated from Peabody and at the church where she was soloist found an organist who became both husband and accompanist. Her operatic debut was in 1912 with the English-language Aborn Opera Company singing Philine in *Mignon* at the Boston Opera House. On the recommendation of the bass Andrés de Segurola, Gatti heard and engaged her without fee for a Sunday-night concert in 1914. So successful were her

Mabel Garrison as Queen of the Night in Die Zauberflöte, *a role she often sang effectively as replacement for Frieda Hempel.*

"Caro nome" and encores that she was placed on the roster the next season for twenty-two weeks at $75 a week. It was a typical Gatti contract with end-of-season renewal options for two additional seasons with escalating pay.

Garrison stayed with the Met for seven seasons, beginning with a mixture of small and leading roles and soon recording for Victor. Met audiences that first encountered her in her 1914 debut role as a Flower Maiden in *Parsifal* learned to appreciate her light lyrical voice when she substituted for Frieda Hempel as the high-ranging Queen of the Night in *Die Zauberflöte,* a role frequently canceled by Hempel. Smaller parts disappeared and she was soon singing only the leading coloratura repertoire: *Lucia, Un Ballo in Maschera, Le Coq d'Or, Marta,* and *Rigoletto.* Aldrich of the *Times* reported of her Adina in *Elisir:* "A charming and sympathetic figure, arch and vivacious in the comedy, she sang with great beauty and purity of voice, with brightness and brilliancy, and with a full command of the style that is essential to the successful portrayal of this genre. Miss Garrison's voice is small; her whole effect is somewhat in miniature [she was surrounded by the robust voices and methods of Caruso, Scotti, and Didur]. . . . But her voice is of a sort that carries and penetrates and there was no doubt of the value and significance of her contribution to the performance."

When Henderson wrote that she was "possessed of a voice crystalline in its clarity and sunny quality and a style marked by smoothness and elegance," it was in review not of an opera but of a 1918 Carnegie Hall recital. Eventually Garrison appeared more often in concert than opera. Following a cordial exchange of letters with Gatti she left the Met at the end of the 1921 season to have a child, which she lost. At the time she was making more than Rosa Ponselle, who had begun in 1918 with a similar beginner's contract. Although she sang in Germany and toured China and Japan, her performances everywhere became fewer. After 1933 she taught at Smith and appeared in one of the few staged performances Handel's *Rodelinda* has had in America.

CHARLES HACKETT

THE MOST ELEGANT OF AMERICAN TENORS was undoubtedly Charles Hackett (1889–1942), who came from a musically cultivated family of Portland, Maine. In one of those fascinating moments when distant vocal eras overlap, the first significant engagement of the twenty-two-year-old singer was a 1911 Rossini *Stabat Mater* in Providence, Rhode Island, that featured soprano Lillian Nordica, whose greatest triumphs were in the nineteenth century. His Carnegie Hall debut

Charles Hackett as Des Grieux in Massenet's Manon *in a photograph probably made backstage at the Metropolitan circa 1919.*

came later the same year in a Verdi *Requiem* with Alma Gluck and Herbert Witherspoon. *Musical America* described "a rare voice, well trained, which the singer handles with great intelligence, always conscious of artistic musical values. . . . He took his high tones with great surety, ringing clear and true against the orchestral accompaniment."

Although a popular and highly paid soloist in concert halls and churches, Hackett elected to sail for Italy in 1912 and further study of operatic repertoire. His operatic debut early in 1915 took place outside Milan when he was summoned to a small theater and asked to sing through the role of Faust in *Mefistofele* for the management. Only then was he informed that he would make his debut that evening, singing the entire role again. His success quickly led to bigger engagements, then to La Scala the following year. In the 1917 Buenos Aires season at the Teatro Colón he shared the leading tenor roles with Caruso, who served as best man at Hackett's marriage to a prima ballerina of La Scala, Virginia Zucchi.

Gatti brought him home for a 1919 debut in *Il Barbiere di Siviglia* with Frieda Hempel and Giuseppe De Luca and praise from public and press: "He has a pure lyric tenor of very agreeable quality, an even scale from top to bottom, clean diction, and great flexibility and finish of phrase. Added to his vocal accomplishments is a youthful physique which adapts itself quite naturally to the requirements of operatic romance."

His vocal graces won him two important Metropolitan premieres, Gounod's *Mireille* with Maria Barrientos and settings designed by the baritone Victor Maurel; and Rossini's *Italiana in Algeri,* in which he was praised as the only cast member capable of performing the florid music. In that period of Metropolitan Opera history, the opera company controlled the outside activities of all but its most famous artists and received annual payments from recording companies for the privilege of contracting Met singers. The Victor Company made the largest payment and usually had first choice. Although in 1917 Gatti had recommended Hackett to Victor as a man with a wonderful future, Hackett signed with Victor's rival, Columbia Records, where he would be its most important operatic tenor rather than another Victor artist competing for attention with Caruso and John McCormack. More than a hundred sides of arias and songs, plus duets with Barrientos, Rosa Ponselle, and Riccardo Stracciari document Hackett's voice at this time.

When Gatti, worried about both Beniamino Gigli's and Caruso's health in the summer of 1921, got around to offering Hackett a fourth season, he had already accepted another Scala contract and scheduled many recitals. He didn't return to the Metropolitan until 1933–34. Until his return to the Met, the Chicago Opera was his home company; he also sang often in Europe, including an appearance as Roméo at Nellie Melba's Covent Garden farewell. He was on the faculty of the Juilliard School when he died.

GABRIELLA BESANZONI

IN THE SPRING OF 1919 THE ITALIAN contralto Gabriella Besanzoni (1888–1962) arrived in New York to be with her lover, the pianist Artur Rubinstein, and to complete her conquest of the Western Hemisphere. She had recently triumphed in Mexico City and Buenos Aires, and Amato had wired Gatti about her big success in Havana (UNUSUAL VOICE GOOD ARTIST HAVE HEARD CAMPANINI IS AFTER BELIEVE IS EXCELLENT ACQUISITION). On Rubinstein's advice, Besanzoni signed a three-year contract with the Metropolitan and arranged a separate agreement for her to make Victor Records. Writing to Met conductor Giuseppe Bamboschek that summer, Gatti was near hysteria worrying about her:

The extravagant Gabriella Besanzoni in a Mishkin portrait from her one Metropolitan Opera season, 1919–20. She was much more successful performing in South America.

"With an extravagant and disorderly woman, it is necessary to remain watchful.... In any case it is necessary to have in her hands the parts that I have already agreed with her. They are *Samson* in French, Marina and *Italiana in Algeri.* If you could teach her the parts, that would be better. But she is a woman who, in New York or out, needs to be constantly watched and checked.... In case Besanzoni is not in Mexico or New York, but in a city of the United States, have the goodness to take the train to find her and find out how things stand."

Gatti needn't have worried. Besanzoni's opening-week debut as Amneris in *Aida* was on schedule. Claudia Muzio sang Aida; Giovanni Martinelli, Radames; and Renato Zanelli debuted as Amonasro. It was an evening of great excitement and promise. "Mr. Gatti-Casazza trained on New York last night the first Big Bertha of his new operatic campaign—to wit, Gabriella Besanzoni. This description applies not to the young lady's physique but to her talent.... The bombardment began shortly after eight last evening, and toward 11:30 it had reached such a pitch of effectiveness that just as the Princess Amneris went down to final defeat a howling mob behind the celebrated railing shouted an uproarious triumph for her impersonation.... [The audience] seemed to like well the range and quality of her voice, its shifting colors and varied registers, to bask luxuriously at discreet distance in its vivid heat. She is a fiery young singer, Miss Besanzoni, and a fiery actress, who saws the air with white-hot metal. Princely pride and princely raiment alike counted for nothing with her Amneris when the life of him she loved was at stake. A woman scorned, from the scorner she turned her fury on the priests marching out of the judgment hall, and, thanks to her knees and the Pharaonic ball gown, the Metropolitan stage could have no use this morning for a vacuum cleaner."

The promise of *Aida* did not follow in the first performance at the Metropolitan of Rossini's *Italiana in Algeri;* one admirer of her Amneris felt she was about as well fitted to act and sing the humors and graces of Isabella as the light-voiced Mabel Garrison would have been for the *Götterdämmerung* Brünnhilde. Her Dalila, in newly acquired French, was also disappointing; Henderson did not find her the seductress that Rubinstein had, "always granting that the act of seduction has remained unchanged since the time of Samson." Gatti did not renew her contract, "for reasons of repertoire," as he explained. She blamed it on Geraldine Farrar and Margarete Matzenauer, Farrar probably for having exclusive rights to *Carmen* and Matzenauer for her stronghold over the other mezzo roles. Besanzoni sang concerts and a handful of performances with the Chicago Opera but had no further U.S. career. During the twenties she sang *Orfeo* and *Carmen* under Toscanini at La Scala. Oddly for a singer so popular in Italy and Latin America, her only solo recordings date from her season at the Met.

RENATO ZANELLI

FOR SOMEONE WHOSE AMERICAN CAreer began so auspiciously, the Chilean Renato Zanelli (1892–1935) was a distinct disappointment in his Metropolitan Opera performances. He had come to New York in 1918 and with the assistance of the bass Andrés de Segurola soon had contracts with Victor Records, Charles L. Wagner for concert tours, and Gatti-Casazza for five seasons in leading roles at the Met. His debut was a December 1919 *Aida* with Claudia Muzio, Giovanni Martinelli, and Gabriella Besanzoni, who also was singing at the Met for the first time. The most favorable notice was in the *Times:* "Mr. Zanelli as Amonasro made an excellent impression by his significant dramatic conception of the part. His voice is rather light, but of excellent metal, directed by intelligence and skill, and promises good things." Despite the beauty of his recordings from this period, however, something was clearly wrong. At his second *Aida,* he "succeeded in making his singing more effective than before, but chiefly by resorting to main force. His voice has sufficient volume and is fresh and of good texture, but his manner of emitting it is unfavorable to resonance and carrying power." His concerts were more numerous and effective than his opera performances. Finally, Zanelli concluded that the baritone register was wrong for his natural voice and that he required more training. After concert tours and four seasons at the Met in which he had little to do except appear at Sunday-night concerts and substitute for Pasquale Amato or Giuseppe De Luca in *Pagliacci* and *Forza,* he sailed to Italy. After a year's study he emerged as a tenor and in a short time graduated to heavier dramatic roles such as Tristan, Siegmund, and Andrea Chénier. Though his appearances at the Met were over, he became known worldwide as the preeminent Otello of his generation, performing the role successfully at La Scala, Covent Garden, and in South America. Zanelli died of cancer in Chile at the age of forty-two.

Renato Zanelli as Manfredo in L'Amore dei Tre Re, *a rare photograph of the future Otello in one of his early baritone roles.*

Orville Harrold as Rodolfo in La Bohème, *the role in which he finally reached the Metropolitan in 1919.*

ORVILLE HARROLD

THE UPS AND DOWNS IN THE CAREER of American tenor Orville Harrold (1878–1933) would provide enough material for at least two rags-to-riches sagas. In early 1908 he was driving a delivery wagon for a coffin manufacturer in Muncie, Indiana; Ernestine Schumann-Heink heard him in oratorio and advised New York and study. Instead, he found small parts with touring Shubert brothers musicals, joined a barbershop quartet, and eventually landed in two-a-day vaudeville at New York's Victoria Theatre. In 1909 the reviewer for *Variety* heard him in "Harold & Wald, Songs" and wrote that "whoever is the tenor has a wonderfully sweet voice, and with a tendency to sound tired before the finish of the act. . . . What the tenor should do, however, is to study for grand opera. It might require more time than he cares or can afford to give, but it would be worth it, for the voice is there." Oscar Hammerstein agreed, put him under the vocal supervision of

Oscar Saenger, and three months later had him singing at a Manhattan Opera Sunday-night concert with Mariette Mazarin, Marguerite D'Alvarez, and Armand Crabbé, touring the Midwest with Luisa Tetrazzini, and finally, in February 1910, singing *Pagliacci* with Lina Cavalieri and Mario Sammarco.

Hammerstein had promised to send Harrold to Paris for study with Jean de Reszke but the next fall presented him as Richard Warrington in the premiere of Victor Herbert's *Naughty Marietta* with Emma Trentini. His big number was "I'm Falling in Love with Someone," in which he was reported to deliver a high E flat with dramatic effect. In 1912, Harrold opened Hammerstein's London opera house as Arnold in Rossini's *William Tell* with Maurice Renaud and for this, *Roméo, Faust,* and *Lucia,* his high notes were intact. Soon, however, he was back permanently in the United States, no longer with Hammerstein, who could not legally produce opera in New York, and singing opera in English at the Century Opera House (formerly the New Theatre). "It is true that his high notes no longer possess the beauty and the brilliancy of those of four years ago, but in their place he showed a feeling, a skill in phrase, a delicacy of expression and a romantic bearing which were worthy of warm praise. In addition his diction was as clear as the most earnest advocate of opera in English could desire."

By 1915 he was touring again in vaudeville, showing off his "magnificent voice which he squanders like a proverbial sailor." He sang at Ravinia unsuccessfully until his third wife, whom he'd met during her days in the *Naughty Marietta* chorus, took him in hand and persuaded him to spend the 1917–18 winter in study. It proved effective: After several auditions Gatti engaged him. He sang with the Met for the first time in *Bohème* performed in Brooklyn in November 1919 and later in Manhattan. He was still popular in New York; according to Henderson, the audience gave "a demonstration of pleasure as the house rarely witnesses when Mr. Caruso is not in the cast. . . . His voice, a big and powerful organ, was in fine condition last night and he sang smoothly, with resonance, and with no small amount of feeling. He took and sustained a brilliant high C in the 'racconto', but more commendable than that feat were his good phrasing and his legato."

Now he made up for the years that had been lost. Gatti tore up his $200-a-week contract for four performances a week, and wrote a new one that paid up to $18,000 a season and called for only three performances a week. Unfortunately, his voice did not hold beyond a few seasons, Metropolitan performances became less frequent, and he left at the end of 1923–24. First-rank tenors on the roster at the time included Beniamino Gigli, Giovanni Martinelli, Giacomo Lauri-Volpi, Edward Johnson, Miguel Fleta, Mario Chamlee, and Armand Tokatyan. It was back one last time to small touring companies and musical comedy for Orville Harrold.

SELMA KURZ

THE FLIRTATION BETWEEN VIENNESE soprano Selma Kurz (1874–1933) and the Metropolitan Opera dated back to 1907 when Heinrich Conried, inspired by the furor of the Manhattan Opera's competition and the anticipated retirement of Marcella Sembrich from his own house, gave Kurz a preposterous contract guaranteeing her eighty performances a season beginning in 1908–1909. (During a six-month period Caruso was only able to perform seventy-seven times.) Kurz was then the reigning soprano at the Vienna Opera, where she would sing leading roles until 1929. Brought to Vienna by Gustav Mahler in 1899, she had begun as Marguerite in *Faust* and had sung Sieglinde in *Walküre* and Elisabeth in *Tannhäuser.* But Mahler persuaded her to add the higher repertoire, and it was to such roles as Gilda, Oscar, Violetta, Queen of the Night, and Lucia that she soon owed her reputation. Her trill seemed endless. In April of 1908 Andreas Dippel, acting for the incoming Gatti, tried to renegotiate her contract for fewer performances at the same fee while she insisted on more money. The contract was canceled when Dippel and Felix Weingartner, who had just succeeded Mahler as Director of the Vienna Opera, signed mutually convenient statements making it impossible for her to sing at the Metropolitan before January 1910. It was rumored again that Gatti had signed her for January 1914 but nothing came of it.

Finally, Kurz arrived in New York in 1921 for concerts. She was interviewed by the press and photographed by Mishkin, and made her American debut in a sold-out concert with full orchestra at the Hippodrome on January 9, 1921. But she had waited too long. Although she was enthusiastically received by the audience, the press was not helpful: "Miss Kurz sang yesterday with a still, small voice that would have resembled the voice of conscience if it had been ruthlessly true to pitch. But it was rather ruthlessly untrue to that quantity—so much so that any prime donne who have been reproached for singing out of tune can now take great comfort. They will be known hereafter as human pitch pipes. On the rare occasion when Miss Kurz vouchsafed a full-voice tone it was clear that her voice is somewhat worn. Her carefully advertised crescendo trill was not much like the crescendo trill for which Dame Nellie Melba was once famous. The pieces she elected to sing—'Deh, vieni non tardar' from *The Marriage of Figaro,* Handel's 'Sweet Bird,' 'Caro Nome' from *Rigoletto,* 'Ah, fors' è lui' from *La Traviata,* and Strauss's 'Voci di Primavera'—are replete with memories of Mmes. Sembrich, Melba, Tetrazzini, Barrientos, and Galli-Curci. At least Miss Kurz must have the credit of admirable courage. . . . In extenuation of any vagaries on [the conductor's] part it must be said that the singer's deliv-

The celebrated Viennese soprano Selma Kurz in a Mishkin portrait made before her only American appearance, January 1921, at the Hippodrome.

ery seldom showed anything like rhythmic incisiveness.'' Although Gatti signed her to two performances the following season, she returned to Vienna. From there in November she wrote to Gatti: "Thank God my voice is in 'full-flight' again and my success has been indescribably great. Now I do not know whether you will have any further use for me at all this season. Eventually perhaps we can hit upon an arrangement concerning next season, if you should happen to think of me.'' By then Gatti had Galli-Curci firmly in hand to open his first Caruso-less season. Kurz never returned to America.

ROSA PONSELLE

DURING 1915 A NUMBER OF OPERA SINGers appeared in vaudeville. At the Palace in New York, Carl Jörn, Orville Harrold, and Carolina White shared the two-a-day stage with a wide range of musical, theatrical, and dance turns. Emma Calvé came from France and played there four weeks to the greatest enthusiasm. However, an event of more lasting operatic significance took place at the Royal and was reported in *Variety,* September 10, 1915, on its page devoted to New Acts: PONZILLO SISTERS, SONGS, 20 MINS.: "This 'sister-act' with appearance and other qualifications, should rearrange its song repertoire before striking out for the big time houses, where it certainly belongs. The girls should have worn a more appropriate costume for the early season opening. Both possess rather pleasing voices, with a wide range that is well used.... The larger of the two continually plays a grand piano, joining her partner for a well harmonized chorus, also handling a ballad splendidly for her only solo number.'' The Ponzillo Sisters were not without experience, having graduated from the local Meriden, Connecticut, performing circuit of churches, movie houses, and cafés. It was the younger sister, Rosa, who played the piano and handled the ballad "splendidly.'' They continued on a round of vaudeville houses for more than two years, played the Palace, and eventually the older sister, Carmela, went to William Thorner for singing lessons. Against his better judgment he also accepted Rosa as a pupil and it is here that we catch up with one of the more fabled operatic legends: the young girl studies for a few months, is heard by Caruso, auditions for the Metropolitan, and six months later makes her debut as Rosa Ponselle (1897–1981) in Verdi's *Forza del Destino* opposite Caruso, Giuseppe De Luca, and José Mardones.

Singing one of the most demanding and rewarding roles in Italian opera, Ponselle began her operatic career at the top. "She is young, she is comely, and she is tall and solidly built. A fine figure of a woman, was the opinion of the experts; and in cavalier costume she was handsome and—embarrassed. Those long boots made her gait awkward, she was too conscious of her legs, and her gait was angular. But what a promising debut! Added to her personal attractiveness, she possesses a voice of natural beauty that may prove a gold mine; it is vocal gold, anyhow, with its luscious lower and middle tones, dark, rich and ductile. Brilliant and flexible in the upper register—if there be such a paradox as a vocal register—she is given to forcing the column of breath with the resultant that the tone becomes hard to steeliness yet a sweet, appealing, sympathetic voice, well placed, well trained. The note of monotony in the tone color that occasionally intruded may be avoided. Nuance, nuance, nuance. That must be mastered. Her nervousness was evident,

C.
MISHKIN
N.Y. 21

Opposite: *A very young Rosa Ponselle was photographed by Mishkin shortly before her first appearance in opera, the Met's 1918* La Forza del Destino. *Caruso felt the shape of her face resembled his and accounted for the richness of her voice.*

but after she sang 'Addio' in Act I she had her audience captured. Her scene and cavatine before the church was astonishingly mature for such a youthful debutante. And she sagged below pitch on her last note. Unless we are greatly mistaken, our opera has in Rosa Ponselle a dramatic soprano of splendid potentialities. But she has an arduous road to traverse before she can call herself a finished artist." Here fact and legend part company, not to converge again until *La Vestale* seven years later, when, her magnificent natural voice under perfect control, the Ponselle people remember and what she made of herself became the same.

ENRICO CARUSO AND *LA JUIVE*

ON OCTOBER 17, 1919, GATTI WROTE TO Caruso in Mexico City at the Teatro Speranza-Iris, where he was appearing. "You are so good, always so reasonable, that you deserve the best of fortune in any undertaking. . . . I have decided to give *La Juive* not as the opening, but still during the first week." Gatti could not know that Caruso's good fortune would soon turn from him, that the approaching season of 1919–20 would be the last complete one for the pride of the Metropolitan.

La Juive opened on November 22, 1919, with Caruso, Rosa Ponselle, Evelyn Scotney, Orville Harrold, and Léon Rothier, with Artur Bodanzky conducting. Caruso was now a mature artist of the theater, at the summit of his powers. As an example of the thought that had gone into his characterization, he described for a newspaper his preparation for the opening scene of the third act,

Enrico Caruso wearing tallith as Eléazar in the La Juive *Passover scene, with fingers separated in traditional priestly blessing. He consulted orthodox rabbis to achieve authentic dress and gesture.*

Opposite: *The last operatic portrait of Enrico Caruso, taken by Mishkin backstage at the Metropolitan during the tenor's final performance, December 24, 1920, in* La Juive.

when the terrified Eléazar must appear before the Tribunal of the Inquisition. To capture the halting steps described in the orchestra, Caruso wore a pair of shoes that fit badly and forced him into an awkward and clumsy walk appropriate for the old man. It was but one small detail in a carefully studied portrait that would have been inconceivable in the young tenor phenomenon at his debut in 1903.

Eléazar was to be Caruso's last new role, his ultimate triumph. His accomplishment was instantly recognized: "Enrico Caruso, who began life as a lyric tenor, aerial of tone and prone to youthful passions of operatic heroes, is now a full fledged tenore robusto, battling with the agonies of fatherhood, the subtleties of political plot and the plangent utterances of French recitative. He has been Renaud, Julien, Samson and John of Leyden, and yesterday afternoon he emerged as Eléazar in Halévy's *La Juive* . . . looking like Shylock, barring a nose which might rather have been a life long burden of Cyrano de Bergerac. No one who is familiar with the achievements of the most popular singer of this time would expect to be told that he met all the requirements of such a role as Eléazar. Nor would anyone of the million devoted admirers of his voice care. Probably no one knows this better than Mr. Caruso himself. All he has to do to evoke thunders of applause, is to linger on a high tone and to emit a final phrase at the full power of his voice. Therefore he commands the respect and admiration of all who regard operatic creations as of more import in art than their interpreters, for he has again and again shown himself a sincere seeker after genuine dramatic results. . . . His Eléazar in *La Juive* will be remembered as one of his highest flights. He had conceived the part in earnest study and he sang and acted it with an art as far removed as possible from that of his familiar Italian roles. There were dignity in his declamation and beauty in his cantilena. His chanting in the second act was a lyric utterance of exquisite character, while his delivery of the pealing air of the fourth act might have excited the envy of Nourrit himself."

During 1919–20 Caruso performed forty-seven times with the Metropolitan, alternating the lighter music of *Marta* and *Elisir* with *Juive, Samson, Prophète, Manon Lescaut,* and *Pagliacci.* He was now idyllically happy. He had a beautiful American wife, and his daughter, Gloria, was born in December 1919. From performances in Atlanta on the Met's spring tour Caruso went to Havana for a short opera season. During an *Aida* performance a bomb exploded in the theater, believed to have been thrown by someone angered by the high price of tickets. At the end of the performance Caruso was told that his home in East Hampton, Long Island, had been burglarized of jewels valued at $150,000. From that point on the events of his life appear to take a steady downhill march to their conclusion. During the summer and fall of 1920 there were concerts; in September he went again to the Victor recording studios in Camden, New Jersey, and made what was to be his last side, "Crucifixus" from Rossini's *Petite Messe Solennelle.* On November 15, Caruso sang Eléazar for the Metropolitan's opening night; there were complaints that he was singing too much, that the voice was tired. On December 3, a falling pillar in the final scene of *Samson* hit him on the head. In *Pagliacci,* on December 8, he was seized by an excruciating pain in his left side as he sang the high A near the end of "Vesti la giubba." At the Brooklyn Academy of Music for *Elisir* on December 11, his throat began to hemorrhage and the audience was dismissed before the first act was over.

Performances of *La Forza del Destino* and *Samson et Dalila* followed without incident, but another *Elisir* was canceled. *La Juive* was repeated on Christmas Eve. It was Caruso's six hundred and seventh performance at the Metropolitan, and at some point during the evening, Herman Mishkin, perhaps aware of the danger to the charmed life of his favorite subject, went backstage to Caruso's dressing room and photographed him for the last time. On Christmas Day, Caruso collapsed from pain and doctors diagnosed pleurisy.

Although there was hope during the following months of operations and recovery, the chief glory of Metropolitan Opera history had passed. Caruso sailed in May to Naples with his wife and young daughter. On July 6 Gatti cabled New York: I VISITED CARUSO MYSELF THREE DAYS AGO HIS CONVALESCENCE IS MORE THAN NORMAL HIS STRENGTH IS RECOVERING DAILY HAVE NO PREOCCUPATIONS FOR HIS FUTURE CONDITION HE WILL SING SURELY COMING SEASON. It was not to be. Caruso's Christmas Eve performance of *La Juive* had been his last with the Metropolitan. He died in Naples August 2, 1921. A few days later Gatti wrote to his widow from Venice: "I do wish to say that the remembrance of our dear Enrico, Artist supreme, a gentleman more than perfect, a man of heart and rectitude above all comparison, shall never leave my memory. I shall always be proud of the friendship, never perturbed for a moment, and of the deference which for twenty years he continuously showed me; a friendship that will constitute the most noble and pure satisfaction of my career. At the Metropolitan, the principal field of his triumphs and where all from the greatest to the smallest admired and adored him, his memory will ever be object of example and of veneration."

Overleaf: *Rosa Ponselle as Selika in* L'Africana.

c Mishkin
NY

PART III

THE GATTI YEARS

1921-1932

FTER WINNING THE OPERatic war with Oscar Hammerstein in 1910, Giulio Gatti-Casazza, the Metropolitan's general manager, experienced a few ideal years at the head of the company. He had his friend Arturo Toscanini, generally acclaimed as the world's finest conductor, leading more than sixty performances a season. Enrico Caruso devoted most of his energies to the Metropolitan, usually singing twice a week from November until May. Almost matching Caruso in public enthusiasm was the glamorous American soprano Geraldine Farrar. There was a strong Wagnerian repertoire with at least one *Ring* cycle and the standard works every season.

Then, citing artistic differences with Gatti, Toscanini returned to Italy in 1915; in fact, his affair with Farrar had reached the point at which she informed him that he must choose between her and his family; he chose his family. The Wagnerian repertoire was banished from the stage in 1917 because of the war with Germany. Finally, the unimaginable happened in the summer of 1921, when Caruso died at the age of forty-eight.

A new era began with opening night, November 14, 1921. That day Gatti-Casazza described the situation to Otto Kahn: "Until a few years ago our institution could be compared to a great machine driven by two principal wheels, one of which could be represented by the Caruso performances and the other by the performances of the Wagnerian repertoire (although the latter is slowly coming to life again). Fatality has willed that successively we should lose the one and the other wheel with the duty to provide to substitutions of a different character. If, as I hope, the substitutions will succeed and our machine can proceed regularly on its way, we can say that we have obtained the greatest of victories."

The 1921 opening performance was *La Traviata,* starring Amelita Galli-Curci in her long-awaited debut, Beniamino Gigli, and Giuseppe De Luca. Galli-Curci had been paid a large fee to rearrange her concert schedule and open the first season since 1903 without Caruso. Additionally for the season Gatti had secured the debut of Titta Ruffo, a baritone with the status of a tenor, and the return of the Russian bass Feodor Chaliapin, who since his one season in New York had become something of a legend.

Most of Gatti's efforts, however, were concentrated on tenors. He had watched Gigli's health that year with almost as much anxiety as he had Caruso's since the younger tenor also had come down with a threatening illness. Once Gigli recovered, Gatti could worry less about some he had considered hiring. He reported to Kahn: "Examined carefully, the situation of the tenors on the European market presents itself in a rather poor light. In the French career during these last times one tenor only has revealed good qualities, Mr. [Fernand] Ansseau of the Opera of Bruxelles. . . . But having asked him his terms for an eventual contract for the season 1922/23, with an unbelievable impudence he put toward some ridiculous demands asking $1500 per performance. [Gigli made less.] In Austria and in Germany there were two tenors for the repertoire of Italian and French operas: 1) The Dalmatian [Tino] Pattiera who has a good presence and a fine voice, but they all tell me he is a singer of very bad taste and bad character. . . . 2) The American tenor [Alfred] Piccaver: a fine voice and good presence but a bad singer who renders his parts in an unartistic and unmusical way. . . . As he was an American, I opened negotiations with him, but he also asked $1500 per performance! For such a ridiculous demand he would deserve to be put in jail without trial. According to me he is worth much less than [Mario] Chamlee to whom we only give $200 a week."

Despite his tenor aggravations, it must be remembered that several things went extremely well for Gatti-Casazza and the Metropolitan. Lucrezia Bori, one of the company's most valuable artists before her throat operations, returned after a long absence in the winter of 1921 to command the lyric soprano repertoire for fifteen more seasons. Rosa Ponselle followed her youthful debut in 1918 with a steady growth that made her one of the great dramatic sopranos of the century. And the years of negotiations with the Viennese star Maria Jeritza finally paid off when she burst upon New York in 1921 and Gatti-Casazza found a box office star for the 1920s to rival Caruso and Farrar.

So effective was Gatti-Casazza in coping with the problems besetting him after Caruso's death that despite his public reticence a new magazine, *Time,* featured him with its cover story published at the opening of the 1923–24 season. Part of the fascination of opera remained in watching a skilled professional deal with the eternal challenges of singers and repertoire. When Gatti's Berlin agent warned in 1922 that bass Michael Bohnen did not want to sing at the same time as soprano Barbara Kemp, Gatti replied with some Met history: "I had here for seven consecutive years Mme. Destinn and Mme. Farrar together, simultaneously during the whole season, two artists having the same merits, who never spoke to each other, nor greeted each other, who could not bear each other and had the same problems in Berlin. Nevertheless, these two artists who sang the same roles, such as *Tosca, Butterfly, Pagliacci, Tannhäuser,* back to back, never gave the administration any trouble, not even the slightest, never caused any inconvenience, but both always had the greatest success with the public. I could say the same thing of Gadski and Fremstad, as well as Hempel and Ober, etc. etc. Also Madame Jeritza came here this year full of apprehensions and worries, but she could be convinced that at the Metropolitan there is a serene atmosphere, impartial and, I repeat, there is room for all." Gatti soon discovered that dealing with Kemp and her husband, Max von Schillings, the composer who managed the Berlin Staatsoper, could be especially unpleasant. After canceling her contract at her request in 1924, the normally taciturn Gatti was forced to make a statement upon finding himself denounced in the papers by von Schillings: "Last year Mme. Kemp arrived here unprepared for many of the roles she was engaged to sing including among others, Selika in *L'Africana* and Brünnhilde in *Die Walküre.* That fact alone gave me the right to cancel her contract. Instead of doing so, out of regard for a woman and an artist of high reputation in Germany, I maintained the contract and not only that but I gave her a new contract for two months of this season and this because she requested it. . . . I have been for twenty-six years at the head of big opera houses and this is the first time that an incident of this calibre has happened to me. It is strange that it should have been perpetrated by a colleague. To my dear colleague I would say: 'You have lost a splendid occasion to remain silent.'"

Jeritza, whose position during the 1920s was impregnable, found a special way of maintaining Gatti's serene atmosphere, as revealed by Otto Kahn in a 1929 letter to Gatti: "I have long thought that we ought to have Lottie [*sic*] Lehmann here. If, as I understood from you, Madame Jeritza has announced her intention not to sing here if Madame Lehmann were at the Metropolitan and if it is granted that we should take such a threat into serious consideration, I cannot see why we should not engage Madame Lehmann during the period that Madame Jeritza does not sing here." Lehmann did not sing for the Met until 1934, after Jeritza's departure.

Gatti-Casazza continued his search for additions to the repertoire, although in 1924 he was not sanguine about the prospects. "The lyric theatre is undoubtedly going through a very serious crisis and the most salient point of such crisis is the lack of artists having a strong personality and the lack of new operas which really interest the public and make them forget the old ones." While before Gatti had tried works by such composers as Wolf-Ferrari, Giordano, and Blech, now he experimented with those of Korngold, Montemezzi, and Respighi. He discussed with Puccini the possible world premiere of his new work on a Chinese theme, *Turandot,* and was assured by the composer that there would be good roles for Jeritza and Gigli. (This was before a feud made their joint appearances impossible.)

Gatti rejected another long-awaited opera: Arrigo Boito's *Nerone,* a treatment of Nero and ancient Rome, to which Boito, the composer of *Mefistofele* and librettist of Verdi's *Otello* and *Falstaff,* had devoted decades without finishing. Completed by Toscanini, *Nerone* premiered at La Scala with Toscanini, a superb cast, and a colossal production, and quickly became a seldom revived curiosity. Gatti notified the Italian publisher Ricordi that he would not produce it in New York; Ricordi responded with pressure through its American agent: "When I called upon Maxwell," wrote Gatti, "to renew the contract for the Puccini operas and for *Falstaff,* they were refused to me! It was only after my strong protests and threats to publish in the newspapers this new kind of hold-up and to begin a campaign for the revisions of the author's rights in America that the good Maxwell was induced to renew the contract upon the same conditions for the coming season."

Although Gatti planned at various times to have either Farrar or Jeritza sing *Salome,* spoke of performing *Ariadne auf Naxos* because Zerbinetta would be such a good role for Galli-Curci, and scheduled *Feuersnot* only to discover he lacked the proper cast, *Rosenkavalier* alone among Strauss operas was regularly performed. Strauss's *Aegyptische Helena* was given in 1928 with Jeritza but did not catch on.

Gatti presented Igor Stravinsky's *Rossignol* in 1926, but there were currents in the contemporary music to which he did not respond. It was left to the visiting Philadelphia Orchestra under Leopold Stokowski to give the New York premieres of both Stravinsky's *Oedipus Rex* and Alban Berg's *Wozzeck* at the Metropolitan in 1931.

Planning to retire at the end of the 1934–35 season, Gatti wrote to Paul D. Cravath, who had succeeded Otto Kahn as chairman of the Metropolitan Board of Directors, "This decision is taken in consideration of my rather mature age and of the continued and exhausting hardships of a long directorial career of forty-two years, twenty-seven of which will have been spent with the Metropolitan." However, Gatti had one final legacy for his opera company. On August 22, 1934, two months after writing to Cravath, Gatti traveled on short notice to St. Moritz and auditioned a Wagnerian soprano as a replacement for Frida Leider, who had demanded release from her contract. Gatti listened to Kirsten Flagstad ("She made an excellent impression," he wrote to New York) and declared himself ready to cancel the arrangements with Leider. Flagstad's debut as Sieglinde in a 1935 Saturday-matinee broadcast performance of *Die Walküre* was a landmark in Metropolitan history. Gatti had spent long years slowly rebuilding his Wagnerian ensemble after the ravages of World War I. Now, just as general manager Maurice Grau in 1903 had bequeathed to his successor Heinrich Conried a priceless contract with Enrico Caruso, Gatti left not merely a voice for Wagner, but in Flagstad a commanding figure to inspire another historic era at the Metropolitan.

FEODOR CHALIAPIN AND *BORIS GODUNOV*

DURING THE SUMMER OF 1921, WHILE the radiant life of Caruso was approaching its end where it had begun near the Bay of Naples, another operatic drama was being played out to the north on the edge of the Baltic Sea. Whiling away his time in Riga was Fred Gaisberg, agent of the Gramophone Company of London, who had made Caruso's influential 1902 Milan recordings. Gaisberg was waiting to meet another old friend: the bass Feodor Chaliapin (1873–1938) was about to emerge from Soviet Russia. At the age of forty-eight, Chaliapin, all his property having been confiscated by the Communists, was faced with leaving his country and rebuilding his life and fortune. Word reached the Metropolitan in early September: "Gaisberg has met Chaliapin in Riga, where, like a great schoolboy, the artist appears to be having a 'bust.' Gaisberg says Riga is full of all sorts of odd impresarios trying to corner Chaliapin. . . . I expect you read about the first concert he gave in Riga. There was such a queue of people waiting to get tickets that they had to call out the soldiers, who finally fired over the heads of people to disperse the crowds. Gaisberg writes me that fabulous prices were paid for the tickets and that speculators seem to have made small fortunes. Gaisberg writes that Chaliapin has gone a bit grey, but that his voice has not lost anything. He sang the Russian folksongs with all the old charm and style and sentiment. Despite a large number of 'Whites' and anti-Bolshevists, who tried to make a demonstration, the rest of the audience were so entranced by his voice that the concert succeeded."

The most vivid of actors, Feodor Chaliapin, as Boris Godunov in a moment of introspection.

Having negotiated a fee higher than Caruso's, Chaliapin returned in triumph to the Metropolitan for six performances of *Boris Godunov* in which he sang Russian to the Italian of everybody else. Whatever the controversy of his first visit in 1907, during subsequent seasons his Boris was the centerpiece, and the critics outdid themselves in attempts to do justice to it. The *Sun* described in the coronation scene "a voice that gave the imperial proclamation such a lyric form as a deity would give who leans down from mountain tops to bless the valleys." Henderson emphasized both voice and drama: "His impersonation better deserves the term elemental than does the opera, for it is a piece of acting in which the sheer overwhelming force of untrammeled virility is the conquering agent. There is much art in the delineation and in the singing. Indeed, Mr. Chaliapin's vocal methods often on the stage and generally on the concert platform result in shattering of melodic lines and alternation of lyric scansion, but his irresistible personality and his power as an actor make him a huge operatic figure. When he revealed his Boris last year, it was said in this place that much of the dialogue and much of the monologue ran to parlando and often to actual speech. But the utterance was always filled with passion and power. 'There was no phase of the anguish of the remorse tortured soul that escaped the searchlight of this brutal art.' It is no exaggeration to say that the operatic stage has furnished no such portrayal of the agonies of a soul since Tamagno's Otello. That Mr. Chaliapin can sing musically, broadly and in a fluent legato style when he wishes to do so was proved by his delivery of the speech of Boris to the people in the first act. It was a truly noble piece of lyric declamation, equalled only by his voicing of the monologue in the chamber scene." Pitts Sanborn stressed the profundity of interpretation: "It was an expression of tragedy which seemed less a personal phenomenon than a universal gesture. This towering, elemental Russian in his fantastic garb of empire, might have been Suffering incarnate. The very majesty of his torment made it as a thing sacred. No wonder that among primitive and oriental peoples those condemned to perpetual sorrow and to madness have been revered as saints and worshipped."

FEODOR CHALIAPIN AND *MEFISTOFELE*

BORN IN POVERTY, FEODOR CHALIAPIN in his youth went on the stage in Kazan almost as soon as his voice had changed, first as a chorister and then singing small parts with a touring Russian provincial company. By the time he was twenty he had sung leading roles, including several with a range or style not later associated with his name—Valentin in *Faust* (sung before taking on Méphistophélès), Tonio in *Pagliacci,* St. Bris in *Les Huguenots,* and Oroveso in *Norma.* He was with the Bolshoi by 1899 and in 1901 Gatti, then at La Scala, brought him to Italy for his first appearances outside Russia. His debuts there and at the Metropolitan in 1907–1908 were in the title role in Boito's *Mefistofele.* Remembered as a disaster for him, that isolated season began in triumph: "Chaliapin, both by necessity and intent, dominated the biggest Broadway stage as no other artist has done in these five years since Conried fell heir to his Caruso contract with Maurice Grau." And: "It took the audience but a brief moment to see that an unusual artist was before them, and when his voice rang out the ear emphasized the impression of the eye." Henderson described "a big, rumbling bass, which resounds immensely in the lower register, yet becomes tractable in the upper ranges and can fine itself away into very musical head tones. In other words, Mr. Chaliapin manages his big voice with a good deal of skill, and while its natural quality makes his singing seem to lack refinement, perhaps he may be said to have paraded that condition as a striking factor in his performance." With Clotilde Bressler-Gianoli, Olive Fremstad, and Maurice Renaud regularly performing, New York was not without superb singing actors. Yet Chaliapin made a vivid impression: "He is an elemental creature, roaring and champing like a bull, charging the poor sinners of this world with the fuss and energy of a 60 horse-power motor and leaving a trail of fire and brimstone behind him. This is the Satan resulting from the union of the Italian creator and the Russian interpreter. His frame, gigantic as it is, cannot contain his nature. He writhes with the emotions that convulse him. His face is drawn into expression of the profoundest agony. . . . All the dramatic action tending to establish this conception of Boito's Satan is accompanied by every helpful aid of light, scenery and mechanical ingenuity. M. Chaliapin takes the utmost pains with his make-up, which combines effectively the use of fleshlings and bare skin. The skin is covered with a shiny, metallic powder which sparkles in the calcium."

His second role, Basilio in *Il Barbiere di Siviglia,* was an instant hit with audiences. "He was made up as a grimy, greasy caricature, his powerful hands and arms pawed the air to get free of his cloth, and the creature's greed and cunning were written large as 'scare headlines,' so to speak, all over the face, from his false chin and painted nose to the raised and distorted crown of a half-hairless wig. All that is admitted freely. But the fact remains that from his first gigantic entrance in the 'Calumny' aria, which had to be repeated, the big, rough Russian bass made his every point a telling one with the house. Only the time-honored reentrance in the 'Goodnight' ensemble fell flat, because the laughing audience had exhausted its applause just before. It is only truth to say that Rossini's opera, the most ancient work into

Opposite: *Feodor Chaliapin arrayed in the coronation robes of Boris Godunov on the occasion of his stunning 1921 return to the Metropolitan Opera.*

Feodor Chaliapin's half-nude Mefistofele shocked New York in 1907 but was an overwhelming success in 1922.

Mishkin's dramatic 1922 portrait of Feodor Chaliapin in the title role of Boito's Mefistofele, *sometimes misidentified as Méphistophélès in Gounod's* Faust.

which the spirit of life and youth is ever breathed today, has not been so boisterously and so heartily enjoyed in a quarter century here, and that no revival on Mr. Conried's stage, save *Meistersinger* or *Hansel and Gretel* alone, has been so greeted with an orderly crescendo of popular smiles, ripples of laughter and, finally, helpless shrieks of delight." But the most influential critics, Aldrich, Henderson, and Krehbiel, denounced the "vulgarity" of his scratching, nose-picking Basilio with such force that by the time he had learned Leporello in a few days and performed it in the Mahler revival of *Don Giovanni,* he was decidedly out of favor. He left New York and threatened never to return.

Other than *Boris Godunov,* nothing from Chaliapin's extensive Russian repertoire was ever seen in New York. For his second season after returning to New York in 1921, Chaliapin had suggested Ivan the Terrible in Rimsky-Korsakov's *Maid of Pskov.* But he reverted instead to the Boito and Gounod Mefistos that had been seen under Conried.

Chaliapin's half-nude Mefistofele was not so sensational in the twenties. As Henderson commented, "Since it became fashionable for prima donnas to strip to the waist there is nothing in it for a mere man." Something of his extraordinary personality may be gathered from his many records and from the extensive excerpts from *Mefistofele, Faust,* and *Boris* that were captured during actual performance at Covent Garden in 1926 and 1928, using the newly invented electrical recording equipment. Photographs and records, however, can only give us hints of the physical impact of Chaliapin. In *Mefistofele,* he was "huge and menacing, shambling about like a great spider, with his long black hair gathered into a sort of scalp-lock that gave his face the look of a Japanese devil-mask." In *Faust,* he could be the incarnation of bestiality in one scene, yet in the Garden Scene, playfully tuck the Siébel under his arm and carry him offstage.

Beniamino Gigli made his 1920 Metropolitan debut as Faust in Mefistofele *only a few weeks before Caruso's final performance.*

BENIAMINO GIGLI

IN JUNE 1919, CALVIN CHILDS OF THE Victor Talking Machine Company wrote to Gatti's assistant, Edward Ziegler, at the Metropolitan: "The Gramophone Company tells me they have signed a contract with a new tenor, Gigly, in Milan, of whom Maestro Sibanio, one of the Assistant Directors of Milan, who is connected with the Gramophone Company says 'Another Caruso'. Of course, you and I have heard this report at least three million times but they are going to forward me sample records of this new wonder as soon as they are finished, and I will give you an opportunity to hear them." "Sibanio" was certainly Carlo Sabajno, the Italian conductor most remembered for his many opera recordings; "Gigly" was Beniamino Gigli (1890–1957), the Italian tenor with whom Gatti-Casazza was then concluding a contract that would bring him to the Met in November 1920, only a few weeks before Caruso's last performance. His New York debut was a new production of *Mefistofele* with Adamo Didur substituting for José Mardones, and Frances Alda. Although no one could replace Caruso, Gigli came closer than any other Italian tenor. "His voice is a lyric tenor of peculiar warmth and mellowness in the middle register, notable for the beauty of its timbre, rather than for power and volume, remarkably elastic, exquisite in mezza voce, luscious in full-throated emission, but decidedly unsensational in its upper range. While Gigli's voice in itself is one of the finest voices of its kind that New Yorkers have heard since the advent of Caruso, the dramatic intensity, the emotional vitality, the expressiveness which informs his singing is even more remarkable. His performance alone of the epilogue—perfect in its delivery of the musical phrase, masterfully worked out in every nuance—would have stamped him as an artist." Gigli was so quickly embraced by the public that Gatti immediately rewrote his contract for future seasons and prolonged the current one. (Caruso had suffered his throat hemorrhage in Brooklyn before the new contract was signed.)

Opposite: *Beniamino Gigli's Edgardo, sung at the Met opposite the first* Lucias *of Amelita Galli-Curci and Lily Pons.*

During the twenties the Met boasted many powerful vocal combinations: Gigli and Claudia Muzio in *Andrea Chénier* and *Loreley;* Gigli and Lucrezia Bori in *Roméo et Juliette* and *Mignon;* Gigli and Rosa Ponselle in *L'Africana* and *La Gioconda;* Gigli and Maria Jeritza in *Tosca* (until he slapped her backstage in a battle over curtain calls, after which they didn't sing together again). The only complaint about Gigli's performances concerned his acting, which seems never to have developed as Caruso's did: "Beniamino Gigli has found in Roméo a role that indulges all the virtues of his voice. There was a hint, in what he did last season in *Le Roi d'Ys,* that he was ready to grapple at any time with that silk covered iron rod, the French style. And on Saturday, he turned this rod into a marshal's baton. For he sang beautifully, artistically, with smoothness and velvety tone, discretion, often with distinction, and with a minimum regard for the gallery. But it was only in the last act that he coupled any emotion of acting to the words he was pronouncing and here, by a silly tumbling down the steps of Juliet's bier, he quashed the doubt as to whether he was dramatic and heroic after all. He was not." (Puccini had been afraid that Gigli's stage appearance would destroy a performance of *La Rondine* in Rome, but after hearing a rehearsal he declared: "I think, after all, that people won't notice the figure when they hear the voice.")

Unfortunately, Gigli's Met career is now remembered for his refusal to accept a 10 percent pay cut in 1932 during the Depression. What isn't known is that he immediately regretted his decision and sent his secretary with a number of compromises, including an offer to sing five or six performances gratis. It is also not generally known that Lily Pons and Rosa Ponselle, two of the singers who publicly assailed Gigli for not contributing his salary to save the Met, had their fees raised the following season. They, however, were making much less than he, and in dismissing Gigli, Gatti saved himself from an expensive contract that would have raised Gigli's 1934-35 salary to Caruso's fee at a time far different financially from the days when Caruso was singing and there were surpluses.

Gigli returned to the Met for five guest appearances in 1938-39. He made movies in the United States (Vitaphone shorts), Italy, Germany, and England; he recorded eight complete operas when such undertakings were not routine. His more than forty years of nonstop barnstorming in opera and concert were testimony to a well-produced voice. While countless tenors have tried to emulate the richness of Caruso, they might just as hopelessly have sought the sweetness of Gigli.

AURELIANO PERTILE

DURING THE SUMMER OF 1921 GATTI surveyed the first-class tenors of the world in preparation for the 1921-22 season. Among those he considered who had never sung at the Metropolitan were Fernand Ansseau, Joseph Hislop, Alfred Piccaver, and Ulysses Lappas. Joseph Mann, the Polish heroic tenor, was actually scheduled to take over many roles for the ailing Caruso, but he dropped dead during a Berlin performance of *Aida* that September. One whom Gatti particularly wanted was the Italian tenor Aureliano Pertile (1885-1952), whose Met engagement Gatti announced to Otto Kahn from Venice on August 7, 1921. "Another tenor, who during the past seasons has had . . . a whole series of simply brilliant successes is Mr. Aureliano Pertile who has sung in all the principal theatres of Italy, Spain and South America. His voice is not a golden voice, it is rather arid but firm and manly. Moreover he is a very serious artist, very musical and possessing a complete repertoire. . . . Mr. Pertile signed his contract the very day in which poor Caruso was in agony, although no one of us knew of it."

It was Pertile's misfortune to make his debut the evening that Maria Jeritza unveiled her sensational Tosca for New York, December 1, 1921. His reviews became footnotes to the soprano's. "His voice has a tendency toward whiteness, but in its fullest volume it is warmer and resonant. He sang his music. He did not shout it, but delivered it with free tones and smoothness."

Pertile soon made a stronger impression of his own. In *Cavalleria* he was described as "a tenor with the mentality of a baritone," and in *Aida* as "a man who gains with closer acquaintance. His voice, to be sure, is not a voice of great sensuous beauty or power. He uses it well, however, and brings intelligence to bear, not only on his singing but on his acting. A dignified, if not actually heroic Radames, he easily won the favor of the audience without indulging in any gesticulatory extravagances." In *Louise* with Farrar there was complete approval. "It was said for him that he first learned the role in Italian, under the French composer's supervision, and enacted it with success in Italy and Spain. On a week's notice, he mastered the French text recently, and a performance in Philadelphia a fortnight ago was in effect his only public rehearsal for Broadway. There need have been no apologies for an impersonation of so high merit as his last night, artistic throughout, refined in phrase, powerful at need, though the tall Italian is no spendthrift of voice. Under his conventional guise of Gallic bohemian, there was a warmth of Southern temperament, as if Julian [*sic*] were newly winner of a Prix de Rome."

Pertile's most successful and frequent part in New York was Dmitri, which had impact opposite the Boris of Chaliapin. "Of the many tenors who have appeared here as the false Dmitri, Mr. Pertile is the first who has

A portrait of Aureliano Pertile, a tenor Gatti-Casazza regretted not being able to reengage after his 1921–22 season.

given the part definite, and even strong, dramatic value. But Mr. Pertile is a rare actor among tenors. He also sang last evening to his marked advantage." When Pertile left in February he had sung his contracted fifteen performances, including two Sunday-night concerts. Though pleased with Pertile, Gatti in his anxiety over Caruso had overloaded his roster with tenors. He waited until April to write in an unusually friendly manner. "Mio caro Pertile, Circumstances are almost always stronger than the will; so that I, who would have been very pleased to renew your contract for the coming season, find myself obliged to let you go. This is all the more difficult for me since you had a brilliant success and your artistic and personal merits earned for you the affection of the public, of colleagues and very much so that of the undersigned."

Pertile's career suffered not at all. At La Scala he became Toscanini's favorite tenor (after Caruso and long before Jan Peerce in New York), singing almost everything from *Lucia* and *Il Trovatore* to *I Maestri Cantori* under his direction; he created the title roles in the *Nerones* of Boito and Mascagni. In December of 1923, although Gatti had the tenors Miguel Fleta, Beniamino Gigli, Giacomo Lauri-Volpi, and Giovanni Martinelli on his roster, with some touch of regret he must have read this message from one of his Italian agents: "As you will read in the papers La Scala has become il teatro 'PERTILE'. All the operas are sung by him, the only tenor!"

THE METROPOLITAN PREMIERE OF *COSÌ FAN TUTTE*

GATTI-CASAZZA HAD WANTED TO PUT on Mozart's *Così fan tutte* as far back as 1911. In 1922 he finally had the right cast for the first Metropolitan performances. *Così* depends for success on the technique of its women; Florence Easton sang brilliantly as Fiordiligi, Frances Peralta was Dorabella, and Lucrezia Bori assumed the comic role of Despina. "The greatest surprise for the knowing was the successful performance of the singers. Nobody who has been on the Metropolitan stage since the departure of Mme. Sembrich could have played the part of Despina more bewitchingly or sung her two airs with more exquisite beauty of tone and phrase than Miss Bori. . . . Mme. Easton conquered the stupendous difficulties of her airs, which, like those of Donna Anna in *Don Giovanni,* are alternately sweepingly dramatic and florid, in a manner that added orbits to her artistic stature, which it has always been a pleasurable duty to recognize, while Miss Peralta disclosed abilities as actress and singer such as she has never given us occasion to guess. And the three gentlemen acted their comedy parts as well as they sang their music." The men in the cast were George Meader as Ferrando, Giuseppe De Luca as Guglielmo, and Adamo Didur as Don Alfonso. When the designer, Joseph Urban, complained that he lost money because of the detailed work required, the Metropolitan responded that "if you think you lost money, you should see our box office receipts." Nonetheless, Gatti insisted on maintaining this critical success in the repertoire, sometimes for only a single performance each season. It did not become a box office hit until Rudolf Bing produced it in 1951–52 with Eleanor Steber, Blanche Thebom, Patrice Munsel, Richard Tucker, Frank Guarrera, and John Brownlee.

Opposite: *Frances Peralta as Dorabella and Florence Easton as Fiordiligi, beguiling sisters in New York's first glimpse of Mozart's* Così fan tutte.

Mishkin
NY 34

C
MISHKIN
N.Y. 40

ROSA PONSELLE AND *LE ROI D'YS*

WHATEVER THE RAGS-TO-RICHES ELEment in the career of Rosa Ponselle, the facts show the glamorous side often overwhelmed by critical disfavor and the years of study overlooked. Gatti had signed her to a beginner's contract, and although she sang leading roles in three Metropolitan premieres that first season—*Forza,* Rezia in *Oberon,* and Carmelita in *The Legend* (a one-act failure by Joseph Breil, composer of the scores for *Birth of a Nation* and *Intolerance*)—she was paid $150 a week, less than her top fee in vaudeville and considerably less than the top sopranos on the Met's roster. That same season Geraldine Farrar received $1,500 a performance; Florence Easton, $50; Frances Alda, $800; and Claudia Muzio $22,000 for the season. On the other hand, Ponselle signed a recording contract with Columbia Records three days after her debut and in the spring began the concert tours that were to occupy a substantial part of her career. When Covent Garden inquired about her in 1919, Gatti replied that her repertoire was extremely limited and "in my opinion, it would neither be in the interest of this artist, nor in the interests of Mr. Higgins to arrange for her appearance in London this year." Instead, he kept her close to home, reviving for her a progression of significant soprano roles. Ponselle's career was made through a curious combination of public acclamation, critical praise and cautions, and constant, steady improvement that could only have been the product of hard work.

Such a progression in Ponselle's career is revealed in reviews of her performances from 1920 to 1924. On her Rezia in *Oberon* (March 1920): "In points of diction, style, phrasing and in revealing histrionism [Florence Easton] was Miss Ponselle's superior. Only in the matter of natural vocal endowment did she yield precedence." As Elisabetta in *Don Carlo* (December 1920), "Rosa Ponselle, on whose big shoulders rested ugly robes, sang with power and a lovely, floating tone. Disappointing as she often is, you feel that the future is hers if she so wills it. The native richness of her vocal and dramatic endowments—for there is plenty of temperament, latent as yet—ought to bear wonderful fruit sometime. A Caruso in petticoats? Who knows what she may achieve with labor rightfully directed (we repeat, rightfully). . . . But, as we said two seasons ago this young woman has an arduous tramp before she attains the peak of the operatic Parnassus." In *Ernani* (December 1921), her Elvira was declared "nothing short of glorious. Hers is a voice that has both the low range and the high range for this exacting role, and she seems to have made distinct progress as a singer." Another critic, who probably had not participated in the standing ovation the performance received, suggested that some of her music had been transposed for convenience.

On her Magared in *Le Roi d'Ys* (January 1922): "The hateful brunette who brought about the disaster of Ys was Rosa Ponselle who made it a sort of study of Ortrud. Her Magared was as sinister as Scotti's Scarpia and she hurled forth her huge tones without restraint. Some restraint, both in singing and acting, will benefit her impersonation." And, as Selika in *L'Africana* in December 1924, "Miss Ponselle also won applause, in the first place because of the superb quality of her voice, secondly, because, although her artistry does not match her natural vocal endowment, she has improved as a singer in later seasons and has, at moments, hints and flashes of the grand manner."

Selika was followed by Leonora in *Il Trovatore* and Gioconda, and then came Giulia in *La Vestale,* a time for acclamation and unimpaired triumph.

GIUSEPPE DANISE

BETWEEN THE REIGNS OF PASQUALE Amato and Lawrence Tibbett there was Giuseppe Danise (1883–1963), the last Italian baritone to dominate the Metropolitan's standard repertoire. After singing in most of the important houses of Italy, Danise came to the Met in 1920–21 during Amato's last season and remained until 1931–32, the season Tibbett first sang *Simon Boccanegra.* He made an immediate impression in his 1920 debut role, Amonasro in *Aida:* "Mr. Danise came here with a fine reputation gained in Latin America as a master of bel canto. But singers worshipped in Havana and Mexico City have been known to get a very cold shoulder in New York—and vice versa. Not so Mr. Danise. He revealed a voice at once rich and brilliant in its upper range, but not lacking a strength lower down." Danise went on to sing not only the Italian baritone's usual lineup of Tonios, Germonts, and Barnabas, but was featured in some unusual Metropolitan performances. He was Gérard in the first Metropolitan *Andrea Chénier* with Beniamino Gigli and Claudia Muzio, Athanaël to the Thaïs of Maria Jeritza, and appeared with Rosa Ponselle in *L'Africana* and *William Tell. The New York Times* singled him out in the first Metropolitan *Loreley* with Muzio: "To be mentioned first because of the beauty and finish and dramatic accent of his singing, the intensive self-control of his acting is the Hermann of Mr. Danise,

Opposite: *Rosa Ponselle as the sinister Margared in Lalo's* Roi d'Ys, *one of a succession of increasingly demanding roles given her in preparation for such important assignments as Gioconda, Giulia in* La Vestale, *and* Norma.

Giuseppe Danise as Karnac in Le Roi d'Ys, *one of thirty baritone roles he sang at the Met between 1920 and 1932.*

one of the finest things he has offered to the New York public." With some four hundred Metropolitan Opera performances behind him, Danise became in the 1930s a respected and demanding teacher of voice. He collaborated in the successful transformation of Regina Resnik from soprano to mezzo. Applying his high standards to his wife, the charming Brazilian soprano Bidú Sayão, he once broke off a coaching session for *Traviata* exclaiming, "They pay you too much at the Metropolitan!"

EMMA CALVÉ

IN THE 1890s, THE CARMEN OF FRENCH soprano Emma Calvé (1858–1942) was a theatrical event comparable in public response and excitement to the Canio in *Pagliacci* of Enrico Caruso a decade later. Calvé made only a bit less money than Nellie Melba and sang several of the same roles, such as Marguerite in *Faust* and Ophélie in *Hamlet*. In 1907 her Carmen for Oscar Hammerstein helped build his Manhattan Opera into a valid rival of the Met. In 1915 she was at the Palace several weeks as headliner (the same season as the Marx Brothers). Sime reported the event in *Variety:* "Nothing better than Deroulede's 'Le Clairon' [The Trumpeter] has ever been done by an operatic star on the vaudeville stage. . . . Vaudeville must have surprised [Calvé] almost as much as she has surprised vaudeville. . . . Previously high operatic singers, whether foreign or native, when in vaudeville, believed in high notes. Calvé is singing. Quite a difference."

On tour in Cincinnati during wartime, she discovered that a large part of the audience was of German origin, walked to the footlights and spat a few times into the auditorium, then launched into "La Marseillaise" without accompaniment. The audience thought it part of the show and cheered.

Back in New York in 1922 she gave a series of recitals in Carnegie Hall. Her renowned ability to mesmerize audiences was still intact: "Mme. Calvé is not only the possessor of a voice and a technic, but she is, as she has been for many years, an interpreter of extraordinary mastery and emotional force." Two months later it was written of her: "Absolutely the most stunning singing heard in New York this season has been the contribution of two veterans of the veterans, Emma Calvé and Ernestine Schumann-Heink, and of a baritone only a little less veteran, Emilio de Gogorza. Figure this out as you will, but let the youngsters all take heed of it! The single fact of knowing how to sing every once in a while asserts its value with a force that is positively startling. . . . Here is a woman who, with forty years of stage career behind her, can sing today contralto, mezzo-soprano, dramatic

The ever-youthful Emma Calvé as she appeared in 1922, twenty-nine years after her Metropolitan Opera debut.

soprano, lyric soprano, canary-bird coloratura. In other words, she can sing—as singers sang before partly arbitrary and largely harmful classifications were so much insisted on. It is unnecessary to speak today of the expressiveness and the magical color of her singing, of the commanding or bewitching way in which her voice and a technic that is second nature become the true medium of thought and feeling. Such singing as Calvé's is not only a ravishment, but the most eloquent of artistic preachments. Some object to her caprices before the public—as when twice she stopped and consulted the music in the habanera from her inveterate *Carmen*!—others object to her use of facial expression and gesture, as when blackrobed she waved an enormous fan of shaded rose hues while she inimitably sang 'L'Eventail.' . . . Calvé, in her carefree, intimate way, sang an impromptu programme quite her own, interspersing it with delightful little announcements. Airs from *Mefistofele,* and from *Carmen,* Santuzza's narrative from *Cavalleria Rusticana* and a variety of songs she delivered in a way that was a rare artistic delight."

During her lifetime she earned and spent a fortune. In 1938 she was forced to sell her manuscript of Massenet's *Sapho,* a creation of hers back in 1897, to the Metropolitan Opera Guild and wrote to Mrs. August Belmont: "I have received your very kind letter, and rejoice at the thought by which, thanks to you and my friend, Mrs. Francis Bacon, this manuscript of Massenet will become part of the Metropolitan Opera library, which reminds me of the enthusiasm of the dear American public to whom I owe the best part of the success of my youth, when I sang for them with all my heart and all my soul! How I should love to come and make a last adieu in a 'farewell' concert. What is your advice? My voice, faithful always, does not want to leave me. It is a child of the ether which carries me away, and I try to follow it. Does this not prove that age counts for nothing when one preserves one's courage and enthusiasm? This fine plan could only take place in the spring during the World's Fair."

She was eighty and had three years to live.

SIGRID ONEGIN

FOR SOME REASON THE METROPOLITAN career of Swedish contralto Sigrid Onegin (1889–1943) did not have the substance that might have been expected. In Europe she had made her operatic debut in a 1912 *Carmen* in Stuttgart and was Dryad in the world premiere of *Ariadne auf Naxos*. Gatti's German agent described her in 1921 as "the artist who, in important centers, receives the biggest fees." However, when negotiations with the Metropolitan began, she declared herself

Sigrid Onegin in a Mishkin portrait made shortly before her 1922 Metropolitan Opera debut as Amneris in Aida, *a performance that introduced Elisabeth Rethberg in the title role.*

Mishkin's official portrait of the Italian soprano Toti Dal Monte, from her one brief Metropolitan season, 1924–25. La Scala was the scene of her greatest successes.

unable to relearn *Carmen* in French and backed out of a commitment to sing Ortrud. After appearing with the Philadelphia Orchestra, she made her Metropolitan debut, as did Elisabeth Rethberg, in a 1922 *Aida* with Giovanni Martinelli. In the five performances she eventually sang with the Metropolitan, her reception was ideal. "Sigrid Onegin, the new Amneris, displayed all the burning dramatic power that the formalities of the concert stage forced her to repress with the Philadelphia Orchestra several weeks ago. . . . Queenly in demeanor and apparel, a similar richness of vesture covered her voice with even hue through all its broad register. Singularly regular the coloring that Mme. Onegin can maintain as far up the scale as she can go." The following week she sang Brangäne in *Tristan:* "The audience was thrilled by sounds such as it has not heard in it since the operatic days of Schumann-Heink. Her voice did roll down from the parapet like an avalanche of sound, yet it was not an avalanche in temperature, but was warm, full-throated, glorious, overwhelming. . . . In the first act, too, Mme. Onegin displayed a voice of singular purity, roundness, and dramatic warmth, and she looked every inch her part. Mme. Matzenauer as Isolde sang splendidly and with tremendous fervor. To be sure the part of Isolde should be sung on a violin, not a viola." It was perhaps Matzenauer's all-round usefulness that prevented Onegin from securing a place on the roster. The *Walküre* Fricka completed her Metropolitan work. Thereafter she went on to a considerable career in the United States as a recitalist, and in the twenties and thirties in Berlin she sang Lady Macbeth, Orfeo, and Fidès in *Prophète.* At her last New York appearance, a Town Hall recital in 1938, *The New York Times* observed: "Not many singers of the past two decades have achieved the record for consistent excellence from both the vocal and the interpretative angle as this richly endowed mistress of song."

TOTI DAL MONTE

GATTI-CASAZZA, WHO LIKED TO KEEP A watchful eye on major operatic enterprises around the world, was particularly wary of events at his former theater, La Scala in Milan, where his one-time partner

Toscanini was in charge during the 1920s. It is likely that one of the first times he was aware of the Italian soprano Toti Dal Monte (1893–1975) was in January 1922, when she appeared at Scala under Toscanini in his *Rigoletto* performances with Giacomo Lauri-Volpi and Carlo Galeffi. Dal Monte had made her 1916 Scala debut in a supporting role in Zandonai's *Francesca da Rimini* with Rosa Raisa in the title role, and had slowly moved toward starring roles of the upper soprano range. In 1923 she appeared at Scala in *Barbiere* and *Lucia.*

About this time Henry Russell, the former director of the Boston Opera, wrote Gatti that he had engaged Dal Monte to support Melba's Australian tour. The reports from Down Under were sensational; Dal Monte's Lucia was said to be the greatest triumph ever witnessed in Australian theaters. Not to be outdone, Melba, still singing well, had come onstage after a performance and proclaimed Dal Monte as her true successor.

Dal Monte came to America and sang with the Chicago Opera before reaching the Met for *Lucia* in December 1924, with Mario Chamlee, Giuseppe De Luca, and José Mardones. Pitts Sanborn used his review to dispose of a few prejudices: "In these piping times when any young thing who can shriek above the staff and simulate a trill while perpetrating operatic dementia is solemnly referred to as a 'coloratura,' one is tempted to write an essay in defence and illustration of an opera which has suffered much abuse, but still is going cheerfully in its ninetieth year, by name *Lucia di Lammermoor.* If a woman can be called a 'coloratura,' why not equally a 'legato,' a 'staccato,' a 'recitative,' alias a 'tremolo.' But the present is hardly the moment for such speculations. The urgent topic is the debut last night. . . . Mme. Dal Monte, a squat, dumpy little woman and a conscientious operatic actress, proved without delay that her voice is by no means one of those vanishing sopranos which are lost in the first outburst of an unsupported flute. If Mme. Barrientos was the sixth echo of La Scala, Mme. Dal Monte is no fainter than the third. Her voice is not the big light soprano (if one may so express the matter) of a Melba or a Tetrazzini, but it is at least an audible and prevailingly serviceable entry. At times last evening her tones were disagreeably white, but oftener the voice was round and pleasant. Of course, it is high and flexible, and Mme. Dal Monte revealed capability, if no remarkable brilliance, in the delivery of fioritura. But that is not the best of the story. The best of it is that Mme. Dal Monte showed herself a musician and a vocal artist. In the role of Lucy Ashton there is far more of sustained song and of lyric declamation than of the trills and runs of reason or unreason. Mme. Dal Monte disclosed a delightful appreciation of this fact."

Two Lucias and a Gilda were the total Metropolitan Opera career. Gatti gave her a contract for the following season, but in November 1925 Charles Wagner, her manager, agreed to the cancellation. In her later years Dal Monte blamed her brief stay on the malignant influence of Amelita Galli-Curci, but the explanation is probably simpler. In 1922 Gatti had written to his agent Lusardi in Milan of another soprano: "La Signorina Angeles Ottein, a leggero soprano you know well, has obtained a real success at the Metropolitan. I must tell you this so that the reason I am not rehiring her next season is not misinterpreted. The only reason is that for the leggero repertoire, we have enough Galli-Curci performances and therefore do not have a position for another noteworthy leggero soprano."

Dal Monte had four seasons with the Chicago Opera during which she included such works as *La Figlia del Reggimento, La Sonnambula,* and *Linda di Chamounix.* She had a long career at La Scala, made recordings in the United States and Italy, and is probably best remembered for a poignant complete *Madama Butterfly* with Gigli recorded in 1939 after she had returned to the more lyrical roles of her early career.

FEODOR CHALIAPIN AND *DON CARLO*

IN 1922 VERDI'S *DON CARLO* WAS NOT A very familiar opera to either the Metropolitan or Feodor Chaliapin. The bass had first assumed the role of Philip II in 1906 in a series of Monte Carlo performances with Geraldine Farrar, Maurice Renaud, and Emilio de Marchi, the original Cavaradossi, and had seldom performed it since.

The first Met *Don Carlo* was in December 1920 with Rosa Ponselle, Margarete Matzenauer, Giovanni Martinelli, Giuseppe De Luca, and Adamo Didur, and two seasons had yielded a handful of performances of this truncated four-act Italian version. Philip was totally different from Chaliapin's other roles; the effect was indelible: "It is easy enough to say that Mr. Chaliapin looked like a great historical portrait, or like such a portrait come to life. But words of that sort convey scarcely so much as a faint notion of his achievement. His Philip was at once the proudest, the craftiest, and the gloomiest of monarchs, and likewise the most imposing to see. Gloves of as white a kid as ever graced the hand of man or woman were positively sinister as he wore them. He lifted a single one of his ten digits and it was as the royal sceptre raised on high. The very curve and angle of his silken knees held the fate of peoples balancing. His face was the cloistered, tortured visage of Mad Joan's grandson, and the whitening russet of his hair betrayed that Spanish House of Austria which sought peace through bloodshed, and burned all heretics, to the greater glory of an approving god. Could Mary Tudor, whose heart in the years of his strength and beauty he had broken, have looked down on this old and broken vestige of a man,

Opposite: *Feodor Chaliapin as the tortured King Philip of Spain in Verdi's* Don Carlo, *an opera in which he made only rare guest appearances.*

his kingly pride cast from him as a useless garment, when in soliloquy he laid bare his soul, wounded to death because his young queen loved another, she would have had to believe that retributive justice does issue from an avenging heaven. Rarely is it given to any mime of song or speech to utter the syllables of the lost despair as the Russian basso did on Saturday in the king's 'Ella giammai m'amo!' The single line 'Dormiro sol nel manto mio regal,' no one who heard it is likely ever to forget. Other basses have sung this air, some of them extremely well; Chaliapin lived it. In honor of Mr. Chaliapin's presence, no doubt, the scene between King Philip and the Grand Inquisitor [Léon Rothier], hitherto omitted at the Metropolitan, was restored. But the great quartet, the most beautiful page in the entire work, was still cut out." Deems Taylor had one serious objection concerning the monologue: "The king sat crouched in his great chair for a moment. Then the king rose and bowed. The yells continued. Feodor Chaliapin walked down to the footlights. 'Da Capo,' he said to the footlights. [Gennaro Papi was the conductor.] And he sang it over again—Hamlet repeated the soliloquy. Mr. Chaliapin did more than break the Metropolitan's 'no-encores' rule; he broke at least one heart as well. We must have had him upon too high a pedestal. Still, it does hurt a little to discover that he is not a great artist at all, only an opera singer."

After Chaliapin sang Philip twice in New York and once on tour in Atlanta, the unfairly neglected *Don Carlo* was not heard again at the Met until Rudolf Bing's first opening night in 1950.

GIACOMO LAURI-VOLPI

FROM ITALIAN AGENT GIUSEPPE LUsardi, Milan, December 23, 1920, to Gatti-Casazza: "The papers have publicized CARUSO's illness and you can imagine with what displeasure I learned such awful news, in every way. Let's hope that it is a curable thing. We have here the greatest tenor in the world: Lauri-Volpi—in twenty years we haven't witnessed such a triumph as this. For whoever heard Masini [Angelo Masini, a favorite of Verdi's in the 1880s] he has the same attributes and can sing all the repertoire that Masini sang. He will now do all the first houses of Italy and Spain. He's already sung in Trieste, Genoa and now in Milan, I repeat, arousing an interest which has no precedent." Gatti engaged Giacomo Lauri-Volpi (1892–1979) and convinced him to sing his January 1923 *Rigoletto,* despite a sore throat, because of a long line of standees surrounding the opera house. At the end of each aria, voices shouted in Italian, and the press hailed him the next day: "His voice is young, fresh, strong, of ample range. There were moments when his delivery of the duke's music was touched with the true divinity of Italian singing. At other times there was an unpleasant roughness in the voice and the use of the voice, due in part, no doubt, to the remnants of a cold. . . . If he will always sing as well as he sang in the duet with Gilda (ending on a top D flat) he will prove a valuable addition to Mr. Gatti-Casazza's forces."

For more than a season Lauri-Volpi sang in operas that partially concealed his true nature, *La Bohème, Il Barbiere di Siviglia, La Traviata, Tosca, Cavalleria Rusticana, Lucia.* Finally, in February 1924, he sang Alim in the first Metropolitan performances of Massenet's *Roi de Lahore* with Delia Reinhardt and Giuseppe De Luca. Here he displayed the qualities for which he is remembered: "It was in this [first-act] finale that Mr. Lauri-Volpi rose to his full height as a singer. He astonished his admirers by suddenly appearing as the kind of singer of whom there are too few today in opera land, a singer of robust and dramatic qualities and by no means the singer of lyrical music which he has been in the past performances of this season. The audience, and quite rightly, responded with special enthusiasm to his performance, and in every respect he fulfilled its desires. The tone was not only brilliant, but often of sensuous beauty, manly, ringing, and, of course, when the opportunities came to send B flats triple fortissimo, crashing against his palate, the audience gave Mr. Lauri an ovation. He was equally successful in the pallid and syrupy love music of the second act. He sobbed, tonally speaking, and sighed, but not inartistically. He waved his hands about in the good old grand opera manner, lay down dying, stabbed by Scindia, when he did not have to sing, and stood up singing when he should have laid [*sic*] down as one about to die; took the middle of the stage with geometrical precision between two wings of the chorus, alternately embraced or parted by a few paces from his soprano, in delivering his amorous address. It was the way to do it. Any other way, truer to drama, would have been infinitely falser to Massenet's opera."

It was only a step away to Calaf in *Turandot,* a role originally planned for Gigli but changed for the Met premiere for Lauri-Volpi, probably because of Gigli's backstage fight with Jeritza as well as his less than stentorian top range, Calaf became Lauri-Volpi's most memorable Metropolitan role. "If we had not known him by his princely garb of purple velvet and jade green and the comely figure that he made, we should have known him by the pealing of his trumpet-voice—as Eve, so she told Adam, recognized the tiger by his stripes. Mr. Lauri-

The temperamental Italian tenor Giacomo Lauri-Volpi, in his 1923 debut role, the Duke in Rigoletto.

Volpi has not forgotten how to fling a high B flat into an enraptured auditorium."

Lauri-Volpi was a frequent partner to Ponselle in *La Vestale, Norma,* and *Luisa Miller,* and on at least one occasion he deeply offended her. At the end of the second scene of *Il Trovatore,* he "held a D flat for eight beats, three beats after Rosa had ended her own bell-like accompaniment!" There was enormous applause, but backstage Ponselle was in tears. There is a peculiar form of arrogance which may only belong to an exceedingly handsome man or a tenor with ringingly secure high notes. Lauri-Volpi was both. Ponselle recalled that Gatti had cast them opposite each other in *Norma* because their personal antagonism would work for the characters portrayed in the opera.

Lauri-Volpi left the Met in 1933 and Gatti-Casazza explained the reasons in a letter to Maestro Bellezza: "It would have been senseless to reengage Lauri-Volpi, even at a reduction, would be too expensive. The fact is, he gave nothing besides having an unspeakable disposition, making enemies of the public and the press." Lauri-Volpi never returned to the United States but continued to sing in Italy until 1959. In 1972, at age eighty, with high notes still intact, he delivered a full-voiced "Nessun dorma" to a cheering gala audience at the Teatro Liceo in Barcelona.

MIGUEL FLETA

BY EARLY 1924 GATTI-CASAZZA HAD gathered about himself so many of the world's leading tenors that he received a plea from Angelo Scandiani, direttore generale of La Scala, asking "that you seek to convince these artists of their artistic availability, and, I would say, of the patriotic duty (for Italians) to accept, even at some financial sacrifice—a luxury which in their fortunate positions they could well afford—to come to La Scala during the time they are not engaged at the Metropolitan. You can well imagine who these artists are: Gigli, Fleta, Martinelli, Lauri-Volpi, and perhaps even Johnson and Chamlee might be useful to me, since it is tenors above all which La Scala needs. To give you an idea of what we might offer them, I am telling you that this year I am giving Pertile L. 7000 per performance [about $315] based on seven performances per month." Although Gatti grudgingly agreed to help, only the Spanish tenor Miguel Fleta (1897–1938) sang immediately with any frequency at La Scala. Among Gatti's [illegible], Fleta was a young man who had been singing professionally only since a 1919 *Francesca da Rimini* in Trieste. Cavaradossi in *Tosca,* his 1923 Met debut role, had established his reputation in New York: "He is a man of rather small stature, but pleasing

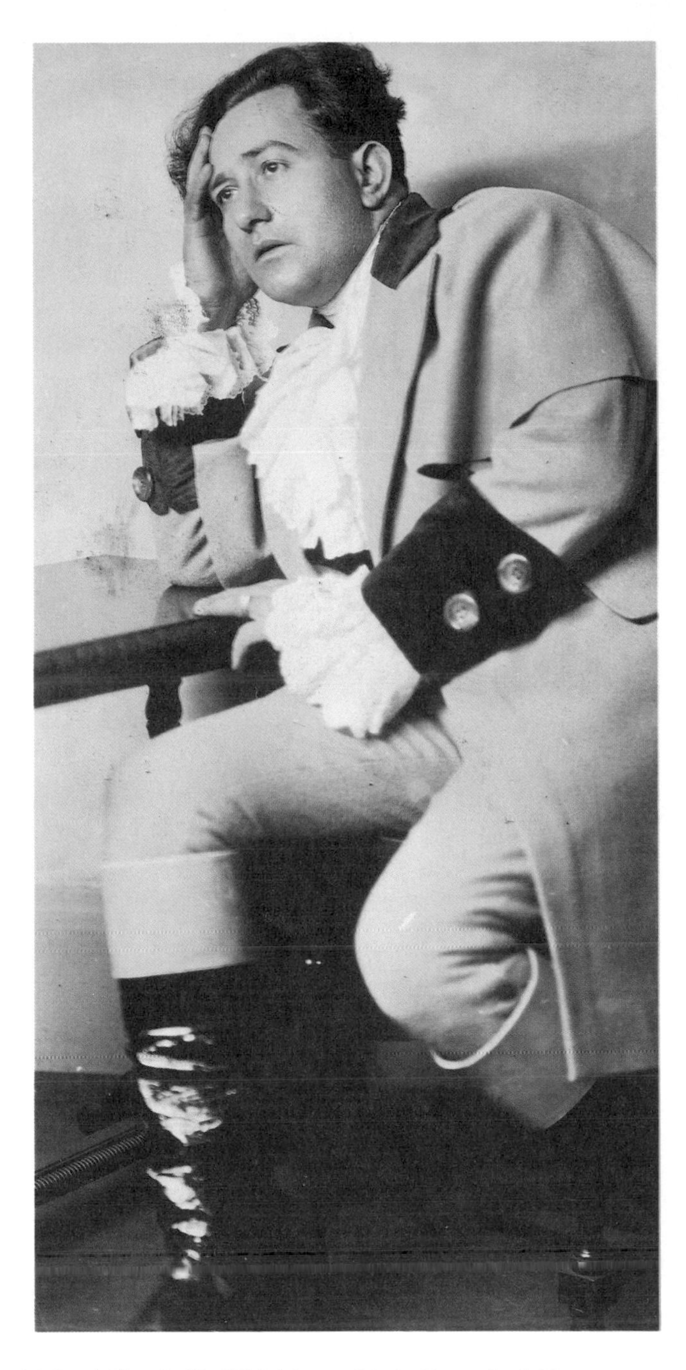

Miguel Fleta in his 1923 debut as Mario Cavaradossi, his most popular role at the Metropolitan before he broke his contract.

appearance. His voice is a fine, manly, vibrant tenor, well equalized in scale, generally well produced, not varied in color nor warm in character, but one that will probably wear well. His style was well suited to the music, and if he was not a particularly impassioned lover, he was certainly a courteous one, even deeply deferential to Mme. Jeritza's hat and feathers in the first act." In two seasons Fleta appeared in the standard repertoire as well as revivals of *L'Amico Fritz* with Lucrezia Bori and *Les Contes d'Hoffmann.* In the latter, "Mr. Fleta put an admirable restraint upon himself for the most part. It is true that he could not help remembering at times that he is an Italian opera tenor; he would now and then dwell too long on a high note, give it a volume that had no relation to the rest of the phrase, and move forward, facing the audience in such a way as to cease to be Hoffmann and become Mr. Fleta appealing for the customary recognition from the audience."

The Spanish government obtained permission for Fleta to postpone his 1925–26 engagement for one season, ostensibly so he could serve in the army. Perhaps by coincidence, he went that season to La Scala for the high point of his career, creating the role of Calaf in the world premiere of *Turandot* under Arturo Toscanini. When he didn't show up for 1926–27 the Metropolitan sued him and eventually won a large cash payment in the Spanish courts. Fleta did not sing opera again in North America and, in fact, his short and meteoric operatic career was all but over. Fleta had been discovered singing popular songs in his father's bar; now with a voice worn and tired from early and strenuous use in opera and long concert tours, he turned increasingly to performances of popular music in his native Spain. He died at the age of forty-one after an operation.

LAWRENCE TIBBETT

A FEW OF GATTI'S SUCCESSES WITH American singers were so spectacular that his long-term hospitality to many young artists might be overlooked. In 1918–19 there was Roa Eaton, a soprano he had intended for Lauretta at the world premiere of *Gianni Schicchi* until illness intervened. In 1920–21 there was Cora Chase, who sang ten performances of *Rigoletto* and *Barbiere* and then disappeared. Another was Martha Attwood, who in 1926–27 was given the enviable assignment of singing Liù in the Met premiere of *Turandot* but made no impression. Balancing the disappointments were Rosa Ponselle and the California baritone Lawrence Tibbett (1896–1960). Tibbett started in 1923 at $60 a week, Attwood's salary and considerably less than Eaton and Chase received. His debut was a small role in *Boris Godunov* with Chaliapin. The following week he was promoted to Valentin in *Faust,* and reportedly "sang his music with a light voice of agreeable quality and generally a commendable style. He showed a lack of stage experience. He may acquire some at the Metropolitan." In his first season he took on twelve roles, a mixture of small parts, such as Marullo in *Rigoletto* and Fléville in *Andrea Chénier,* with Escamillo in *Carmen* and two parts traditionally given to budding baritones, Silvio in *Pagliacci* and the Herald in *Lohengrin.* Then, in January 1925, came Ford in *Falstaff* and with it an incident

Opposite: *Lawrence Tibbett as Ford in* Falstaff, *the role that thrust him securely into the public eye.*

Lawrence Tibbett as a youthful Valentin in Faust, *his first important role at the Metropolitan Opera.*

C
MISHKIN
NY

that "occasioned considerable excitement and was quite without precedent in the annals of the organization. The evening also produced the most brilliant performance that has been given in the opera house this season. The Falstaff was Antonio Scotti, whose art requires no description or laurels today. The Ford was the young American Lawrence Tibbett, who last season became a member of the Metropolitan Opera Company, and who has since advanced very rapidly as a singer and dramatic interpreter. At the end of the second act comes the scene between Ford and Falstaff, in which Ford becomes convinced that his spouse is actually plotting infidelity, and, alone on the stage, intones his monologue of suspicion and jealousy, 'E sogno.' This scene Mr. Tibbett delivered with a quality of vocalism and interpretation which constituted one of the highest points, and one of the strongest individual performances of the evening. As the curtain fell the house burst into prolonged applause. In response to the applause, which kept up and increased in volume for many minutes, various of the principals appeared. Then Mr. Tibbett and Mr. Scotti appeared together and received ovations. At last it was evident that the audience wished Mr. Tibbett and none other for its attentions. But this singer did not come before the curtain alone. The commotion in the theatre increased. Some began to stamp, whistle and catcall. Cries of 'Tibbett' came from various parts of the house. There was no response. For a while no one appeared before the curtain; the lights were lowered and Mr. Serafin, the conductor, raised his baton for the next scene to begin. He found it impossible to proceed. Pandemonium grew. Even the elect in the boxes began to take more than a polite interest in the proceedings. The audience, justly or unjustly, had gained the impression that Mr. Tibbett was not allowed to come before them and receive their appreciation and had determined that the performance should go no farther until he had done so.

"It was Mr. Serafin who ended the business. He sent one of the orchestra players back stage to request that Mr. Tibbett be allowed to appear. The curtains parted, the young singer stepped to the front of the stage, bowed low and repeatedly to the excited assembly, and the performance proceeded. An American audience had decided that one of its own nationality should be properly recognized for his talent, and that ended the incident." Tibbett was quoted in the *Times* as saying that Scotti had motioned him to take a solo bow but that he had held back from timidity.

For all practical purposes, *Falstaff* ended his brief apprenticeship. His agents negotiated a contract in March 1926 that specified casting only in leading parts, with the exception of the Herald, Silvio, and Ford. From then on the important revivals and premieres were his, and they ranged from the Deems Taylor operas *The King's Henchman* and *Peter Ibbetson,* to Gruenberg's *Emperor Jones,* to *Peter Grimes* and *Khovanchina* at the end of his career. With Martinelli in 1937 he was Iago in the first complete *Otello* since Slezak's time. When his turn came to sing the title role in *Falstaff* the following season, legend has it that, with an eye to history, he refused to permit the promising young baritone Leonard Warren to sing Ford.

Equally successful in movies, concerts, and radio, Tibbett was at his finest in the title role of the first American *Simon Boccanegra* with Maria Müller, Giovanni Martinelli, and Ezio Pinza in 1932: "The feature of the Metropolitan's production is the Boccanegra of Mr. Tibbett—happily, for Simon is almost constantly in evidence. Mr. Tibbett makes him an engrossing and impressive figure, almost a great one. His denotement of the Doge's magnanimity, his courage, his tenderness, his will, his imperial dignity, his tragic pathos, is quite the finest thing that Mr. Tibbett has accomplished in opera. This is a remarkable embodiment—in its truth, its power, its authority, its ease, its fluency and grace. It was interesting to observe last night the inability of the claque (whose activities were especially pestiferous) to manufacture enthusiasm, in contrast with the obviously real thing which the audience attended to unaided when Mr. Tibbett finally took a curtain call by himself. One wondered if, after all, the claque earns its pay."

MICHAEL BOHNEN

IN *PAGLIACCI* MICHAEL BOHNEN (1887–1965) as Tonio made his entrance walking on his hands; in the Met lobby he picked up a telephone booth and laid it on its side, with his friend Lawrence Tibbett in it; at all times onstage he repaid the audience's constant attention. In a 1926 *Walküre* with Friedrich Schorr, Nanny Larsén-Todsen, and Florence Easton, "you might have guessed that Mr. Bohnen was the Hunding, before ever he entered his dwelling in the first act, and whether or not you had read his name in the program. Most Hundings announce their approach, to the accompaniment of their proper motive on the horns, by a decorous clanking of chains and a reticent suggestion of equine stampling. ('Sieglinde,' say the stage directions at this point, 'starts, listens and hears Hunding outside, leading his horse to the stable.') But yesterday the ominous staccato rhythm of the horns was accompanied by a crash outside the door which suggested that an overnourished Walkyr had been thrown from her steed in some celes-

Opposite: *Michael Bohnen's threatening characterization of Caspar in the 1924 revival of Weber's* Der Freischütz, *performed opposite Elisabeth Rethberg.*

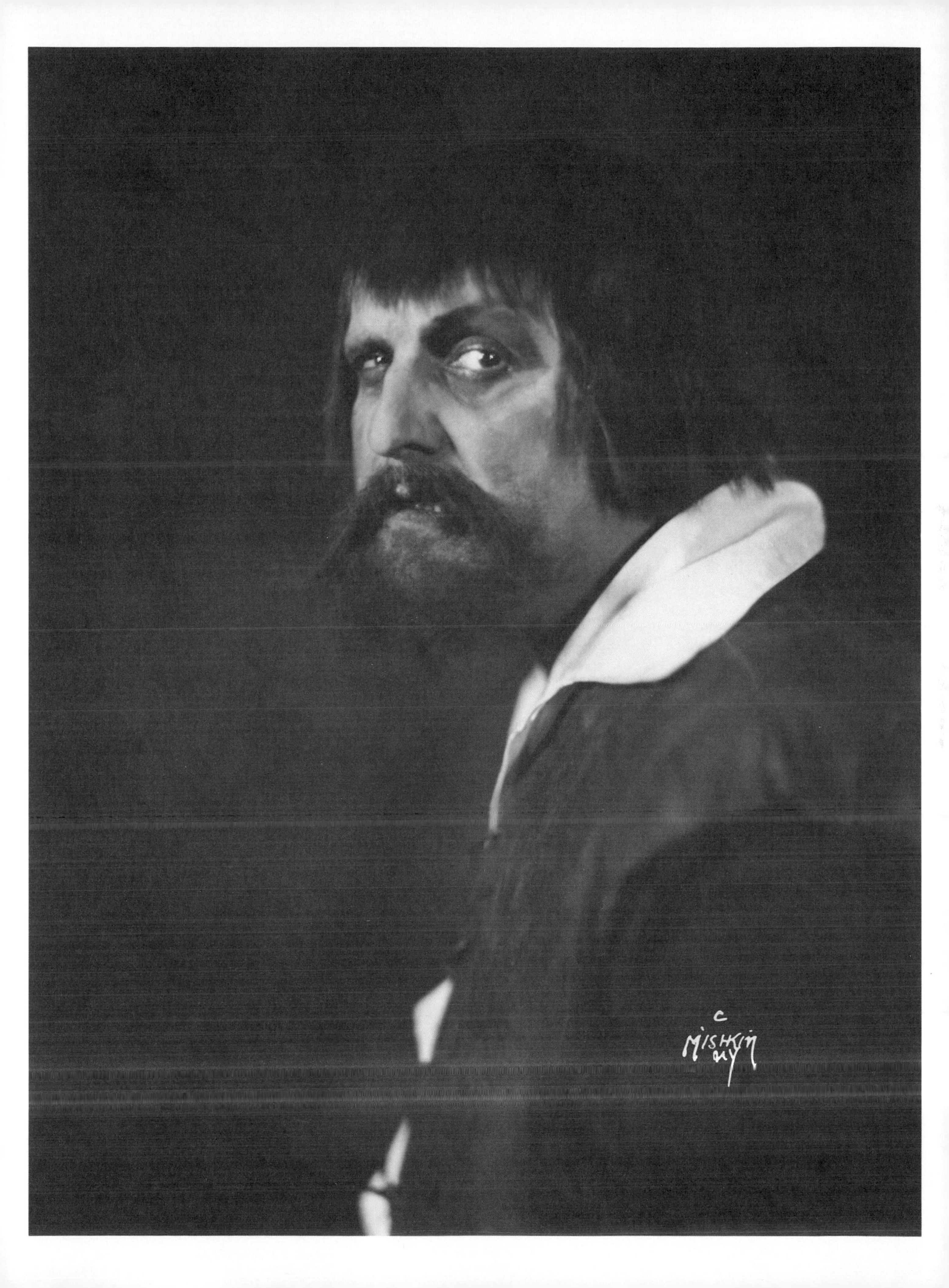
c
MISHKIN
NY

tial galaxy and precipitated upon Hunding's doorstep. After which the door opened and Mr. Bohnen, as Hunding, escorted by his quintet of tubas, appeared upon the threshold. It was a superb entrance—you would have trusted Mr. Bohnen for that. Barbarically accoutered, his black bearskins reaching to his ankles, his mask ferociously contrived, he was a sinister and savage figure—menacing, brutal and perturbing."

Gatti had assured Otto Kahn that he was "the greatest artist in all the opera houses of Austria-Germany" and promised a magnificent result. Bohnen debuted at the Metropolitan in 1923 in von Schillings's *Mona Lisa* with the composer's wife, Barbara Kemp, in the title role. Deems Taylor reported that "once on the stage he dominated it, a tall, prowling, black-cloaked figure whose movements were effortless and graceful and whose moments of repose had sculpturesque solidity and plastic beauty. He is famous in Germany as a motion picture actor as well as singer and his screen experience has served him well, for his pantomime is extraordinarily sure and vital. . . . His voice has not the golden mellowness of Chaliapin's, but it is rich and powerful and equally expressive throughout its entire range—which is a wide one. Again, like Chaliapin, he seems to have his voice under such exceptional control that he can color his singing to create the illusion of speech."

Gatti considered Kemp's two-season engagement, with her inability to sing the roles specified in her contract, an exceedingly unpleasant experience; he must have been gratified that Bohnen's large salary was repaid with seemingly endless invention, full houses, and enthusiastic notices. "He will sing four Hagens a season, and he will not wear the same wig and make-up twice. He will show himself once as a fierce Hunnish warrior, forehead shaven, topknot of black hair, long, drooping mustaches and heavy beard. He will appear the next time with flowing wig and no beard, or a third time clean shaven. He will not hesitate to alter, impromptu, the stage business assigned him: instead of dueling with Gunther in the third act of *Götterdämmerung,* he will lunge with his spear at the unhappy Gibichung. One masterstroke he maintains performance after performance, season after season: listening to Siegfried's narrative, he stoops to the ground to pluck herbs which he presently mixes in a drink that fatally restores the memory of the Volsung hero."

Bohnen's Wagnerian roles also included Gurnemanz, King Marke, Wotan, and Hans Sachs. He sang Amonasro as well, and his Caspar seemed justification enough for a 1924 revival of *Freischütz* with Elisabeth Rethberg and Curt Taucher, in which "the chief singers are competent, and in the case of Mr. Bohnen brilliant. His Caspar is a very fine piece of acting and singing. Indeed, it would astonish most of the skeptical to go to the opera and hear him deliver Weber's sweeping bravura in the first act."

After his operatic debut as Caspar in 1910, Bohnen had sung at the Bayreuth Festival and throughout Germany. A versatile man, he produced, directed, and acted in films, was a professional boxer and wrestler, and excelled at swimming and billiards.

Bohnen left the Metropolitan in 1932, a time when the company drastically reduced its roster of major artists. Although a member of the State Opera in Berlin, he was mainly occupied with films. His lack of cooperation with their regime prompted the Nazis to make him a porter in a Siemens radio factory. He emerged after the war to help rebuild the Berlin State Opera during two years as director. Late in life he looked back on his years with the Metropolitan and remembered: "I owe this wonderful house my greatest honors and much of my fame."

KARIN BRANZELL

ONE OF THE STURDIER METROPOLITAN careers was built by the Swedish contralto Karin Branzell (1891–1974), who was discovered by Crown Princess Margaret when she heard Branzell's voice sticking out from the sound of a small church choir. Beginning in 1912, her career was concentrated in Stockholm and Berlin until Gatti heard her in 1923 and hired her for the Metropolitan.

New York first heard Branzell as Fricka in a 1924 *Walküre* with Margarete Matzenauer and Michael Bohnen. Her appearance was brief but impressive: "She is a woman of fine presence and disclosed last evening a valuable knowledge of action and pose. She is the fortunate possessor of a very beautiful mezzo soprano voice which has a vein of contralto in its timbre. In the music of Fricka it was noble and fluent and reposeful. The newcomer sang like an artist of fine instincts and intelligence. The passage 'Deiner ew'gen Gattin heilige Ehre' was delivered with genuine grandeur of style. The less critical operagoer will recognize the fresh and opulent quality of this singer's voice, but last evening's brief appearance indicated that art might furnish the voice with large resources."

Inevitably, with her strong young voice and lower salary, Branzell was chosen by Gatti to sing Matzenauer's repertoire; two nights after the debut it was Ortrud in *Lohengrin:* "There remains . . . Mme. Branzell as the sinister, vindictive and impassioned Ortrud—all these she was and with a large limbed appearance and action well-

Opposite: *Karin Branzell as a seemingly placid Ortrud in* Lohengrin, *one of her first roles at the Metropolitan.*

© MISHKIN
NY

planned, vigorous, sometimes moving.... She sang all the music artistically but without penetrating its heart. Her invocation of the old gods, however, was sung with much power and plenitude of voice." Erda in *Siegfried* and Brangäne soon followed. Less successful was an attempt to duplicate Matzenauer's Brünnhilde in *Walküre* and her non-Wagnerian repertoire. In her Dalila, for instance, "Her seductive art is neither wily nor subtle and there is little of the sensual about it. In fact, in the garden scene her solicitous attitude placed Mr. Martinelli's Samson in the light of a small boy forced to come in the house out of the rain. But Mme. Branzell sang her music with all her fine somber richness of tone, her opulent if restricted coloring and a style at once tender and impassioned. Her costumes were somewhat disappointingly modest." Matzenauer left the Metropolitan in 1930 and Branzell became an important part of the notable Wagnerian performances of the thirties and forties. She left the Metropolitan in 1944 with her husband's public explanation, "She hopes she is making a place for some gifted young American singer." However, she wrote a close friend, "They told me in the last performance that I have to sing Waltraute [in *Götterdämmerung*] with a big cut—all the beautiful things I love in that part they have taken away and when I looked in my score I just couldn't do it." Later she added, "Now I will remember only the beauty of all these performances—I will not sing there any more but I can go down there and I will sit and listen."

During Rudolf Bing's first Metropolitan season Branzell returned to sing Erda in the historic 1951 *Ring* cycles that alternated Flagstad and Traubel as Brünnhilde.

LAURITZ MELCHIOR

IN METROPOLITAN HISTORY THE SUBlime and the ridiculous have sometimes unintentionally combined. Seldom have they been in greater proximity than Wednesday, February 17, 1926, when in an evening *Rigoletto* a young soprano named Marion Talley from Kansas City, Kansas, made her operatic debut as Gilda. Gatti had sent her to Milan for study several years earlier and her return to a marshaling of publicity was overwhelming. According to Pitts Sanborn, "to parallel at all the Talley debut one would have to go back to the birth of Venus or of Eve." That same afternoon, almost unnoticed and singing the Paris version of *Tannhäuser* for the first time without a rehearsal, appeared a little-known singer, Lauritz Melchior (1890–1973), in a cast that included Maria Jeritza, Karin Branzell, Michael Bohnen, and Friedrich Schorr. It was an inauspicious beginning for the twentieth-century's greatest heldentenor: "Mr. Melchior came back from his interview with the Pope in much better vocal condition than when he left the Wartburg festival hall. His vocal displays in the first act were not happy. The color of his voice was distinctly barytone and he revealed most of those familiar characteristics of constriction and forced tone so common in tenors from the land just south of his own native heath. He used few head tones, much of his upper range was not congenial to him and the quality of tone was far from lyric. Neither did Mr. Melchior's appearance resemble a man racked with the inner conflicts of a tormented soul. . . . Very evidently, however, he found inspiration if not solace in Rome. Warmth and fervor crept into his work in the last act. A touch of velvet softened the edges of his voice and his whole interpretation increased in stature, dramatic conviction and profundity of feeling."

Opposite: *Lauritz Melchior photographed in 1926 as Tannhäuser, the first of his memorable Wagnerian portrayals to be heard at the Metropolitan Opera.*

Melchior had begun operatic life as a baritone with Danish opera companies. The American contralto Mme. Charles Cahier sang with him and suggested that he was really a tenor with a lid on the top of his voice. She recommended that he restudy his technique. For several years he worked and alternated baritone with higher roles before emerging in the twenties as a leading Wagnerian tenor. By the end of his first Met season Melchior had revealed his complete Wagnerian repertoire, *Parsifal, Die Walküre,* and *Siegfried,* and under less than ideal conditions. At his first *Siegfried,* again unrehearsed, he had to ask where on the stage in Act III he would find the sleeping Brünnhilde, whom he was required to waken with a kiss.

At the same time the Met continued its search for heldentenors, stimulated perhaps by Melchior's reluctance to learn Max in *Der Freischütz,* Walther in *Die Meistersinger,* or Loge in *Das Rheingold.* For 1928–29 Melchior agreed that he would prepare Tristan and sing it elsewhere before his arrival. In March 1929, on his thirty-ninth birthday, Melchior gave a New York audience its first glimpse of what would become one of the opera's classic portrayals: "Mr. Melchior's very first gesture was revolutionary—he bowed to Isolde [Gertrude Kappel], as, of course, any well brought up knight would do on finding himself in the presence of a lady. Never to my knowledge had a Metropolitan Tristan shown that common courtesy to a Metropolitan Isolde." Lawrence Gilman could not recall a Tristan since the dim days before the war who had sung the music so well: "There was often beauty of tone, beauty of phrasing, beauty and a delicate thrust of sentiment, in Mr. Melchior's singing—especially in the quieter passages of the love duo ('O sink' hernieder' was sung almost wholly in tune by

th the enraptured lovers). In the Vision scene of the hird Act, Mr. Melchior's 'Siehst du sie? Siehst du sie noch nicht?' was of rare tonal loveliness—even more poetic in timbre and texture than the tone-color achieved by the horn quartet in the succeeding cantilena that sustains the wondrous song of the dream-haunted lover. Mr. Melchior's medium register is especially responsive; and when the music's tessitura favors him, and he can sing mezza voce, the results are grateful to a degree that can be understood only by those who have suffered, as so many of us have, from the hideous, brazen bawling, the tonal mayhem committed by a majority of the Metropolitan's Heldentenors during recent years. Mr. Melchior did not yell, and most Tristans, sooner or later in that terrific Third Act, resort to yelling. In aspect the new Tristan is surprisingly personable. His generous size is shrewdly turned to account. The face is bearded—acquires gravity and hint of epic romance."

This was to be Marion Talley's last Metropolitan season, while Melchior's Metropolitan career would extend for twenty-one more years. Frida Leider sang with him for two seasons in the thirties and then began that unparalleled outpouring of Wagnerian heroines—Kirsten Flagstad, Marjorie Lawrence, Helen Traubel, and Astrid Varnay. For all of them Melchior was a noble partner.

With his jovial personality and his ability to laugh at himself, Melchior soon acquired a reputation totally in contrast to the utter seriousness of his Wagnerian heroes. At a Met fund-raising performance in the 1930s he and tiny Lily Pons performed a Parisian Apache dance. A big-game hunter when it was still fashionable, Melchior provided costumes for Siegmund and Siegfried from animals he had bagged. Over the years he became less willing to rehearse; in Act I of *Parsifal* he would become bored at standing onstage while not singing and wander off for a beer. Occasionally, he needed special help from conductors. Bruno Walter once tactfully advised him, "Melchior, my left hand is exclusively yours."

Melchior left the Metropolitan in 1950 in a battle with Rudolf Bing over rehearsals and contracts. Although he was welcome in Hollywood to make popular musical films, Melchior will always be remembered for Wagner. While our own time has witnessed Birgit Nilsson continuing the grand line of Lilli Lehmann and Flagstad, Lauritz Melchior has had no one who might be said to have followed him.

Gertrude Kappel as Brünnhilde in Die Walküre, *one of the heroines that made her a Wagnerian mainstay during the late 1920s and early 1930s.*

GERTRUDE KAPPEL

AFTER THE WAR GATTI-CASAZZA WAS willing to experiment with a succession of singers while he maintained the Wagner works as a central part of his repertoire. The Swedish soprano Nanny Larsén-Todsen was one of those who arrived in the 1920s, but her 1925 debut was postponed because, in the words of the Met pay book, "horse at reh. of Gottung. stepped upon her."

W. J. Henderson used her first Isolde to summarize Wagnerian singing in New York: "The performance of *Tristan und Isolde* on Saturday afternoon did much toward sweeping the Wagnerian department of the Metropolitan Opera House back into the atmosphere of the eighties. The younger generation of operagoers does not know Mme. Katherine Klafsky [with the Damrosch Opera Company] or her name would now be coupled with that of Mme. Nanny Larsén-Todsen, who was the Isolde. Mme. Klafsky radiated vast quantities of superheated temperament and sang Wagner's music with immensity of voice and physical vigor. Her Isolde was tumultuous, irresistible, and unmusical. It was the antipodes of the Isoldes of Mme. Rosa Sucher and Mme. Ternina. Mme. Lehmann, who trumpeted the role in clarion tones and wore a regal majesty, was the one mighty Isolde of those times. Mme. Larsén-Todsen cannot be called unmusical since she shows a sense of melodic line and an appreciation of phrase. But on Saturday she was said to be still suffering from a cold and this may have accounted for some of the stridency of her singing and the unsteadiness of her tone. But her Isolde was conceived in the heroic mold and had theatrical force and authority. This kind of impersonation, however, is likely to restore life to the long dead theory that operas can be given without good singing. In spite of Lehmann and [Emil] Fischer, this theory prevailed here up to the time when the De Reszkes, Nordica and their associates proved that the tragic Wagner dramas could be beautifully sung and that they were all the greater when so presented."

By far the most successful of the Wagnerian sopranos whom Gatti presented during the 1920s was the German Gertrude Kappel (1884–1971), who had been singing since 1906. Her New York debut was a 1928 *Tristan* with Rudolf Laubenthal, Karin Branzell, Friedrich Schorr, and Michael Bohnen. Immediately she proved herself worthy of such colleagues: "Mme. Kappel is 'new,' of course, only to New York. In Europe her sweeping, exalted, and fiery embodiments of major Wagner heroines—Isolde, Brünnhilde, Kundry—have been familiar and acclaimed for several years, at the Festival performances in Munich, at Covent Garden, London, and in Vienna. . . . Mme. Kappel is plenteously endowed with voice. It is a true Wagner organ that she brings to us, rich, warm, enduring. She employs it with a subtlety and finesse that no Isolde within our memory has brought to the singing of this role since Ternina's day. She phrases with the sensibility of an accomplished Lieder singer; with a continual play of varied color and nuance, with an exquisite use of mezza voce." In addition to her Wagnerian repertoire, she sang Leonore in *Fidelio*, and, not very happily, was the Metropolitan's first Elektra in 1932. She was singing the *Walküre* Brünnhilde the afternoon in 1935 when Kirsten Flagstad made her debut as Sieglinde, and she retired two years later.

Maria Müller as Aida, her most frequent role in a Met career that easily mixed Italian and German parts, Verdi and Wagner.

MARIA MÜLLER

DURING THE TWENTIES AND EARLY thirties the Metropolitan had two sopranos who passed freely across the boundaries of German and Italian opera, varying the lighter Wagnerian parts Eva, Elsa, and Elisabeth, with Aida, Mimi, Cio-Cio-San, and assorted novelties. One was Elisabeth Rethberg; the other was Maria Müller (1898–1958), who made her 1925 debut in a *Walküre* with Michael Bohnen as Wotan and Julia Claussen coming to "contralto grief" in Brünnhilde's demanding battle cry. "Last night we had a new [Sieglinde], Maria Müller, a Czechoslovakian soprano who was born near Prague twenty-three years ago [*sic*], made her debut at Linz as Elsa, sang thereafter in Prague and went from there to Munich, whence she was acquired for the Metropolitan. Miss Müller is first of all good to look upon; and that to our mind is a cardinal virtue in a singing actress. The hasty might even call her beautiful. She exhibits a sense of the stage; her acting has both intensity and repose. Her suggestion of the sympathy, the swiftly waxing passion, the ecstasy, the despair and terror of the 'Schwester und Geliebte' of Siegmund, were as touching as they were simply accomplished. Her voice has loveliness of texture, and she uses it—especially in its lower and middle ranges—with skill and taste; she knows the worth and beauty of a fine-drawn pianissimo and the value of emotionally characterizing tone color." Müller also sang Octavian (in which part one critic complained you could see her thinking about what she should do next but not doing it), Donna Elvira, and, in 1932, Amelia in the American premiere of *Simon Boccanegra*. At Bayreuth she sang every Sieglinde between 1931 and 1942 except 1934, when she shared the part with Kirsten Flagstad.

Rosa Ponselle in one of Mishkin's unforgettable studies, the title role of La Gioconda, *her most frequent Met portrayal after Leonora in* La Forza del Destino *and Santuzza in* Cavalleria Rusticana.

ROSA PONSELLE AND *LA GIOCONDA*

IN 1925–26, WHEN THE METROPOLITAN Opera opened its new season with Ponchielli's *Gioconda* for the fourth time in its history, the opera house was just forty-two years old. Traditions and legends had begun to spring up almost from the first night; *La Gioconda* itself had appeared during the Met's first season and enjoyed a succession of stirring protagonists over the years.

Inspired by long experience, Lawrence Gilman honored *La Gioconda's* fourth opening night with an evocative bit of fantasy: "The dozing music critic tossed restlessly in his comfortable crimson opera seat. . . . But he roused himself with what even a music critic could recognize as a guilty start, when his eardrums told him that Gioconda had scaled her high B flat at the climax of her famous duet with Laura in the second act. Thoroughly awake now—for the Metropolitan orchestra and the two Venetians on the stage were making a prodigious clamor, and the audience was exploding with excited rapture—the reviewer scribbled on his program a sketch of his opening sentences. They were not difficult to write—for had he not heard many performances of *La Gioconda*?

> The Metropolitan season opened last night with a performance of Ponchielli's *La Gioconda*. The occasion, as is usual with opening nights at the Metropolitan, was more notable for its brilliancy as a spectacle than for its artistic importance. Mme. Nordica, Mme. Homer, Mr. Caruso and Mr. Plançon were cast for their familiar roles. Arturo Vigna conducted.

Arturo Vigna? Nordica, Caruso, Plançon? What was this? The music critic opened his eyes very wide and stared at the stage. Nordica had certainly lost weight (marvelous how these sopranos can bant when they want to!). And was that Caruso, sustaining his high A on 'Addio' as he made ready to plunge into the moonlight waters of the Adriatic that run so deep in the neighborhood of Thirty-ninth Street and Seventh Avenue? It did not sound quite like Caruso's A. And then, realizing at last where and when he was, the music critic got up, adjusted his Opening Night waistcoat, sighed profoundly and made for the Press Room, babbling to himself of old, forgotten, far-off things and battles long ago. As he pushed his way through the throng behind the rail he could have sworn that he heard Nordica's deep golden laugh just behind his shoulder, in the darkness; and as he crossed the foyer behind the grand tier boxes he saw (he will swear it to the end of time) the tall, erect figure of Pol Plançon, bearded, majestic, aloof, disappearing around the turn of the stairway.

"Yes, the Opera House was full of ghosts tonight. And then he remembered that it was almost twenty years ago that the Metropolitan had opened with this very opera of Ponchielli's, and he had reviewed it, as he was about to review this. He must be careful: instead of Nordica, Ponselle as La Gioconda; instead of Caruso, Gigli as Enzo; instead of Plançon—[Mardones]. But why worry? He, for one, would not deserve the reproach of Stewart Mitchell that 'critics, like brides, throw their bouquets backwards.' He might, he reflected, have turned sixty . . . but he was quite as capable as he ever was of recognizing new talent, new conceptions of histrionic style and dramatic effect; and certainly Mr. Gigli had a voice of uncommon beauty, and was by way of being an excellent artist, when he didn't force his tone and sing to the gallery and the railbirds. And so, dexterously settling his opera hat just a semitone off the pitch (he must try not to look his years), he entered the Press Room, trailing clouds of nineteenth century glory."

JOSÉ MARDONES

UNTIL HENRY RUSSELL DISCOVERED him singing at the San Carlo in Lisbon and hired him for the opening season of his Boston Opera in 1909, the Spanish bass José Mardones (1869–1932) had been limited to appearing in the more obscure opera and Spanish zarzuela houses of Europe and South America. When all organized opera failed in Boston, Mardones moved on to the Metropolitan for a November 1917 opening-night debut in *Aida*. It was wartime and after the triumphal scene, chorus and principals, Claudia Muzio, Margarete Matzenauer, Caruso (struggling manfully with the words on a sheet of paper), Amato, and Mardones, appeared onstage to sing the "Star-Spangled Banner" with waving flags. The United States had declared war on Germany that spring; German opera and artists had been banished from the Metropolitan stage. In the outburst of patriotic fervor Mardones's debut was almost overlooked. However, the Met's roster of basses included Andrés de Segurola, Adamo Didur, and Léon Rothier, all by then more noted for characterization than sheer voice; Mardones was needed. A Brooklyn reviewer welcomed him later in the season: "Mardones, who fills the very necessary position of a genuine basso—a position long vacant in the Metropolitan's forces—was the High Priest. He is a well-schooled artist in whom one finds no particular individual art but the serviceable reliable kind that just falls short of supreme excellence." His first-season roles included Don Basilio in *Barbiere*, "giving the 'Calumny' air with vast volume of tone, never rough and roaring, but mellow as a fine Spanish oil, a triumph of bass singing," and Archibaldo in *L'Amore dei Tre Re* with Caruso: " . . . though his act-

José Mardones as the vindictive Alvise in La Gioconda, *which he sang on opening night of the Metropolitan's 1925–26 season.*

ing lacked that gnarled bitterness which goes so effectively into Mr. Didur's interpretation, it was full of nobleness and grandeur. Those who held their breaths to see him duplicate the renowned Didur strength of arm saw him lift Miss Muzio across his shoulder with acrobatic ease." He was Guardiano in the first Met *Forza* with Ponselle and Caruso and appeared in most of the Met's important Italian revivals of the period. During the twenties he was considered a superbly reliable, rather calming singer, an antidote to the ceaselessly inventive antics of his bass colleague Michael Bohnen. "He projects nothing but profundity of tone, a solemn and sobering sonority, which if unsupported by other elements of opera would perhaps be found of peacefully soporific quality."

His last new role was Pontifex Maximus in the 1925 *Vestale* with Rosa Ponselle. Gatti, who valued him highly, declined to bring in the promising young bass Ezio Pinza until Mardones decided to retire in 1926.

ANGELO BADA

IN 1921 W. J. HENDERSON WROTE ABOUT the importance of good secondary singers, mentioning Mario Laurenti, Marie Sundelius, Mary Ellis, and especially Angelo Bada (1876–1941). "The priceless value of the gift of voice is often demonstrated by the minor singer's possession of almost all the qualities of greatness except the splendor of brilliant tone. At the Metropolitan Opera House, for example, there is a secondary singer who might be one of the greatest stars in the operatic firmament if he had a voice of the first order. His name is Angelo Bada, and what most people do not know about him is that he is an excellent singer as well as a remarkably accomplished actor. Naturally a man occupying such a position as that of Mr. Bada is not often called on to do any important singing, but occasionally some of the crumbs go to him. One recalls with pleasure his admirable singing of the call of the Muezzin in *Marouf,* of the few cantabile phrases of Wagner in *Mefistofele,* and Triquet in *Eugene Onegin* and the old

Angelo Bada as Torquemada in the 1925 Met premiere of L'Heure Espagnole *in a rare onstage photograph.*

clothes man in *Louise.* But when it comes to the composition of 'character bits,' as they are called in the theatre, no one in the Metropolitan company can surpass this secondary singer. Recall his exquisitely finished impersonation of the dancing master in *Mme. Sans-Gêne,* his complete photograph of the spy in *Andrea Chénier,* his perfect Goro in *Madama Butterfly.* . . . The repertory is large, many operas are given each season, rehearsals are numerous and exhausting, and hence only some such tireless human as Angelo Bada can be expected to sing in everything. There is plenty to read about how the celebrated stars who sing twice a week keep themselves in condition. But Bada sings almost every night. How does he do it? What does he eat? How does he exercise? When does he sleep? Some day he too will be interviewed and then we shall know things."

Bada always sang small roles and had the good fortune to make his debut surrounded by friends and neighbors in his hometown in Italy. The opera was *Aida* and his part that of the Messenger who arrives in Scene I with a few lines warning of approaching danger. The friendly audience greeted him with such enthusiasm that he had to encore the message. *Aida* was also his Met debut opera in 1908 when Gatti brought him from La Scala, along with Amato and Toscanini. He did not retire until thirty seasons later, after many hundreds of performances and dozens of roles, everything from Don Alvaro in *L'Africana* to Marlardot in *Zazà.*

George Meader as the dwarf Mime who appears in both Das Rheingold *and* Siegfried, *a classic portrayal from the 1920s.*

GEORGE MEADER

ONE OF THE FORGOTTEN ARTISTS OF Metropolitan history is the American tenor George Meader (1888–1961). He began as a boy soprano in Minneapolis, whereupon success rapidly took him to Chicago, New York, and a national tour before his voice could change. After college he followed his teacher, Mme. Anna Schoen-René, to Berlin and made his operatic debut in Leipzig as the Steuermann in *Der Fliegende Holländer.* In Europe he combined the lighter tenor roles with lieder, and it was in an Aeolian Hall recital that he was heard again in New York in 1919. Two years later, in November 1921, came his Metropolitan debut as Victorin in *Die Tote Stadt.* Averaging more than thirty-five performances a season, Meader had a contract second only to Florence Easton's for the variety of roles required. In his first season he was the Shepherd in *Tristan,* Third Esquire in *Parsifal,* and Remendado in *Carmen,* and then he emerged from obscurity to sing Fernando in the Met's first *Così fan tutte* with Easton, Peralta, Bori, De Luca, and Didur.

In the first postwar *Die Meistersinger* Meader found one of his enduring roles: "Mr. Meader as David was almost perfect, bringing to the role a vocal artistry that revealed hitherto unsuspected beauties in the music and giving an impersonation of the young apprentice that had a boyish impulsiveness and touching awkwardness, quite irresistible. Already he sings the role better than anyone we have ever heard, and when he has ripened his impersonation a little more he ought to give a performance that should match the almost matchless David of Albert Reiss himself." In *Siegfried* was another definitive role: "Mr. Meader's Mime was without question the best the Metropolitan has known. The action was subdued but adequate. In spite of a cold, however, Mr. Meader sang all his music with extraordinary finesse. His command of vocal color, his clarity of diction and, above all, his supreme skill in giving a correct and convincing dramatic reading to every line contributed an achievement in Wagnerian art that calls for nothing but enthusiastic praise." After ten seasons Meader was lured to Broadway by Max Gordon to perform in *Cat and the Fiddle;* as an itinerant street musician he introduced a Jerome Kern standard, "The Night Was Made for Love." A variety of character roles followed, including several with the Lunts, and these led naturally westward to Hollywood, where he concluded his career making movies.

FEODOR CHALIAPIN AND *DON QUICHOTTE*

AMONG TWENTIETH-CENTURY SINGERS perhaps only Beniamino Gigli came close to matching the year-in, year-out routine of opera and concert appearances that Feodor Chaliapin made in a career lasting more than forty years. It was inevitable in all this performing that some of the music could not match the quality of *Boris Godunov* or *Don Carlo.* Even Chaliapin, however, must have been surprised at the critical reaction to Massenet's *Don Quichotte,* an opera he had created in Monte Carlo back in 1910, when Gatti staged it for him in 1926. Critic Samuel Chotzinoff pointed out that writing an opera with Chaliapin in mind "is not the best way to write an opera, because you can leave so much to Chaliapin. This superb artist, when he is at his best, can vitalize the most insipid music."

Lawrence Gilman was more amusing. "There have been brave men in France; but of them all, surely the bravest was the late Jules Emile Frédéric Massenet. This intrepid composer, gifted with the spiritual distinction of a butler, the compassionate understanding of a telephone girl, and the expressive capacity of an amorous tomtit, had the courage to choose as a subject for music the greatest of all tragi-comedies, the most exquisitely piteous figure in the imaginative literature of the world. Monsieur Massenet, composer of *Manon* and the *Méditation Religieuse,* selected as the theme for an opera the Don Quixote of Cervantes, and with it he did his worst. The result of this incredible adventure was displayed to us on Saturday afternoon.

Chaliapin as Don Quichotte displays the histrionic genius that led one critic to observe that composers writing for him could neglect their jobs because the singer brought so much to his performances.

"The thing, as drama, never comes to life. It has no continuity of pattern, no tension, no substance. It is operatic sawdust of the most unnourishing kind. A composer of imagination, even of fancy, might have given it flavor of a sort; but not Jules Massenet! . . . Cervantes' creation goes to the roots of compassionate tenderness, pitiful laughter: Massenet's humanity and sensibility as an artist were never more than skindeep. The humor of *Don Quixote* is the profoundest, the most philosophical, the most touching, in all literature: the humor of Massenet is to seek.

"Its only conceivable excuse for survival is that it gives Mr. Chaliapin a stalking-horse for a superb impersonation. This extraordinary artist has gone beyond Massenet. . . He has gone, evidently, to the figure of the nobly fanatical dreamer as he exists for us all in Cervantes, and has recreated him almost in defiance of the shabby trio who defaced a masterpiece. In Chaliapin the true Don Quixote comes alive across the footlights.

"Visually, the character stands before you, aided by a make-up that is in itself a creative triumph—save that the figure is a little over-stalwart for the spare, worn frame of Cervantes' Knight. Mr. Chaliapin evokes for you the image of the man and the projection of his burning spirit almost wholly by means of his consummate genius as an actor. He sings the music very badly—with persistent disregard of the pitch, with defective rhythm, poor tone. But these things, under the circumstances, hardly matter. It would indeed be far better if Mr. Chaliapin should frankly content himself with speaking his lines, as the Bandits are required to do. What matters is the superb, transfiguring histrionism of this unrivalled artist, who has taken the poor empty skin of the librettist and filled it with the body and soul of Don Quixote,

©
Mishkin Studio
120 N.Y.

Opposite: *Feodor Chaliapin in the title role of Massenet's* Don Quichotte, *an opera written for him, first performed at the Met in 1926.*

making it luminous with his incandescent ecstasy, his shining belief in a world of fantasy that is more actual to him than the stupid realities that balk and defeat him, the beautiful dignity and exaltation that never desert him even in those abysses of absurdity which only so great a spirit could survive."

Ironically, it is a *Don Quixote,* though not by Massenet, that provides us with the best representation on film of an important singer. Chaliapin stars in the 1932 G. W. Pabst film, with music by Jacques Ibert, in French and English versions that are both eloquent.

CLARENCE WHITEHILL

ONE OF THE CENTURY'S MOST DISTINguished artists, now almost forgotten, was the American baritone Clarence Whitehill (1871–1932), whose first performances at the Metropolitan were in an equally obscure 1900 season by the "Metropolitan English Grand Opera Company." The year before Whitehill had been the first American man to sing at the Opéra-Comique in Paris and was returning home for eight varied roles, from Escamillo, Méfistophélès in *Faust,* and Lothario in *Mignon,* to Pooh-Bah in *The Mikado* and King Henry in *Lohengrin.* In 1904 as Wolfram he sang the first of two seasons at Bayreuth. In spite of his promise to Cosima Wagner that he would respect the Wagner family's proscription against performances of *Parsifal* outside Bayreuth, his official Metropolitan debut in 1909 was as a highly praised Amfortas: "His voice is a fine and resonant baritone, his singing is marked by skill, and the potency of emotional expression. The sufferings, the remorse, the passionate protestations of the delinquent King were given a truly moving embodiment." Soon after the *Parsifal* debut, Henderson used Whitehill's Wotan in *Walküre* as the basis for an essay on the "Bayreuth" school of singing. "In Germany the theory of Wagnerian declamation is that beauty of tone and clarity of enunciation are irreconcilable, because beautiful tone means dwelling on the vowel sounds and enunciation demands that these be made secondary to the consonants. This theory of singing was not entertained by one Richard Wagner, who has very plainly stated his belief that the vowels must be generators of musical tone and the publishers thereby of dramatic emotions. He did demand that his text be clearly articulated, but so did Charles Gounod. The correct method of Wagner singing is that employed in the artistic delivery of lieder. It unites beauty of tone, musical phrasing and nuancing with intelligible delivery of the words. This is the kind of Wagner singing that Mr. Whitehill does, and he does it extremely well, with much nobility of tone and dignity of style. He is a decided acquisition to the list of local singers, and his Wotan, conceived, according to the contemporaneous German idea, as a very human personage, is a noteworthy contribution to the gallery of Wagnerian portraits."

One of America's most distinguished singers, Clarence Whitehill, as Golaud, with Louise Hunter as Yniold, in the 1925 Met premiere of Pelléas et Mélisande.

When Wagner was revived in English after the war, Whitehill became the leading baritone; in *Lohengrin* he "declaimed the text so distinctly and eloquently that for once translated opera took on the inevitableness of opera in the original." His several Covent Garden seasons included the first *Ring* in English with the British National Opera Company in 1922. Later in the decade, while Gatti-Casazza struggled with the paucity of Wagnerian sopranos and tenors, he enjoyed the luxury, unparalleled since, of having both Whitehill and Friedrich Schorr on the roster to share the lower roles. Schorr's Hans Sachs has rightly become a legend. But here is Henderson in 1924, months after Schorr had sung his first Sachs in New York, writing of Whitehill's: "Finally, there was the manly, tender, lovable Hans Sachs of Clarence Whitehill, an operatic impersonation that will long dwell in the memory.... Mr. Whitehill (closely seconded by Mme. Easton) gave a brilliant demonstration of the possibilities of creating the illusion of spoken articulation without loss of the lyric flow of the music. He and the soprano gave a remarkably fine exhibition of the most finished and effective type of Wagner singing."

Whitehill was also singled out by critics in the annual revivals of *Pelléas et Mélisande*: "Mr. Whitehill's Golaud is destined to be remembered as one of the great tragic figures of the contemporaneous opera stage. There will be debate about it; and some will cavil at his methods in certain moments; but of the power and authority of the impersonation the future will entertain no doubt."

Whitehill's Metropolitan career ended badly. He had always been known for great dignity, an aura of good breeding emphasized by an ability to wear clothes of any period with ease and style. When Gatti failed to rehire him in 1932, an unpleasant public squabble ensued, the men denouncing each other in the press. This was a year of great change at the Metropolitan; moreover, critics had noted that Whitehill's voice was often frayed. Whitehill left the Metropolitan after eighteen seasons and died of a heart attack before the year was out.

FRIEDRICH SCHORR

ON OCTOBER 27, 1922, BERLIN AGENT Norbert Salter wrote Gatti-Casazza: "The heroic baritone Friedrich Schorr who sang for you the summer of 1921 in Vienna has received an offer to join the German troupe that will begin February with popular performances of Wagner operas in America. You would have a good opportunity then to hear him and see whether he pleases you or not." The German Opera Company opened just five blocks downtown from the Metropolitan at the Manhattan Opera House. The company, directed by Leo Blech, not only brought back two former Metropolitan tenors, Heinrich Knote and Jacques Urlus, but also introduced several important singers to the United States, including the sopranos Meta Seinemeyer and Elsa Alsen and the bass Alexander Kipnis. The Hungarian-born bass-baritone Friedrich Schorr (1888–1953) made his New York debut on the company's second night in *Tannhäuser,* and was singled out: "The finest singer in the cast was Friedrich Schorr, who took the part of Wolfram; a singer with a noble and beautiful quality of voice, used with fine intelligence and expressiveness, and with a modulation of its power not always at the command of the German singer." Schorr sang in *Der Fliegende Holländer, Die Walküre,* and *Fidelio,* and when he sang his first New York *Die Meistersinger* on February 28, 1923, it was probably a celebration; that same day he had signed a five-year contract with the Metropolitan. It is usually forgotten that Schorr's first stage performances had been in small roles with the Chicago Opera in 1912. The career as usually remembered began later the same year when he sang Wotan in *Die Walküre* with the Graz Opera. Not long after, he met his first wife, a dramatic soprano, during the second act of an unrehearsed *Fliegende Holländer* performance in Cologne at the moment when the Dutchman enters and beholds Senta. The onstage romance resulted in marriage a few weeks later.

Opposite: *Friedrich Schorr as Don Pizarro in the 1927 revival of* Fidelio, *with Nanny Larsén-Todsen in the title role, performed for the centenary of Beethoven's death.*

His Metropolitan debut the following season was again as Wolfram, succeeded by his first Metropolitan *Meistersinger* with Delia Reinhardt (who fainted at the end of the quintet). It was a triumph: "Beauty, indeed, was present in abundance at yesterday's performance. Mr. Schorr's remarkable Hans Sachs possesses, no doubt, the largest share of it. It was his first appearance in the role at the Metropolitan.... We have seen few finer Sachses than Mr. Schorr's. Perhaps, if we had to testify under oath, we should have to confess that we do not remember a more persuasive one since Emil Fischer's great performance in the old days; though Fischer never sang this music, within our recollection, as Mr. Schorr did yesterday. Mr. Schorr has a voice of exceptional beauty, and he sings like a musician. Some of his mezza-voce and pianissimo singing yesterday was of astonishing delicacy, purity and finesse—we shall not soon forget the rare tenderness of 'Dem Vogel, der heut sang' or the musing poetry of the great monologue in the third act, and Mr. Schorr's phrasing is that of an artist of fine taste and sensibility.... This complex and subtle character came to life under Mr. Schorr's hands and moved before us in humaneness and truth. It was largely planned but was none the less full of significant and revealing detail—as in that moment of Sachs's difficult self-control when Eva throws herself into his arms and unknowingly torments him with her gratitude that she swears is love. Here, for an instant, we saw the anguished middle-aged lover of Wagner's poignant conception, with his sorrow, his fortitude, his resignation, his magnitude of soul, his humorous acceptance of his own tragedy, his tenderness that is never for himself."

In a departure from the humanity of his Wotan, Wanderer, and Amfortas, Schorr was the villain in the 1927 *Fidelio* revival with Nanny Larsén-Todsen, Rudolf Laubenthal, and Michael Bohnen performing Bodanzky's version with orchestrated dialogue and a final scene that omitted the C major chorus. Here he showed his grandeur could as easily be corruption. "In Mr. Schorr's Pizarro, beetling hate and vindictive cruelty hurtled through a coating of eighteenth century magnificence, a carriage of acrid pride of place."

Schorr continued to sing in Covent Garden summer seasons until 1933, although he had dropped Berlin and Bayreuth after 1931 because of the presence of the Nazis. The focus of his career became the Western Hemisphere. He was Orest in the first Metropolitan *Elektra* and sang in the American premieres of *Jonny Spielt Auf* and *Schwanda*. Wagner, however, was his life's work; he performed the bass-baritone roles more often than anyone else in the Metropolitan's history.

Schorr's achievement lay not in statistics but in the compelling quality of everything he did. He insisted that Wotan's farewell be sung with a flowing cantabile line equally appropriate for Renato's "Eri tu" in *Un Ballo in Maschera*. His favorite and most memorable role was Hans Sachs, a part he spent over twenty years in mastering only to confess on his retirement that he was still discovering new things in it. Schorr was the middle link in an interesting chain of Metropolitan baritones. He studied with Adolf Robinson, who appeared in five early Met seasons and was the first Wolfram, Pizarro, and William Tell there; he taught the American baritone Cornell MacNeil, first on the Met roster in 1959. As a teacher Schorr was known for his honesty and directness. One unpromising student who had been encouraged by several well-known instructors found different advice from Schorr: go out and play baseball with your friends.

MARIA JERITZA

THE PHENOMENAL NEW YORK CAREER of Czech-born Maria Jeritza (1887–1982) might never have begun. Gatti-Casazza complained in 1915 to Otto Kahn that Jeritza, having promised to come, "took advantage of my offer to obtain a ten years contract with Vienna at very good terms, without however, reserving for herself a leave of absence for New York." By 1920 she had become more demanding, as Gatti informed Ziegler: "Nothing arranged with Jeritza her pretensions being absurd. . . . Find out about value of Soprano Lotti [*sic*] Lehmann." Finally, in November 1921, she arrived in New York and began a twelve-year reign that encompassed both New York and Vienna. In her debut as Marietta in Erich Korngold's *Tote Stadt* she was: "tall as a grenadier. . . . Mrs. Jeritza looked a composite portrait of Mary Lawton, the actress, Maude Fay, the singer, and the goddess H_2O_2. Under the mass of white-gold hair, the features are piquant. She is a wonderful frame for clothes—for snowy silks and velvets of deep rose or jade. She is an actress and with all her length, almost an acrobat. She can leap cleanly on a table or jump upright on to the seat of a chair. She can twist and twirl in all the many movements of the dance. She is of a volcanic energy, she strikes out with the punch of a kicking pony, she has more than a slap or two for the clumsy male." A few days later came her spectacular *Tosca*. In a staging that earned Puccini's sanction, Jeritza sang "Vissi d'arte" crouched against a sofa after Scarpia (Scotti) had thrown her to the ground. "It was more significantly unconventional in the larger sense, in that it put a new and enthralling vitality into the role which has threatened to become constrained by routine. Mme. Jeritza does not look the ideal Tosca but she sang and acted the part entrancingly. Her singing was her principal histrionic asset, as singing always must be with a really great operatic artist. The short recitative passages, which have so often gone without apparent meaning, she read with luminous intelligence, giving every phrase, every word, every syllable a value. In the broader lyric passages she revealed an amazing range of tonal coloring used with an unerring judgment that made her singing—not always technically flawless—alive with dramatic eloquence. . . . [She] reserved outbursts of full voice for those passionate outbreaks without which Tosca cannot be made real for an audience. Her tones in the caressing measures in the scene with Cavaradossi in the first act were liquid and melting. When she pealed out her rage at the Attavanti's picture they were of hammered steel. In 'Vissi d'arte' they were moist with tears. Such a vocal colorist could not fail to make Tosca human. Her action had dignity and grace in the first act and panther fierceness in the gory climax of the second. There was no mistaking her discovery of the fatal knife and the dawning on her mind of desperate and bloody purpose. Her pantomime over the dead body of Scarpia was that of an excellent judge of theatrical values, a mistress of stage technic. The whole second act was tragically done." In his autobiography, Gatti reported that the ovation by a cheering, screaming audience after "Vissi d'arte" was the longest one he'd witnessed in his professional career.

Not only did Jeritza become the box office successor to Caruso in the 1920s, but her triumphs with public and press were so great that both Geraldine Farrar and Clau-

Opposite: *Giacomo Lauri-Volpi as Calaf and Maria Jeritza as Turandot, photographed onstage at the dress rehearsal of the 1926 Met premiere of* Turandot.

c
Mishkin
NY

Maria Jeritza in her distinctive 1928 portrayal of Carmen.

dia Muzio left the company rather than compete. No problems arose with Rosa Ponselle, since they had only Santuzza in common. Jeritza commanded the German repertoire and a series of theatrical novelties including *Fedora, Jenůfa,* and *I Gioielli della Madonna.* During this time of her greatest fame she even had a newspaper column in which she answered beauty questions. On wrinkles: "Avoid eye strain, nervous strain, worry and disagreeable thoughts."

In 1926 came Puccini's *Turandot.* Both Jeritza and Rosa Raisa had argued in print that the title role was written for her; whatever the case, it is probable that Ponselle, who summered near Puccini in Italy, was the first soprano to sing through part of Turandot's music. In any event, Jeritza was chosen for the title role in the grandest production in the history of the Metropolitan. "Puccini's portrait, a more than life-size photograph framed in laurel branches and violet satin bows, was hung over the parterre box promenade rail in the Broadway entrance. During the performance a census of those singing on the stage and mostly visible to the house showed these large totals: 120 opera chorus, 120 chorus school, 60 boy choir singers, 60 ballet girls, 30 male dancers and procession leaders, 30 stage musicians, 230 extra 'supers'—650 persons, all told, besides the eleven-star cast and a hundred orchestra players in the pit."

For Jeritza, it provided several of her most theatrical moments: "It was a magnificent entrance as Jeritza accomplished it last night: the sudden, gleaming apparition, making its sovereign patibulary gesture toward the moonlight youth upon the wall—one recalls no entrance quite so superb in opera hereabout since an unforgettable Thaïs strode upon the stage of the Manhattan Opera House nineteen years ago disguised as Mary of Paris and Alexandria. This conquering bit of histrionism (Turandot sings not a note until the second act) set the key for a triumphant impersonation. . . . She has done nothing more brilliant in New York, nothing more completely imagined and integritive and fused, than her enactment of the merciless Oriental princess."

Her later novelties, all less successful, included Tchaikovsky's *Iolanta,* Strauss's *Aegyptische Helena, Fanciulla,* and Von Suppe's *Boccaccio* and *Donna Juanita.* Her 1928 Carmen was a distinct failure. "Her voice had the consistency of cotton-wool and its disclosures of pitch were foggy. Part of the 'Seguidilla' she sang on her back on the garrison table (recalling by contraries her prayer in *Tosca*)."

In 1932, Gatti wired her in Vienna that the executive committee of the Metropolitan had instructed him not to reengage her. Jeritza's salary had risen to $2,500, the same as Caruso's and the highest in the company; even with her acceptance of the 10 percent pay cut requested of everyone, it was still more than the Met could afford. Moreover, her performances no longer drew audiences as they had in the past. Jeritza's career continued elsewhere but never again on the exalted level she held at the Metropolitan. In his first season as general manager, Rudolf Bing brought her back with much of her verve intact for a gala appearance as Rosalinda in *Die Fledermaus.* Later, she was a familiar figure in broadbrimmed hats and dark glasses at many Metropolitan performances, occupying her regular seats—in the first row, naturally.

GRACE MOORE

A HEALTHY VOICE, THE FIGURE OF A showgirl, and the pretensions of a prima donna combined in Grace Moore (1901–1947) to produce an unusually interesting American soprano between the two world wars. The gulf in those days between Broadway and an operatic career was not the insuperable divide that the use of microphones has made it today, and Grace Moore went from singing "Yes, We Have No Bananas" in the 1923 *Music Box Review* to study in Paris. From there Otto Kahn cabled Gatti in 1927: JUST HEARD GRACE MOORE. SHE HAS MADE REMARKABLE PROGRESS CONTRARY TO MY EXPECTATION AND DESERVES IN MY OPINION SERIOUS CONSIDERATION ESPECIALLY FOR FRENCH PARTS EVEN LOUISE. Gatti evidently agreed, since her debut in *La Bohème* occurred the following February. Despite trainloads of fellow Tennesseeans cheering out

Grace Moore in Mishkin's portrait made for her 1928 Met debut as Mimi in La Bohème, *a performance that brought trainloads of friends from Tennessee.*

front and baskets of flowers backstage, most critics were not particularly impressed. "Unfortunately the Metropolitan itself has more than once demonstrated that the appearance of a donna on its stage did not necessarily mean that she is of prime order. . . . This soprano has a pretty voice of lyric quality, the color tending toward mellowness and capable of more warmth than the singer knew how to evoke from it. The range was sufficient for Mimi. . . . In the third act, when she had rid herself of the nervousness, she sang her upper tones with more freedom and something more like focus. . . . Two or three constrained gestures used over and over and an alternation of facial expression from smile to no smile seemed to exhaust her pictorial resources." From this inauspicious beginning Grace Moore built a career that included Juliette, Manon, and Tosca at the Metropolitan, concerts, and recordings, but one most significant for movies. *One Night of Love* was one of the most successful of musical films and *Louise* with Georges Thill, directed by Abel Gance, one of the best. She died in 1947 in a plane crash outside Copenhagen. By then the principles of photo-journalism required that a picture of her charred body be widely published.

ROSA PONSELLE AND *NORMA*

IN THE WORLD OF THE OPERATIC soprano, Bellini's *Norma* rises like some mysterious Stonehenge on a plain of lesser monuments. The first Metropolitan Norma was Lilli Lehmann in 1890, who, when questioned about singing out at a *Götterdämmerung* rehearsal, replied: "Don't be alarmed about my voice. It is easier to sing all three Brünnhildes than one Norma. You are so carried away by the dramatic emotion, the action, and the scene that you do not have to think how to sing the words. That comes of itself. But in Bellini you must always have a care for beauty of tone and correct emission." Lehmann has been quoted so often that one forgets her own problems with the role: "Mme. Lehmann's voice does not lend itself readily to the rapid utterance of scales, but she invested Bellini's measures with a fine fervor, and in her acting there was an unfailing reverence for artistic verisimilitude." Two-thirds of a century later came Maria Meneghini Callas, in 1956, never at her best in her New York *Normas*, but so mesmerizing everywhere that she deluded succeeding sopranos into believing the role was performable.

Between Lehmann and Callas there was Rosa Ponselle. In 1920 Ponselle had heard Rosa Raisa's tempestuous traversal of the score and assumed that the part would always be beyond her. Gatti must have planned otherwise. How else explain Ponselle's steady progression that leads from *Ernani* in 1921, goes through *William Tell* and *L'Africana* in 1923, and culminates in a triumphant performance of Spontini's *Vestale* in 1925? "In singing Julia Rosa Ponselle has taken that big step forward which it has always been in her power to take, but which her more exacting admirers had begun to despair of her ever taking, so easy is it in these days of neglected vocal art to let well enough alone. Though her vocal performance on Thursday was somewhat uneven, at its best it achieved such nobility of tone and purity and elevation of style that it really seems today as though Mme. Ponselle might wake up one morning to find herself the 'grande chanteuse classique' which our stage has sorely lacked for years. And her acting, in its dignity, its plasticity, its significant directness, its fine new reticence, kept pace with her singing."

Two years later she sang her first Norma. Here at last the lovers of vocal richness could unite with the bearers of critical standards. "Bellini wrote for a style of song, for a manner of operatic acting, that must be now regained. As Miss Ponselle proved in the part of Norma, it may be reconquered. . . . Bellini prefered the quill pen to the stub when he took ink from a crystal inkstand and set notes on music paper. . . . [Ponselle's] semblance and carriage arrest the eye and stimulate imagination. She has learned to strike the attitudes and outfling the gestures that were essential parts of 'the grand style.' She can sustain the long Bellinian melody; hold it serene and crystalline; give it depth and abundance, stir its sensibility and suggestion. She does not fall too short of the full-bodied, quasi-ecstatic ornament. She lacks only that infusion of exalted passion which was crown upon 'the grand style'—in the final scene really gains it. An operatic past stands renewed in her operatic present. In these days there is no rarer feat of the theater."

Such was the acclaim for *Norma* that *The New York Times* reported that singers who proverbially stood in awe of the opera had thronged to the second performance, even paying their way into the house. And in 1930 W. J. Henderson paid Ponselle his ultimate tribute: "Rosa Ponselle's attainment of the level on which she carved out her Giulia in *La Vestale* and her Norma is due first and last to Rosa Ponselle. If she had not had the good sense to see her own deficiencies and to set about improving her art, she would have sunk into comparative insignificance in spite of the exceptional voice which nature bestowed upon her. As it is now, she is without doubt the foremost dramatic soprano of the Italian opera."

Norma was followed by Luisa Miller, Donna Anna in *Don Giovanni,* and Violetta in *La Traviata.* After only thirteen years on the Metropolitan stage, her career began to wind down when she sang Montemezzi's *Notte di Zoraima.* No one could have suspected her approaching retirement in 1931: "It was a night of splendor for Miss Ponselle. Never has her gorgeous voice swept its noble scale with greater certainty or more theatrical effect. If the opera does not retain a place in the repertory, it will be a pity, for it will be worthwhile to go occasionally to hear Miss Ponselle breathe the breath of life into Montemezzi's manufactured song. The music afforded her scope for that sweeping phraseology and grandiloquence of style in which she is so impressive. The grand proportions of her voice are untrammeled, while it beautifully tempered itself to tenderer passages. There is no use blinking the fact that new roles for Miss Ponselle are greatly needed. This opera was probably produced in order to supply her with one, and for that reason we should hope that it will please the public."

After this there was only one new role, Carmen, which she unveiled in 1935 after years of preparation. Gatti had exercised all his skill in programming roles for the major discovery of his career. With Gatti gone earlier in 1935, the problem was clearly beyond the ability of Edward Johnson as general manager; he refused to stage Cilèa's *Adriana Lecouvreur* for her and she determined to leave. Ponselle sang with the Met for the last time on tour in Cleveland in a *Carmen* on April 17, 1937.

Opposite: *Mishkin's definitive portrait of Rosa Ponselle in the title role in* Norma, *made for her first performances of the role in 1927.*

It was just under nineteen years since Caruso had first heard her in the studio of her teacher. Concerts, radio, a fascinating screen test as Carmen for MGM followed, and eventually there were no performances at all. Instead, a long and happy retirement at her home Villa Pace in Maryland, whence guests would return with tantalizing tales of a voice that still retained much of its magnificence.

EZIO PINZA

ON JANUARY 15, 1929, GATTI-CASAZZA wrote to Otto Kahn: "For several years, from time to time, you have asked me when we shall give a good revival of Mozart's *Don Giovanni* at the Metropolitan and until now I could only answer you negatively, because I did not have a company that could guarantee an execution worthy of the great master-piece. But to-day having at last been able to solve the difficult problem, I take pleasure in advising you definitely that during next November or December we shall give the revival, with the following cast:

Donna Anna	Rosa Ponselle
Donna Elvira	Elisabeth Rethberg
Zerlina	Editha Fleischer
Don Giovanni	Ezio Pinza
Don Ottavio	Beniamino Gigli
Leporello	Pavel Ludikar
Commendatore	Léon Rothier
Masetto	Louis D'Angelo
Conductor	Tullio Serafin
Stage Director	Wilhelm von Wymetal
Scenery by	Joseph Urban

"The reasons which induced me to give the role of the protagonist to Pinza, who is a basso cantante and not a baritone, are the following:

"1. That if it is true that traditionally and with very few exceptions the part of Don Giovanni was performed by a baritone it is also true that Mozart, in the original score, mentions as protagonist a basso cantante and not a baritone, and that he has written the part in a way that is perfectly adapted to the vocal means of a basso cantante, without having to change a single note.

"2. That none of the baritones of our company has the requisites of the role. Bohnen would never have succeeded in learning the role in Italian, and, on the other hand, his voice is heavy and lends itself very little to the bel-canto. Tibbett too has a voice not well adaptable to the bel-canto and moreover it seems that instead of progressing he has gone back of late. De Luca, excellent singer and with a good declamation, has absolutely no physique du rôle.

"Now, it is absolutely indispensable, for obvious reasons, that Don Giovanni be a handsome man. This is a requisite that cannot be overlooked. In regard to Pinza, only one objection can be made: the color of his voice of basso. But this is a very little thing if we consider that on the stage he is a very handsome man, intelligent, good actor, and naturally elegant. In addition he enjoys the sympathy of the public and critics; furthermore, he sings at present the role of the 'Toréador' in *Carmen,* which is a role for baritone, with a genuine great success. Pinza has already studied the part of Don Giovanni with Mo. Serafin. I had the occasion of hearing him myself in the principal parts and received the impression that we could take a chance to give him the role."

With hindsight one knows that Gatti was inspired in his choice of Ezio Pinza (1892–1957) for Don Giovanni, a performance that became one of the classics of the twentieth century. However, from the point of view of the twenties the choice was not so obvious. When an Italian agent wrote Gatti early in 1924 that Pinza was "probably the best we have," Gatti replied: "The bass Pinza has been repeatedly offered to me by Comm. Lusardi, but I have done nothing: first, I have a very valuable group of basses [in addition to Chaliapin, on the roster were Didur, Mardones, and Rothier], none of which merits being replaced; second, because I don't wish to seem to lessen the already scarce group of Scala artists and thereby create problems for my friend Scandiani."

Pinza eventually made his New York debut in the opening-night *Vestale* of 1926; W. J. Henderson thought him "useful," Sanborn "promising," and only Gilman really approved. The good reviews slowly developed, and with *Norma* in November 1927 it was noted that "In Mr. Pinza, who essayed the part of the high Priest, Miss Ponselle found the only member of the cast whose voice and manner of singing most nearly approximated the requirements of Bellini's music."

There were other priests, fathers, and villains, and Pimen to Chaliapin's Boris Godunov, before a double bill of *Coq d'Or* and Alfano's *Madonna Imperia* in 1928 when Pinza was said to look like a Titian portrait and sing and act "with pithy incisiveness and address worthy of better things."

Don Giovanni came the next year and was not initially successful. "Mr. Pinza has the presence for the title role and in time he will doubtless cut out the hop-and-skip-and-jumping and comport himself more like a grand seigneur." But Gatti persisted and the future held two Mozartean triumphs for Pinza, both *Don Giovanni* and *Le Nozze di Figaro,* as well as *Faust, Boris* (in Italian), and almost all the standard bass repertoire. Emile de Becque

Opposite: *Ezio Pinza as Oroveso, the stern father of Norma, a performance in which he was said to match the skilled vocalism of Rosa Ponselle.*

Ezio Pinza as Chancellor of Ragusa in Alfano's Madonna Imperia, *a 1928 portrayal that led Gatti-Casazza to cast him as Don Giovanni.*

Opposite: *Elisabeth Rethberg as the reluctant Donna Elvira of the 1929 revival of Mozart's* Don Giovanni *with Ezio Pinza.*

in *South Pacific* followed on Broadway in 1949, and Pinza made several films. The first of his many recordings had been made as early as 1923 in Rome. Quite often, record companies have recognized vocal gold before anyone else.

ELISABETH RETHBERG

IN A QUANDARY WHETHER TO HIRE Delia Reinhardt or Elisabeth Rethberg (1894–1976) since his Berlin agent, Norbert Salter, kept insisting that first one and then the other was superior, Gatti-Casazza eventually engaged them both for 1922–23. Reinhardt's first season began with Sieglinde; her roles eventually included Mimi, Fiordiligi, Octavian, and Sita in *Le Roi de Lahore.* But her engagement was complicated by illness and she left after two seasons. Nor was Rethberg in good health during her first year, although her 1922 *Aida* debut with Giovanni Martinelli and Sigrid Onegin was a success: "Mme. Elisabeth Rethberg, who hails from old Schwarzenberg in Erzgebirge and later from well-won triumphs in Dresden, Berlin and most of the capitals of Europe, was the new Aida and by the sheer beauty of her soprano voice and her sincere if not always convincing acting won for herself a high place." Her first season in what was to be a significant Metropolitan career brought her roles that illustrated her value to the company. In one December week she sang both Sieglinde and Sophie. In *Die Walküre,* "Even when she came now to the sturdy Wagnerian strophes there was a hint of cis-Alpine grace and smoothness. Yet under the velvet strode a strong, free body of tone, unfaltering and always eager. . . . The golden regality that Jeritza is wont to bring the role was melted down in Mme. Rethberg to a simpler, perhaps a readier sympathy." In *Rosenkavalier,* six days later, "The extremely difficult pages following the entrance of Octavian in the second act she sang with good intonation and a lovely quality of tone, both of which she attained by refraining from forcing her voice."

From a German repertoire that included *Der Freischütz, Lohengrin,* and *Tannhäuser,* she moved freely to *Madama Butterfly, Andrea Chénier,* and *Faust.* Lawrence Gilman, speaking of "the limpid and solacing beauty of Madame Rethberg's voice in *Meistersinger,*" maintained that "you might easily be reminded, by her phrasing, of the art of a master of bowed instruments, so just is her sense of the shape and balance and musical designs, her delicate instinct for line and cadence and proportion."

Although she sang the title role in the 1928 Dresden premiere of Strauss's *Aegyptische Helena,* the part went to Jeritza in New York. Several critics felt she was lucky to be assigned Rautendelein in the American premiere of Respighi's *Campana Sommersa* instead.

In 1929, as he prepared his revival of *Don Giovanni,* Gatti was forced to remind Rethberg of the fact that Sophie was not a role she sang often. Informed by his assistant, Edward Ziegler, that Rethberg didn't want to sing Donna Elvira because of Ponselle's presence in the cast as Donna Anna, Gatti replied: "You will also point out to Rethberg that, apart from all the questions of right, one of the first consequences which she would face if she refuses to sing Donna Elvira, would be to force us to have her sing necessarily Sophie in performances of *Der Rosenkavalier* with Mme. Jeritza, because we naturally counted on her singing Donna Elvira to make up

c
Mishkin
N.Y.

The young baritone George Cehanovsky, who made his debut in 1926–27 and his last appearance in 1965–66, one of the Met's longest careers.

her guaranteed number of performances." She capitulated, and succeeded: "Mme. Rethberg's enameled art is superbly wedded to the music of Mozart."

Before her twenty-season Metropolitan career ended in 1942, Rethberg was in the cast of two significant revivals, *Otello* in 1935 with Martinelli and Lawrence Tibbett and *Le Nozze di Figaro* in 1940 with Ezio Pinza, Bidú Sayão, and Risë Stevens. Years later Rethberg formed another Metropolitan alliance with her marriage to the distinguished baritone George Cehanovsky, who sang there between 1926 and 1966. In featured roles, Cehanovsky appeared more than two thousand times and continues, after his singing career, as an adviser to the Met on language and style.

EDWARD JOHNSON

IN 1923 HENRY E. KREHBIEL REPORTED that "an old stage manager once remarked to us that in the place of torment to which he would be consigned after death his punishment would consist in being doomed to make tenors act." Neither stage manager nor Krehbiel could have been referring to Edward Johnson (1878–1959), the tenor from Guelph, Ontario, who came to the Metropolitan with experience on Broadway, seven years singing under the name Edoardo di Giovanni in Italian theaters (at La Scala he was the first Parsifal in Italy), and three seasons with the Chicago Opera. Whatever the appraisal of his voice, Johnson was always singled out for his stage demeanor. "Grace, stature, and superior good looks, true and effective acting" were noted at his 1922 Metropolitan debut in *L'Amore dei Tre Re* with Lucrezia Bori. In *Roméo et Juliette* and *Pelléas et Mélisande,* Johnson and Bori formed a romantic onstage partnership noted for its grace, elegance, and warmth. In 1931 they appeared in *Peter Ibbetson,* Deems Taylor's second opera for the Met. "The great feature of this performance was Mr. Johnson's Peter, bilingual, like the original character, and admirable in song. . . . In the very finest sense of the word, this figure was adolescent, his passion pure, intense, idealistic as only the passion of young poet and dreamer could have been. Mr. Johnson created not only drama but poetry. He ornamented his dramatic performance, in which every gesture was a picture and every lineament an emotion, with song which also had in it youth and intense feeling." Bori and Johnson worked together in fund-raising drives to support the Metropolitan during the Depression. A year after his last Met performance in 1934, Johnson became general manager upon Herbert Witherspoon's death shortly after taking the job. As Conried had inherited Caruso's contract from Maurice Grau, Johnson was heir to the well-maintained Wagnerian repertoire of Gatti and its recent phenomenon, Kirsten Flagstad. (After World War II he declined to reengage her and pretended that this was not a political decision.) The displacements of war strengthened his conducting staff; during two remarkable seasons, 1942–43 and 1943–44, the roster included Bruno Walter, Sir Thomas Beecham, and George Szell. His regime fostered a whole generation of important American artists, including Helen Traubel, Risë Stevens, Leonard Warren, Eleanor Steber, Jan Peerce, Astrid Varnay, Regina Resnik, Richard Tucker, Robert Merrill, and Jerome Hines.

LUCREZIA BORI

THE HISTORY OF OPERA IS LITTERED with singers who encountered vocal difficulties and never returned to their former excellence. Toward the end of 1914–15, increasing strain led Lucrezia Bori to have nodes removed from her vocal cords. The operation was not a success and her scheduled Metropolitan performances the next season were canceled. In Milan a surgeon who had cured Caruso of the same problem op-

The Canadian tenor Edward Johnson in the title role of Deems Taylor's 1931 opera Peter Ibbetson, *four years before he became the Met's general manager.*

Lucrezia Bori as an elegant Mary, Duchess of Towers, in Peter Ibbetson, *the last of her twenty-nine Metropolitan roles.*

erated in 1916 and prescribed a long period of silence as the only guarantee for recovery of the voice. Rest in the mountains of Spain followed, long periods of isolation, more than a year without speaking a word. Stumbling on a path one day and giving a little cry of surprise convinced Bori that her voice was well; then began the slow process of learning how to sing all over again.

Gatti found it easy to dispense with problem singers and move on to others. However, he watched over Bori with concern and encouragement. He asked for reviews from her 1919 return to opera in Monte Carlo, scolded her for making a bad impression when she canceled a scheduled performance in Barcelona (she never sang opera in her homeland) and made what he regarded as a "very prudent contract" for her return to the Metropolitan. He reported to New York from Milan in June 1920 that "I saw here Miss Bori in good condition and I found her with plenty of courage and confidence in herself. Several artists who sang with her at Montecarlo have assured me that her vocal conditions are excellent: from what they have told me, it may be that her voice has become smaller in volume, but it is more beautiful in quality and above all more equal. Well, we shall see." Bori reappeared in New York in January 1921 with the Met's new tenor, Beniamino Gigli, in *La Bohème,* and sang "with a voice more beautiful than it was six years ago and a much improved art." Gatti exulted in a cable to his Milanese agent, Lusardi: BORI ABSOLUTE SUCCESS CONDITION VOICE ACKNOWLEDGED UNANIMOUSLY PERFECT VOLUME QUALITY RESONANCE.

Bori's prewar years now became prelude to sixteen seasons of unmatchable elegance. Rosa Ponselle had her magnificent vocal instrument, Jeritza her flamboyant personality. Bori's special province was the repertoire demanding charm and musicality, grace and sincerity. She was Manon and Violetta, Mimi, Juliette, Mignon, and Mélisande, moving easily between Italian and French schools without offending either. The qualities that W. J. Henderson found in her 1922 *Snegourotchka* help define her skill in portraying twenty-eight other parts at the Metropolitan: "Who could have been the fragile, hesitating, doubt haunted little Snow Maiden but Miss Lucrezia Bori? She flutters pathetically through the drama, a northern butterfly, the sport of fate, a sweet little winter blossom doomed to death in the warmth of the sun. It would be easy to spoil such a role by striving to elaborate it, but Miss Bori wisely kept herself within the lines of the picture. She was simple, tender, sympathetic, captivating. She sang beautifully. The composer did not give her any opportunity to excite raptures by her vocal proclamation, but she was always pleasing.... The audience may not have thundered its approval of her art, but without doubt, it loved her."

Jean de Reszke had predicted at her 1910 debut that she would "take her place at the top of the list of the world's great singers." She was a great singer but also something more. She repaid the love of Metropolitan audiences with a second career after her 1936 retirement. Her tireless efforts supported the Metropolitan through periods of stress and need until the day of her death.

LILY PONS

THE AUDITION CARD IN THE METROpolitan Opera Archives for March 20, 1930 reads: "PONS, LILY, coloratura soprano, Maria Gay. Very good voice, Very good style, 'Vera coloratura.' Exceptional element." Lily Pons (1898–1976) had been discovered by Gay and her husband, Giovanni Zenatello, not by chance in a small theater in South of France as the newspapers gullibly reported, but by appointment in the Paris studio of her teacher, Alberti de Gorostiaga, who had been Florencio Constantino's valet. Impressed, Gay and Zenatello signed a management contract with her and sent her across the Atlantic for Gatti to hear. With Metropolitan contract in hand Pons returned to France. Gay wrote Gatti in October: "We leave with Lily Pons on November 12 for New York on the *Ile de France.* Lily wanted to leave so long before the beginning of her contract because she wants to work on the repertoire she's going to sing at the Metropolitan under the wise advice of Maestro Serafin. She's worked very hard during the summer with an Italian pianist, Zecchi, at our home in Verona and I can tell you that she's made great progress and you'll be very happy with her—especially in *Lucia* she's absolutely splendid."

Her January 1931 debut as Lucia with Beniamino Gigli, Giuseppe De Luca, and Ezio Pinza was dazzling. W. J. Henderson enthusiastically examined her: "Miss Pons is several years under thirty [*sic*], slender and prepossessing, if not strikingly beautiful, gifted with a voice of pure and pleasing quality and a technic far above the slovenly average of today.... The tones were forward even to the top of the scale. The breath control when at its best was substantial and the singer in numerous places showed ability to 'spin' tone, as the old masters called it, with skill.... She sang the mad scene well, but failed to establish the mood.... The cadenza with the flute was delivered with beauty of tone, elegance of phrasing and exquisite observance of melodic line, but there was no great brilliance in it.... She concluded the scene with a clear and well sustained high E flat."

After performances of *Lucia* and *Rigoletto* it became

Opposite: *Lily Pons in one of the last of Mishkin's official portraits, taken before her successful 1931 Metropolitan debut as Lucia di Lammermoor.*

MISHKIN
N.Y.

evident that Pons was a godsend to an opera house that was beginning to reflect the gloom of national depression. Lawrence Gilman celebrated her arrival: "Now is the Gatti of our discontent made glorious by this sun of Cannes: opera is once more as popular as an uncut dividend and as public as the Fourth of July. . . . The mistress of the top E flat (to say nothing of the E naturals and Fs which Mme. Pons so profitably employs) is assured of eternal operatic life. She sleeps, and becomes inactive, from time to time, like Kundry, until she is needed by her operatic masters for service or enchantment; but, like Kundry, she has a hundred incarnations, and is never dead for long. Last night, once more, you might have heard her, revived and influential, at her old work of tonal conjuration, flinging top notes into the blue, and garlanding the enraptured air (a bit heavy with Coty from the boxes and the Allium sativum of the claque) with blossoms of fioriture, well content to let the dead past bury its legendary divas."

By March the agreement with Gay had fallen apart, Pons claiming so many charges were made against her salary that nothing was left for her. Gay took Pons to court and claimed in an affidavit that "she found the singer with a fair voice and talent but with imperfect diction, dramatic ability, poise, expression, intonation and voice control. She asserts that by her efforts Miss Pons developed into a sensation." An out-of-court settlement separated the antagonists permanently.

Pons's skill and allure secured her one of the Met's enduring popular careers during the thirties and forties. Long-neglected operas such as *Lakmé, La Sonnambula, Linda di Chamounix,* and *La Fille du Régiment* were revived for her; she sang more *Lucias* than anyone else in Met history. Hollywood musicals enhanced a reputation already reinforced by cross-country recitals. She spent much of her time during World War II in hazardous tours singing before the armed forces within the sound of battle. Although she suffered from chronic nervousness, she said the wartime service was the only time her stage fright left her.

Long after celebrating the twenty-fifth anniversary of her Metropolitan debut, Lily Pons reappeared in 1972 at a New York Philharmonic Promenade concert conducted by her ex-husband, André Kostelanetz. "Radiating chic, as ever . . . Miss Pons made an entrance that could only have been the product of nearly fifty years' practice in perfecting the unreality that is every true prima donna. The exquisite way in which she was turned out assured her a triumph by sight alone." Vocally, she unveiled another miracle: "It was a kind of afterglow, a final flaring up of the barely smoldering vocal flame, a stirring about of the all but exhausted embers that recalled the equally memorable exhibition—perhaps the last previous one of its kind—that the great baritone Giuseppe De Luca gave in Town Hall, aged seventy."

NOTES

Most of the following citations are from daily newspapers. All New York City newspapers are listed without the prefix "New York"; thus *The New York Times* appears below as *Times.* Out-of-town newspapers are identified by city.

The most frequently quoted critics are Richard Aldrich, Lawrence Gilman, William J. Henderson, Henry T. Parker, Pitts Sanborn, and Algernon St. John-Brenon, and they have been identified by their initials.

Several quotes cited below come from unidentified newspaper clippings in the Metropolitan Archives and the New York Public Library. Some have been attributed to a probable author or date, and are so identified with a question mark enclosed within parentheses.

INTRODUCTION: THE GOLDEN AGE OF OPERA

page

3 "It must have been a success . . .": A. St. J.B., *Telegraph,* 28 Apr. 1914.

Opera Singers in New York

page

4 "the silver tones of the Signorina . . .": *American,* 30 Nov. 1825.

4 "Compass, sweetness, taste . . .": *Evening Post,* 30 Nov. 1825.

4 "excepting Malibran, no singer . . .": Richard Grant White, *The Century Magazine,* May 1882.

4 "incomparably fine—brilliant, powerful, impetuous . . .": *Courier & Enquirer,* 11 Sept. 1854.

4 "with such exquisite appreciation . . .": White, *The Century Magazine,* June 1882.

4 "Her appearance was that . . .": *Herald,* 25 Nov. 1859.

5 "He is young . . .": *Herald,* 2 Oct. 1873.

5 "a style that reminded the hearers . . .": *Herald,* 11 Apr. 1876.

6 "Mme. Sembrich was announced . . .": W.J.H., *Sun,* date unknown, circa 1 Feb. 1909.

6 "Her voice is true . . .": Henry E. Krehbiel, *The Musical Season 1885–86* (New York: Novello Ewer & Co., 1886), p. 44.

6 "His noble stage appearance . . .": W.J.H., *Harper's Weekly,* 16 Feb. 1895.

6 "the greatest basso of the time. . . .": ibid.

6 "the foremost living exponent . . .": ibid.

6 "a singer of true dramatic instincts . . .": Krehbiel, *Tribune,* 30 Nov. 1893.

6 "with the splendor of the trumpet . . .": W.J.H., *Harper's Weekly,* 16 Feb. 1895.

8 "that Jean de Reszke left the Metropolitan . . .": W.J.H., *Sun,* 2 May 1932.

The Critics

page

9 "The Swedish Swan . . .": Walt Whitman quoted by Robert D. Fanner, *Walt Whitman and Opera* (Carbondale: Southern University Illinois Press, 1951), p. 62.

9 "When the twenty-first century . . .": W.J.H., *Sun,* 2 Mar. 1913.

9 "If it is out of tune . . .": W.J.H., *Sun,* 2 Feb. 1908.

10 "Mme. Tetrazzini has many gifts . . .": W.J.H., *Sun,* 27 Feb. 1909.

10 "It has not perceptibly lost anything . . .": R.A., *Times,* 17 Nov. 1912.

10 "In this impersonation . . .": ibid.

10 "Madame Tetrazzini is not 'chic' . . .": P.S., *Globe,* (?) 1913.

12 "The fly in the ointment . . .": *Times,* 6 Dec. 1903.

12 "Miss Liebling's voice . . .": *Tribune,* 6 Dec. 1903.

12 "The lady looked . . .": unidentified newspaper, 23 Mar. 1908.

12 "But, then, everyone who goes to opera . . .": James G. Huneker, Philadelphia Press, 26 Nov. 1917.

The Opera Photographers

page

16 "to perpetuate the artistic side . . .": *Sun,* 4 Apr. 1909.

16 "It would probably never have been possible . . .": ibid.

19 "that other picture syndicates . . .": William Freese to Frank Wenker, 22 Nov. 1933, Metropolitan Opera Archives

Herman Mishkin

page

23 "MISHKIN—Photographer and great camouflage artist . . .": G. Viafora, *Caricature* (New York: privately published, 1919), p. 15.

25 "photographs necessary to advertising . . .": contract dated 22 Apr. 1910, Met Archives.
25 "The scores of dead . . .": W.J.H., *Sun*, 3 Mar. 1913.
26 "Dear Mr. Mishkin . . .": Enrico Caruso to Herman Mishkin, 31 Dec. 1917, Met Archives.
26 "As you know I am very well . . .": Caruso to Mishkin, 13 Dec. 1920, Met Archives.
29 "Several weeks ago . . .": Mishkin to Giulio Gatti-Casazza, 2 May 1932, Met Archives.
29 "Mr. Ziegler informed me . . .": Mishkin to Gatti, 13 May 1932, Met Archives.
29 "You have rendered faithful . . .": Gatti to Mishkin, 14 May 1932, Met Archives.

PART I: THE HAMMERSTEIN YEARS: 1906–1910

---

page
33 "She has been making scenes . . .": *Sun*, 1 May 1910.
34 "sent his secretary to tell her . . .": ibid.
34 "He was allowed as many performances . . .": ibid.
34 "Nobody who knows . . .": ibid.
34 "On the morning of the appointment . . .": *Musical America*, 29 Dec. 1906.
34 "the voice was one of 'splendid promise' ": ibid.
34 "the Oscar Hammerstein of ten years ago . . .": Edward Ziegler to Gatti, 9 July 1919, Metropolitan Archives.

Alessandro Bonci

page
34 "It is a voice that will sound small . . .": R.A. (?), *Times*, 4 Dec. 1906.
34 " . . . his repertoire is limited . . .": *Times*, 28 Feb. 1907.
34 "In his first phrases he answered . . .": W.J.H. (?), *Sun*, 23 Nov. 1907.
35 "As an operatic team . . .": Reginald de Koven, *World*, 28 Nov. 1907.
35 "The most temperate in the audience . . .": *Musical America*, 7 Feb. 1920.

Mario Ancona

page
35 "a light baritone voice . . .": *Times*, 12 Dec. 1893.
36 "Signor Ancona as Rigoletto . . .": *Times*, 30 Dec. 1893.
36 "If Dalmorès can go . . .": *Musical America*, 23 Mar. 1907.
36 "The possible effect of this edict . . .": ibid.
37 "sang with beautiful quality . . .": *Times*, 5 Nov 1907.
37 "His clear baritone is imperishable . . .": Boston *Advertiser*, date unknown, circa 25 Nov. 1913.

Mario Sammarco

page
37 " . . . a singer of uncommon gifts . . .": *World*, 2 Feb. 1907.
37 "sang the music with great purity . . .": *Times*, 15 Feb. 1907.
37 "a singing actor who nonchalantly . . .": H.T.P., Boston *Evening Transcript*, 9 (?) April 1909.
38 "Sammarco was the spirit . . .": Chicago *Evening Post*, date unknown.
38 "animated by the desire . . .": *Musical America*, 11 Jan. 1913.
38 "In London for three seasons . . .": ibid.

Eleonora de Cisneros

page
38 "To say that Mme. de Cisneros . . .": P.S., *Globe*, 20 Dec. 1906.

Amedeo Bassi

page
39 "Mr. Bassi, while not a Bonci . . .": *Musical America*, 29 Dec. 1906.
39 "It is a strong and flexible organ . . .": *Times*, 20 Dec. 1906.
39 "a fervor that took . . .": *Evening World*, 28 Mar. 1908.
40 "I engaged Bassi . . .": *Musical America*, 24 July 1909.
40 "yet where in America . . .": *Globe*, 6 Mar. 1912.

Giannina Russ

page
41 "made a far better impression . . .": *Globe*, 19 Dec. 1906.
41 "so satisfying vocally . . .": *Telegraph*, 26 Dec. 1906.
41 "something between an Alaskan squaw . . .": P.S. (?), *Globe*, 20 Dec. 1906.
41 "the most matronly exponent . . .": unidentified newspaper, 23 Mar. 1907.

Clotilde Bressler-Gianoli

page
42 "I have never known anyone . . .": A. St. J.-B., *Telegraph*, date unknown.
42 "It was the apparently unstudied . . .": Henry E. Krehbiel, *Tribune*, 15 Dec. 1906.
42 "Bressler-Gianoli's impersonation . . .": Sylvester Rawling, *World*, 19 Mar. 1907.

Charles Dalmorès

page
42 "I want to engage you . . .": *Musical America*, 15 Apr. 1911.
42 "Faust, José, Samson . . .": H.T.P., Boston *Evening Transcript*, 24 Mar. 1909.
43 "A genuine artist. . . .": W.J.H., *Ladies' Home Journal*, Mar. 1910.
43 "I sang tenor roles . . .": *Musical America*, 11 Dec. 1909.
43 "blowing thousands of dollars . . .": Philadelphia *Times*, 28 Apr. 1910.

Jeanne Gerville-Réache

page

44 "Her voice was not to be forgotten . . .": H.T.P., Boston *Evening Transcript,* 7 Jan. 1915.

Hector Dufranne

page

44 "one of the greatest artists . . .": W.J.H., *Sun,* 20 Feb. 1908.

44 "Mr. Dufranne has a baritone voice . . .": R.A., *Times,* 20 Feb. 1908.

44 "As Jochanaan Mr. Dufranne . . .": R.A., *Times,* 29 Jan. 1908.

44 "That Mr. Dufranne would do vocal . . .": unidentified newspaper.

Armand Crabbé

page

46 "His voice, while not of great power . . .": *Times,* 6 Nov. 1907.

46 "policy of this organization . . .": Felix Borowski, Chicago *Record Herald,* 5 May 1913.

Maurice Renaud

page

46 "Where Renaud sits . . .": Henry T. Finck, *My Adventures in the Golden Age of Music* (New York: Funk & Wagnalls, 1926), p. 356.

48 "Renaud's voice was not a big voice . . .": H.T.P., *Eighth Notes* (New York: Dodd, Mead, 1922), p. 49.

48 "a performance of pathos . . .": *Globe,* 12 Jan. 1909.

48 "exquisite finesse . . .": *Times,* 17 Jan. 1907.

48 "whose high-heeled buskin . . .": *Evening Sun,* date unknown.

48 "he towered above her . . .": Finck, *My Adventures,* p. 358.

48 "Mr. Scotti's is no more than . . .": H.T.P., Boston *Evening Transcript,* 1 Dec. 1910.

48 "For those who make no distinction . . .": W.J.H., *Sun,* 11 Jan. 1911.

Mary Garden

page

49 "made in it a new disclosure . . .": R.A., *Times,* 20 Feb. 1908.

49 "What a glorious work . . .": *Musical America,* 10 Oct. 1908.

49 "To add to the public interest . . .": W.J.H., *Sun,* 28 Mar. 1909.

49 "without question the important thing . . .": W.J.H., *Sun,* 29 Jan. 1909.

49 "I have no objection . . .": *Evening Sun,* 19 Jan. 1909.

49 "In this action you have taken . . .": Garden to Hammerstein, undated letter, author's collection.

49 "It is an achievement to have made . . .": *Times,* 9 Dec. 1909.

53 "I consider the newspaper reviews . . .": *Times,* 3 Feb. 1910.

53 "Miss Garden then went on . . .": *Herald Tribune,* 18 Jan. 1954.

53 "Garden had no school . . .": Vincent Sheehan, *Opera News,* 4 Feb. 1967.

Florencio Constantino

page

53 "His voice, though not in volume . . .": *Times,* 6 Nov. 1907.

54 "From the glittering diamond . . .": A. St. J.-B., unidentified newspaper.

Carmen Melis

page

54 "she possesses to an unusual degree . . .": Philadelphia *Record,* 7 Dec. 1909.

54 "Mme. Melis lays aside . . .": Philip Hale, Boston *Herald,* 23 Jan. 1911.

55 "Her Tosca can be almost as distinguished . . .": Boston *Transcript,* 2 Jan. 1912.

Maria Gay

page

55 "Her Carmen may or may not . . .": *Times,* 4 Dec. 1908.

55 "A big woman, not over tall . . .": *Evening Sun,* 4 Dec. 1908.

55 "Last night at the Boston House . . .": Boston *Post,* 1 Jan. 1911.

55 "(the voice when correctly used . . .": Chicago *Tribune,* 18 Jan. 1910.

Giovanni Zenatello

page

57 "Her voice, with its original freshness . . .": *Tribune,* 26 Dec. 1908.

57 "This, too, was because he treated . . .": W.J.H., *Sun,* 26 Dec. 1908.

57 "What discount ought we to . . .": *Musical Opinion* (London), date unknown.

57 "impersonation of the betrayed . . .": *World Telegram,* 15 Jan. 1933.

Marguerite d'Alvarez

page

57 "A really excellent contralto . . .": *Evening Sun,* 31 Aug. 1909.

57 "To Amneris the composer . . .": Hale, Boston *Herald,* 13 Dec. 1913.

58 "She did the greater feat. . . .": H.T.P., Boston *Transcript,* 19 Jan. 1914.

58 "To the singing of words . . .": John H. Raftery, *Telegraph,* 13 Feb. 1920.

58 "Robed in lustreless black . . .": R.A., *Times,* 2 Nov. 1920.

[illegible]

page

59 "In nothing has she shown . . .": R.A., *Times,* 2 Feb. 1910.

59 "This French dramatic soprano . . .": W.J.H., *Sun,* 2 Feb. 1910.

PART II:
THE GATTI YEARS: 1910-1921

page

63 "all sorts of snippets . . .": A. St. J.-B., *Telegraph,* 27 Dec. 1905.

64 "Merely because I wish to salute . . .": *World,* (?) 1912.

64 "bombarded throughout the year . . .": A. St. J.-B., *Telegraph,* 29 Nov. 1914.

64 "Although he is known . . .": *Herald,* 23 Nov. 1913.

64 "One thing is certain . . .": Giulio Gatti-Casazza to Otto Kahn, 6 Sept. 1915, Otto Kahn papers, William Seymour Theater Collection, Firestone Library, Princeton University.

64 "a mad-house soaked with blood . . .": ibid.

64 "As an Italian . . .": Gatti to Kahn, 1 Nov. 1917, Otto Kahn papers.

65 "In strange contradiction . . .": A. St. J.-B., *Telegraph,* 4 Dec. 1913.

65 "The dreamy and artistic author . . .": ibid.

65 "It is now high time . . .": A. St. J.-B., *Telegraph,* 1 Mar. 1914.

65 "Bonci did not draw . . .": Gatti to Giuseppe Lusardi, 20 Mar. 1920, Metropolitan Opera Archives.

65 "(the only one except Caruso . . .": Geraldine Farrar to Gatti, 2 May 1920, Met Archives.

65 "My dear friend . . .": Gatti to Farrar, 7 May 1920, Met Archives.

The World Premiere of *La Fanciulla del West*

page

67 "It is 10:30 in the morning . . .": *Sun,* 11 Dec. 1910.

68 "For Act III the stage is converted . . .": *Times,* 5 Dec. 1910.

69 "The dullest imagination can figure . . .": A. St. J.-B., *Telegraph,* 11 Dec. 1910.

71 "Tito Ricordi, of the Milan . . .": *Musical America,* 17 Dec. 1910.

Dinh Gilly

page

72 "He gave them a distinction . . .": *Times,* 25 Nov. 1909.

72 "Mr. Dinh Gilly as Rigoletto . . .": *Telegraph,* 12 Jan. 1912.

72 "The French baritone never has . . .": *Press,* 11 Jan. 1913.

Emmy Destinn

page

72 "I wish you would write to me . . .": Maurice Grau to Nahan Franko, 4 Aug. 1902, Met Archives.

74 "Miss Destinn might have been appearing . . .": P.S., *Globe,* 17 Nov. 1908.

74 "Her face is of that peculiar type . . .": W.J.H., *Sun,* 14 Dec. 1913.

74 "She at any rate has solved . . .": ibid.

74 "The climax was the Bohemian . . .": *Evening Sun,* 20 Feb. 1909.

Léon Rothier

page

76 "it should be called *Arkel* . . .": P.S., *Telegram,* 2 Feb. 1929.

Albert Reiss

page

76 "the best Mime New York has yet enjoyed . . .": *World,* 5 Mar. 1902.

76 "There is always . . .": *Times,* 27 Dec. 1910.

Alma Gluck

page

77 "displayed a very pretty . . .": *Sun,* 17 Nov. 1909.

77 "With a pleasing personality . . .": Philip Hale, Boston *Herald,* 1 Apr. 1910.

77 "We have few concert singers . . .": Henry E. Krehbiel, *Tribune,* 20 Oct. 1910.

77 "apply herself to the study . . .": Agreement dated 17 Apr. 1912, Met Archives.

78 "It is specially stipulated . . .": Agreement dated March 1913, Met Archives.

78 "as Miss Gluck's voice now stands . . .": W.J.H. (?), *Sun,* 1 Nov. 1914.

Leo Slezak

page

78 "Out of the aggregation . . .": *Press,* 18 Nov. 1909.

78 "his voice is less robust . . .": Reginald de Koven, *World,* 18 Nov. 1909.

78 "The scenes of his jealousy . . .": *Evening Globe,* 18 Nov. 1909.

78 "I was bawling alongside him . . .": Leo Slezak, *Song of Motley* (London: William Hodge & Co., 1938), p. 18.

80 "Verdi's hero of high C's . . .": unidentified newspaper, 2 Dec. 1909.

80 "Best of all he shows . . .": W.J.H., *Sun,* 23 Jan. 1910.

Herman Jadlowker

page

80 "This is my Lohengrin. . . .": Dalia Carmel, "My Uncle Hermann," *Metropolitan Opera Program,* February 1968, p. 12.

80 "A voice of more than usual richness . . .": *Telegraph,* 24 Jan. 1910.

80 "the first Faust in the memory . . .": Boston *Transcript,* 15 Nov. 1910.

81 "Had I that voice . . .": *Musical America,* date unknown.

81 At a *Bohème* performance . . . : *Musical America,* 24 Dec. 1910.

81 "had the title role . . .": W.J.H., *Sun,* 9 Nov. 1911.

81 "since Jean de Reszke's . . .": *Sun,* 30 Jan. 1912.

81 "I want to teach young people . . .": Carmel, "My Uncle Hermann," p. 11.

Riccardo Martin

page

81 "If we are not very much . . .": Henry T. Finck, *Evening Post,* 21 Nov. 1907.

81 "The prospect of singing Manrico . . .": *Evening Globe,* 11 Mar. 1909.

82 "Riccardo Martin sang the music . . .": W.J.H., *Sun,* 21 Nov. 1911.

Dmitri Smirnoff

page

82 "Mr. Smirnoff is in many respects . . .": *Musical America,* 7 Jan. 1911.

82 "If this Juliette had vowed . . .": W.J.H., *Sun,* 14 Jan. 1911.

83 "In the finale . . .": Brooklyn *Eagle,* 12 Jan. 1912.

83 "It is a land of Italians . . .": *Times,* 15 Feb. 1912.

Geraldine Farrar

page

83 "I want professional rates.": unidentified magazine.

85 "She has had her ascents . . .": W.J.H., *Sun,* 24 Feb. 1914.

85 "The higher notes of Miss Farrar's voice . . .": A. St. J.-B., *Telegraph,* 17 Dec. 1910.

85 "Whatever faults Miss Farrar . . .": W.J.H., *Sun,* 30 Jan. 1915.

85 "She has a new costume . . .": W.J.H. (?), *Sun,* 6 Jan. 1918.

85 "She was indeed a vision . . .": W.J.H., *Sun,* 20 Nov. 1914.

85 "Her voice, which last season was dull . . .": W.J.H., *Sun Herald,* 1 Feb. 1920.

87 "Are you coming back?": unidentified newspaper, 8 Apr. 1922.

87 "Geraldine Farrar with vocal . . .": *Sun,* 17 Jan. 1920.

87 "Has George M. Cohan stopped . . .": unidentified newspaper, 24 Apr. 1922.

Enrico Caruso

page

89 "It is like gold . . ." Francis Robinson, *Caruso: His Life in Pictures* (New York: Studio Publications, 1957), p. 18.

89 "It also seems to me . . .": ibid, p. 42.

89 "In the first act he kept . . .": *Sun,* 24 Nov. 1903.

89 " . . . a finer Ramphis": *Commercial Advertiser,* 1 Dec. 1903.

89 "was naturally very careful . . .": ibid.

91 "godsend": *Herald,* 1 Dec. 1903.

91 "the year's popular idol": *Press,* 1 Dec. 1903.

91 "The worship of Caruso . . .": Newark *Evening News,* 1 Dec. 1903.

91 "His fire is unbounded.": *Press,* 1 Dec. 1903.

Olive Fremstad

page

91 "She was always an epic . . .": Mary Watkins Cushing, *The Rainbow Bridge* (New York: G. P. Putnam's Sons, 1954), p. 120.

91 "She was the [illegible] . . .": Cushing, *Rainbow Bridge,* p. 72.

91 "Mme. Fremstad's performance . . .": *Times,* 26 Nov. 1903.

91 "Miss Fremstad (last night in green . . .": A. St. J.-B., *Telegraph,* 20 Mar. 1906.

91 "Mme. Fremstad's voice . . .": R.A., *Times,* 2 Jan. 1908.

91 "Mme. Fremstad is the one . . .": *Christian Science Monitor,* 18 Jan. 1910.

95 "Her management of the high tones . . .": *Sun,* 19 Dec. 1909.

95 "I do not claim . . .": Willa Cather, *McClure's Magazine,* Dec. 1913.

95 "I spring into life . . .": Cushing, *Rainbow Bridge,* p. 119.

95 "Mishkin, the photographer . . .": John Brown to Gatti, 10 Nov. 1911, Met Archives.

95 "The tint and glory . . .": A. St. J.-B., *Telegraph,* 20 Feb. 1914.

95 "It recalled to wistful . . .": L.G., *Herald Tribune,* 3 Feb. 1935.

Jacques Urlus

page

96 "Much had been hoped . . .": unidentified newspaper, 10 Feb. 1913.

96 "splendid display of nerve . . .": *Evening Sun,* 10 Feb. 1913.

96 "perhaps most gratifying . . .": P.S., *Globe,* 13 Feb. 1913.

96 "In the final act he finally . . .": *Herald,* 13 Feb. 1913.

96 "one of the most profoundly moving . . .": *Evening Journal,* 13 Feb. 1913.

96 "rarely has the love duet . . .": unidentified newspaper, 1 Mar. 1913.

Johanna Gadski

page

97 "One portion of it . . .": A. St. J.-B., *Telegraph,* date unknown.

97 "Fräulein Gadski, who made her debut . . .": *Times,* 2 Mar. 1895.

97 "It was full of superb vigor . . .": *Times,* 26 Nov. 1903.

97 "Miss Gadski showed herself . . .": *Sun,* 1 Dec. 1903.

97 "Mme. Gadski reappeared . . .": W.J.H., *Sun,* 15 Jan. 1929.

99 "Her vocal technique was well-founded . . .": W.J.H., *Sun,* 17 Mar. 1931.

Adamo Didur

page

99 "Maurice Renaud recently gave . . .": *Times,* date unknown.

99 "In action forcible . . .": De Koven, *World,* date unknown.

99 "Hitherto he has seemed . . .": H.T.P., *Boston Transcript,* 21 Mar. 1913.

101 "This is not true.": unidentified newspaper.

101 "Such a triumph as came to Didur . . .": *Times,* (?) Mar. 1913.

Paul Althouse

page

102 "He is comely to see . . .": H.T.P., Boston *Transcript,* 21 Mar. 1913.

102 "Mr. Althouse was not a Wagnerian hero . . .": W.J.H., *Sun,* 5 Feb. 1934.

Antonio Scotti

page

102 "When Jean de Reszke left . . .": W.J.H., *Herald,* 5 Jan. 1924.

105 "Not only in make-up . . .": Max Smith, *Press,* 5 Feb. 1915.

Enrico Caruso and *Pagliacci*

page

105 "and the more the house cheered . . .": *Evening Sun,* 1 Feb. 1906.

105 "From year to year he amplified . . .": H.T.P., *Eighth Notes* (New York: Dodd, Mead, 1922), p. 62.

Lucrezia Bori

page

107 "She gives it the Italian . . .": P.S., *Globe,* 21 Nov. 1912.

108 "her voice, firm and clear . . .": *Telegraph,* 21 Nov. 1912.

108 "took her deathblow . . .": *Evening Sun,* 21 Nov. 1912.

108 "It was the most important opportunity . . .": R.A., *Times,* (?) Jan. 1914.

109 "What a flower-like . . .": A. St. J.-B., *Telegraph,* 3 Jan. 1914.

Edoardo Ferrari-Fontana

page

110 "His voice is unmistakably an Italian voice . . .": H.T.P., Boston *Evening Transcript,* 12 Feb. 1913.

110 "Mr. Fontana is the most romantic . . .": Philip Hale, Boston *Herald,* 12 Feb. 1913.

110 "It may be said of him without hesitation . . .": W.J.H., *Sun,* 3 Jan. 1914.

Margarete Matzenauer

page

110 "The majestic Matzenauer . . .": W.J.H., *Singing Magazine,* Feb. 1926.

112 "in many respects was strikingly successful.": R.A. (?), *Times,* 27 Feb. 1912.

112 "revelled in the gorgeous opulence . . .": Krehbiel, *Tribune,* 21 Jan. 1920.

113 "She is a cathedral . . .": James G. Huneker, unidentified newspaper.

113 "to avoid the flowers . . .": *World,* 17 Feb. 1930.

Frieda Hempel

page

113 "It was not the voice . . .": R.A., *Times,* 28 Dec. 1912.

113 "Hempel has made *Traviata* . . .": *Times,* 30 Jan. 1913.

113 "The personages were clothed . . .": ibid.

113 "Her impersonation was truly beautiful . . .": W.J.H., *Sun,* 14 Dec. 1913.

115 "I have had so many disillusionments . . .": Frieda Hempel to Gatti, 18 Dec. 1934, Met Archives.

115 "the musicality, the knowing phrasing . . .": *Times,* 3 Oct. 1948.

Anna Case

page

115 "the happiest of all happy shades . . .": W.J.H., *Sun,* 11 Dec. 1921.

116 "the most perfect scale . . .": Francis Robinson, *Opera News,* 28 Feb. 1970.

116 "It is a light soprano . . .": R.A., *Times,* 13 Oct. 1916.

Frances Alda

page

116 "Does the care of home . . .": unidentified newspaper, 1908.

116 "Mme. Alda was the Manon. . . .": W.J.H., *Sun,* 27 Feb. 1909.

118 "It was a night in which Mme. Alda . . .": H.T.P., Boston *Evening Transcript,* 15 Apr. 1916.

118 "Three is a crowd. . . .": Brooklyn *Daily Eagle,* 15 June 1933.

118 "The chief difference . . .": Dale Warren, *The Music Magazine,* Oct. 1962.

118 "in the best of voice . . .": P.S., *Telegram,* 30 Dec. 1929.

118 "The two most grievous errors . . .": *Sun,* 1937.

118 "Half a dozen kings . . .": Frances Alda, *Men, Women and Tenors* (Boston: Houghton Mifflin, 1937), p. 4.

Lina Cavalieri

page

118 "white Caucasian ermine . . .": Quaintance Eaton, *The Boston Opera Company* (New York: Appleton-Century, 1968), p. 242.

120 "She has fire . . .": A. St. J.-B., *Telegraph,* 20 Dec. 1907.

Lucien Muratore

page

120 "There were moments last night . . .": *Evening Post,* 24 Jan. 1918.

120 "true to his art": unidentified newspaper.

120 "There's always one in the theatre . . .": Gustave Huberdeau, as reported by Leo Riemens, album notes for *Muratore* (Toronto: Rococo Records No. 5327, circa 1968).

Louise Homer

page

121 "Of course, if you do not want to arrive in New York . . .": Gatti to Louise Homer, 26 Oct. 1918, Met Archives.

121 "The only singing we hear is from the thrushes and robins . . .": Homer to Gatti, 1 June 1919, Met Archives.

121 "During the entr'acte . . .": *Musical America*, 28 May 1910.

121 "Don't you make our mother cry": Anne Homer, *Louise Homer and the Golden Age of Opera* (New York: William Morrow, 1974), p. 323.

Giovanni Martinelli

page

122 "to terminate this contract . . .": Contract dated 14 Sept. 1908, Met Archives.

122 " . . . to win the plaudits of the house . . .": *Globe*, 21 Nov. 1913.

122 "Since the days of Mr. Jadlowker . . .": H.T.P., Boston *Evening Transcript*, 13 Apr. 1916.

123 "Arnold is the high part . . .": P.S., *Telegram*, 13 Nov. 1923.

123 "Mr. Martinelli ascended . . .": W.J.H., *Sun*, 7 Jan. 1928.

Enrico Caruso and *Samson et Dalila*

page

123 "Never could a season have had . . .": A. St. J.-B., *Telegraph*, 16 Nov. 1915.

126 "In physical appearance Madame Matzenauer . . .": ibid.

126 "Mr. Caruso was in better voice . . .": *Tribune*, 26 Nov. 1915.

126 "as the opera progressed . . .": Finck, *Evening Post*, 11 Dec. 1919.

Ernestine Schumann-Heink

page

126 "The splendor of tone . . .": W. J. H. *Sun*, 21 Oct. 1906.

126 "During the war her family . . .": Brooklyn *Eagle*, 25 Feb. 1926.

126 "I never in my life smoked . . .": *Singing Magazine*, Oct. 1927.

126 "Now she is [at the Metropolitan] . . .": P.S., *Telegram*, 26 Feb. 1926.

John McCormack

page

128 "He is a pure lyric tenor . . .": *Evening Post*, 11 Nov. 1910.

128 "His command of breath . . .": Philip Hale, Boston *Herald*, 2 Feb. 1913.

128 "Mr. McCormack was almost equal . . .": W.J.H., *Sun*, 1 Mar. 1911.

128 " . . . what Mr. McCormack contributed . . .": R.A., *Times*, 17 Nov. 1917.

Margaret Ober

page

129 "a singer of uncommon excellence . . .": R.A., *Times*, 22 Nov. 1913.

129 GERMAN SHE SEVERS . . . : *Tribune*, 3 Feb. 1916.

Melanie Kurt

page

130 "It is a veritable sporano . . .": R.A., *Times*, 3 Feb. 1915.

Elisabeth Schumann

page

131 One day while still at sea . . . : from conversation between Elisabeth Schumann and Gustl Breuer, as reported to author by Breuer, 1982.

131 "As anyone who heard Miss Case . . .": Smith, *Press*, 22 Nov. 1914.

131 "Her artistic sincerity . . .": *Press*, 21 Nov. 1914.

131 "disclosed the surprising fact . . .": *Press*, 8 Feb. 1915.

Andrés de Segurola

page

132 "The best acting of the evening . . .": *Evening Post*, 20 Mar. 1913.

Pasquale Amato

page

132 "won for himself immediate welcome . . .": *Sun*, 21 Nov. 1908.

132 "as far as voice and physique . . .": W.J.H., *Ladies' Home Journal*, Mar. 1910.

134 "Mr. Amato apparelled . . .": H.T.P., Boston *Evening Transcript*, 11 Feb. 1911.

134 "profound and elaborate unction . . .": A. St. J.-B., *Telegraph*, 28 Nov. 1912.

134 "In the prologue he demonstrated . . .": *Sun*, 21 Nov. 1912.

134 "With Ruffo's singing . . .": *Evening Telegram*, 21 Nov. 1912.

Anna Fitziu

page

134 "Miss Fitziu also has a voice . . .": unidentified newspaper, 29 Jan. 1916.

135 "this full blooded, passionate utterance . . .": *Times*, 29 Jan. 1916.

Maria Barrientos

page

135 "Her voice is exceedingly light . . .": H.T.P., Boston *Evening Transcript*, 7 Apr. 1916.

136 One reviewer complimented her . . . : *Evening Sun*, 16 Mar. 1916.

Edith Mason

page

137 "She is pretty and her manner . . .": *Herald*, 20 Nov. 1915.

137 "This part of Sophie . . .": R.A., *Times*, 18 Jan. 1916.

137 "Miss Mason's arrival . . .": Chicago *Evening American*, date unknown, 1917.

137 "At last we heard *Thaïs* . . .": Herman Devries, Chicago *Evening American*, date unknown, 1919.

Giuseppe De Luca

page

137 "won the audience . . .": *Herald*, 26 Nov. 1915.

139 "His acting is charged . . .": *Herald*, 12 Feb. 1916.

139 "a restored duet . . .": *Evening Sun*, 12 Feb. 1916.

139 "the most distinguished singing . . .": *Sun,* 4 Dec. 1922.

139 "For five years, I was playing . . .": *Time,* 25 Mar. 1946.

139 "A life well and continently spent . . .": Irving Kolodin, *Sun,* 12 Mar. 1946.

Claudia Muzio

page

140 "The baggage master . . .": *Times,* 10 Dec. 1916.

140 "She has beautiful speaking eyes . . .": *Evening Post,* 5 Dec. 1916.

140 "warm and sympathetic in quality . . .": Krehbiel, *Tribune,* 5 Dec. 1916.

140 "She was always willing . . .": R.A., *Times,* 5 Dec. 1916.

140 "Miss Muzio was entirely too busy . . .": Paul Morris, *Herald,* 10 Dec. 1916.

140 "like flint and steel together.": Brooklyn *Standard Union,* 9 Dec. 1917.

142 "as a dramatic soprano . . .": Brooklyn *Standard Union,* 29 Jan. 1920.

142 "As for Muzio . . .": Gatti to Angelo Scandiani, 8 Apr. 1922, Met Archives.

Amelita Galli-Curci

page

143 "Last year during the winter . . .": Gatti to Kahn, 2 May 1917, Otto Kahn papers.

143 "have made sounds like those . . .": W.J.H., *Sun,* 17 Feb. 1918.

143 "She stole out on the stage . . .": *Times,* (?) Feb. 1918.

Lydia Lipkowska

page

144 "A more than comely . . .": Krehbiel, *Tribune,* 19 Nov. 1909.

144 "Not within recollection . . .": H.T.P., Boston *Evening Transcript,* 12 Feb. 1910.

145 "she wore so many diamonds . . .": A. St. J.-B. *Telegraph,* 19 Nov. 1909.

Rosa Raisa

page

145 "I never know what step . . .": Rosa Raisa, unpublished autobiography.

145 "Luckily your repetition . . .": ibid.

147 "Miss Raisa has a voice . . .": *Times,* 25 Jan. 1918.

147 "in the florid 'Ah, bello a me ritorno' . . .": P.S., *Globe,* 4 Feb. 1920.

147 "many of the elaborate passages . . .": W.J.H., *Sun,* 8 Feb. 1920.

147 " . . . she had made no progress . . .": W.J.H., *Herald,* date unknown, 1921.

147 "You should hear me in South America . . .": Edward C. Moore, *Forty Years of Opera in Chicago* (New York: Horace Liveright, 1930), p. 126.

147 "There remained in her singing . . .": Eugene Stinson, Chicago *Daily News,* (?) July 1938.

Titta Ruffo

page

147 "What are you doing here?": Leopold Salzman, "The Victor Cafe," *Opera News,* 19 Feb. 1966, p. 7.

148 "His voice is extraordinary . . .": unidentified Philadelphia newspaper, 4 Nov. 1912.

148 "He has a splendid pair . . .": W.J.H., *Sun,* 24 Nov. 1912.

149 "Tell Melba that she . . .": Titta Ruffo, *La Mia Parabola* (Rome: Staderini Editore, 1977), p. 181.

149 "The recitative secco . . .": W.J.H., *Herald,* 20 Jan. 1922.

149 "Mr. Ruffo's Neri . . .": Boston *Evening Transcript,* (?) Jan. 1926.

Maggie Teyte

page

150 "accomplished a portrait . . .": *Tribune,* 24 Sept. 1918.

150 "by virtue not only of pure . . .": P.S., *Globe,* 24 Oct. 1918.

Florence Easton

page

150 "Miss Easton in her turn . . .": H.T.P., Boston *Transcript,* 5 Nov. 1906.

151 "considerable audience bore up . . .": P.S., *Globe,* 4 Jan 1918.

151 "She sang with an emotional expressiveness . . .": Smith, *American,* 4 Jan. 1918.

151 "To accomplish at short notice . . .": Smith, *American,* 22 Jan. 1918.

151 "first of all because . . .": Gatti to Florence Easton, 25 Apr. 1924, Met Archives.

151 "was voiced in ringing tones . . .": Noel Straus, *Times,* 1 Mar. 1936.

The World Premiere of *Trittico*

page

151 "Could I have foreseen . . .": Puccini to Gatti, quoted in *Herald,* 2 Dec. 1918.

151 "The opening work provides . . .": Brooklyn *Eagle,* 16 Dec. 1918.

151 "Mr. Crimi as the lover . . .": Huneker, *Times,* 15 Dec. 1918.

153 "as a one-act thriller . . .": P.S., *Globe,* 16 Dec. 1918.

153 "Seldom has Miss Farrar . . .": H.T.P., Boston *Evening Transcript,* 18 Dec. 1918.

153 " . . . the only notable lyric . . .": Huneker, *Times,* 15 Dec. 1918.

153 "Even the mechanics . . .": H.T.P., Boston *Evening Transcript,* 18 Dec. 1918.

153 " . . . made the crafty Gianni Schicchi . . .": *Evening Mail,* 16 Dec. 1918.

153 "The pearl of the evening . . .": *Evening Sun,* 16 Dec. 1918.

153 "Mr. and Mrs. Oscar Hammerstein . . .": Huneker, *Times,* 15 Dec. 1918.

Mabel Garrison

page
154 "A charming and sympathetic figure . . .": R.A., *Times,* 20 Dec. 1919.
154 "possessed of a voice . . .": W.J.H., *Sun,* 3 Nov. 1918.

Charles Hackett

page
155 "a rare voice, well trained . . .": *Musical America,* 23 Dec. 1911.
155 "He has a pure lyric tenor . . .": P.S., *Telegram,* 1 Feb. 1918.

Gabriella Besanzoni

page
155 UNUSUAL VOICE . . . : Pasquale Amato to Gatti, 20 Jan. 1919, Met Archives.
156 "With an extravagant and disorderly woman . . .": Gatti to Giuseppe Bamboschek, 20 Aug. 1919, Met Archives.
156 "Mr. Gatti-Casazza trained . . .": P.S., *Globe,* 20 Nov. 1919.
156 "always granting that the act . . .": W.J.H., *Sun,* 11 Dec. 1919.
156 "for reasons of repertoire": Gatti to Besanzoni, 30 Mar. 1920, Met Archives.

Renato Zanelli

page
156 "Mr. Zanelli as Amonasro . . .": R.A., *Times,* 20 Dec. 1919.
157 "succeeded in making his singing . . .": P.S., *Globe,* 9 Dec. 1919.

Orville Harrold

page
157 "whoever is the tenor . . .": *Variety,* 9 Oct. 1909.
158 "It is true that his high notes . . .": *Tribune,* 28 Jan. 1914.
158 "magnificent voice which he squanders . . .": Chicago *Examiner,* 5 Oct. 1916.
158 "a demonstration of pleasure . . .": W.J.H., *Sun,* 30 Dec. 1919.

Selma Kurz

page
158 "Miss Kurz sang . . .": P.S., *Globe,* 10 Jan. 1921.
159 "Thank God my voice . . .": Selma Kurz to Gatti, 30 Nov. 1921, Met Archives.

Rosa Ponselle

page
159 PONZILLO SISTERS, SONGS . . . : *Variety,* 10 Sept. 1915.
159 "She is young, she is comely . . .": Huneker, *Times,* 16 Nov. 1918.

Enrico Caruso and *La Juive*

page
161 "You are so good . . .": Gatti to Enrico Caruso, 17 Oct. 1919, Met Archives.
163 "Enrico Caruso, who began life . . .": W.J.H., *Sun,* 23 Nov. 1919.
163 I VISITED CARUSO MYSELF . . . : Gatti to Edward Ziegler, 6 July 1921, Met Archives.
163 "I do wish to say . . .": Gatti to Mrs. Caruso, 7 Aug. 1921, Met Archives.

PART III:
THE GATTI YEARS 1921–1932

---

page
167 "Until a few years ago . . .": Guilio Gatti-Casazza to Otto Kahn, 12 Nov. 1921, Metropolitan Opera Archives.
167 "Examined carefully, the situation . . .": Gatti to Kahn, 7 Aug. 1921, Met Archives.
167 "I had here for seven . . .": Gatti to Norbert Salter, 9 Apr. 1921, Met Archives.
168 "Last year Mme. Kemp . . .": Gatti statement, Mar. 1924, Met Archives.
168 " . . . we ought to have Lottie [*sic*] Lehmann . . .": Kahn to Gatti, 27 Nov. 1929, Otto Kahn papers, William Seymour Theater Collection, Firestone Library, Princeton University.
168 "The lyric theatre is undoubtedly . . .": Gatti to Kahn, 19 Nov. 1924, Met Archives.
168 "When I called upon Maxwell . . .": Gatti to Kahn, 26 May 1925, Met Archives.
168 "This decision is taken . . .": Gatti to Paul D. Cravath, 16 Jan. 1934, Met Archives.
168 "She made an excellent impression . . .": Gatti to Ziegler, 6 Sept. 1934, Met Archives.

Feodor Chaliapin and *Boris Godunov*

page
169 "Gaisberg has met Chaliapin . . .": Sydney W. Atkins to Gatti, 29 Aug. 1921, Met Archives.
169 "a voice that gave the imperial . . .": The Listener, *Sun,* 16 Nov. 1922.
169 "His impersonation better deserves . . .": W.J.H., *Herald,* 16 Nov. 1922.
169 "It was an expression of tragedy . . .": P.S., *Globe,* 10 Dec. 1924.

Feodor Chaliapin and *Mefistofele*

page
171 "Chaliapin, both by necessity . . .": *Evening Sun,* 21 Nov. 1907.
171 "It took the audience . . .": *Herald,* 21 Nov. 1907.
171 "a big, rumbling . . .": W.J.H., *Sun,* 21 Nov. 1907.
171 "He is an elemental creature . . .": W.J.H., *Sun,* 5 Jan. 1900.
171 "He was made up . . .": *Evening Sun,* 13 Dec. 1907.
173 "Since it became fashionable . . .": W.J.H., *Herald,* 19 Nov. 1922.
173 "huge and menacing, shambling about . . .": Deems Taylor, *World,* 20 Nov. 1922.

Beniamino Gigli

page

173 "The Gramophone Company tells me . . .": Calvin Childs to Ziegler, 12 June 1919, Met Archives.

173 "His voice is a lyric tenor . . .": Max Smith, *American,* 27 Nov. 1920.

175 "Beniamino Gigli has found . . .": W.J.H., *Herald,* 27 Nov. 1922.

175 "I think, after all, that people . . .": Beniamino Gigli, *The Gigli Memoirs* (London, Cassell & Co., 1957), p. 92.

Aureliano Pertile

page

175 "Another tenor, who during . . .": Gatti to Kahn, 7 Aug. 1921, Met Archives.

175 "His voice has . . .": W.J.H., *Herald,* 2 Dec. 1921.

175 "a tenor with the mentality . . .": Smith, *American,* 25 Dec. 1921.

175 "a man who gains . . .": *American,* 21 Dec. 1921.

175 "It was sad for him . . .": *Times,* 31 Dec. 1921.

175 "Of the many tenors who have appeared . . .": P.S., *Globe,* 13 Jan. 1922.

176 "Mio caro Pertile . . .": Gatti to Pertile, 5 Apr. 1922, Met Archives.

176 "As you will read . . .": Luigi Broglio to Gatti, 23 Dec. 1923, Met Archives.

The Metropolitan premiere of *Così fan Tutte*

page

176 "The greatest surprise for the knowing . . .": *Tribune,* 25 Mar. 1922.

176 "if you think you lost . . .": (?) to Joseph Urban, (?) 1922, Met Archives.

Rosa Ponselle and *Le Roi d'Ys*

page

179 "in my opinion, it would neither be . . .": Gatti to Kahn, 31 Jan. 1919, Met Archives.

179 "In points of diction . . .": Brooklyn *Eagle,* 6 Mar. 1920.

179 "Rosa Ponselle, on whose big shoulders . . .": James G. Huneker, *World,* 24 Dec. 1920.

179 "nothing short of glorious . . .": P.S. *Globe,* 9 Dec. 1921.

179 "the hateful brunette . . .": Henry T. Finck, *Evening Post,* 6 Jan. 1922.

179 "Miss Ponselle also won . . .": Olin Downes, *Times,* 28 Dec. 1924.

Giuseppe Danise

page

179 "Mr. Danise came here . . .": P.S., *Globe,* 18 Dec. 1920.

179 "To be mentioned . . .": R.A., *Times,* 5 Mar. 1922.

180 "They pay you too much . . .": *Metropolitan Opera Program,* 15 Oct. 1962, p. 33.

Emma Calvé

page

180 "Nothing better than Deroulede's . . .": Sime, *Variety,* 12 Mar. 1915.

180 "Mme. Calvé is not only the possessor . . .": P.S., *Globe,* 22 Mar. 1922.

180 "Absolutely the most stunning . . .": P.S. *Globe,* 6 May 1922.

181 "I have received . . .": Emma Calvé to Eleanor Belmont, 9 Dec. 1938, Met Archives.

Sigrid Onegin

page

181 "the artist who, in important centers . . .": Salter to Gatti, 1921, Met Archives.

182 "Sigrid Onegin, the new Amneris . . .": *Sun,* 23 Nov. 1922.

182 "The audience was thrilled . . .": Finck, *Post,* 28 Nov. 1922.

182 "Not many singers of the past . . .": Noel Straus, *Times,* 31 Jan. 1938.

Toti Dal Monte

page

183 "In these piping times . . .": P.S., *Telegram,* 6 Dec. 1924.

183 "La Signorina Angeles Ottein . . .": Gatti to Giuseppe Lusardi, (?) 1922, Met Archives.

Feodor Chaliapin and *Don Carlo*

page

183 "It is easy enough . . .": P.S., *Globe,* 4 Dec. 1922.

185 "The king sat crouched . . .": Taylor, *World,* 3 Dec. 1922.

Giacomo Lauri-Volpi

page

185 "The papers have publicized . . .": Lusardi to Gatti, 23 Dec. 1920, Met Archives.

185 "His voice is young . . .": P.S., *Globe,* 27 Jan. 1923.

185 "It was in this [first act] finale . . .": Downes, *Times,* 1 Mar. 1924.

185 "If we had not known him . . .": L.G., *Herald Tribune,* 1 Nov. 1927.

187 "held a D flat . . .": *Journal,* 26 Jan. 1929.

187 "It would have been senseless . . .": Gatti to Vincenzo Bellezza, 14 Apr. 1933, Met Archives.

Miguel Fleta

page

187 "that you seek to convince these artists . . .": Angelo Scandiani to Gatti, 5 Feb. 1924, Met Archives.

187 "He is a man of rather small stature . . .": *Herald,* 9 Nov. 1923.

187 "Mr. Fleta put an admirable restraint . . .": Ernest Newman, *Post,* 14 Nov. 1924.

Lawrence Tibbett

page

188 "sang his music with a light voice . . .": W.J.H., *Herald,* 1 Dec. 1923.

190 "occasioned considerable excitement and was . . .": Downes, *Times,* 3 Jan. 1925.

190 "The feature of the Metropolitan's . . .": L.G., *Herald Tribune,* 29 Jan. 1932.

Michael Bohnen

page

190 "you might have guessed . . .": L.G., *Tribune,* 5 Mar. 1926.

192 "the greatest artist . . .": Gatti to Kahn, (?) 1922, Met Archives.

192 "once on the stage . . .": Taylor, *World,* 2 Mar. 1922.

192 "He will sing four Hagens . . .": Edward Cushing, Brooklyn *Eagle,* 1 Apr. 1928.

192 "the chief singers are competent . . .": W.J.H., *Sun,* 1 Apr. 1924.

192 "I owe this wonderful house . . .": David E. Prosser, "Unruly Giants," *Opera News,* 31 Jan. 1970, p. 5.

Karin Branzell

page

192 "She is a woman of fine presence . . .": W.J.H., *Herald,* 7 Feb. 1924.

192 " . . . Mme. Branzell as the sinister . . .": W.J.H., *Herald,* 9 Feb. 1924.

194 "Her seductive art . . .": W.J.H., *Sun,* 20 Mar. 1925.

194 "She hopes she is making a place . . .": Mary Ellis Peltz, *Opera News,* 25 Jan. 1925.

194 "They told me in the last performance . . .": ibid.

194 "Now I will remember . . .": ibid.

Lauritz Melchior

page

194 "to parallel at all the Talley debut . . .": P.S., *Telegram,* 18 Feb. 1926.

194 "Mr. Melchior came back . . .": W.J.H., *Sun,* 18 Feb. 1926.

194 "Mr. Melchior's very first gesture . . .": Samuel Chotzinoff, *World,* 21 Nov. 1929.

194 "There was often beauty . . .": L.G., *Herald Tribune,* 21 Mar. 1929.

Gertrude Kappel

page

196 "The performance . . .": W.J.H., *Sun,* 16 Feb. 1925.

197 "Mme. Kappel is 'new' . . .": L.G., *Herald Tribune,* 17 Jan. 1928.

Maria Müller

page

197 "Contralto grief": P.S., *Telegram,* 22 Jan. 1925.

197 "Last night we had a new . . .": L.G., *Tribune,* 22 Jan. 1925.

Rosa Ponselle and *La Gioconda*

page

199 "The dozing music critic . . .": L.G., *Tribune,* 3 Nov. 1925.

Jose Mardones

page

199 "Mardones, who fills . . .": Brooklyn *Eagle,* 2 Jan. 1918.

199 "giving the 'Calumny' air . . .": R.A., *Times,* 23 Feb. 1918.

199 " . . . though his acting lacked . . .": *Evening Sun,* 23 Nov. 1918.

200 "He projects nothing but profundity . . .": W.J.H., *Singing Magazine,* 1923.

Angelo Bada

page

200 "The priceless value . . .": W.J.H., *Herald,* 11 Dec. 1921.

George Meader

page

201 "Mr. Meader as David . . .": Taylor, *World,* 10 Nov. 1924.

201 "Mr. Meader's Mime . . .": W.J.H., *Herald,* 3 Feb. 1924.

Feodor Chaliapin and *Don Quichotte*

page

202 "is not the best way to write . . .": Chotzinoff, *World,* 5 Apr. 1926.

202 "There have been brave men . . .": L.G., *Tribune,* 5 Apr. 1926.

Clarence Whitehill

page

205 "His voice is a fine and resonant baritone . . .": *Times,* 26 Nov. 1909.

205 "In Germany the theory . . .": W.J.H., *Sun,* 9 Jan. 1910.

205 "declaimed the text . . .": P.S., *Globe,* 17 Nov. 1921.

206 "Finally, there was the manly . . .": W.J.H., *Herald,* 20 Nov. 1924.

206 "Mr. Whitehill's Golaud . . .": W.J.H., *Sun,* 24 Nov. 1925.

Friedrich Schorr

page

206 "The heroic baritone . . .": Salter to Gatti, 27 Oct. 1922, Met Archives.

206 "The finest singer in the cast . . .": R.A., *Times,* (?) Feb. 1923.

206 "Beauty, indeed, was present . . .": L.G., *Tribune,* 24 Feb. 1924.

208 "In Mr. Schorr's Pizarro . . .": H.T.P., Boston *Evening Transcript,* 27 Jan. 1927.

Maria Jeritza

page

208 "took advantage of my offer . . .": Gatti to Kahn, 16 July 1915, Otto Kahn papers.

208 "Nothing arranged with Jeritza . . .": Gatti to Ziegler, 11 Aug. 1920, Met Archives.

208 "tall as a grenadier . . .": P.S., *Globe,* 21 Nov. 1921.

208 "It was more significantly unconventional . . .": W.J.H., *Herald,* 1 Dec. 1921.

210 "Avoid eye strain . . .": *Journal,* 11 Dec. 1926.

210 "Puccini's portrait . . .": *Times,* 17 Nov. 1926.

210 "It was a magnificent entrance . . .": L.G., *Herald Tribune,* 17 Nov. 1926.

211 "Her voice had the consistency . . .": P.S., *Telegram,* 14 Jan. 1928.

Grace Moore

page

211 JUST HEARD GRACE MOORE . . .: Kahn to Gatti, 15 Nov. 1927, Met Archives.

211 "Unfortunately the Metropolitan itself . . .": W.J.H., *Sun,* 8 Feb. 1928.

Rosa Ponselle and *Norma*

page

213 "Don't be alarmed . . .": Henry E. Krehbiel, *Chapters of Opera* (New York: Henry Holt & Co., 1911), p. 150.

213 "Mme. Lehmann's voice does not lend itself . . .": L.G., *Herald Tribune,* 13 Nov. 1927.

213 "In singing Julia . . .": The Melomane, *Town Topics,* 19 Nov. 1925.

213 "Bellini wrote for a style . . .": H.T.P., Boston *Evening Transcript,* 18 Nov. 1927.

213 "Rosa Ponselle's attainment . . .": W.J.H., *Sun,* 18 Feb. 1930.

213 "It was a night of splendor . . .": W.J.H., *Sun,* 3 Dec. 1931.

Ezio Pinza

page

214 "For several years, from time to time . . .": Gatti to Kahn, 15 Jan. 1929, Met Archives.

214 "probably the best we have": Amodeo Indelicato to Gatti, (?) 1924, Met Archives.

214 "The bass Pinza . . .": Gatti to Indelicato, 14 Feb. 1924, Met Archives.

214 "In Mr. Pinza, who essayed . . .": Chotzinoff, *World,* 17 Nov. 1927.

214 "with pithy incisiveness . . .": P.S., *Telegram,* 29 Feb. 1928.

214 "Mr. Pinza has the presence . . .": P.S., *Telegram,* 30 Nov. 1929.

Elisabeth Rethberg

page

216 "Mme. Elisabeth Rethberg, who hails . . .": John H. Raftery, *Telegraph,* 23 Nov. 1922.

216 "Even when she came now . . .": *Sun,* 19 Dec. 1922.

216 "The extremely difficult pages . . .": W.J.H., *Sun,* 24 Dec. 1922.

216 "the limpid and solacing beauty . . .": L.G., *Herald Tribune,* 13 Nov. 1928.

216 "You will also point out . . .": Gatti to Ziegler, 8 June 1929, Met Archives.

218 "Mme. Rethberg's enameled art . . .": Edward Cushing, Brooklyn *Eagle,* 30 Nov. 1929.

Edward Johnson

page

218 "an old stage manager once remarked . . .": Krehbiel, *Tribune,* 21 Feb. 1923.

218 "Grace, stature, and superior . . .": *Sun,* 17 Nov. 1922.

218 "The great feature of this performance . . .": Downes, *Times,* 8 Feb. 1931.

Lucrezia Bori

page

220 "very prudent contract": Gatti to Kahn, 20 Aug. 1919, Otto Kahn papers.

220 "I saw here Miss Bori . . .": Gatti to Ziegler, 28 June 1920, Met Archives.

220 "with a voice more beautiful . . .": W.J.H., *Herald,* 29 Jan. 1921.

220 "Bori absolute success . . .": Gatti to Lusardi, 29 Jan. 1921, Met Archives.

220 "Who could have been the fragile . . .": W.J.H., *Herald,* 24 Jan. 1922.

220 "take her place at the top . . .": *Musical America,* 2 July 1910.

Lily Pons

page

220 "PONS, LILY, coloratura . . .": unsigned audition card, 29 Mar. 1930, Met Archives.

220 "We leave with Lily Pons . . .": Maria Gay to Gatti, 20 Oct. 1930, Met Archives.

220 "Miss Pons is several years under thirty . . .": W.J.H., *Sun,* 3 Jan. 1931.

222 "Now is the Gatti of our discontent . . .": L.G., *Herald Tribune,* 20 Jan. 1931.

222 "she found the singer with a fair voice . . .": *Times,* 27 Mar. 1931.

222 "Radiating chic, as ever . . .": Kolodin, *Saturday Review,* 24 June 1972.

222 "It was a kind of afterglow . . .": ibid.

INDEX